Cross-Platform
Power Tools®

Cross-Platform Power Tools®

Application Development
for the Macintosh®, Windows™,
and Windows NT®

Steve Petrucci

RANDOM HOUSE
ELECTRONIC PUBLISHING

Cross-Platform Power Tools®: Application Development for the Macintosh®, Windows™, and Windows NT®

New York   Toronto   London   Sydney   Auckland

To Ann and Lucas

Contents

Part Two

Part 3

User Interface Implementation 281

Preface

In the mid-1940s the first computers to possess program storage motivated the scientists and mathematicians that used them to design ways to allow programs to be easily constructed and executed using sequences of numbers. Soon after, the first programming languages emerged which allowed abstract representations of a program to exist. Whether the designers knew it or not, this signalled the beginning of portable coding. As different varieties of computers were created and connected together, a program from one machine eventually made its way to another machine.

Time went on and graphical user interfaces were designed and constructed to make it easier to use computers. This made it more difficult to port an application from one computer to another. Not only did the program have to run, but it had to bridge the different user interfaces. Portable coding techniques evolved to become cross-platform development.

In 1981, while at Bell Laboratories, I took a course on writing portable programs in C; I understood the rationale, but didn't really understand the need. Most UNIX systems at Bell Labs were pretty much equivalent with respect to tools, and the personal computer really wasn't able to provide the kind of computing power, services, or tools that were necessary to program in a high-level language, except for simple types of programs.

In 1986, when I started working for Aldus, I had my first taste of cross-platform development. While working on simultaneous versions of PageMaker for the Macintosh and Windows 1.0 platforms, it became obvious that unless a cross-platform strategy was used, we would never be able to complete the task.

As Macintosh and Windows systems became more and more powerful and substantial numbers of these systems entered the mainstream computing population, I was convinced that any successful application had to be written (or rewritten) to run on more than one platform (at least Macintoshes and Windows systems).

In 1988 I purchased a book entitled *The Viewport Technician: A Guide to Portable Software Design*, by Michael Brian Bentley. It talked about writing programs for the Windows, Gem, Macintosh, Amiga, and Apple IIGS platforms. It presented comparisons of the functions and features of each of the platforms. Some of the material in the book is now dated, and some of the material a bit superficial, but the ideas and concepts were ahead of their time.

Most of the time cross-platform development doesn't require a hacker's knowledge of one or many operating systems. It requires an understanding of what the operating systems provide, what tools are available, what the problem you need to solve is, and how much time you have to do it.

In this book I present an introduction to cross-platform development. There are too many features and platforms to consider for a complete discussion of the topic. My hope is that you learn enough about the general topic and the specifics of implementation so that you are better able to make a decision about purchasing or developing a cross-platform solution.

THE BOOK

This book was developed cross platform, using Microsoft Word for the Macintosh and Windows. *Cross-Platform Power Tools* is organized into four parts:

- Part 1 Foundation — presents an overview of cross-platform development and discusses some specific comparsions for equipment and software

- Part 2 Basic Implementation — discusses specifics of the implementation of general cross-platform application program interface (API), not including user interfaces

- Part 3 User Interface Implementation — compares the different UIs and and functions and discusses the implementation of a cross-platform user interface API

- Part 4 Advanced Topics — talks about what to do next and discusses more advanced cross-platform topics

The parts of the book are organized from general cross-platform information to specific issues of implementation and examples. Likewise every chapter in the book proceeds from the general to the specific. This allows you to come up to speed with a topic that you might not be familiar with. It also makes it easier for nonprogrammers to understand the issues of particular topics without needing to read the entire chapter.

Part 1   Foundation

Chapter 1 Cross-Platform Issues. Covers definitions and background information, the reasons for cross-platform development, types of cross-platform solutions, the economics of cross-platform development, and the levels of cross-platform development.

Chapter 2 Platform Specifics. Gets more specific about the platforms discussed in this book—Macintosh, Windows 3.1, and Win32 subsystem in Windows NT. It compares the three platforms, the equipment required for developers and users, and the processors involved in the discussion of cross-platform development.

Chapter 3 Cross-Platform Tools. Talks about general language issues and the software tools available for cross-platform development, including languages, resource tools, editors, and version control.

Part 2   Basic Implementation

Chapter 4 Program Structure. Begins the discussion of implementing a cross-platform solution. It discusses the definition of a cross-platform architecture, some basic data types, programming style, a presentation of a cross-platform program skeleton, and the necessary program entry point and initialization functions.

Chapter 5 Memory Management. Discusses a simple memory management solution using the ANSI C libraries and a presentation of a practical cross-platform memory management solution. This compares API functions across platforms, data types, and several code samples. Some advanced memory management considerations are presented at the end of the chapter.

Chapter 6 File Management. Looks at a simple cross-platform file management solution using the ANSI C libraries, presents a practical solution, and then discusses some advanced file management topics. The implementation compares file functions, file features, and disk formats across platforms, then presents some necessary data types and values before presenting several samples of code.

Chapter 7 Events. Investigates the differences in the event (or messaging) systems of the three platforms, discusses how to define a cross-platform event system, and considers the details of implementing a cross-platform solution—covering specific event messages, data types, functions, event decoding, and keyboard events. Several next-step considerations are also discussed.

Chapter 8 Graphics. Compares the native API graphic models, terminology, and graphic functions and presents a cross-platform graphics implementation strategy that includes necessary data structures, global variables, and graphics functions. Advanced topics are also discussed.

Chapter 9 Text and Fonts. Looks at the different font technologies, native font and text functionality, font metrics, and font styles. It then presents an implementation for a simple cross-platform font and text API that includes data structures and functions. Advanced considerations are also discussed.

Chapter 10 Bitmaps. Compares the bitmap features of the native platforms and discusses bit transfer operations. A basic bitmap implementation is discussed and covers data types, global data, and cross-platform bitmap functions. Additional features and functions are also presented.

Chapter 11 Printing. Printing issues are discussed and platform-specific functions are discussed and compared. A collection of basic cross-platform printing functions and data types are presented, as well as some advanced printing topics.

Chapter 12 Miscellaneous Functions. Discusses and compares character, string, point, rectangle, and date and time issues and presents some basic solutions to these functional areas across platforms.

Part 3   User Interface Implementation

Chapter 13 Menus. Basic terminology is presented and comparisons of menu features and functionality across platforms lead into a discussion of selecting a basic menu feature set. The discussion of a cross-platform implementation covers data types, menu bar, menu list, and menu item functions. Advanced issues are also presented.

Chapter 14 Windows. Issues of defining cross-platform window management functions are disussed, which include basic terminology, comparisons of window user interface features, and comparisons of window functionality across platforms. Implementing a cross-platform window solution requires defining some cross-platform data types and values, then implementing basic functions. Some advanced considerations are discussed.

Chapter 15 Dialogs. Various platform-specific types of dialogs are discussed, including alerts (message boxes) and modal and modeless dialogs. Dialog functions are compared across platforms and implementation specifics for alert dialogs and modal dialogs are discussed and presented. Additional capabilities are also discussed.

Chapter 16 Controls. The process of defining a reasonable subset of user interface controls is discussed, which includes a discussion of terminology, capabilites, and available functionality. Discussions of implementing cross-platform button-control functions and edit text-controls are also included. Some additional considerations are also presented.

Chapter 17 Cursors. Specific platform cursors and cursor capabilities are discussed and compared and a cross-platform cursor data type, resource identifiers, and functions are presented.

Part 4   Advanced Topics

Chapter 18 The Next Step. Discusses how to further develop the functionality discussed in Part 2 and Part 3. This includes improving event support, multiple documents, supporting the clipboard, expanding user interface support, providing more standard dialogs, enhancing graphics and text functionality, advanced printing issues, other file management issues, application initialization information, and compound documents.

Chapter 19 Advanced Resource Considerations. Deals specifically with the problems of resources: what types of cross-platform solutions exist, how to support more features, and methods of abstracting resource tools.

Chapter 20 Extensions. Discusses ways to provide cross-platform extensions to your application, for example, providing external code, internationalization, and file import and export modules.

CD-ROM: XPLib Reference

Documentation for XPLib appears on the CD-ROM that comes with this book (for both the Windows environment and the Macintosh).

XPLib Architecture. Discussion of the criteria for the XPLib software, its architecture, and overview of the basic cross-platform application construction process.

XPLib Quick Reference. Discussions of each of the major function groups that comprise the XPAPI appropriately cross-referenced.

XPLib Function Reference.   Details of each of the functions in XPLib that make up the XPAPI.

XPLib Data Types.   Presentation and explanation of the data types and structures for the XPLib software.

 XPLib Events.   Discussion of XPLib event messages and notification codes. Every event message is discussed in detail including the encoding of information for each of the three platforms.

Simple Example.   Presentation of a simple cross-platform application using XPLib that illustrates basic program structure, window handling functions, and text and graphics. Emphasis is on program organization and not functionality.

Advanced Example.   Discusses all phases of the cross-platform application construction process using XPLib by presenting the source code for graphics and text drawing program and the necessary resources.

THE SOFTWARE

First my disclaimer: the examples in this book are meant for illustration purposes only and should not be taken as a complete implementation of a cross-platform solution. They solve pieces of the cross-platform solution, but they should not be taken too far out of context.

A working cross-platform solution is presented in the form of the XPLib software provided with this book on the CD-ROM. XPLib is a set of three libraries (one each for the Macintosh, Windows 3.1, and Windows NT) that provide a cross-platform functional API for developers, called XPAPI. The libraries don't provide a complete solution to the cross-platform development problem, but they do provide you with the ability to solve many problems and gain an understanding of the benefits of cross-platform design. (Currently XPLib only supports the most common menu forms, resource types, window styles, events, and graphics and text features.)

System Information

In this book Macintosh refers to a Macintosh computer running System 6.0.5 or a later version and running Finder or MultiFinder, or a Macintosh computer running System 7.0 or a later version; unless, specifically indicated otherwise.

Windows 3.1 refers to a PC-compatible computer running DOS 4.0 or a later version and running Microsoft Windows 3.1. Many of the examples of Windows 3.1 solutions do not utilize Windows 3.1-specific functions, but rather opt for the Windows 3.0 subset.

Win32 refers to a computer running Windows NT with Win32 Version 3.1 or a later version.

Windows refers to a computer running Windows 3.1 or Win32.

About XPLib

Macintosh.   XPLib was developed using a Macintosh IIci computer with 8 MB of RAM, a 200 MB hard disk drive, running System 6.0.7 with Finder and MultiFinder, and running System

7.0 and 7.1. In addition the software was developed using THINK C version 5.0, which is published by Symantec.

Windows 3.1. XPLib was initially developed using a Gateway 2000 486/33C computer with 8MB of RAM and a 200 MB hard disk drive, running Microsoft DOS 5.0 and Windows 3.1. In addition the software was developed using Borland C/C++ version 3.1.

Win32. XPLib was developed using a Gateway 2000 486/33C computer with 40 MB of RAM, a 700 MB hard disk drive, running Microsoft, the Win32 subsystem of Windows NT pre-Beta, Beta 1, and Beta 2. In addition the software was developed using the 32-bit version of Microsoft C version 8.0.

XPLib Requirements

Macintosh. To use XPLib, we recommend that you have a Macintosh computer with at least a 68030 processor, 4 MB of RAM, a 100 MB hard disk drive, and System 6.0.7 running MultiFinder or System 7.0. THINK C 6.0 or Symantec C++ is recommended, but the Macintosh Programmer's Workbench (MPW) can be used with the understanding that some conversion is required.

Windows 3.1. To use XPLib, we recommend that you have an IBM PC or 100 percent compatible computer with at least a 25 MHz 80386 processor, 4 MB of RAM (it's better to have 8 MB), a 100 MB hard disk drive, DOS 5.0 or later, and Windows 3.1. Borland C/C++ version 3.1 or later is recommended because its interface is very similar to THINK C and its build process is straightforward. Microsoft C version 6.0 or 7.0 can be used because the XPLib library is in a standard linkable library. A Symantec C++ version of XPLib will be available soon.

Win32. To use XPLib, we recommended that you have a PC or 100 percent compatible computer capable of running Windows NT, with at least a 33 MHz 80486 processor, 16 MB of RAM, a 200 MB hard disk drive, and the most recent version of the Windows NT/Win32 SDK, Borland C/C++, or Symantec C++. Non-PC Windows NT computers are all powerful enough to use XPLib, but we have not generated MIPS or DEC Alpha AXP binary versions of XPLib yet.

Refer to the README files on the CD-ROM that accompanies this book for information about the organization and content of the software. The Macintosh README file is a TeachText file and the Windows README file is plain text. Also, included on the CD-ROM are a text-only bug report (BUGS.TXT) and registration (REG.TXT) forms. You can reach me using email at:

MCI:	504-5758 or spetrucci
CIS:	71052,2577
Internet:	0005045758@mcimail.com

Have fun and good luck!

Steve Petrucci

ACKNOWLEDGMENTS

Ron Petrusha (previously at Random House) for asking me to do this book, Paul Mace at Paul Mace Software for planting the bug in Ron's ear, and Jeff Angus for introducing me to Paul.

Geoff LeBlond and Bill LeBlond from The LeBlond Group for information about production issues, Ann Becherer for editorial assistance, and Paul Bariteau for technical advice and moral support.

Scott Suhy for evaluating and testing the software in this book and answering many of my questions about Windows NT, and without whom, I would have been lost.

Tom Tenerowicz, Tom Croswell, Andy Keene, and Bill Baggett from Silicon Graphics, for providing me with information about the MIPS processors and the MIPS version of Windows NT and tools.

Nan Borreson and Linda Grier at Borland International, for providing me with beta copies of Borland's C/C++ compiler for Windows NT.

Trudy Edelson at Farallon for background information about networks and network products.

Jim DeLaHunt at Adobe Systems Inc., for helping me to understand some PostScript font issues.

Ben Schreiber, David Price, Kelly Phillips, David Pursel, and Bob Schneider from Digital Equipment Corporation for information about the Alpha AXP processor and the Alpha version of Windows NT and its tools.

Eric Engstrom, Adam Waalkes, Bob Taniguchi, Dave Beaver, and Mike Flora at Microsoft for help with my Windows NT questions ranging from the general to the specific.

Allen Bannon and Steven Levine at Symantec Corporation for information about the Symantec compilers and information about the Bedrock cross-platform application framework.

Mike DeLaurentis and Tammi Tsujikawa at ElseWare Corporation for information and discussion about PANOSE and parametric font synthesis.

Finally, thanks to everyone who provided me with bits and pieces of information that helped to fill many of the holes in the subject matter of this book and those that made me think about things that I hadn't initially thought of.

Part One

Foundation

1

Cross-Platform Issues

If there were only one microprocessor architecture, one brand of computer system, one operating system, and one graphical user interface, then any program written would run on all computers. But this is the real world.

Two major microprocessor architectures are used in consumer and corporate computer machinery, the Intel 80x86 and the Motorola 680x0.[1] There are scores of computer hardware manufacturers: for example, Apple, IBM, Compaq, and Dell. On top of this add the various flavors of a single platform: the Macintosh Toolbox running System 6, System 6 with MultiFinder, or System 7; various versions of DOS (MS-DOS and DR-DOS) running Windows 3.1 (some still running Windows 3.0); OS/2 2.1; NeXTSTEP; and Windows NT running the Win32, Win16, OS/2, or POSIX subsystems. Not all systems are created equal, and each computer user has a favorite.

As you plan your product, you have to decide which microprocessor, computer system, and operating system to support. Obviously you make this decision with the buyer in mind. Who

---

[1] There are numerous types of microprocessors within the common processor families as well. The 80x86 family contains the 8086, 80286, 80386, 80486, Pentium, and others. The 680x0 family contains the 68000, 68020, 68030, 68040, and others. Workstation computers utilize an even more diverse selection of microprocessors: Sun Microsystem's SPARC family, the MIPS family of RISC processors, Hewlett-Packard's PA-RISC processor, Digital Equipment's Alpha AXP, and IBM's RS/6000, for example.

3

will buy the product? What types of computers do these potential customers use? If they use one type of computer, then the answer to your first question is simple. If they use just two, the answer might depend on which computer is the most popular. If they use three, the answer is less clear.

When users of many computer system types, or platforms, require a broad range of software solutions, the application developer must eventually select one or two platforms to develop for. Alternatively, you may develop or purchase a solution that will allow you to support many platforms, allowing you to easily migrate to new systems or to systems that have become more popular.

The key to success in the competitive marketplace may very well be using cross-platform design and implementation techniques to provide products for more than one computer platform with minimal implementation redundancy.

Why is cross-platform development necessary? What techniques do cross-platform developers use to design and implement a single product for multiple platforms? How does developing for multiple platforms affect engineering? Management? Marketing? In this chapter we'll lay the groundwork for the discussion by:

- defining terms used in this book
- presenting the different types of cross-platform development
- exploring the reasons for cross-platform development
- looking at the economics of cross-platform development
- surveying the various types of cross-platform solutions

BACKGROUND

Cross-platform development evolved from portable coding practices. Portable source code will compile and execute on another computer system even if the underlying hardware is different.

The problems that portability solves represent a subset of the problems that a cross-platform solution must solve. Portability deals with differences in hardware and operating system features, like memory and file management. Many of the differences are masked by compiler-specific data types, careful coding practices, and using standard libraries (the ANSI C language has the standard C libraries, for example).

A cross-platform solution must solve the portability problems and also the problems specific to platforms: graphical user interfaces, event-driven operating systems, resource management, drawing graphics, displaying images, rendering fonts, and interprocess communications. Because every platform is different, a cross-platform solution is often tailored to the task of the application for which it is being designed.

Companies want cross-platform products so that the information can be shared across platforms. Software developers use cross-platform development techniques to produce these cross-platform products. Aldus Corporation was one of the first companies to use cross-platform development techniques for a commercial software product, PageMaker. Microsoft ships cross-platform versions of its word processor (Word) and spreadsheet applications (Excel) that were developed using a common cross-platform code base. Many products are successful because they run on multiple platforms and have the ability to read and write the data from other programs and other platforms.

As the number of popular types of computers increases, the need to share information and to provide products capable of sharing information becomes more important. Cross-platform development is one way to do this.

To provide a cross-platform solution, you need to provide a cross-platform API. Figure 1.1 illustrates some of the components and the relationships between many of these components of single-platform and cross-platform applications. These components are defined in the next section.

DEFINITIONS

To understand the principles of cross-platform development, you needn't be familiar with the intricacies of many platforms. A reasonable understanding of just one platform is all you need (preferably the Macintosh or Windows). It is helpful to understand the meanings of the components that make up the big picture shown in Figure 1.1. These terms and others are discussed in this section.

Hardware Platform.   A hardware platform is a computer hardware design that incorporates a certain type of microprocessor; for example, an IBM PC (or PC for short) or compatible, which is based on the 80x86 microprocessor, is a hardware platform and a Macintosh, which is based on the 680x0 microprocessor, is another hardware platform. A hardware platform is *capable* of running any type of operating system. Some hardware platforms run only one type, while others run more than one type; for example, the Macintosh runs System 6, System 7, or A/UX; the PC runs DOS, Windows NT, OS/2, UNIX, NeXTSTEP, Solaris, etc.

Graphical User Interface (GUI).   A GUI lets the user access software through a graphical (usually non-textual) paradigm. Typically a GUI uses icons to represent an application or documents. An application usually maintains one or more windows, a menu bar, and dialog boxes with which the user will interact. Typically the user positions a mouse cursor over an icon

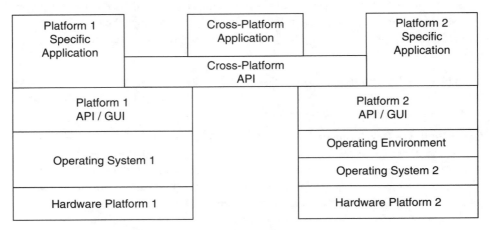

Figure 1.1 Multiple- and cross-platform architectures.

and double-clicks to start up the application or document. Other methods of interaction include clicking and dragging files to copy or move them from one directory to another. A platform's GUI is unique but still shares many anatomical features of most other GUIs. The Macintosh, Windows 3.1, Win32 (Windows NT), Presentation Manager (OS/2), and Motif (X Windows) are a few of the most popular GUIs.

Operating System.   An operating system is a program that runs very close to the computer hardware (usually just above the ROM code or BIOS). It gives the user a way to access system and file information and run applications. An operating system also provides the developer with a set of access points which an application uses to access operating system information or perform low-level tasks, like reading the contents of a file. The user interacts with the operating system using a text-based command line (as in MS-DOS) or using a GUI (as in Macintosh). In this book, I refer to these types of operating systems as text-based operating systems and graphical operating systems, respectively.

Operating Environment.   An operating environment provides a GUI for operating systems that do not inherently possess one, such as Windows 3.1, which is an operating environment that runs on top of MS-DOS. That way, the combination of text-based operating system and operating environment look and act like a graphical operating system.

Application Program Interface (API).   The API is a set of operating system or environment functions that the application developer uses to access the features and capabilities of the system. In a graphical operating system or environment, an API lets the application developer access and control the GUI. A typical API provides access to memory allocation, file management, windowing, and menu management functions.

Platform.   For the purposes of this book a platform is a computer running a graphical-based operating system (for example, Macintosh with System 6 or 7 or Windows NT with Win32) or a graphical-based operating environment on top of an operating system (for example, Windows 3.1 and DOS). It is the combination of a hardware platform and a specific operating system or environment that constitutes a platform. A graphical-based operating system or environment maintains a graphical user interface (GUI) with which the user will interact. This differs from more traditional portable coding practices where the user interface is assumed to be text-based.

Per-Platform Development.   Per-platform development is the design and development of software that will run on a single platform. It's impossible to port software developed in this manner to other platforms without significantly rewriting it.

Cross-Platform Development.   Cross-platform development is the design and development of software that can be recompiled to run on more than one platform. A true cross-platform application requires no special effort to recompile and run on different platforms. You simply move the source code to the new platform and *make* the application. Developing for multiple platforms isn't easy because most platforms have capabilities, limitations, or tools that differ significantly from those on other platforms. Cross-platform design is the method used to produce a cross-platform application.

Platform-Dependent or Platform-Specific Feature or Code. A platform-dependent or platform-specific feature is unique to that platform (for example, a single desktop menu bar is unique to the Macintosh). A platform-dependent or platform-specific piece of source code will run only on a specific platform (for example, a function that includes inline 8086 assembler code used to call up a PC BIOS function is specific to the Windows 3.1 platform).

Platform-Independent Feature or Code. A platform-independent feature is independent of the platform it will run on. For example, all platforms discussed in this book have windows; thus, a window is a platform-independent feature. A platform-independent piece of source code can be compiled to run on any platform. When an entire application is produced in a platform-independent way, it is a cross-platform application.

Resource. A resource is data that is bound to an application and is necessary for that application to run. For example, an application's resources might define a new cursor shape, an icon, or the contents of a dialog box. In the Macintosh a resource can be modified when an application is running. In Windows 3.1 a resource is usually statically bound to the executable file during the development process and is not modifiable at run-time.

WHY CONSIDER CROSS-PLATFORM DEVELOPMENT?

There are many reasons for you to consider cross-platform development. The most obvious reason is so that your software will run on multiple computer platforms. Many of the other reasons for cross-platform development are justified because it is an economical way to produce a product on multiple platforms. For example:

- Platforms gain and lose popularity.
- New platforms are always emerging.
- Cross-platform software makes efficient use of development resources.
- Cross-platform software is easy to maintain.
- Cross-platform support can be used as a marketing tool.

Each of these reasons will be described in this section.

Recognizing Opportunities

Each of the well-established platforms has strengths and weaknesses that attract and repel certain types of users. For example, many Windows users think Macintoshes are still toys and are too expensive, but Macintosh users think Windows is difficult to learn and PCs are difficult to set up. No matter how much better another platform might be for a certain task, dedicated users of a specific platform usually remain loyal.

Do you target an additional platform and its users or ignore the potential market? When the number of users of a platform reaches the point where the cost of developing and marketing a product for that platform is substantially less than the potential revenue, you'll want to support that platform. Using cross-platform development techniques allows you port to new platforms with minimal effort.

Also consider that a platform's popularity can change. As some platforms age and lose popularity, others emerge with great acclaim. Still others emerge slowly and become popular over time.[2] Track the shifting tides of popularity. Anticipating the popularity of a platform can translate to market success. Failing to detect ebbing popularity can compound quarterly losses as you continue to support and maintain a marginally successful product.[3]

Supporting New Platforms Easily

Viable new platforms do not emerge often, and the long-term success of a new platform is often difficult to predict. Even successful platforms have a life cycle that is usually dictated by the success of a particular type of computer hardware and the applications that are available for that system. Some successful desktop platforms include CP/M (without which there would be no PCs), Apple II, DOS, Windows, Macintosh, and UNIX. Some less successful platforms include Gem, TOS, and TopView. The future of other platforms, for example, OS/2 and Windows NT, are not yet clear.

The failure of a platform is relative to your viewpoint. The ability to provide a reasonable product for a reasonable period of time at a reasonable cost may often indicate success to the user and the developer but can also indicate failure to the personal computer market as a whole. As a software developer it is often difficult to discern the difference between a potentially successful platform and one that is not so successful. Careful analysis of the market is essential for the success of a product on any platform, even one that is relatively short-lived.

Nonetheless, it is important to be aware of new platforms *before* they emerge. This allows you to gain experience with the platform and get a jump on potential market opportunities. The cost is that you must work with incomplete software, and the risk is that the platform may not be accepted by the users as rapidly as you anticipate. However, a good cross-platform design will allow migration to new platforms with minimal cost.

Using Resources More Efficiently

Producing a single product on a single platform requires a development staff that knows the API of the platform and the functional components of your product. Producing a single product on three platforms without using cross-platform development techniques requires either three groups, each familiar with a particular platform and the various functional components of each product, or a single group that is familiar with all three platforms and the various functional

---

[2] In the early days of Windows, PC users were slow to give up their DOS applications. It wasn't until Windows 3.0 was released that Windows became a dominant platform. Also, look at UNIX and its long bumpy ride from the laboratories of AT&T to its various incarnations.

[3] Take, for example, OS/2 1.0 and the companies that had tied their success to this system only to discover that because the PC market wasn't accepting it, Microsoft decided not to continue marketing it. Their products may be great and still in demand, but without the support of Microsoft, the market for these products dried up and yet the cost to maintain these orphan products is high. This is not to say that IBM won't pull off the reincarnation of OS/2 in version 2.1 and cause a new shift in its popularity.

components. It's rare to find developers with these qualifications, and it is often costly to bring new developers up to speed. It's much simpler to buy a cross-platform solution or hire developers who understand a particular platform to develop the cross-platform tools you'll need. Then the developers who understand the nuances of the product and its functional components use the tools for development.

In a small development environment it is simpler to spend the time up front developing the cross-platform tools and then use those tools to produce your product on various platforms. More often, it is more economical to purchase the cross-platform tools so that you can concentrate on developing your product and not on the implementation details of the individual platforms.

Simplifying Maintenance

The time and staff needed to produce an application represents only a part of the cost associated with a product during its life. Each product on each platform requires continual improvements, expansions, or shifts of their feature sets, problem fixes, and customer support. A product that takes eighteen months to develop can remain viable for ten years. During the product's life cycle, you must keep the product in a marketable condition. Supporting and maintaining a single product across multiple platforms is not a simple task. If all platform-related issues of development are handled by a group or by another company that provides a cross-platform solution, maintenance requires modifying only a single set of source files for all platforms.

Capitalizing on Marketing Advantages

Positioning a product is integral to its success. It's important to realize the market potential for your product across all viable platforms. You must be aware of the shifts in popularity of a platform, the emergence of new platforms, and the existence of all relevant platforms to make intelligent decisions about the feasibility and lifespan of your product, as well as its potential market size and market growth.

Also, advertising that your product works on a particular platform or multiple platforms can often lead customers to buy your product rather than another. Availability on multiple platforms might give the sense of security to a user or might solve an in-house standardization problem for a company that uses multiple platforms and wants to provide compatible file formats across those platforms.

THE ECONOMICS OF CROSS-PLATFORM DEVELOPMENT

Choosing a platform or platforms for which to develop a product is really a matter of economics. Do you have the time and resources available to perform the tasks? Do you have enough of a market to which to sell to justify the expense of development? Is the market window for your product on a platform long enough to realize the product? Here we will present some simple quantitative support for cross-platform development and look at the time, personnel, and market economics of cross-platform development.

Time Considerations

It takes time to evaluate all potential platforms and your software needs to produce a cross-platform architecture. It takes time to design, develop, and debug a cross-platform solution for a single platform. If it takes M time units to develop an application for a single platform, then using per-platform development techniques, it takes $M*N$ time units to develop the same product for N platforms. For per-platform development you must consider the time it takes to implement and debug a per-platform solution for each platform that you want to support. For cross-platform development you must consider the time required to implement and debug each cross-platform solution plus the time required to produce the application, once. To get a complete picture of the time you will invest for development, you must also factor in the time to produce new versions of the product and the time required to maintain it—we will ignore these factors in this discussion.

To develop the simplest cross-platform solution will require about one month per platform to develop. This will provide you with a reasonable solution to a reasonable set of cross-platform solutions. A middle-of-the-road solution will require about six months per platform to develop and should suffice for all but the most demanding software needs. A complete cross-platform solution will require a year or more per platform to develop, but will give you a lot of functionality and should solve all of your software needs.

To minimize the time required to provide a cross-platform solution, consider a commercially available product. In this case you will only need to consider the time required to learn the cross-platform API and to learn the development processes of the product on each platform.

Resource Requirements

To provide a cross-platform solution, you need to have the necessary resources—either the people to implement the solution or the funds to buy, and possibly augment, an existing solution. If you are producing your own cross-platform solution, you need to have or hire people experienced in all platforms or you must be willing to train them. If you are buying a cross-platform solution, then you must be sure that the vendor supports all relevant platforms and has sufficient support resources or documentation to assist you in learning his or her product. Both people and product resources require that you be aware of your future plans. You must keep on top of market trends and your need to migrate to other less-important platforms.

Cost to Implement or Ignore

To properly evaluate the cost to develop a software application, you must find the proper balance between the cost to ignore other platforms, the cost to implement a per-platform solution, the cost to develop your own cross-platform solution, and the cost to purchase an existing solution. This isn't an easy task. It requires a thorough understanding of your development capabilities and market needs, the amount of time available, the importance of control over the solution (in-house or supplied sources versus precompiled libraries), and your need to understand the cross-platform solution.

Market Advantage of Cross-Platform Implementation

Providing multiple-platform support is sometimes a marketing plus. It makes your product more visible and perhaps more appealing to multiple-platform customers. Providing a solution on a popular platform gives your product a lot of attention. By shortening your time-to-market you can satisfy changing market needs without a lot of development overhead. This allows you to change your direction quickly, with little development cost.

Here is a simple example of the effect of migrating to another popular platform that has a smaller market share—both platforms are assumed to have the same number of units in the field. If platform A has a 50 percent market share for your product and platform B has a 20 percent market share, and if you assume a long-term market saturation of 20 percent on both platforms, then you can increase your sales by 40 percent by providing a product for platform B.

Simple Analysis of Cross-Platform Economics

Here we will look at a simple analysis of the costs to develop a product using per-platform and cross-platform techniques. We make the following assumptions:

- One person performs the work. The efforts of several additional developers can be factored in later.
- The amount of time to develop a cross-platform solution is known. The up-front time to design a cross-platform solution is factored into the time to produce each platform solution.
- The time required to complete a software application is the same regardless of whether we use a cross-platform solution or a per-platform solution. This means that the cross-platform solution does not provide solutions to application-specific problems.
- Cross-platform solutions are applied to produce a single software application across multiple platforms.
- We know the number of platforms for which we will be producing a product.
- Developers are assumed to be experienced and not to require any ramp-up time.

we can infer the following relationship between a per-platform and a cross-platform solution:

$T_{product}$ = time to develop the product

T_{cross} = time to develop a cross-platform solution

N = number of platforms

If $N * T_{product}$ represents the time required to produce a per-platform solution and $T_{product} + N * T_{cross}$ represents the time required to produce a cross-platform solution, then if $N * T_{product} > T_{product} + N * T_{cross}$, a cross-platform solution is a better choice than a per-platform solution. This relationship simplifies to $T_{product}/T_{cross} > N/(N-1)$.

A graph of per-platform development compared with cross-platform development is shown in Figure 1.2. This graph assumes $T_{product}$ is twelve months and T_{cross} is six months. For an application that is run on a single platform, a per-platform solution is always a better choice.

For two platforms a cross-platform solution is better if it takes more than twice as long to develop the per-platform product as it does to develop a cross-platform solution. One person

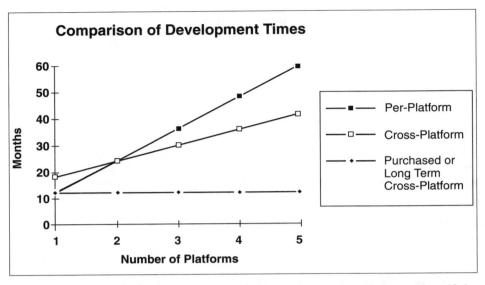

Figure 1.2 Comparison of the times to produce a multiple-platform product if the per-platform product takes twelve months to develop.

working on a one-year product will require an additional six months for each platform solution (one year), which results in two years to complete two versions of the product using a cross-platform solution. One person will require two one-year product cycles or two years for a per-platform solution of the same products. Both solutions are equally viable.

Two people, working efficiently and each skilled in a single platform and possessing an understanding of the software problem, could probably produce two platform versions of a product in less than two years with a cross-platform solution.

For three platforms a cross-platform solution is better if it takes more than 1.5 times as long to develop the product as it does to develop the cross-platform solution. Again, if a product requires twelve months to develop and each platform requires six months, then this equals 18 + 12, or thirty months (maximum) to produce the product for three platforms. Compare this to thirty-six months for three separate twelve-month per-platform solutions.

If the cross-platform solutions you have previously crafted or purchased are robust enough for your product line, then you can save a lot of time, namely, $T_{product} * (N - 1)$ time units minimum, using cross-platform development techniques. If $T_{product}$ is a year, then you can save at least two years with one person producing the same product for three platforms. This is also illustrated in Figure 1.2.

Figure 1.3 shows what happens to development times if $T_{product}$ is eighteen months (a more realistic time to produce a complex application) and T_{cross} is six months. Notice that even for two platforms it is more efficient to use a cross-platform solution even when the solution is performed in house.

Obviously this analysis is very simple and makes some assumptions about a product cycle, the abilities of the developer, what happens if there is more than one developer, and the

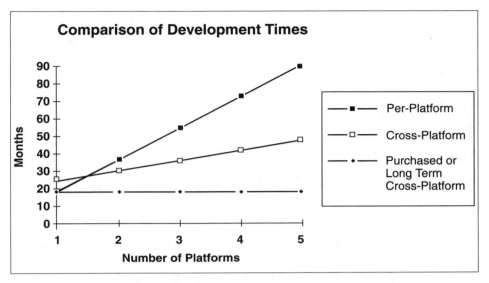

Figure 1.3 Comparison of the times to produce a multiple-platform product if the per-platform product takes eighteen months to develop.

cross-platform solution process. It could be made quite a bit more formal by including variables for personnel, etc., but that is not the intent of this book. This analysis is included to illustrate how much time can be saved when cross-platform techniques are utilized.

TYPES OF PLATFORM INDEPENDENCE

There are four types of platform independence:

- syntactic independence
- data independence or data structure equivalence
- file format and transfer independence
- look and feel equivalence

Syntactic Independence

The most basic form of platform independence is in the syntactic representation of the source code for an application. It allows the software developer to write a product once and compile it to execute on all relevant platforms. It does not imply that data or file forms are equivalent. It only makes the developer's job easier. Syntactic independence is the simplest and fastest form of cross-platform solution to implement. This is provided by macros, function abstraction, and object class libraries, which are discussed later in this chapter.

Data Independence

To provide an open architecture that allows a developer, after-market developer, or a power user to access certain features of your product across multiple platforms, you must provide equivalent forms for important data structures. It isn't really necessary to provide this level of platform independence for internal development purposes. It is only important to provide data independence if you plan to open up your product's architecture to the world or to facilitate cross-platform file formats.

File Independence

A true cross-platform application allows you read and write files that can be used on a variety of platforms. For example, Microsoft Word for Windows and Macintosh can read or write files in a variety of formats but are especially useful if you want to use a Macintosh Word document in Windows and vice versa. The user does not (and should not) have to worry about the details of the format. The user only needs to know that whatever work he or she does will not be lost when someone on another platform wants to read, edit, or print the document. This transparency of form is a very important asset of a cross-platform application from the user perspective.

Look and Feel Equivalence

When you set out to design your cross-platform solution, you will need to balance how the solution and the resulting application will look and feel to the user. This is more complicated than it seems. You will need to maintain a familiar look and feel on a particular platform to keep the users happy while they use your application and other platform-specific applications. You will also need to maintain a consistent look and feel for the application across all of the platforms you are supporting for those who use your particular application across platforms.

Discussion of Types of Platform Independence

To satisfy normal user cross-platform needs, you only need to provide file format and transfer independence and look and feel equivalence. The user doesn't care what the code base is that provides these features; he or she only cares that these features exist.

If you want to provide a product or products for third-party and power users, you need to concentrate on providing file format and transfer independence and data independence. Again, the power user doesn't care how these features are implemented.

If you are developing a cross-platform solution, you need to develop a cross-platform code base. To do this you need to provide syntactic independence and possibly data independence. The other types of platform independence may be necessary depending on who your customers are and the features you want to provide.

As a developer you will need to consider what solution you will need to allow a single set of sources to generate an application on multiple platforms. This involves satisfying syntactic and data independence. You will also need to consider how the application will be used and to consider file independence and look and feel equivalence. One of your biggest challenges will be to provide look and feel equivalence. You will need to provide a solution that considers the number of users, the number of platforms, and the number of applications that are used in a working environment. This presents a three-dimensional problem space that is illustrated in Figure 1.4.

It's simple to provide a consistent look and feel to a single user on one machine using one application because the entire range of experience is defined by one application. When you have an environment that has either many users or many platforms, or many applications and only one or both of the other two variables, the problem of providing an acceptable look and feel is more complicated but is still defined by the factor that is variable. If you have many users–many platforms, many users–many applications, or many platforms–many applications, the look and feel problem becomes complex. You must satisfy two varying quantities to best solve the problem. The most complex situation is if you have many users, many platforms, and many applications in an environment. You will probably have to make some tradeoffs in look and feel consistency if you are designing a single cross-platform solution, or you will have to implement a not-so-pure cross-platform solution. These relationships are also shown in Table 1-1.

The problem should be approached by defining the market or markets that you are selling to and by defining the scope of the application you are developing. By mapping that information into the problem space described in Figure 1.4, you can determine the difficulty level of the problem. Then, based on the resources that are available for your development effort, you can decide if and where you will need to cut corners in the product's look and feel.

Simple Scenario. Develop a product for multiple platforms that is used by single users in isolation as the sole solution; for example, a program that general contractors use to manage their jobs in the field on a specific machine. You can be more flexible in your cross-platform

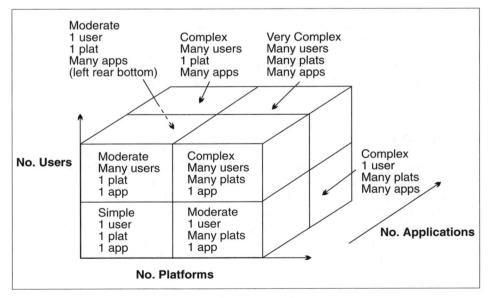

Figure 1.4 Cross-platform look and feel problem space.

Table 1.1 Cross-platform look and feel problem.

Level of Difficulty	Situations		
simple	1 user 1 platform 1 application		
moderate	1 user 1 platform many applications	1 user many platforms 1 application	many users 1 platform 1 application
complex	1 user many platforms many applications	many users many platforms 1 application	many users 1 platform many applications
very complex	many users many platforms many applications		

solution and the look and feel of the product because the product will not be shared by users across multiple platforms.

Complex Scenario. Develop a cross-platform application that is used by a large corporation that has multiple platforms and many applications that are used in tandem with your product. You will need to be more careful and thorough when you design your cross-platform solution or you will need to allow for more platform-specific exceptions in your design to provide an adequate solution in this case.

The types of platform independence that you must support depend on whether cross-platform is to be the method of development, the method of use, or both.

CROSS-PLATFORM SOLUTIONS

There are numerous methods and techniques that are used in cross-platform development. Some of these methods are straightforward and don't affect performance but will limit the complexity of the resulting application. Others are more complex and may ultimately affect performance but imply no limit to the application's final complexity. As with most solutions, there is a tradeoff of time and usability. You must fully understand the needs of the application you are writing to determine a course of action before you implement your cross-platform solution.

This section briefly describes the full spectrum of cross-platform solutions, including:

- using the ANSI C library
- finding a common denominator

- synthesizing missing functionality
- rewriting inadequate functionality
- replacing the API
- using or creating an object class library
- finding a suitable cross-compiler
- abstracting internal or external data types
- buying an existing cross-platform solution

Using the ANSI C Library

The ANSI C standard regulates the form of the C language and the standard support libraries.[4] Any program written in the ANSI C dialect will be understandable by all ANSI C compilers and should be syntactically correct. The ANSI C library solves the portability problem.

However, the ANSI library does not provide a way to access features of a platform's API, operating system specific functionality, or any GUI features. Also, the standard doesn't necessarily resolve specific hardware issues, such as byte order, but it does allow the code to be compiled. You must take care to ensure that hardware issues are considered.

You can construct simple, non-GUI, cross-platform applications using the ANSI C libraries provided you use portable coding techniques. ANSI C libraries can also provide cross-platform solutions to very specific areas of a cross-platform implementation, for example, file management, string management, character identification, date and time management, and memory management. Take care to understand the limits of a particular platform implementation using ANSI C, because not all platforms provide equivalent functionality.

The ANSI C library does not adequately address user interface issues. Nor does it address event driven platform models. The ANSI C library often doesn't provide a consistent international solution and doesn't address interprocess communications. File operations don't necessarily take into account all of the features of the platform's file management functions. Memory allocation isn't consistent, nor is it necessarily based on the same underlying model. Resources are also overlooked in the ANSI C libraries.

Ideally the industry should develop a cross-platform standard that encompasses the needs of specific hardware platforms and the GUI environment. This would allow a language, like C, to provide a broader solution across platforms. As it is, however, GUIs are not very compatible, and many issues, such as international character representations, are still evolving.

For more information on the specific hardware and platform limitations of an ANSI C cross-platform solution, see Platform Comparisons in Chapter 2.

Finding a Common Denominator

Probably the most common approach to cross-platform development is finding a common denominator method. With this approach, you analyze your target platforms and their APIs to

---

[4] ANSI C refers to the 1989 standard for the C programming language and is formally known as American National Standard X3.159-1989.

determine a subset of features that your application requires. Once you've defined the feature set, you find the functions that provide the required functionality on each platform. You design a new API or layer to remove existing platform dependencies. You design this cross-platform API to produce applications that run on all supported platforms.

If you choose the smallest functional subset common to your target platforms, then you have found the least (or smallest) common denominator, and you will need to synthesize a lot of other necessary functionality. If you choose the largest subset common to your target platform (the union), then you have found the greatest common denominator and you will synthesize the minimum amount of other necessary functionality. The least common denominator is easier to find but will be less efficient if you need a complete cross-platform solution.

The common denominator method can be implemented two ways: using macros to define a new API and using functions to define a new API.

Macro Definitions

In the simplest case the common denominator method can be a compile-time abstraction, usually in the form of macros, that maps the various platform functions to the new API, as shown in Figure 1.5. This is only useful in the simplest cases where differences in platform capabilities are minimal, for example, to abstract the Windows 3.1 and Win32 APIs. When you use macros, the cross-platform API has little or no effect on the performance of the resulting application or program. Unfortunately, macros are rarely useful for applications that provide a broad range of functionality or operate across more than two platforms.

Further, using macros to map functionality creates a problem when debugging the application. Because a macro can expand, it can cause problems at compile time and run-time that are not always evident from the syntax of the macro definition. For example, an error in the macro definition can cause syntax errors when the macro is expanded at compile time that may seem

```
#ifdef __PLATA__
// these macros are for platform 1
#define XPMOVETO (x, y) P1MoveTo (y, x)
#define XPLINETO (x, y) P1LineTo (y, x)

#else
// these macros are for platform 2
#define XPMOVETO (x, y) P2MoveTo (x, y)
#define XPLINETO (x, y) P2LineTo (x, y)
#endif
```

Cross-Platform	Platform A Expansion	Platform B Expansion
XPMOVETO(0,100);	P1MoveTo(100,0);	P2MoveTo(0,100);
XPLINETO(100,200);	P1LineTo(200,100);	P2LineTo(200,100);

Figure 1.5 Example of using macros to define a cross-platform API.

inconsistent with the original source code. Or it can cause improper expansion that might be syntactically correct but functionally incorrect. Run-time problems arise when the macro isn't fully debugged, or when you step through the code during symbolic debugging and the source code that you see does not match the expanded source code (that you don't see) or doesn't map in a one-to-one manner.

Functional Abstraction

Normally the common denominator method requires you to construct a new functional interface, or layer, that calls the corresponding function or functions in the underlying platform API, as illustrated in Figure 1.6. Ideally this functional abstraction is kept to a minimum to allow the cross-platform solution to be as fast as possible. An indirection of one function call rarely appreciably degrades performance on most platforms.[5]

A call to an abstracted function will indirectly call the native API function. When you use an abstracted function, be careful to avoid iterative or recursive calls to it. Instead, try to find a way to provide the iterative solution by creating an additional function in your cross-platform API that provides the iteration option but implements it at the platform API level.

In some instances it isn't possible to find a functional equivalent on all platforms. When this happens, you need to find the best fit for as many platforms as you can and then synthesize the functionality on the other platforms.

I primarily used the function abstraction approach to implement the XPLib cross-platform solution discussed in this book, but I also had to rewrite and synthesize certain functions.

Synthesizing Missing Functionality

Creating, or synthesizing, functionality that is not present in a platform isn't a distinct cross-platform implementation technique. Rather, it is a way to augment another technique when a platform is deficient in one or more areas. For example, if one platform API did not support round rectangles, you could synthesize them by drawing arcs and lines. Another example is that Macintosh and Win32 platforms provide direct API functions for getting the date and time, but Windows 3.1 does not. A cross-platform date and time function needs to synthesize this by calling low-level DOS functions. Unless all of the platforms for which you are developing a cross-platform API provide the same feature set, you will need to synthesize some functionality.

If your cross-platform API is too broad, it may be very difficult or even impossible to synthesize the required functionality across all platforms. For example, if some platforms support preemptive multitasking and others don't, it would be complicated to synthesize this functionality. In these cases it might be better to settle for less functionality. Because synthesis is very labor intensive, the decision to use this method really depends on how important a certain class of functionality is and how much time and how many resources you have to solve the problem.

---

[5] Be aware that the overhead of a function call in Windows 3.1 is greater than in other platforms. There are often many non-obvious intermediate levels of code that need to be executed to perform Windows API calls, for example, the device drivers, virtual device drivers, and helper code that changes the mode of the 80x86 processor.

```
// example of Functional Abstraction
void XPMoveTo (int x, int y)
{
  #ifdef __PLATA__
  P1MoveTo (y, x);

  #else
  P2MoveTo (x, y);
  #endif
}

void XPLineTo (int x, int y)
{
  #ifdef __PLATA__
  P1LineTo (y, x);

  #else
  P2LineTo (x, y);
  #endif
}

void Function ()
{
  XPMoveTo(0,100);
  XPLineTo(100,200);
}
```

platform A flow	*platform B flow*

`XPMoveTo(0,100);`
`  P1MoveTo(100,0);`
`XPLineTo(100,200);`
`  P1LineTo(200,100);`
	`XPMoveTo(0,100);`
	`  P2MoveTo(0,100);`
	`XPLineTo(100,200);`
	`  P2LineTo(100,200);`

Figure 1.6 Example of functional abstraction.

Rewriting Inadequate Functionality

Sometimes the implementation of a particular class of functions in a platform's API is inadequate. In this case you'll have to rewrite certain portions of the platform's API to provide a better or more flexible solution. This might sound a lot like synthesis, but there is an important difference. You rewrite when platform functionality is inadequate, and you synthesize when a platform is missing functionality. Like synthesis, rewriting isn't a distinct cross-platform implementation technique; rather, it is used to augment another approach when a platform is deficient in one or more areas.

A good example of rewriting is if you want to implement line drawing on the Macintosh without the crazy end caps provided by QuickDraw (see Chapter 8 for more information). Rather that implementing a cross-platform "move to" as a call to the QuickDraw MoveTo() function, you might want to draw the line using a borderless, filled polygon.

Replacing an API

If you decide that a particular platform differs radically from other target platforms, you may want to replace all or parts of the problem platform API with another. This approach is a more encompassing version of rewriting and synthesis. Avoid replacing the API unless you have no other options or unless replacement solves a particular problem. For example, suppose you are a very good Macintosh programmer but you don't like to program in Windows. You could specify your cross-platform API so that it is equivalent to the Macintosh API. The Macintosh implementation would be handled by the Macintosh API and the Windows implementation would be equivalent to porting the Macintosh API to the PC platform. This might seem like an attractive solution for a Macintosh programmer, but to port the Macintosh API would require a very thorough understanding of the Windows API to properly replace and emulate the functionality of the Macintosh.

You may also choose to replace an API when you have decided that the APIs of all platforms are inadequate or inappropriate for the task at hand. In this case, you start from scratch and write a new API to be used on all platforms. You would need to implement the new API at a very low level to make it as portable as possible on each of the target hardware platforms. This solution is reserved for cross-platform operating system developers—for example, for Microsoft developing Win32 to run with Windows NT for the Intel processors, for the MIPS processors, and for Digital Equipment's Alpha processor.

Abstracting Data

Data abstraction (hiding) isn't a method unto itself, but is a necessary component of all the other methods. Data abstraction, illustrated in Figure 1.7, means that certain platform-dependent data types are abstracted or hidden, and sometimes enhanced, in order to produce a new (common) data type to be used by relevant platform-independent functions. Data abstraction is inherent in an object-oriented cross-platform solution and is part of an object class definition.

The required degree of abstraction depends on the complexity of the functions that will use the data type. For example, if you are developing a cross-platform solution for two platforms, P_a and P_b, with corresponding data types, D_a and D_b, it might be necessary to create a new data type D_c to produce a workable cross-platform functional interface. However, in other cases you might decide that the cross-platform data type should be equivalent to D_a or D_b.

Task X on Platform A	Task X on Platform B	Cross-Platform Task X on Platform A	Cross-Platform Task X on Platform B
data A1	data B	data C:	data C:
data A2		data A1	data B
data A3		data A2,	
		data A3	

Figure 1.7 Example of data abstraction.

Data abstraction allows you to specify additional data fields, modify data fields, or hide certain necessary (platform-dependent) data fields. Try to minimize your use of data abstraction. Include, add, modify, or hide fields only when necessary. Unnecessary data abstraction leads to confusion and inefficient data access.

A specific example would be abstracting the printing data structure of the Macintosh, TPrPort, and the data structures needed by Windows, a DEVMODE and a DEVNAMES structure. The cross-platform type PRINTDATA hides these inconsistencies. (See Chapter 11 for more information.)

Using Object Class Libraries

An object class library is essentially the object-oriented equivalent of the common denominator method of cross-platform development coupled with data abstraction (see Figure 1.8). I mention it separately because this method always uses an object-oriented language, like C++. To their disadvantage, object-oriented languages typically do not provide a direct way to dynamically manage the memory associated with objects in accordance with most platform memory managers or task or process managers. In Windows 3.1, for example, a task that is iconized might want to free up as much memory as possible to provide another task with as much non-virtual memory as possible. If many objects are defined, running and switching between

Task X on Platform A	Task X on Platform B	Object C on Platform A	Object C on Platform B
data A1	data B1	data C:	data C:
data A2	function B1	data A1	data B1
data A3	function B2	data A2	internal data
function A1		data A3	method C1:
function A2		method C1	function B1
		function A1	method C2:
		method C2:	function B2
		function A2	
		Cross-Platform Task X on Platform A	**Cross-Platform Task X on Platform B**
		object C:method C1	object C:method C1
		function A1	function B1
		object C:method C2	object C:method C2
		function A2	function B2

Figure 1.8 Object-oriented cross-platform solution.

multiple tasks could lead to memory fragmentation unless the objects are intelligently defined and managed.

Another disadvantage of using an object-oriented language is the introduction of another level of indirection in the execution of an object method over the equivalent functional implementation. In non-demanding applications this creates an acceptable amount of overhead, but it can cause a marginally responsive application to become unacceptable or tedious for a user. In some object-oriented implementations, using a method that is inherited from a superclass several times removed can cause even greater inefficiencies, as each object class is sequentially searched until the defining class is found and the method is executed. My preference is to keep the cross-platform API functional and then build by objects on top of that.

As object-oriented languages mature to encompass the needs of the GUI-based platform and as hardware becomes more powerful, object class libraries will become more useful cross-platform development tools.

Using Cross-Compilers

A cross-platform compiler is the ideal solution to cross-platform development problems. The ideal cross-compiler could be a portable compiler with the necessary extensions to support the underlying GUI in a platform-independent manner. This means a common source code could be compiled for a target platform, as shown in Figure 1.9. Smalltalk (in a general way because it is an interpreter) or some custom cross-compiler implementation would fit this description. A cross-platform compiler might also be a portable operating system that provides a common API across multiple platforms. Windows NT and certain forms of UNIX meet this qualification, as does the Win32s API that runs in Windows 3.1 and under Windows NT.

A cross-compiler, in some ways, is very similar to an object class library, or a functional library, except that it is a solution provided by the compiler maker or the operating system vendor. It is a cross-platform solution that is designed into the language or system and is not an issue for a third-party vendor or the application software developer.

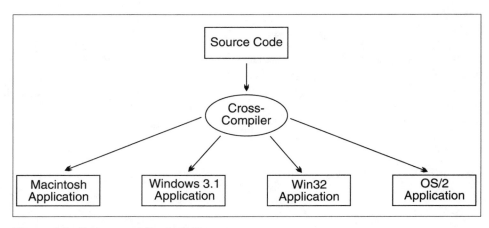

Figure 1.9 Cross-compiler building process.

Generally you will not want to implement a cross-compiler solution to solve your cross-platform problems. It is a solution that is usually implemented by the supplier of cross-platform solutions, languages, or operating systems. Implementing a cross-compiler involves much more time than other cross-platform techniques.

Buying a Cross-Platform Solution

Unless you have sufficient time, sufficient personnel, or a specific cross-platform need, it is more economical to purchase a cross-platform solution from a company that has already spent the time to design, develop, and debug it.

Before you invest the time and money in a cross-platform solution, carefully assess your needs. Some solutions are object-oriented; some work with only a subset of platforms; some specialize in user interface design; some provide a minimal cross-platform solution in exchange for speed, flexibility, and proximity to the underlying platform; and some provide a complete cross-platform solution and abstract all aspects of program development. Some commercially available solutions are discussed in more detail in Chapter 3.

Be certain of the demands of your product or product line to ensure that a particular cross-platform solution is efficient and sufficient for your near-term and long-term needs. Don't forget to consider the per-platform cost, support costs, and royalty costs if applicable. And be sure that the solution is available and stable, or easily fixed by you or the supplier.

SUMMARY OF CROSS-PLATFORM ISSUES

There are many reasons for you to consider cross-platform development. The most obvious reason is so that your software will run on multiple computer platforms. Many of the other reasons for cross-platform development are justified because it is an economical way to produce a product on multiple platforms.

Also, there are many design issues that you need to consider when you develop for multiple platforms. The most important issues to consider first are:

- Whether your application is to be developed using cross-platform techniques
- Whether your application is to run as a cross-platform application

You will also need to determine the most appropriate cross-platform solution for your situation. You will need to look at the extent of use of the software, the needs of the user, the lifetime of the product, the most viable platforms for the product and the tools that are available, the amount of time available to you, and the total dollar and personnel resources that are available.

2

Platform Specifics

Of the many platforms for software applications, the most important for developers of main-stream applications that require cross-platform solutions are:

- Macintosh using System 6 and Finder, System 6 and MultiFinder, and System 7
- PCs running a viable DOS (MS-DOS or DR-DOS, for example) and Windows 3.1
- computer systems running Windows NT and the Win32 subsystem

The remainder of this book will concentrate on these three platforms. In this chapter we will discuss the specifics about the three target platforms with respect to:

- platform comparisons
- equipment requirements
- processor issues

PLATFORM COMPARISONS

The Macintosh, Windows 3.1, and Win32 platforms share a number of features:

- the contents of the screen, or the desktop, and other user interface features
- file system features
- the event or message dispatching system

- resources
- the availability of the ANSI C library

In this section we will look at how these features map across the three major platforms. We'll also discuss features that are platform-specific and those that present particular problems for developers attempting to port applications to the other platforms.

The Macintosh Platform

Macintosh computers are based on the Motorola 680x0 family of microporcessors (some future machines will use the PowerPC RISC processor). The basic architecture of this platform is shown in Figure 2.1. Macintoshes are unique in that a large portion of the operating system and other functionality (the Toolbox) resides in ROM. Most other operating systems minimize the software that is in ROM.

Also, there isn't a rigid hierarchy of functional layers in the Macintosh operating system. Any layer has free access to the other layers. This is one of the reasons that the Macintosh operating system is so efficient.

Macintosh User Interface

Figure 2.2 provides a sample of the Macintosh System 6 user interface and Figure 2.3 illustrates the user interface of System 7.

Macintosh File Anatomy

In the Macintosh every file can have a data fork and a resource fork, as shown in Figure 2.4. Resources, which include menu definitions, window definitions, strings, and executable code segments, are maintained in the resource fork and accessed using the Resource Manager. The data fork is reserved for storing data and usually contains the information associated with a document. The information in the data fork is accessed in an application-specific way.

The resource fork contains all of the resources needed by an application. Some document files also have a resource fork to maintain information. The Macintosh system software provides the Resource Manager as a mechanism to access and maintain the resource data contained within

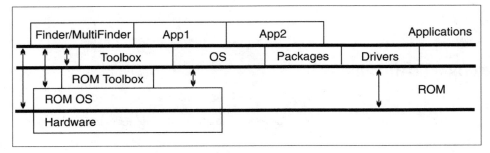

Figure 2.1 Macintosh architecture.

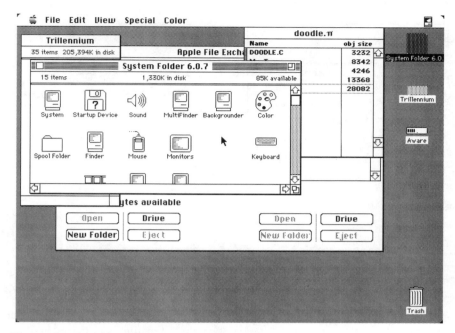

Figure 2.2 Macintosh System 6 user interface.

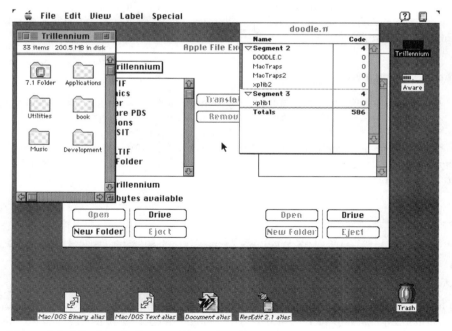

Figure 2.3 Macintosh System 7 user interface.

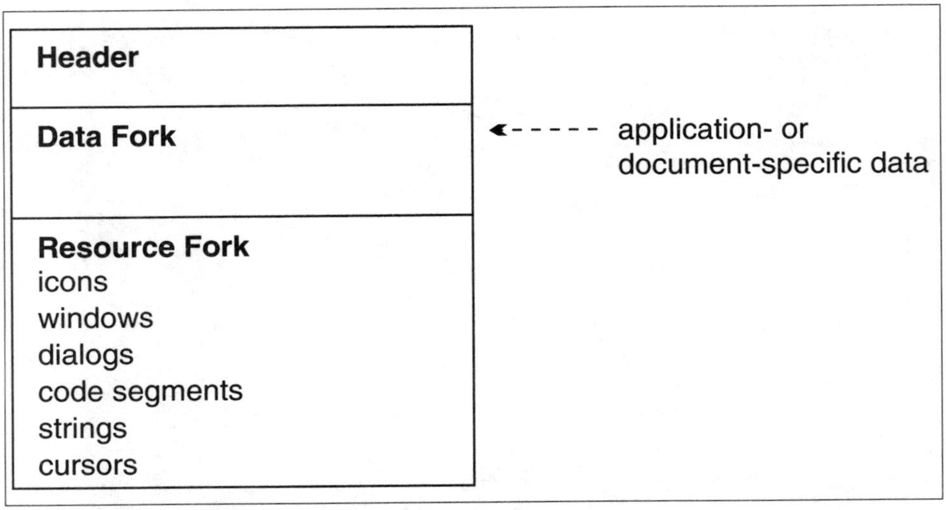

Header
Data Fork
Resource Fork icons windows dialogs code segments strings cursors

◄ - - - - - application- or
document-specific data

Figure 2.4 Basic Macintosh file structure.

the resource fork. This makes the resource fork a convenient place to store information that you want easily accessible; you don't have to worry about providing functions to read and write the information.

Resource forks contain dynamic information. Using functions in the Resource Manager, an application can read and write information to the resource fork of a file as needed—even to and from its own resource fork. For example, this allows an application to maintain some initialization information within itself.

The Windows 3.1 Platform

The Windows 3.1 platform is an operating environment that runs on top of DOS on PC-based (80x86) computer systems. The basic architecture for Windows 3.1 is shown in Figure 2.5. One of the first things you'll notice is that there are many layers in the Windows 3.1 architecture. Many of the layers are accessible from all other layers, but certain Windows function calls, especially those that are associated with virtual device drivers, must proceed through the hierarchy of layers.

Windows 3.1 User Interface

Figure 2.6 shows an example of the Windows 3.1 desktop and some basic user interface features.

Windows 3.1 File Anatomy

Windows 3.1 uses two basic types of files: executable files and data files. Data files contain information in application-specific formats. The contents of data files can represent documents, object files, and library files. Executable files have a special identifying header that is recognized

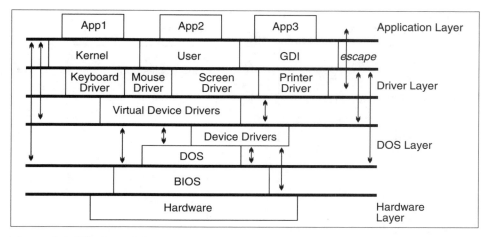

Figure 2.5 Windows 3.1 system architecture.

by the system loader. This header contains information that allows the file to be loaded and executed. Executable files also maintain resource data that is appended to the code information, as illustrated in Figure 2.7. Normally the resource data is static. It is compiled and added to the executable file when the application is being built.

Figure 2.6 Windows 3.1 user interface.

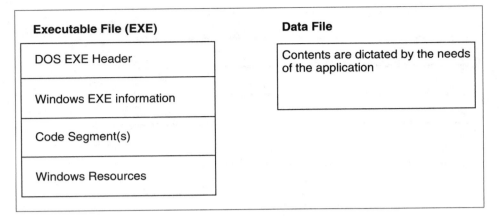

Figure 2.7   Windows 3.1 file types.

Actually, there are four executable file types: EXE files, DLL files, COM files, and VxD files. COM files represent a more limited version of the standalone executable file (EXE) that cannot represent a Windows application. For our discussion, we will ignore COM files. DLLs, or Dynamic Link Libraries, represent executable libraries of code but are not standalone executable like EXE files. Many of the executable pieces of Windows are DLLs. VxDs, Virtual Device Drivers, are 32-bit programs that run in the enhanced mode of Windows and allow access to hardware to be virtualized or simulated. Many of the components that characterize the enhanced mode of Windows are VxDs.

The Windows NT Platform

Windows NT is an operating system that is designed with a portable kernal and can run on any number of hardware platforms. Currently Windows NT runs on the Intel 80x86 family of processors, the MIPS R4x00 family of RISC processors, and the Digital Equipment Alpha AXP family of RISC processors. The basic architecture of Windows NT is shown in Figure 2.8.

What makes Windows NT different from other operating systems is that it is designed to be portable. The Hardware Abstraction Layer (or HAL) provides the interface between the kernel and the hardware. Normally many low-level interfaces to hardware are performed by software that is in ROM—the BIOS in a standard PC, for example. This allows Windows NT to be ported to other platforms with essentially only a rewrite of the HAL.

Windows NT User Interface

In Windows NT components of the user interface depend on the subsystem that is in use. If you are running the Win32 or the Win16 subsystem, the user interface is almost identical to the Windows 3.1 interface (see Figure 2.9). We will limit our discussion to the interface based on the Win32 subsystem.

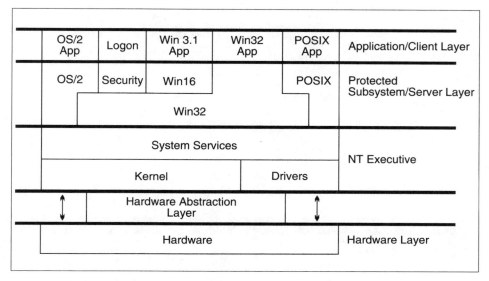

Figure 2.8 Windows NT architecture.

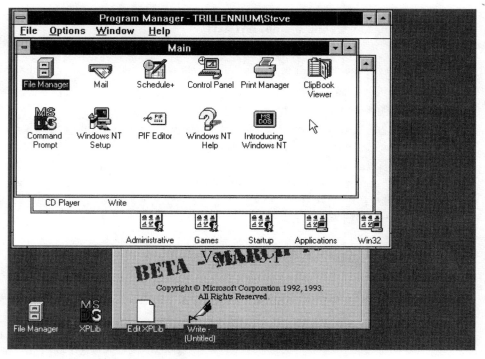

Figure 2.9 WIN32 user interface.

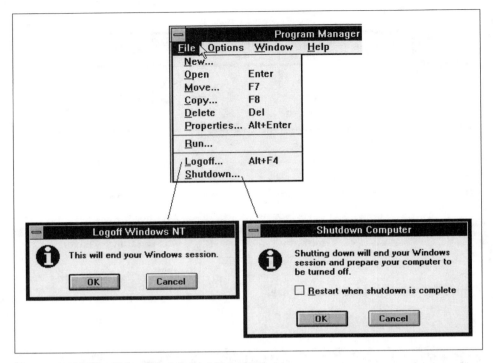

Figure 2.10 Win32 logoff and shutdown/restart.

The Windows NT interface differs from the Windows 3.1 interface in several ways. In Windows NT:

- You have to log on to the system to start working.

- You can log off, restart, or shut down the system to terminate, as illustrated in Figure 2.10.

- Each process maintains its own cursor state.

- The "wait" cursor is displayed in conjunction with the process cursor, which is called the "start glass" cursor. For example, an arrow cursor can contain an hourglass cursor, as illustrated in Figure 2.11. This cursor informs the user that a process has started but other work can still be done.

Figure 2.11 Win32 combined cursor.

Windows NT File Anatomy

The general file anatomy of Windows NT is the same as that of Windows 3.1 even though Windows NT supports the FAT (File Allocation Table), HPFS (High Performance File System), and NTFS (New Technology File System) disk formats; has a different EXE file format, called "*coff*"; and has some minor differences in the way resources are organized. The details of the disk formats are discussed in Chapter 6. Windows NT still provides the two basic types of files: executable files (EXEs and DLLs) and data files.

Cross-Platform Considerations

When you develop a product for an individual platform, you normally define the functionality required for your application, then use a subset of the platform's API to implement the application's functionality. Defining the functionality required by the application and the necessary functions in the platform's API helps to limit the scope of the development effort and helps you focus on solving the problem.

The same is true for developing a cross-platform product. If you are developing a cross-platform solution for your product, first you define the limits of the problem and then you define the limits of the functionality required to solve the problem. Next you consider the cross-platform API needed to provide the functionality and look at how you can provide the API based on information about the target platform APIs. This process of distillation forms the framework for the cross-platform solution.

Alternatively, if you use an existing cross-platform solution, you must decide which areas of functionality to use, which areas need to be enhanced, and which areas need to be addressed on a platform-by-platform basis. At times you must use the same approach when looking at variations of system versions on the same platform. With a good commercial cross-platform solution, you can proceed with your development in much the same way as you would if the product was being developed for an individual platform.

In this section we will look at the differences in some basic features between:

- System 6 and System 7
- Macintosh and Windows
- Windows 3.1 and Windows NT

Differences in specific areas of API functionality will be discussed in Part 2 and Part 3 of this book.

Comparing Macintosh System 6 and System 7

There are some basic differences between the GUIs of System 6 and System 7. For a thorough discussion of the Macintosh GUI for System 6 see *Inside Macintosh*, Volumes I, IV, and V, and *Human Interface Guidelines: The Apple Desktop Interface*. For a thorough discussion of the GUI features of System 7, see *Inside Macintosh*, Volume VI, Chapter 2.

Essentially the user interfaces of System 6 and System 7 are identical, except for:

- The System 7 interface has 3D-looking windows and controls.
- The System 7 interface has two icons on the right end of the menu bar. The right icon represents the executing application and lets the user switch between applications. The left icon controls the popup Balloon Help options.
- The trash can in System 7 can be moved and is not automatically emptied.
- Documents and applications can be represented by aliases.

Beyond the visual differences there are many differences between System 6 and System 7 that are described in *Inside Macintosh*, Volume VI, Chapter 3. For example, System 7:

- supports TrueType fonts
- has better international support
- provides file sharing across networks
- allows interapplication communication
- supports virtual memory

In your cross-platform design you will need to consider if System 6 support is important to your application. All new Macintoshes use System 7, but older Macintoshes might not be upgraded. Some users of System 6 discount the added functionality of System 7 in preference to the increased speed of System 6.

If you want your application to run on System 6 and System 7, you must use only those features of System 7 that are also present in System 6. In addition, if you consider that MultiFinder may be used with System 6, you must consider this option in your design. Some applications, such as Microsoft Word, conditionally turn on features depending on the version of Macintosh system software that is running; for example, publish and subscribe capabilities or embedding objects are available only if you are running System 7.

You will have to decide how important a feature is, then consider whether it is worth adding conditional run-time logic. It is more complicated to include run-time conditional features if you need to consider running across non-Macintosh platforms as well. In general the less system-specific code you include in your program, the easier it is to provide a cross-platform solution. The difficulties (both in the long-term and in the short-term) must be weighed against the value of the feature or features that you will conditionally support.

Comparing Windows and Macintosh

The user interface of Windows (3.1 and Win32 under Windows NT) is visually quite different from that of the Macintosh. But even with the differences, both platforms have the same basic anatomical features and both allow the user to do the same things. In addition to addressing these differences the developer must consider several fundamental differences between the two platforms—specifically, differences in:

- underlying processors
- file anatomies
- resource philosophies
- types of users

In this section we will discuss the basic issues that you should consider when you are writing an application that will run on both the Macintosh and the Windows platforms.

User Interface Differences. Table 2.1 lists the differences between the user interface models of the Macintosh and Windows. More specific information about user interface differences are discussed in Part 4 of this book.

Processor Differences. Currently all Macintosh machines use a 680x0 processor, although future machines will use the PowerPC RISC processor. Windows 3.1 machines use the 80x86 processors. Windows NT machines use the 80x86, MIPS R4x00, and DEC Alpha AXP processors.

The types of processors used affect register availability for variable declarations. See Appendix L for information about processor differences.

File Anatomy Differences. If you are developing a program that will share data across platforms, you need to consider how the data is stored. You don't want to store data in a Macintosh implementation in the resource fork because you can't assume that a file transfer will copy the resource fork. Generally, only the data fork is copied and a cross-platform application should only use the data fork.

Resource Philosophy Differences. On the Macintosh all resources (in the resource fork) can be read or written at run time. In Windows 3.1, except during the building of the executable or the sculpting of a user interface, resources are read-only.

User Differences. Most users prefer to use one type of machine over another. Consider the types of users that will buy your product and what they expect from a platform when you are developing your application. In addition you must try to maintain the look and feel of the native platform while ensuring a consistent look and feel for your product across platforms.

Comparing Windows 3.1 and Windows NT

If you are writing an application that you want to port between Windows 3.1 and Windows NT, you must consider the differences between processors and hardware, some user interface and

Table 2.1 Comparison of user interface features between Macintosh and Windows.

UI Feature	Macintosh	Windows
menu bar	desktop	each window or application
menu text		underline designates keyboard sequence
command-key	Apple or COMMAND key	ALT key
system menu	Apple in menu bar	system icon in title bar
close window	in title bar	menu item in system menu or double-click system menu icon
zoom window	left side of title bar	left side of title bar
size window	size icon in lower-right corner of window	size border around window

operational differences, like the meaning of CTRL-ALT-DELETE, and internal differences, like Windows NT is a preemptive multitasking operating system and Windows 3.1 is not. The degree of difficulty of porting between versions of Windows, as shown in Figure 2.12, should also be considered.

Different Processors. Unlike Windows 3.1 Windows NT can run on different hardware platforms: the MIPS R4x00 and DEC Alpha AXP in addtion to standard PCs. Don't rely on inline assembly code being portable. You also can't assume that a particular register is used on both processors to point to the stack or to return data from a function call. Nor can you assume that register allocation of variables is consistent. You should assume that the fewest number of registers are available, based on an 80x86 compiler implementation. See Appendix L for some specific information about register usage. (This information is provided for general comparison purposes of the organization and usage of registers on various platforms with certain compilers.)

Also, pay attention to structure alignment. On RISC processors compilers typically want to align data based on the data size; for example, a 1-byte variable can be aligned on any boundary, 2-byte variables can be aligned only on addresses that are multiples of 2, and 4-byte variables can only be aligned on 2- or 4-byte boundaries.

Different Support of Hardware. Windows 3.1 uses the BIOS (the code in ROM) to provide the fundamental low-level access to critical hardware subsystems. Windows NT relies on the HAL (Hardware Access Layer) to provide similar low-level support, which provides a virtual-ized access to hardware. Windows 3.1 programs can directly access DOS functions and BIOS functions if they want. In Windows NT, this type of coding is not possible because you can't assume you know the type or method of interaction with hardware—this is dependent on the hardware platform and the particular implementation of the HAL. Applications should access Windows NT features using the Win32 API.

CTRL-ALT-DELETE. On a DOS-based PC the infamous three-finger salute will cause Windows 3.1 to stop executing your program. The user can then choose whether to continue the

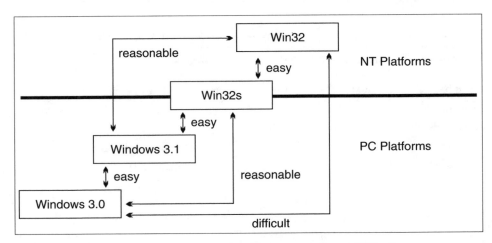

Figure 2.12 Level of difficulty in porting between versions of Windows.

application, stop the application, or reboot the machine. In Windows NT this is a signal to the system to perform a logon, a logoff, change your password, shut down the system, etc.

Logging On and Off. In Windows NT the user needs to log on to the system before using it. In Windows 3.1, logging on and off are not necessary.

Portability Between Windows 3.1 and Win16. All (well-behaved) applications that run in Windows 3.1 will run on the Win16 subsystem in Windows NT. This allows you to support 80x86 implementations of Windows NT without rewriting or recompiling your application. See Figure 2.12.

Using Win32s. If you write your application to the Win32s specification, you will be able to port it without modification from Windows 3.1 to any Windows NT system provided that you haven't done anything processor-specific (for example, inline assembly). See Figure 2.12.

Windows 3.0 Support. If you need to support a category of users that have not migrated to Windows 3.1, you will need to consider an even smaller subset of functionality that allows Win32 applications to be ported to the Windows 3.0 environment. Don't consider doing this unless you have a very urgent need. In general, if you don't need to worry about Windows 3.0, then don't. Porting from Windows 3.1 to Win32 or any variation thereof is much easier if you ignore Windows 3.0-specific functions.

Various File Systems. Windows 3.1 directly supports FAT (File Allocation Table) formatted disks. Windows NT directly supports FAT, HPFS (OS/2), CDFS (CD-ROM File System), and NTFS formatted disks. Using additional drivers, Windows 3.1 will support the CD-ROM CDFS formats, but CDs are directly supported by Windows NT. Basically you can't assume anything about the format for file names and paths; this information is best abstracted by dialog boxes. See Chapter 6 for more information about file management.

EQUIPMENT NEEDS

To develop and test a software application efficiently, you must invest in two types of systems: a development system and one or more end-user systems.

Developers require more powerful and costly systems. This usually means a faster computer, with more RAM and more disk space than the end user would require, development tools, and applications software. You should always work with the latest release of system software, as well as at least one previous version. You should also ensure that all the features of your application operate properly and that the product performs adequately on the lowest class of equipment that an end user might own. This ensures that your product is accepted by the largest segment of your market.

End-user systems are specified by the developer and depend on the target platforms and the application. Generally end-user equipment is less expensive than developer equipment. Table 2.2 lists equipment for typical developer and end-user systems on the major platforms. The end-user needs are provided to indicate typical new product equipment needs. Your product needs may exceed those listed or may not be as great as those listed.

Table 2.2 Developer and end-user equipment needs.

Platform	Developer Configuration	End-User Configuration
Macintosh	68030 @ 25 MHz System 6 w/ Finder System 6 w/ MultiFinder System 7 8 MB RAM 200 MB hard disk	Newer low-end Macintosh configurations are a good starting point. Certain features may require System 7 to function. 4 MB RAM 80 MB hard disk
Windows 3.1	80486DX @ 33 MHz DOS 5.0 8 MB RAM 200 MB hard disk	80386 @ 25 MHz DOS 4.0 or above 4 MB RAM 100 MB hard disk
Windows NT (PC)*	80486DX @ 33 MHz 16 MB RAM 400 MB hard disk High Density Floppy CD-ROM Drive	80386 @ 25 MHz 12 MB RAM 100 100 MB hard disk High Density Floppy
Windows NT (MIPS)	R4000 @ 50 MHz 32 MB RAM 400 MB hard disk SCSI CD-ROM drive	R4000 @ 50 MHz 16 MB RAM 200 MB Hard Disk SCSI CD-ROM drive
Windows NT (DEC)	21064 @ 150 MHz 32 MB RAM 400 MB hard disk SCSI CD-ROM drive	21064 @ 150 MHz 16 MB RAM 240 MB hard disk SCSI CD-ROM drive

* A suitable PC-based Windows NT equipment solution is usually sufficient to also provide a Windows 3.1 solution.

Windows NT Equipment

Macintosh and Windows 3.1 systems are available from a variety of sources. Windows NT systems can be:

- an IBM PC or 100 percent compatible with at least a 386 processor
- a MIPS R4x00–based computer; for example, the ACER ARC1
- a DEC Alpha AXP–based computer from Digital Equipment Corporation

For information about cost and availability of non-PC–based Windows NT systems, refer to Appendix E for some contact information.

Porting to NT Systems

MIPS provides porting centers to allow developers to port their Windows NT applications to the MIPS hardware platform. Similarly, DEC provides Alpha migration centers to facilitate porting NT applications to the Alpha AXP hardware platform. Appendix E contains porting center information.

Network Equipment

The network equipment you will need for cross-platform development depends on your needs, your tolerance, and the size of your project team. A minimal solution for small teams (of one or two people) does not require any specialized network hardware. Files can be transferred by floppy from one platform or station to another using Apple File Exchange or PC Exchange on the Macintosh or Mac-In-DOS on Windows. These programs convert files on Macintosh disks to PC (FAT formatted) disks and vice versa.

If you have a larger team (of three to six people), you will need to invest in network hardware. Before you research your options, ask yourself two questions:

- What type of network hardware do you want to use?
- Do you want a peer-to-peer network or one that is file server based?

Network hardware products include: LocalTalk, Ethernet, Token Ring, ARCNET, FDDI, etc. LocalTalk support is included with every Macintosh (old and new). Ethernet is included with many new Macintoshes but requires a card for older Macintoshes. Token Ring support requires an additional card.

For 80x86-based computers, any network hardware requires a network card (unless you purchased a file server or similar system). For MIPS- and Alpha AXP–based computers you will also need to purchase a network card and software.

Probably the least expensive solution for Windows 3.1 is to invest in a LocalTalk card for your 80x86 machines and some networking software. For example, Farallon offers *Timbuktu for Windows PhoneNET Kit* that includes all necessary software and hardware to allow a PC to connect to a LocalTalk network. This allows you to connect your Macintosh to your PC machine and transfer files back and forth. If you purchase *Timbuktu* for the Macintosh, you can control your Macintosh system from Windows and vice versa.

If the bandwidth of LocalTalk is insufficient for your needs (perhaps you will be transferring many files often), you might want to use Ethernet instead. If your Macintosh is already equipped with Ethernet support, you need only purchase an Ethernet card for your PC or other system. If not, you will have to buy an Ethernet card for your Macintosh as well. If you plan to use Ethernet over unshielded twisted pair cable, you will also need a repeating hub.

If you have more demanding needs (larger teams or large projects), you will probably need to invest in a dedicated file server that will maintain your project files, provide services to developers (installations, updates, etc.), and facilitate backing up files. A file server is normally a high-end computer with lots of RAM and lots of disk space. Don't get more than you need, but don't get something that will strangle your development after a short time.

For cross-platform development involving Windows NT, you might want to look at Windows NT Advanced Server (NTAS). It provides the software necessary to support AppleTalk, Ethernet, and other networks. For network-aware applications and development environments, you will also want to investigate Windows for Workgroups.

Printing Equipment

A cross-platform development environment must also include appropriate printing devices. A certain amount of this printing problem can be solved with a robust network solution—a dedicated server connected to one or more standard types of printing devices. For small-scale work or development environments or those that do not have large operating environments, limit your printing options to the most common printing hardware and printing languages; for example, printers that support PCL-4 or PCL-5—that is, the HP LaserJet family or 100 percent clones—and printers that support PostScript Level 1 or Level 2.

You also need to consider the printing needs of the end user of your product. If your product has certain needs that aren't addressed by PostScript or PCL types of printers, for example, plotting or carbon copies, then consider your options carefully to ensure that a suitable solution, i.e., a printer driver, exists for all target platforms.

SOME PROCESSOR ISSUES

There are three areas of processor-specific information that you should consider when you do cross-platform development:

- the structure packing restrictions
- the representation of integer data
- the representation of floating point data

Structure Packing

Structure packing is important when you want to ensure that the representation of data structures is equivalent on all of your target platforms. Many times there are compile-time options that you can use to control the way structures are aligned. Other times, you need to be careful when you define the contents of structures. Generally it's a good idea to put the larger data types before the smaller ones, to minimize data packing problems. Also, make sure that 8-byte data types are aligned on 8-byte boundaries, 4-byte types on 4-byte boundaries, and so on.

Refer to Appendix L for general processor information, register usage, and information about integer and floating point data organizations for the 80x86, 680x0, and RISC processors.

Integer Representations

There are four things to be careful of when you are working with integers:

- maximum intrinsic integer size
- the bit order within a byte
- the byte order within 2-byte or 4-byte integers
- importance of compatible file access of integer data

Bit and byte order affect your ability to read and write data to file and how you use bit-field information. On most common processors today the bit order within a byte is always represented as 8 consecutive bits numbered from 0 through 7 (right to left). There are two types of data packing organizations in processors: little-endian and big-endian. Little-endian means that the bytes are packed into consecutive bytes of memory, least-significant byte first, as in the 80x86 and Alpha AXP processors. Big-endian means that data bytes are packed into consecutive bytes of memory, most-significant byte first, as in the 680x0 processor. The MIPS R4x00 processor can be configured as a big- or little-endian processor—in Windows NT systems it is configured as little-endian.

Be aware what the intrinsic integer size is for your compiler. This can often be controlled using a compile-time option. Macintosh and Windows 3.1 normally work with 16-bit integers, but Windows NT assumes that an integer is 32 bits.

High performance processors, like RISC and the Pentium, support 64-bit integers. For our purposes we will ignore 64-bit integers.

> *Sixty-four bit integers are also called quadwords, if you are familiar with CISC processors, where a word is normally 16 bits. They are called double words in RISC nomenclature, where words are normally 32 bits. C compilers that work with Windows NT will represent 64-bit integers as a "long long" data type.*

Floating Point Representations

Like integers, you need to be careful with the representation and organization of floating point numbers. When you use them be aware of:

- intrinsic floating point size
- availability of IEEE floating point representation
- importance of speed
- importance of compatible file access of floating point data

In the Macintosh and Windows 3.1 floating point numbers are commonly (and efficiently) referenced as 80-bit data types. On RISC processors the standard representation for floating point numbers is as 64-bit data types. Both the 80-bit and 64-bit types conform to the ANSI/IEEE 754-1985 standard.

If you want to store a common representation of a floating point number across platforms, the greatest denominator is to use 64-bit floating point numbers. Unfortunately this representation is often not as efficient to work with on 680x0 and 80x86 processors. It might be necessary to use 80-bit floating point numbers on these processors and convert to 64-bit when you are saving information in a form that will be shared across platforms.

SUMMARY OF PLATFORM SPECIFICS

Table 2.3 summarizes the platform-specific details for the Macintosh, Windows 3.1, and Windows NT platforms. There are many factors to consider as you design your product or purchase a cross-platform solution. Be specific about your needs. Look only at what you require, but don't ignore your long-term needs in the process. It is very easy to go overboard in your purchases or your designs when multiple platforms are involved.

Don't overlook the fact that your equipment needs as a developer are often substantially more than those of the end user. Make sure that your product will function properly on end-user system configurations.

This chapter only briefly discussed file and user interface issues. File management issues are discussed in detail in Chapter 6. Details about user interface issues are discussed in Part 3 (Chapters 13 through Chapter 17).

Table 2.3   Platform comparison summary.

Item	*Macintosh*	*Windows 3.1*	*Windows NT*
processor	680x0	80x86	PC: 80x86 DEC: Alpha AXP 2106x MIPS: R4x00 Intergraph-Clipper[*]
ROM	Toolbox	BIOS	PC: BIOS + HAL MIPS: System firmware and HAL DEC: System firmware and HAL
format	Macintosh FAT	FAT	FAT HPFS NTFS CDFS

operating system	System 6 + Finder
	System 6 + MF
	System 7
		DOS plus
		Windows
		   DOS
		   Windows 3.1
		   Win32s
			Windows NT
			   OS/2
			   Posix
			   DOS
			   Win16
			   Win32
			   Win32s

network	LocalTalk Token Ring[***]	LocalTalk[**] Token Ring[**]	LocalTalk[**] Token Ring[**]
printer	PostScript PCL[****]	PostScript PCL	PostScript PCL

[*]   Others are in development, such as Motorola's Power PC RISC chip.

[**]   Requires additional hardware.

[***]   Might require additional hardware.

[****]   Will require a driver that is not part of the standard Macintosh setup.

3
Cross-Platform Tools

Now that you understand a little about the three target platforms that we are discussing in this book, let's look at some of the tools that are available to help in the cross-platform development process. In this chapter we will look at:

- choosing a cross-platform language
- some compilers that are available
- commercially available cross-platform solutions
- some resource management tools
- file transfer problems
- some version control systems
- considerations when using C

CHOOSING A LANGUAGE

If you are careful, you can probably develop in just about any language. But certain languages provide solutions for certain types of problems more efficiently than other languages. When considering which language to use for cross-platfrom development, you must make sure that equivalent forms of the language exist on all target platforms.

However, if you are creating a cross-platform API that you intend to use as a general solution to the cross-platform development problem, then you should restrict your language choice to those that are the most robust·and the most widely used.

43

The language you choose should:

- be consistently specified across platforms
- execute efficiently on all platforms
- be widely used so that you can find programmers
- provide a consistent development environment across platforms

Function-Based Languages

Choosing a language in which to implement or utilize a function-based cross-platform API is not difficult. First you must consider the type of work that will be performed, who will do the work, and who will use the results. For in-house business applications a cross-platform COBOL implementation might be a good choice if the personnel is already in place to do the work (assuming that the language exists).

Pascal is a possible candidate, but the language is not always standardized across platforms or even between implementations on an individual platform. The most obvious choice is ANSI C. The syntax is specified by the ANSI standard, it is available on many platforms, and is used by many Macintosh and Windows programmers.

Object-Oriented Languages

Choosing an object-oriented programming language, and, optionally, a class library, is more difficult than choosing a functional language. The object-oriented languages that are defined consistently across many platforms are not necessarily the best languages for developing compiled applications. For example, certain versions of Smalltalk are defined equivalently for multiple platforms, but they do not allow you to produce standalone applications. Programs written in Smalltalk are interpreted and cannot deliver the same level of performance as programs written in compiled languages.

Implementations of C++ are not always consistent across multiple platforms, as there is no official standard,[6] but C++ is probably the best object-oriented language to use. You can find a cross-plaform C++ implementation from a single manufacturer or from multiple manufacturers that will work on your target platforms. For example, Symantec C++ is available on the Macintosh, Windows 3.1, and OS/2 platforms, and MetaWare C++ is available for most non-Macintosh platforms. Both compilers have a reasonably high per-platform cost. In general, it is safest to use different platform versions of C++ from the same manufacturer to ensure cross-platform compatibility of the language specification and implementation.

Weighing the Language Choices

C++ is a cross-platform development language candidate if you are careful when you choose the manufacturer. Compliance with the same AT&T standard is essential for maintaining your

---

[6] At present there is no ANSI standard defined for the C++ language. Many developers of C++ compilers use the AT&T CFRONT 3.0 definition of the language.

sanity. I choose not to use C++ to write XPLib because I find that C++ code executes slower than C.

Pascal is also acceptable if you are careful about the specification of the language. If you select a manufacturer of Pascal that provides multiple-platform support for your target platforms, you are ensured that the specifications are equivalent. For example, Borland provides a version for MS-DOS and Windows 3.1.

The language I have selected is C. Many language developers provide ANSI implementations of the C programming language and the Macintosh and Windows development tools have pretty much standardized on it. Consequently, many GUI-based platform software developers are familiar with the C language. That is why I chose C as the language in which to implement my cross-platform solution. All examples presented in this book, as well as the code in XPLib, are written in a minor superset of ANSI C.

COMPILERS

To use cross-platform development techniques properly, you must provide a standard development environment or consistent development environments. This isn't as easy to do as you might think. In deciding which development environments to consider in this book, I looked for the following features:

- ANSI C support plus C++ comments
- an integrated development environment running on the platform
- an integrated source-level debugger
- interactive resource and dialog creation
- consistency in development environment with other platforms solutions
- fast compile times
- ability to produce small and large applications
- flexible control of floating point formats
- reasonable cost

My main criteria in selecting a compiler for three platforms were ease of use, consistency with other platform solutions, and cost. An easy to use product and those that present a consistent working environment across platforms minimize the confusion of using three compilers and switching between them. This makes the development process simple and reduces the time and cost to deliver a cross-platform product. Although it wasn't possible to find three compilers that function identically, my goal was to find compilers that provide the same language features, and roughly the same development capabilities for a reasonable price. I also opted to use products with an integrated development environment, which makes it easier to manage the many files that make up a sofware project and makes the process of building the application simpler.

Compilers that provide a source-level debugger, an ANSI C implementation with the standard C library, access to various floating point formats, and the ability to create complex software applications are available for all the major platforms.

I prefer to work with C compilers that support C++ style comments, //, as well as standard C comments, /* */. C++ style comments make it easier to comment out a line of code and to add a multiline comment (you don't have to look for the close-comment sequence).

C++ comments can take the standard C comment form:

```
/* begins a comment
and ends a comment */
for (i=1; i<5; /* i+=2 */ i++);
```

Or they can look like this:

```
// this whole line is a comment
i=j+k/m; // ignore the rest of this line
```

Macintosh C Compilers

Two development environments are available for the Macintosh: Macintosh Programmer's Workshop (MPW), published by Apple, and the THINK Project Manager, published by Symantec. MPW provides the broadest range of solutions and the most flexibility for complex development problems. THINK provides a less arduous environment in which to work but is simpler in scope. The compile-link-execute cycle in THINK is very fast and provides a very efficient development environment. Some of the Macintosh C and C++ compilers are listed in Table 3.1.

THINK Project Manager is less expensive than MPW and requires a smaller investment in equipment to be useful. MPW is the better investment if you want a total development environment for a broad range of probems and languages. In instances where a project produces multiple executable files (for example, large libraries or drivers), Symantec's THINK C may not be the best choice. (Recently, Apple and Symantec have agreed that Symantec will produce the next generation of Macintosh development tools. So expect changes and improvements to the development tools.)

Also, THINK C is a C compiler that also provides an object-oriented version of C but is not C++. If you intend to use C++ for your development, you should use Symantec C++ or MPW C++.

Table 3.1 Macintosh C and C++ compilers.

Compiler Name	Publisher	Environment
MPW C	Apple	MPW
MPW C++	Apple	MPW
Symantec C++ for MPW	Symantec	MPW
THINK C	Symantec	THINK Project Manager
Symantec C++	Symantec	THINK Project Manager

Table 3.2 C and C++ compilers for Windows 3.1.

Compiler Name	Publisher	Windows IDE
Microsoft C/C++	Microsoft	no
Visual C++	Microsoft	yes
Borland C/C++	Borland	yes
Symantec C/C++	Symantec	yes
MetaWare	MetaWare	no
WATCOM C	WATCOM	no

Windows 3.1 C Compilers

In the Windows 3.1 environment numerous C and C++ compilers are available, as listed in Table 3.2. However, there are three compiler publishers that you should consider if cost is a high priority: Microsoft, Borland, and Symantec. These publishers offer an integrated development environment, the ability to produce large applications, a C compiler, and a C++ compiler. The primary differences are environment and speed.

Microsoft C does not provide a Windows-based development environment, the project construction process is more tedious, and compile times are slower. Because of this, I consider Borland C a better solution. Borland C also provides an environment and feel that is similar to the integrated environment of Symantec's THINK C. Borland also provides a solution for OS/2.

Visual C++ is a newcomer in Microsoft's product line. It offers an integrated Windows-based development environment, but its main benefit comes from using the Microsoft Foundation Classes and AppWizard (an application framework). It is available for Windows NT but is not available for other platforms. Prior to Visual C++, Microsoft had Quick C for Windows, which provided a Windows-based development environment, but this product has been superceded by Visual C++.

Symantec C++ is a good choice for compatibility across multiple platforms (especially between the Macintosh and Windows) and is in the same price range as the Microsoft or Borland products. It provides a Windows-based development environment and supports Windows, DOS, and Win32s applications. Symantec's product has the most sophisticated development environment of all Windows development tools.

MetaWare and WATCOM C are high-end products that provide good solutions but at higher prices. They also support a diverse selection of platforms and can be used to generate 32-bit DOS, Windows, and OS/2 applications. The MetaWare compiler(s) can also generate code for embedded processors.

Windows NT C Compilers

Table 3.3 lists several sources for C and C++ compilers for various Windows NT hardware platforms. Microsoft currently provides a 32-bit version of its 80x86-based C/C++ compiler, as well as compilers for the MIPS R4x00–based computers and Digital's Alpha AXP–based

Table 3.3 C and C++ compilers for Windows NT.

Compiler Name	Publisher	NT Hardware Platform
Microsoft C/C++	Microsoft	80x86 and MIPS
Visual C++	Microsoft	80x86
Borland C/C++	Borland	80x86*
Symantec C++	Symantec	80x86*
MetaWare	MetaWare	80x86**
WATCOM C	WATCOM	80x86
DEC C++	Digital Equipment	Alpha AXP

*   Supports Win32s only

** Talk to manufacturer for more information about other platforms.

computers. These compilers do not provide an integrated development environment and are more cumbersome to use than the THINK C and Borland C/C++.

Symantec C++ provides a complete selection of development tools for 80x86-based Win32s and is a decent alternative to Borland C/C++, but it is a little more expensive. But because Symantec provides C/C++ development tools for Macintosh, Windows 3.1, and Win32s, it provides a good deal of continuity in terms of language implementation, product features, and look and feel. It also has the nicest working environment of any compiler. As with Windows 3.1 compilers, MetaWare and WATCOM C represent higher-end compilers for a diverse selection of platforms and target processors.

> *Many of the tools for Windows NT weren't in final release when I wrote this book and developed the XPLib software. At times, I used the following roundabout approach to develop the Win32 version of the XPLib software: I first wrote the XPLib software for this book on the Macintosh using THINK C, modified and repaired it to run on Windows 3.1 using Borland C, ported it back to the Macintosh, transferred it back to Windows 3.1 and recompiled it, then ported it to Win32. I did this to minimize the development time on the Windows NT platform and to ensure that many of the basic features of XPLib functioned in Windows 3.1 before trying them in Win32.*

COMMERCIAL CROSS-PLATFORM PRODUCTS

Table 3.4 lists the commercial function-based cross-platform products that are based on C. Table 3.5 lists the object-oriented cross-platform products that are generally based on C++. Object-oriented products usually take one of two forms: a class library or an application framework. A class library is the object-oriented equivalent to a functional API. An application framework provides an integrated way to produce all aspects of a GUI-based application, including the user interface, the code to support the user interface, compiling, linking, and debugging. Products that are indicated as RC type provide a platform-independent resource format that can be used

Table 3.4 Function-based cross-platform products.

Company	Product(s)	Type
Guild Systems	Guild	UI, FL, RC
Liant Software	C-scape	FL
	Look & Feel	UI
Neuron Data	Neuron Data Open Interface	FL, UI, RC
WNDX	WNDX	FL
	OPUS	RC, UI
XVT Software	XVT Design	UI
	XVT Portability Toolkit	FL

Legend
FL   function library
UI   user interface designer
RC   resource compiler

Table 3.5 Object-oriented cross-platform products.

Company	Product(s)	Type
Borland International	OWL	CL
	Resource Workshop	UI
Computer Associates International	Glockenspiel Common View	CL
Digitalk	Smalltalk/V*	AF
Inmark	zApp	AF
Liant Software	C++/Views	CL
Microsoft	Foundation Classes	CL
	AppStudio	RC, UI
	AppWizard	AF
Neuron Data	Neuron Data Open Interface	CL, UI, RC
StarDivision	StarView	CL
	DesignEd	RC
Stepstone	ICPak 201**	CL
Symantec	Bedrock***	AF, RC
XVT Software	XVT Design++	UI
	XVT Portability Toolkit	CL
Zinc Software	Zinc Application Framework	CL

Legend
CL   object class library   UI   user interface designer
AF   application framework   RC   resource editor

  *   Uses the Smalltalk language.

 **   Uses the Objective-C language.

***   Talk to Symantec about availability.

to create and use resources across platforms—some specify common resource scripts and some specify common resource binary formats.

Table 3.6 lists all of the cross-plaform products and indicates which platform each of the products supports.

RESOURCE TOOLS

Unless you use a product that specifies its own resource format that is the same across platforms, you won't find resource management tools that provide the same functionality and the same development features across multiple platforms. This is the case in our discussions in this book because the Macintosh and Windows platforms support different resource formats, have different resource needs, and interact with resources differently. Even the resource formats (RES) for Windows 3.1 and Win32 differ, although the resource script is the same. (The RES format for Win32 is a superset of the RES format for Windows 3.1.)

If we assume resources exist and are ready for use, we can avoid having to know the format of the contents. This minimizes the time required to develop a cross-platform resource solution. Providing API functions that create and modify resources requires some understanding of the underlying resource format or requires a common resource description. Abstracting and specifying resources at run-time requires a significant amount of time to implement. Because the

Table 3.6 Platforms supported by cross-platform products.

Product or Company	*Mac*	*Win3.1*	*Win32*	*OS/2*	*DOS*	*Motif*	*Other*
XVT	x	x	x	x	C	x	OpenLook
WNDX	x	x	x	x	x	x	OpenLook
Zinc	x	x	x	x	x	x	OpenLook
MFC		x	x				
StarView	x	x	x	x		x	OpenLook
zApp	S	x	x	x	x	S	
OWL		x	x	x			
Liant		x		x		x	
Stepstone	x	x		x	x	x	various
Guild	x	x	x	x		S	
CommonView		x	x	x		x	SCO
Neuron Data	x	x	x	x		x	OpenLook
Smalltalk/V	x	x	x	x			
Bedrock	S	S	S				

Legend
C   supports character-mode only
S   will be released soon

compiler manufacturers have provided very complete resource management tools, it isn't necessary to duplicate them unless you have the need and the time to do it.

Table 3.7 lists the resource management tools that are provided for our target platforms. Most of the existing tools for managing resources are easy to use. They are also cost effective because they come bundled with the rest of the development software. However, you can't consistently create resources or design dialog boxes across a wide range of platforms with these tools—there are no common resource scripts or resource file formats. If this is a problem, see Chapter 19, Advanced Resource Considerations, for more information about resource solutions.

> *In XPLIb I chose to provide a common API access to resources that were created using a platform's native resource management tool or tools. There are no cross-platform functions for creating resources in the XPAPI. This restriction allows you to load and use resources without having to know about the organization of the information.*

SOURCE CODE CONSIDERATIONS

Here we discuss how to transfer source code from one platform to another and the general problem of managing the source code that makes up a sofware project.

Source Code File Transfer

Source code file formats (text files) differ across platforms. Consider the difference between a new line on the Macintosh and Windows (DOS):

Macintosh:	0x0D (return) terminates a line of text
DOS:	0x0D 0x0A (return and linefeed) terminates a line of text

To properly share source files between these two platforms, you must provide a way to convert between these two formats. On the Macintosh you can use Apple File Exchange or PC Exchange

Table 3.7 Summary of resource management and design tools.

Product	*Publisher*	*Platform or Platforms*
ResEdit[*]	Apple	Macintosh
Resource Workshop	Borland	Windows 3.1 and Win32
Dialog Editor	Microsoft	Windows 3.1 and Win32
AppStudio (Visual C++)	Microsoft	Windows 3.1 and Win32
Symantec Resource Toolkit	Symantec	Windows 3.1
ResourceSHIELD	Stirling Group	Windows 3.1 and OS/2

* Symantec includes ResEdit with its THINK C and Symantec C++ Macintosh compilers. They do not provide their own interactive resource management tool.

(System 7.1 only) to convert formats. To convert from Macintosh text to DOS text and vice versa on a PC, you need to write two simple programs, one to convert Macintosh text files to DOS text files and one to convert from DOS to Macintosh. This conversion process is necessary when you convert text files between Macintosh and Windows 3.1 and between Macintosh and Windows NT.

Source Code Management

There are two types of source code management: single-project source code management and true version control. Single project allows one user to define a project based on a set of source code files. When a file is modified, the manager knows which files have changed and compiles them and any files dependent on them to rebuild the project. There is no way to coordinate the activity of multiple developers or easily work with multiple-project configurations (for example, debug and release versions).

Version control provides the developer or group of developers with a way to limit write access to source code files to one person at a time and to provide a modification history. Maintaining a history of changes to a file allows you to revert to any previous version. You can also recreate a particular version of the entire project, for example, version 1 of a project while you are working on version 2.

Source Code Management on the Macintosh

In MPW, Projector is a local (non–cross-platform) source code manager with some version control features. Projector is integrated into the MPW Shell to provide individuals and project teams access to a common set of source files. Unfortunately it doesn't lend itself to cross-platform development.

Prior to THINK C 6.0, THINK had an integrated single-project source code manager, but it offered no direct way to provide version control for a cross-platform project or multiple-developer project—you had to do it as another step outside the THINK C environment. In THINK C 6.0 or Symantec C++ 6.0, Symantec introduced the THINK Project Manager which has the ability to check files in and out using information in a Projector database. Previously this feature was only available in MPW. If you choose not to run the SourceServer (provides access to Projector), you will have the same level of source code management as prior to THINK C 6.0.

Projector is fine for Macintosh-specific development but does not lend itself to cross-platform projects. There is no way to access the features of Projector from multiple computers, unless the computers are Macintoshes running AppleShare and all file check-ins and check-outs are performed from the THINK C Project Manager.

Source Code Management in Windows

Microsoft C, Borland C, and Symantec C all provide an integrated single-project source code manager. Borland C and Symantec C provide a way to work with multiple-project configurations (debug and release, for example). None of the compilers incorporate version control features and there is no direct access to this functionality over a network. Consequently there is no way for these types of project managers to function as version control systems—they are not suitable

Table 3.8 List of version control software available on DOS and Windows.

Product	Manufacturer	DOS	Windows*
Sourcerer's Apprentice	Borland		x
PVCS	InterSolv	x	x
RCS	Mortice Kern Software (MKS)	x	
SourceSafe	One Tree Software		x
Microsoft Delta	Microsoft		x
Source_Manager	TransWare Enterprises	x	
TLIB	Burton Systems Software	x	
Curran's Bench**	MicroQuill		x
CCC/Manager	Softool Corporation		x

* Check with the vendor for the availability of NT versions of the version control products available for Windows 3.1.

** Written using XVT, this should be portable to other platforms.

as multiple-developer or cross-platform version control systems. This functionality is usually provided by separate version control software.

Development environments that require a separate text editor for entering and modifying source code provide a way to manage individual or multiple-developer projects. This management process is handled by the editor—for example, by Brief, Codewright, ED, or Multi-Edit. With these editors, opening a file transparently and automatically accesses a version control system. The controlled sources might reside locally or on a network server. Version control system software that run in DOS and Windows are listed in Table 3.8.

A version control system introduces an additional step in the development process if you use a compiler with an integrated development environment: the files you want to work on must first be checked out. For individual projects, this means that you check out all of the files before you work on the project and check them all back in when you are finished. For projects with multiple developers, each developer needs to check out the files that he or she wants to work on, modify them, then check them back in. Borland C and Symantec C/C++ for Windows 3.1 and Win32 provide ways to access a version control system from their project managers. Even though this doesn't provide the best solution if you also want version control for the Macintosh, it does provide you with a way to access version control for 16-bit and 32-bit Windows projects. Symantec's method of integrating version control features is coupled to the development environment a little better than Borland's, although the latter is a little more flexible.

Source Code Management Across Platforms

The two types of multiple-platform projects, those written by a single developer and those written by more than one developer, present their own unique source code management challenges.

Single-developer projects are easier to maintain. You have two options:

- Designate one machine to maintain the master copy of sources or act as the file server—a stationary file server.

- Designate the current development machine as the file server—a floating file server.

Either of these options will work and neither has any special equipment requirements. Transporting sources using a floppy (sneakernet) is acceptable if the project is reasonably simple and the sources will fit on a single floppy. This also provides an automatic backup mechanism.

Maintaining source code for multiple-developer projects is more complicated, especially across platforms. There are three options:

- Designate one developer and machine as the file server.

- Provide a separate network file server.

- Provide a distributed file server using a peer-to-peer network—the most recent version of a file on a particular developer's machine is the server for that file.

The first option is acceptable only if the project is simple and the number of developers is small. Otherwise the file server developer must have a powerful machine or little development responsibility. Ideally the third option is the most elegant solution and perhaps the best choice, but no real distributed file server solutions exist for multiple platforms.

Realistically the best choice is the second: provide a separate network file server. This dedicated machine should be reasonably powerful, should have a large hard disk capacity and a lot of RAM, and should be accessible to all of the developers through a network. The least costly server is a PC. Conveniently the best choices in version control software are also available for PCs and were previously listed in Table 3.8. Remember, for a cross-plaform solution you will also need to provide software to convert between the Macintosh and Windows text file formats.

CONSIDERATIONS WHEN USING C

Even though the C programming language may be implemented according to a standard specification, all features of a particular implementation may not match those of another. Certain platform-specific features may not be available on other platforms, or the interpretation of a standard feature on one platform might not match that on another platform. Some C language features that you want to be careful using are:

- command line arguments
- standard file streams
- pragma directives
- error constructs
- ANSI C memory functions
- inline assembly code

You should also be careful in specifying the format for the contents of your source files; inconsistent source file formats can cause you a lot of headaches.

Command Line Arguments

Command line arguments are formally specified to part of the main() function in C programs, but they are not necessarily used or supported by all platforms and by all software users. The Macintosh does not provide a mechanism to specify command line arguments other than through the Finder mechanism. Symantec's THINK C compiler allows your application to prompt the user for command line arguments if you compile with a special header file and library, but this is not standard, nor is it representative of Macintosh applications.

In Windows some users start programs by double-clicking on the application icon or a document's icon. Others start programs by choosing Run from the File menu in the Program Manager or the File Manager. In Windows NT, all Win16, Win32, and DOS applications can be started from a DOS session command line. The main entry point for a Windows program, WinMain(), is given a pointer to a command line string, which contains the information about the method of invocation for the program. You can't be guaranteed the number or existence of suitable command line information. So be careful if and when you support them.

To avoid problems in cross-platform programs, don't insist that the proper invocation of your program rely on command line arguments. If you need to specify parameters, use a dialog box that is common to all versions of your program.

Standard File

Unless you are using the standard C libraries, you probably won't be using the standard file stream designations: stdin, stdout, or stderr. Because most platforms are GUI-based, standard file streams are not always consistently implemented. On the Macintosh with a THINK C application, using stdout or stderr creates a separate window and directs all output there. In Windows 3.1 standard files are not available from the operating environment. In Windows NT standard files are available if you write a console (DOS equivalent) application but are not available if you are using the Win32 subsystem.

Generally you wouldn't want to use standard file features in a GUI-based, commercial-type software product, unless you really need to and you fully understand how these features behave on all target platforms. I recommend using them only if the software will not be distributed widely or if standard files serve a debugging purpose.

Pragma Directives

Pragma directives, or pragmas, are used to extend the C preprocessor functionality or to allow the developer to specify compiler options or features in the source code. Pragmas are very useful and very powerful; however, you need to be careful when you use them. Always place them within the protective custody of compile-time, compiler-specific, and platform-specific conditionals. You don't want to inadvertently reference a pragma that just happens to have a different meaning than what you intended out of context.

Error Constructs and Error Directives

Don't confuse error constructs with error directives. Error directives control what happens when an error condition occurs at the preprocess phase of compiling and should be used as carefully as pragmas.

Error constructs control the flow of execution when an error condition occurs as a result of a function call. They are also called error or exception handlers. Avoid using error constructs in cross-platform development for platform-independent code because error contstructs are implementation-specific. For example, THINK C or Symantec C++ uses:

```
TRY {
  //try to do something here
}CATCH{
  //if it fails, catch it here
}ENDTRY;
```

Microsoft C/C++ 7.0 in NT has one of two possible forms:

```
Method 1:                         Method 2:

try{                              try{
  //try to do something here        //try to do something here
}except (exceptionCode){          }finally{
  //if it fails, process it         //upon completion, do this
}                                 }
```

However, you are free to use error constructs in platform-specific sections of code without restriction. But if you plan to implement a cross-platform error handler using a compiler's native error constructs, you should be very careful, even restrictive, when you abstract them.

ANSI C Functions

If you plan to use ANSI C libraries, study the functional area that you intend to use and compare it very carefully to the same set of functions on the other platforms. Look at the functional descriptions, as well as the range of data and the numbers that a function's parameters might use. Even though the form of the functions may be the same, the way the data is generated may not be. Consider, for example, the ANSI C function time(). The THINK C time base assumes a start year of 1904, while Borland and Microsoft C assume a start year of 1970; see Chapter 12 for more information.

There are a few peculiarities of the ANSI C functions with respect to THINK C. If you use the file functions, for example, fopen(), you cannot directly specify the type or creator of the file; these types default to 'TEXT' and '????.' Also, if you are planning to produce an international version of your software, you will have trouble with THINK C's character checking isxxx() functions and string comparison strcmp() and strcmpi() functions. Nor will you be able to use THINK C's implementation of the multi-byte string functions mbxxx() to work with Macintosh international character sets. Refer to Chapter 6 for more information about file management and Chapter 20 for some guidance about internationalization.

Another thing is to avoid using the ANSI C memory functions, for example, malloc() and free(). They operate differently on different platforms and often do not manage memory in the way you intend. See Chapter 5 for information about the ANSI C memory functions.

Inline Assembly

Inline assembly allows the programmer to insert snippets of assembly instructions inline within C code. On some compilers the assembly code is inserted into the code generation stream, so you need to be careful about register usage. On other compilers the code is inserted, but critical registers are saved before and restored after the code fragment. If you use different compilers on the same platform, be careful when you use inline assembly because compiler behavior may vary.

Exercise caution when you use inline assembly across platforms, too. You can't always assume that different compilers on similar platforms will expect the same syntax or handle the inline code the same way. Nor can you assume that a platform will consistently compile to the same processor. For example, Windows NT will run on an 80x86 platform, and inline 80x86 assembly will probably work fine on Windows 3.1 (though you can't make assumptions about the specific type of 80x86 processor) and on PC-based Windows NT platforms running Win32 or Win16. But native RISC code will not port easily to non-native RISC platforms or to Intel-based Windows NT platforms. Nor will 80x86 inline assembly port easily to RISC platforms. If you must use inline assembly, you will need to enclose it in compile-time conditionals that are dependent on the particular NT hardware that you are compiling for.

You need to be aware of what happens to inline assembly when you use it. On some platforms improper code can easily compromise the system's integrity. Fortunately improper use of inline assembly is usually a compile-time or development-time problem. If the code is bad, either it won't compile or it will cause a serious problem the first time it is executed.

If you need to use inline assembly code, use the most generic form for the most basic form of target processor; for example, on the Macintosh use basic 68000 assembly instructions, and on a PC use 8086 assembly if you want to be really safe about the target processor (generally, with Windows 3.1, you are safe in using 80386 assembly).

Inconsistent Source File Formats

Anyone who has worked on a project where there is no standard source code editor or editor configuration knows how much of a problem tabs are. Not all editors treat tabs the same. Some let you choose whether tabs are expanded to spaces while you are typing or whether tabs remain as TAB characters. Some editors save the file with or without tabs and convert the text to the desired form after you open the file.

Another problem with tabs is deciding where to put the default tab stops. Some people like two spaces, others like four spaces, and still others like eight. It can be very confusing and frustrating to leave a file one way and read it back the next day and it looks totally different. A project team should set some standards about how tabs are used and interpreted.

The other source of source file inconsistency is line termination. Lines in Macintosh text files end in a RETURN and lines in PC text files end in a RETURN-LINEFEED. This issue was discussed in the section Source Code Considerations.

Table 3.9 Summary of compilers and platforms.

Compiler Name	Publisher	Mac	DOS	Win3.1	NT	OS/2 2.0	Other	Processors
Microsoft C/C++	Microsoft		x	x	x			80x86, MIPS
Visual C++	Microsoft		x					80x86
Borland C/C++	Borland		x	x	x	x		80x86
Symantec C++	Symantec	x	x	x	x	x	x	80x86, 680x0
THINK C	Symantec	x						680x0
MPW C/C++	Apple	x						680x0
WATCOM C	WATCOM		x	x	x	x		80x86
DEC C++	Digital				x		x	Alpha AXP
MetaWare C++	MetaWare		x	x	x	x	x	80x86, 680x0, SPARC, MIPS, HP-PA, AM29K, and others*

* Talk to manufacturer for more information.

LANGUAGE AND TOOLS SUMMARY

Table 3.9 summarizes the compilers and the platforms that they support. The essence of this chapter is:

- The best choice in function-type language is ANSI C.

- Currently the best choice in an object-oriented language is C++ that conforms to the AT&T CFRONT 3.0 standard.

- For a cost-effective solution use Symantec's THINK C on the Macintosh and Borland C/C+++ for Windows 3.1 and Win32s (or Microsoft C/C++ 8.0 for Win32).

- A slightly more expensive but more consistent solution is to use THINK C/Symantec C++ on the Macintosh and Symantec C/C++ on Windows 3.1 and Win32s.

- You need to convert between Macintosh and Windows text files.

- Use version control if you need to access multiple versions or configurations of your product or if there are multiple developers working on the project.

- Be careful using implementation-specific features of compilers.

- Refer to Tables 3.4 and 3.5 for information about function-based and object-oriented cross-platform products.

For more information about the companies and products discussed in this chapter, refer to Appendix E.

Part Two

Basic Implementation

4

Program Structure

Cross-platform development allows an application to be written once and then compiled to run on each supported platform. Ideally the recompilation process does not require any platform-specific switches. This means that the source code is identical for all platforms.

To attain true platform independence, you must hide many platform-specific features, including data, specific functional groups, event or message dispatching, program initialization, and termination. Using a robust naming convention and robust grammatical conventions allows you to minimize syntactical and semantic problems during development.

In this chapter we will discuss the cross-platform issues related to general program structure. These include:

- establishing some basic data types
- defining the program entry point
- performing program initialization and termination
- outlining the basic requirements of the event system
- defining a basic programming style

These components comprise the first step in the development of a cross-platform application.

CROSS-PLATFORM ARCHITECTURE

In this book and the XPLib software, we have assumed that the cross-platform solution is a layer on top of the platform's API, as shown in Figure 4.1.

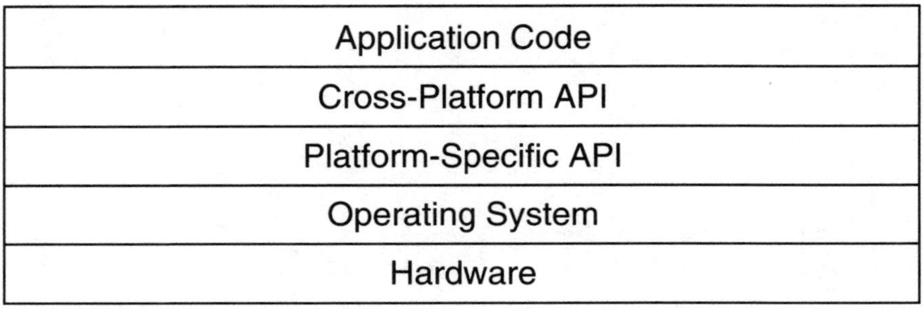

Application Code
Cross-Platform API
Platform-Specific API
Operating System
Hardware

Figure 4.1 Architectural layers of a cross-platform application.

Further, we have chosen to use the common denominator method (finding the greatest-common denominator whenever possible) and synthesize any functionality that is not available. Our primary goal was to produce as thin a cross-platform layer as possible to minimize performance degradation. This means that we will not nest a platform's native API call more than one function level beyond the cross-platform API call, unless it is necessary and doesn't occur in a frequently used function. This nesting detail is illustrated below:

```
XPFunctionToDoThing1 ()
{
    .
    .
    .
    NativeFunctionToDoThing1 ();
    .
    .
    .
}
```

Sometimes, this means giving up some modularity in order to minimize the function call overhead.

BASIC CROSS-PLATFORM DATA TYPES

The necessary cross-platform data types fall into two categories: simple data types—those that are based on a single other data type—and data structures—those that are based on more than one other data type. Some of these essential data types are described in the next two sections and are used in the code samples and discussions in the remainder of this book.

Simple Data Types

Simple cross-platform data types can be monomorphic (platform-independent) and polymorphic (platform-dependent). We present examples of both types and some essential predefined data values. Other data types are necessary and will be discussed in their appropriate contexts in the following chapters.

Platform-Independent Data Types

Type	Definition	Description
UINT1	unsigned char	unsigned byte
UINT2	unsigned short	unsigned word (2 bytes)
UINT4	unsigned long	unsigned double word (4 bytes)
SINT1	signed char	signed byte
SINT2	signed short	signed word (2 bytes)
SINT4	signed long	signed double word (4 bytes)
BOOL1	signed char	1-byte boolean
BOOL2	signed short	2-byte boolean
PTR	char *	32-bit pointer
ERR	signed short	signed word (2 bytes)

Platform- or Compiler-Specific (Polymorphic) Data Types

Type	Definition	Description
UINT	unsigned int	unsigned word or long
SINT	signed int	signed word or long
INT	int	signed or unsigned word or long (compiler dependent)

Common Data Values

Type	Value ID	Value
ERR	ERR_No	0
	ERR_Yes	1
BOOLx	TRUE	1
	FALSE	0
general	NULL	0
PTR	NULLPTR	(PTR) 0

Basic Data Structures

There are many cross-platform data structures, but POINT and RECT are essential to the general discussion. Others will be described in the chapters that follow.

Point Structure

Whenever we specify a point, we are specifying a point in a platform-specific manner, dictated by the graphics model. Consequently, we must define a POINT in a polymorphic way:

Field	Type	Description
x	SINT	polymorphic signed integer for *x* value
y	SINT	polymorphic signed integer for *y* value

This allows us to pass point information to graphics functions, for example, without having to define a cross-platform (non-polymorphic) point type that must be converted or coerced to a platform-specific type before it is used. This gives us a simple and efficient way to implement functions that require this type of information. An alternative is to specify a monomorphic POINT using 4-byte integers and require an intermediate conversion for systems that define points using 2-byte integers. Polymorphic data types can cause confusion when you are coding if you are doing arithmetic operations on them or make assumptions about their intrinsic sizes, but for our discussion we opt for performance over some confusion.

Rectangle Structure

As with a POINT structure, we define a RECT in a polymorphic way:

Field	Type	Description
left	SINT	polymorphic signed integer for leftmost *x* value
top	SINT	polymorphic signed integer for topmost *y* value
right	SINT	polymorphic signed integer for rightmost *x* value
bottom	SINT	polymorphic signed integer for bottommost *y* value

PROGRAMMING STYLE

Programming style is divided into two areas: naming conventions and coding style. A naming convention ensures that we can understand the meaning of a variable or function without having to know its entire context and the platform for which it is intended. Coding style specifies the manner in which we will use the syntax of the C language throughout this book.

Cross-Platform Naming Conventions

In producing a cross-platform solution, it is important to follow portable coding practices and to adhere to a strict naming convention. In this section we will outline the basics of a variable

Table 4.1 Common variable name prefix characters.

Prefix	Meaning
_	platform-specific variable
g	global
u	unsigned integer
s	signed integer
z	null-terminated string
p	pointer
h	handle
1	single byte or 8-bit quantity (modifier)
2	2 bytes or 16-bit quantity (modifier)
4	4 bytes or 32-bit quantity (modifier)

and function naming convention which is similar to Hungarian Notation.[1] It can be modified to suit your particular needs. For a detailed description of the cross-platform coding style, see Appendix C.

Variable Naming Convention

The cross-platform variable naming convention is made of the following rules:

- A variable name begins with one or more prefix descriptor characters or numbers that indicate the underlying type of a variable.
- All data types are given in uppercase.
- All variables begin with any number of lowercase prefix characters, a lowercase first letter, and separate words are capitalized. No underscores are used to separate words.
- All macros are given in uppercase.
- All globals begin with a lowercase "G."
- Platform-specific variable names begin with an underscore.
- A three-character prefix is used to indicate a specific platform name.

Table 4.1 lists some of the common variable name prefixes. Here are some examples of using the naming convention:

u2Num refers to a 16-bit unsigned number.
f10Num refers to an 80-bit floating point number.
gpu4Num means a global variable that is a pointer to a 4-byte unsigned integer.

---

[1] Hungarian Notation is a term used to describe a coding style that is used at Microsoft and by other Windows application developers. It was named in honor of Charles Simonyi, who formalized the notation.

When an integer size is not specified, the default size for the compiler is used. Be careful when you use this type of variable because it can be platform-dependent (polymorphic). At the same time, by using a polymorphic data type, you can effectively hide platform-dependent data types to platform API functions that are fundamentally different. For example, the coordinate values of the Macintosh and Windows 3.1 are specified as 16-bit signed integers, whereas in Win32 they are 32-bit signed integers. By defining an integer type for coordinate values as polymorphic, we can effectively hide the difference. (This is what the Windows header files do between Windows 3.1 and Win32.)

If you use polymorphic data, you cannot make assumptions about the size of the underlying data type. This means that you must provide polymorphic maximum and minimum values and cross-platform ways to manipulate and perform arithmetic operations on these data types, if necessary.

Function Naming Convention

The function naming convention is made of the following set of rules:

- All function names begin with an uppercase character and contain both upper- and lowercase characters and numbers, as necessary.
- Functional groups all begin with the same prefix letter or letters.
- The descriptive words within a function name are organized from most significant to least significant.
- Platform-specific function names begin with an underscore.
- A three-character prefix is used to indicate a specific platform name.

Here are some sample function names:

```
GroupDataRead ()
GroupDataWrite ()
_MacGroupDataRead ()
_MacGroupDataWrite ()
_Win31GroupDataRead ()
_Win31GroupDataWrite ()
```

Not only does this technique allow us to know what functional group a function belongs to without searching through the name but it allows us to sort easily our functions by group, category, and subcategory.

Cross-Platform Coding Style

The coding style that we have developed in writing this book and the accompanying code specifies a method of expressing C syntax to minimize semantic errors and to make the code easier to read. It is specified in detail in Appendix C, but a few of the important rules of the coding style are:

- Simple *if-* or *if-else* statements are made of a simple expression and simple statement that appear on the same line as the if or else keywords.

```
if (a==b) a++;
else b++;
```

- Multiple-line *if-* or *if-else* statements are always enclosed in curly braces and none of the statements contained therein are on the same lines as the curly braces.

```
if (a==b){
    a+=b;

    b=b+a;

}else{
    //only increment variable b
    b++;
}
```

- Return values or expressions are always enclosed in parenthesis.

```
return (TRUE);
return (a+(b/c));
```

- There is no space between an operand and a conditional operator.

```
if (var1<2 && var2>3) var1=var2;
```

- Curly braces that define a function are always left justified.
- All functions are declared using a parameter-type list rather than an identifier list. For example:

```
int Function1 (int parameter1, long parameter2)
{
}
```

the right way, but:

```
int Function1 (parameter1, parameter2)
    int parameter1;
    long parameter2;
{
}
```

is the wrong way. Duplicating the parameter name is unnecessary, confusing, and leads to syntax errors.

- Simple iteration statements (*do*, *for*, *do-while*) and *switch* statements have the opening brace at the end of the beginning statement line:

```
do{
}while (1);
for (i=0; i<10; i++){
}
```

About Sample Code in this Book

The code samples in this book are designed for clarity and do not perform robust error checking or generate detailed error codes. At times I have used unnecessary program structure or inappropriate coding practice to make the examples easier to understand and present during the discussion.

THE PROGRAM SKELETON

The basic anatomic components of a cross-platform application are:

- program entry point
- program initialization function
- event processing function or loop
- program termination function

A simple cross-platform application might look like this. (We will fill in some of the missing information in the sections that follow.)

```
// Define the main cross-platform entry point
XPMain (/* common parameters*/)
{
    // perform any necessary initializations
    XPInit (/* common parameters*/);

    // create a window and then process its events
    WinCreate (/* window creation parameters*/);
    EventLoop (/* common parameters*/);

    // clean up before we exit
    XPExit (/* common parameters*/);

    return;
}
```

Essential Global Variables

Before we describe the components of the skeletal cross-platform program, we will define some globals that will be used during initialization and in other functional areas of our cross-platform solution.

Macintosh Globals

BOOL2	_gb2MacMultiApps= FALSE	If the operating system can run multiple applications, the value is TRUE (MultiFinder or System 7); otherwise it is FALSE.

SINT2	_gs2MacSysVers=6	This maintains the current version of the operating system: System 6 or 7.
BOOL2	_gb2MacColorQD= FALSE	If this Macintosh is running Color Quick-Draw, the value is TRUE; otherwise it is FALSE.
HANDLER	_gfnMacHandler	This keeps a pointer to the handler function for Macintosh event processing. In effect, this is the class information for a Macintosh window.
MenuHandle	_ghMacAppleMenu	the handle to the Macintosh system menu list (Apple menu)
SINT2	_gs2MacAppleMenuID=1	the id of the system (Apple) menu list

Windows Globals

HINSTANCE	_ghWinInstance	a copy of the instance handle for this application
LPSTR	_gzWinCmdLine	a copy of the command line passed to us by WinMain()
int	_gnWinCmdShow	a copy of the show command passed to us by WinMain()
UINT1	_gzWinClassName= "XPLibClass"	the class name for cross-platform windows

Program Entry Point

Every program begins with an entry point to the platform's API. This special function is called by the operating system either directly or by the run-time environment that is set up by the compiler. There are two ways to abstract a program entry point: use a macro definition or tie into the run-time prolog.

Most compilers insert some run-time code at the beginning and end of a program—the run-time prolog and epilog, respectively. These allow the compiler to prepare to run the program and to clean up after the program has terminated. Tying in to the prolog allows you to define a common functional interface or set up some global data that can be used by an application.

A macro definition allows you to hide platform-dependent features of an entry point. These features include the function name, its parameters, and its return value. It isn't the most elegant method, but it is quick to implement and safe. We have used this method in the XPLib software and describe it here.

We specify the prototype for the cross-platform entry point as:

```
INT XPMain();
```

We assume that the main procedure returns some information to the operating system that is either used or ignored. There are no arguments because these are hidden by macro definitions that we will define for each platform.

In the Macintosh using THINK C we define the entry point as:

```
#define XPMain() main (void)
```

THINK C does not assume that the main() procedure has a return value—you can define it to have one or not. For general applications the value is ignored. (If you were writing a code resource for a window definition procedure, you would need to specify the entry point to return a long integer.)

In Windows we define the entry point as:

```
#define XPMain() PASCAL WinMain (HINSTANCE hInst, \
    HINSTANCE hPrevInst, LPSTR zCmdLine, int sCmdShow)
```

The Windows entry point, WinMain(), provides us with several parameters. They are used by the Windows program initialization function that is described next. Because these aren't necessarily useful to other platforms, we will hide them from the cross-platform application. The WinMain() function is prototyped in the WINDOWS.H file as:

```
int PASCAL WinMain (HINSTANCE hInst, HINSTANCE hPrevInst,
    LPSTR zCmdLine, int sCmdShow)
```

Currently the Windows ignores return value from WinMain(). Be aware that because the int type is polymorphic between Windows 3.1 and Windows NT (2 bytes and 4 bytes, respectively), if the return value is to be significant relative to other cross-platform applications, a program will need to limit the return value to a number representable by a 2-byte integer.

We can now define the simplest cross-platform application as:

```
INT XPMain()
{
    return (0);
}
```

Program Initialization

When a program is started, some sort of initialization is usually required. Some of the necessary steps of program initialization are platform-dependent and some are application-dependent. Here we are concerned only with platform-dependent initialization. Because the information that is used during initialization is also platform-dependent, it isn't always easy to specify a simple functional interface to perform the initialization.

Consider the Macintosh and Windows platforms. Those portions of initialization that need to be specified can be represented by a single function call:

```
BOOL2 XPInit (SINT2 s2Masters, BOOL2 b2Copies,
    HANDLER fnHandler);
```

In the Macintosh the b2Copies parameter is ignored because you can have only one instance of a specific application running at a time. But the s2Masters parameter is necessary to specify additional master memory pointers that must be allocated during program initialization. The fnHandler parameter is used to specify the default window handler function. The macro definition for the Macintosh initialization function is:

```
// b2Copies is ignored
#define XPInit (s2Masters, b2Copies, fnHandler) \
    _MacInit (s2Masters, fnHandler)
```

Then we define the Macintosh program initialization procedure. It is responsible for initializing the Toolbox managers, getting some information about the configuration of the system, the _MacSystemInfo() function, and setting up a default system (Apple) menu that can be used by all menu bars created in this application.

```
//-------------------------------------------------------
BOOL2 _MacInit (SINT2 s2Masters, HANDLER fnHandler)
//-------------------------------------------------------
// s2Masters - number of additional master pointers to
//             allocate
// fnHandler - pointer to the window handler procedure
// RETURNS   - TRUE if successful and FALSE if not
//-------------------------------------------------------
{
    do{
        MoreMasters ();
    }while (s2Masters--);

    MaxApplZone ();
    InitGraf (&thePort);
    InitFonts ();
    FlushEvents (everyEvent, 0);

    InitWindows ();
    InitCursor ();
    InitMenus ();
    TEInit ();
    InitDialogs (0L);

    // Get some information about this Macintosh:
    //   system 6 or system 7?
    //   do multiple applications?
    //   have Color QuickDraw?
    _MacSystemInfo ();

    // Initialize the global containing the default window
```

```
            // handler routine...a minimal window class. All
            // windows will use this handler to process events.
            _gfnMacHandler=fnHandler;
            // set up the system menu to include "About..."
            // and "Help..." grayed out (disabled)
            {
            Str255 pPStr;    // Pascal string

            pPStr[0]=1;
            pPStr[1]=appleMark;

            _ghMacAppleMenu=NewMenu (_gs2MacAppleMenuID, pPStr);
            AppendMenu (_ghMacAppleMenu, "\p(About...");
            AppendMenu (_ghMacAppleMenu, "\p(Help...");
            AppendMenu (_ghMacAppleMenu, "\p(-");

            //load all desk accessories and append them
            //to the Apple (system) menu
            AddResMenu (_ghMacAppleMenu, 'DRVR');

            ClearMenuBar ();
            InsertMenu (_ghMacAppleMenu, 0);
            DrawMenuBar ();
            }

            return (TRUE);
        }
```

In Windows the s2Masters parameter is ignored, but b2Copies is needed if we want to run multiple instances of the application; fnHandler is needed to allow us to create a window class. In addition we need to pass the other parameters that were supplied to us by the WinMain() entry point but were invisible to our cross-platform application because they were hidden by our XPMain() entry point. We define a macro to map our XPInit() macro function call to the WinInit() function.

```
// s2Masters is ignored

// hInst, hPrevInst, zCmdLine, and sCmdShow were provided
// by WinMain()
#define XPInit (s2Masters, b2Copies, fnHandler) \
    _WinInit (hInst, hPrevInst, zCmdLine, sCmdShow, \
      b2Copies, fnHandler)
```

Then we define the initialization routine. The first four parameters are identical to those of WinMain(). The last is a pointer to the function that will be the callback procedure for all of our windows—we support only a single window class.

```
//------------------------------------------------------
BOOL2 _WinInit (HINSTANCE hInst, HINSTANCE hPrevInst,
    LPSTR zCmdLine, int nCmdShow, BOOL2 b2Copies,
    HANDLER fnHandler)
//------------------------------------------------------
// hInst      - handle of this instance of the application
// hPrevInst  - handle to the previous instance of this
//                 application
// zCmdLine   - command line string
// nCmdShow   - show command for the application's window
// b2Copies   - TRUE means allow multiple copies of this
//                 application
// fnHandler  - pointer to the window handler procedure
// RETURNS    - TRUE if successful and FALSE if not
//------------------------------------------------------
{
    // check if we are supposed to allow multiple copies
    // of this application to run
    if (hPrevInst && !b2Copies) return (FALSE);

    // save a copy of the instance provided by Windows
    _ghWinInstance=hInst;

    // save a copy of the command line
    StrCopy (_gzWinCmdLine, zCmdLine);
    _gnWinCmdShow=nCmdShow;

    if (!hPrevInst){
        WNDCLASS wc;

        //each window gets a DC & receives double clicks
        wc.style=CS_OWNDC|CS_DBLCLKS;
        // specify the window handler procedure, remember
        // to export this procedure in the DEF file.
        wc.lpfnWndProc=fnHandler;
        wc.cbClsExtra=0;
        //reserve some space for XP extra data
        wc.cbWndExtra=sizeof (WNDX);
        // the window belongs to this application
        wc.hInstance=_ghWinInstance;
        // specify an icon for this application (default)
        wc.hIcon=LoadIcon (NULL, IDI_APPLICATION);
        // specify our default cursor
        wc.hCursor=LoadCursor (NULL, IDC_ARROW);
        // this window's default background is white
```

```
            wc.hbrBackground=GetStockObject (WHITE_BRUSH);
            // this window has no default menu
            wc.lpszMenuName=NULL;
            // specify our cross-platform window class name
            wc.lpszClassName=_gzWinClassName;

            // register the window with Windows
            if (!RegisterClass (&wc)) return (FALSE);
    }


    return (TRUE);
}
```

Basic Event Loop

Our program model assumes that a window is necessary to process events; see Chapter 7 for more information about the event model. Before we can process events, we need to create a window whose events we will process. In XPInit() we have already specified a window handler procedure that will process events for all windows that we create. So we need to create a window. Then we wait for events to occur.

The details of the event loop function are also discussed in Chapter 7. Its primary purpose is to loop indefinitely and retrieve event messages that your application needs to process. In a GUI-based application the event loop calls the window handler function and allows the application to do its work. Normally an event loop looks like this:

```
create a window
while we have an event{
    process the event
}
```

If your program does not require a window or will not be processing events you can simply insert code to do some work or perform some calculations and then exit. For example:

```
SINT XPMain ()
{
    XPInit (0, FALSE, NULLPTR);
    FunctionToDoWork ();
    XPExit (0);
    return (0);
}
```

Regardless, the spot between program initialization and program termination is reserved for "the stuff that does all the work." This can be processing events or adding numbers.

Program Termination

Just before we exit the application, we need to clean up any platform-specific stuff. Here we define the exit procedure that allows us to specify an exit code. This parameter is currently ignored, but is a placeholder for a feature that might be nice to include in a more sophisticated implementation.

```
//----------------------------------------------------
VOID XPExit (SINT2 s2ExitCode)
//----------------------------------------------------
// s2ExitCode - not currently used
// RETURNS    - nothing
//----------------------------------------------------
{
```

In the Macintosh we delete all items in the system (Apple) menu list and then free up the memory associated with it.

```
if (_ghMacAppleMenu){
    DeleteMenu (_gs2MacAppleMenuID);
    DisposeMenu (_ghMacAppleMenu);
}
```

Nothing is required by Windows 3.1 or Win32 during program termination, so we can just end the function.

```
}
```

Now that we have described how a cross-platform looks in a general sense, let's look at some of the pieces that provide the services that do the real work.

5

Memory Management

At the heart of an operating system or application is the memory manager. All other major groups of functionality rely on the memory manager's ability to perform its job accurately and efficiently. The same must be true of the memory manager layer that you construct to provide a common memory manager interface on all platforms that you plan to support. If you spend more time ensuring that the cross-platform memory manager works, you will probably spend less time debugging other parts of your cross-platform library and applications. The first step in finding a cross-platform solution is to find a solution to a cross-platform memory manager.

This chapter presents:

- a simple cross-platform memory management solution using the standard C library functions
- a practical cross-platform memory management solution and its components
- a discussion of advanced memory management issues

The function samples presented in this chapter are not necessarily equivalent to the XPLib memory management functions. The samples are meant to illustrate the basic cross-platform memory management issues and do not a provide a total solution to the memory management problem. The XPLib software provides a more thorough cross-platform memory management solution.

SIMPLE MEMORY MANAGEMENT SOLUTIONS

The simplest and most expedient solution to the memory management problem is to not need or use a memory manager. This means that you don't use dynamically allocated memory in your software applications. Instead use statically allocated memory, which is specified at compile time and allocated or reserved when the program is loaded; or use automatically allocated memory, which is specified at compile time and allocated from the processor's run-time stack.

Not providing a memory manager is fine if a program does not need to work with large amounts of memory or with memory blocks of unpredictable sizes. However, it is not suitable for most software applications. You should consider static and automatic data to be limited resources that should be used wisely. You must be aware of the total size of static memory declared. Some environments limit the total static memory; for example, Windows 3.1 imposes a limit of 64K bytes per static data segment. Some programmers, especially those using object-oriented languages, insist that using static (or global) data should be minimized or avoided.

You must also be careful if you use large amounts of automatically allocated memory. This type of memory is typically allocated from the processor's stack. Defining reentrant or recursive functions that declare large automatic variables can cause stack overflows if you are not careful.

A better, but still simple, cross-platform memory management solution is to use the ANSI C standard library memory allocation routines—for example, malloc(), realloc(), and free(). This solution lets your program dynamically allocate memory with little or no platform-specific code and provides a portable function syntax. The problem with this method is that in some environments the compilers use a limited memory resource for this type of dynamic memory; for example, in Windows 3.1 the memory is allocated from the application's local heap and is limited to 64K bytes.

If you decide to use the standard C library solution, you should realize that memory allocated using these routines cannot be unlocked. The functional specification for the standard C library memory functions does not provide a way to lock or unlock memory and consequently relocate it. This might not be a problem for your application, but fixed memory can lead to memory fragmentation or memory waste. On platforms that allow multitasking and that provide a reserved memory space for each task, allocating fixed memory will cause memory problems. Programs that run on sophisticated platforms should be aware of, and utilize, the functionality provided by the platform's native memory functions.

IMPLEMENTING A MEMORY MANAGEMENT SOLUTION

The criteria for creating a memory manager for multiple event-driven platforms are:

- The memory manager functions need to be fast.
- Large memory blocks should be easily allocated.
- Numerous, small memory blocks should be efficiently allocated.
- The memory manager functions must represent the highest subset of available functionality.

The memory manager functions must be fast. The routines in the memory manager will be called often by many other functions in your application and by other functions in the cross-platform library. It is unwise to use any unnecessary indirection; nested function calls should be minimized. When you have to implement platform-specific features, you should do so in the most efficient native form. This means using assembly language if you have to (except on platforms where assembly code is impractical—for example, on Windows NT, where there can be numerous underlying processors, depending on the computer system it is running on). If you do use assembly language, use it consistently and wisely, and concentrate its use in specific functions and files—don't spread it around.

No unnecessary limitations on memory block size or on the number of memory blocks should be imposed by the memory manager. In the solution presented in this section and in the XPLib software, numerous, small memory objects are not efficiently allocated using Windows 3.1. This is a flaw in the Windows 3.1 memory management functions and is discussed in Advanced Memory Management Considerations, later in this chapter.

To take advantage of as many features of a platform's API as possible, you must not limit the functional scope of the more basic components of the cross-platform solution—for example, memory management. You don't want to find out that you are precluded from implementing a feature because you scrimped on the memory manager.

Comparing Available Memory Functionality

The first step in creating a cross-platform memory manager is to look at the functionality that you want to provide and to find the closest matches to that functionality on all of the platforms you will be developing for. A map of desired memory management functionality, to the closest platform-specific function that can provide that functionality, is shown in Table 5.1.

Note the important distinction between the Macintosh and Windows memory allocation models. In the Macintosh a handle is a pointer to a pointer. This means that to generate the pointer associated with a memory handle, you only need to dereference the handle. Also, be

Table 5.1 Comparison of memory management functionality across platforms.

Function	*Macintosh*	*Windows*[*]
allocate pointer	NewPtr	GlobalAllocPtr[**]
free pointer	DisposPtr	GlobalfreePtr[**]
allocate handle	NewHandle	GlobalAlloc
free handle	DisposHandle	GlobalFree
lock handle	HLock	GlobalLock
unlock handle	HUnlock	GlobalUnlock
reallocate handle	SetHandleSize	GlobalReAlloc
handle size	GetHandleSize	GlobalSize
compact memory	CompactMem	GlobalCompact
maximize memory	MaxMem	GlobalCompact

[*] Windows 3.1 and Win32 are considered jointly in the Windows column because the functions are syntactically the same, even though there are some differences in the definitions of some data types on the two platforms. For example, GlobalLock() returns an LPSTR in Windows 3.1 and Win32, but an LPSTR refers to a selector and offset in Windows 3.1 and a 32-bit linear address in Win32.

[**] These are macros defined for Windows 3.1, Win32s, and Win32.

careful when using pointers that are associated with unlocked handles for long periods of time. Unless the handle is locked, it is possible for the Macintosh operating system to relocate the memory block without you knowing it.

In Windows 3.1 a handle is a selector. To resolve the pointer you have to look up the pointer associated with the selector. Because this is done at the operating system level, this process also locks the memory to prevent it from moving around while you are using it.

To make cross-platform functions equivalent, you must ensure that a Macintosh pointer is not generated by just dereferencing it. The handle must be locked and then dereferenced.

Comparing Memory Pointers

The great disparity among the platform APIs and data types presents a problem for cross-platform development. This is true for memory management. There are many things to consider when choosing the appropriate data representation for a memory pointer:

- the intrinsic pointer size on a platform
- the pointer organization on a platform
- the maximum memory block size that a pointer can refer to on a platform

For each of the platforms and their incarnations, you must look at all of the options for memory pointers. These options are compared in Table 5.2. As you can see, there is quite a bit of variation. Windows 3.1, with its many models and modes, poses the greatest problem. For simplicity I have chosen to work with the large model and generally have ignored the underlying physical limitations of the operating mode. I did not choose the small or medium memory models because

Table 5.2 Comparison of memory pointers across platforms.

Macintosh	*Windows 3.1*[*]	*Windows NT*[**]
System 6	small model: 16 bits	32 bits
24 bits physical	medium model: 16 bits	
32-bit type	large model, standard mode	
	24 bits physical	
System 7	32-bit type	
32 bits	max 64K block size	
	large model, enhanced mode	
	26 bits physical	
	32-bit type	
	max 64K block size	
	huge model: 32 bits	

[*]   Windows 3.0 had real mode which allowed 20-bit physical addresses, a 64K maximum block size, and no virtual memory management.

[**] The Alpha AXP and R4x00 processors allow 64-bit memory addressing, but NT is a 32-bit operating system.

Table 5.3 Virtual memory support across platforms.

Macintosh	*Windows 3.1**	*Windows NT*
System 6: no	standard mode: yes	yes
System 7: yes	enhanced mode: yes	

* Windows 3.0 had a real mode that did not support virtual memory.

the intrinsic pointer type cannot represent memory blocks larger than 64K bytes. I did not choose the huge memory model because the overhead of using pointers of this type makes it inefficient.

Using the large memory model does not prevent you from allocating arbitrarily large memory blocks; it only defines the intrinsic data type associated with a char * declaration. The large memory model prevents you from accessing more than 64K bytes of memory using pointer indexing, but it does not limit the size of the memory block pointed to by the pointer to be less than or equal to 64K bytes. In addition the large memory model produces intrinsic pointer types that are consistent with the definition of pointer types in the Windows API functions.

Comparing Virtual Memory Availability

You must also consider whether the platforms support virtual memory; see Table 5.3. Virtual memory support allows an application to access more memory than is physically available by using the system's hard disk to swap out the contents of physical memory when more memory is needed. Of all the platforms considered in this book, only the Macintosh running System 6 does not directly support virtual memory.

Be aware that improperly using virtual memory can significantly decrease your application's performance. Avoid using virtual memory to create many frequently accessed memory blocks. Instead use virtual memory for data that is related to specific, reasonably static, nonoverlapping areas of program functionality. Incur the performance penalty of unloading physical memory to disk and loading from disk only when necessary.

Essential Memory Data Types

To properly abstract the functionality associated with dynamic memory blocks, you must provide a way to isolate the application from the underlying allocation processes. You can do this by abstracting the memory functions, the memory handle data type, and the memory pointer type. The cross-platform memory handle and pointer data types are define as follows:

Data Type	*Declaration*	*Description*
HMEM	UINT4	the 32-bit handle to the memory block
PTR	char *	the 32-bit pointer to the memory block

The cross-platform memory handle data type, HMEM, is defined as an unsigned 4-byte integer on all platforms, but the platform-specific memory handles have these types and sizes:

Macintosh	*Windows 3.1*	*Win32*
handle	HANDLE or HGLOBAL	HANDLE or HGLOBAL
4 bytes	2 bytes	4 bytes

Incidently the null memory handle value, MNULL, is defined as zero on all platforms. And the null pointer value, NULLPTR, is defined as (PTR)0 on all platforms.

Because handles and their pointers are usually used near each other, it is more efficient to define a data type to use for all memory operations and to hide the handle, pointer, and other information necessary for cross-platform abstraction. In XPLib this was done using a data structure called MEM, which is made of the following components:

Data Type	*Name*	*Description*
PTR	ptr	the 32-bit pointer to the memory block
HMEM	h	the handle to the memory block
UINT2	u2Lock	the lock count of the memory block

The u2Lock entry allows the Macintosh to have the same memory locking capability as Windows 3.1 and Win32. If you are not concerned about multiple locks to the same memory block, you can omit the u2Lock entry in the data structure.

Because the components of the MEM data structure are all defined with the same intrinsic data types, the structure is the same size on all platforms. This makes the MEM data structure syntactically and spatially equivalent on all of the platforms.

Implementing Essential Memory Functionality

A broad range of memory management functions must be defined to suit the needs of a sophisticated application. However, we can use a limited number of basic memory management functions to illustrate the process of constructing a cross-platform memory manager. This section describes the following basic memory management functions:

- memory allocation—to allocate a block of memory
- memory locking—to lock down a block of memory so it can be used
- memory unlocking—to unlock a block of memory so it can be relocated if necessary
- memory freeing—to free up a block of memory when it is no longer needed

- memory compaction—to compact memory to ensure the success of a subsequent memory allocation

- memory block size—to retrieve the size of an allocated memory block

Once you understand the basic issues of providing cross-platform memory management functionality, all other features are fairly straightforward to understand and to implement.

Allocating a Block of Memory

The first memory management function that is needed is the ability to allocate a block of memory. To specify a block of memory to allocate, we need one essential piece of information: the number of bytes to allocate. The memory allocation routine in XPLib works with a MEM data structure to allocate memory of the specified size and return a valid handle to the memory block if the allocation is successful. The XPLib function also includes a boolean parameter that indicates if the memory block is to be initialized to zeros. This parameter is omitted to simplify the sample code.

To start we declare the memory allocation function, MAllock(). It requires a valid pointer to a MEM structure and the number of bytes that we want to allocate; then we initialize the memory structure.

```
//-------------------------------------------------------
PMEM MAlloc (PMEM pMem, UINT4 u4Bytes)
//-------------------------------------------------------
// pMem    - pointer to a MEM structure
// u4Bytes - number of bytes to allocate
// RETURNS - pMem if successful, NULLPTR otherwise
//-------------------------------------------------------
{
    // initialize the memory structure properly
    pMem->ptr = NULLPTR;
    pMem->u2Lock = 0;
```

Next we need to allocate the memory. On the Macintosh, a new handle is created that references a block of memory of the specified size.

```
    pMem->h = (HMEM)NewHandle (u4Bytes);
```

In Windows 3.1 and Win32 we allocate some memory from the global heap and save the handle. We specify the size of block that we want to allocate and the attributes of that block. For consistency with the Macintosh we specify that the block be moveable and discardable.

```
    pMem->h = (HMEM)GlobalAlloc(
        GMEM_MOVEABLE|GMEM_DISCARDABLE, (DWORD)u4Bytes);
```

On exit from the allocate function, indicate the success or failure of the allocation. A non-null value indicates success and a null value indicates failure.

```
    return (pMem->h ? pMem : NULL);
}
```

The declared type of a cross-platform memory handle HMEM is a 4-byte unsigned integer. This is equivalent with the intrinsic size of a handle in the Macintosh and Win32 platforms. In Windows 3.1, the intrinsic size of a memory handle is 2 bytes. On all platforms we cast the handle returned by the platform's allocation routine to type HMEM. This does two things: it ensures that the type of the handle returned is the same as the type of the cross-platform handle, and it visually indicates that there may be a difference between the two handle types.

Locking a Block of Memory

After a block of memory has been allocated, but before it can be used to store information or the information in the block is accessed, the memory block must be locked down and an actual pointer to a physical memory block must be retrieved.

A memory block can be locked more than once. This allows different functions to use the memory block and ensures that the physical memory pointer is valid when it is being used. Each time the memory block is locked, the lock count increases by one. When a memory block is first allocated or when it is completely unlocked, the lock count is zero.

We begin by declaring the memory lock function MLock() and pass it the pointer to a valid MEM structure. We will eventually return a pointer to the locked-down memory block. But before we proceed with the locking process, we must check to ensure that the memory handle contained in the MEM structure represents a valid block of memory.

```
//----------------------------------------------------
PTR MLock (PMEM pMem)
//----------------------------------------------------
// pMem     - pointer to a MEM structure referencing
//              allocated memory
// RETURNS - pointer to locked memory if successful
//----------------------------------------------------
{
    //has the memory been allocated?
    if (pMem->h==MNULL){
        return (NULLPTR);
    }
```

After we have verified that the memory handle value is valid, we continue with the locking process. In the Macintosh the handle is locked and the handle is dereferenced to produce a pointer to the physical memory.

```
    // we only need to lock if we haven't done so before
    if (!pMem->u2Lock){

        SINT2 s2Result;
        Handle hMem=(Handle)pMem->h;
        asm{
            MOVE.L hMem,A0;
            HLock;
            MOVE.W D0, s2Result;
        }
```

```
// check the Mac return code
if (s2Result!=noErr){
    // error: can't lock memory handle
    return (NULLPTR);
}


// dereference the handle: Macintosh handle is
// a pointer to a pointer
pMem->ptr=*((Handle)pMem->h);
}
```

In Windows 3.1 and Win32 the memory handle is locked and the physical memory pointer is returned by the Windows API function GlobalLock(). In Windows 3.1 a memory handle refers to a selector—a handle does not directly refer to a physical memory location but is an index into a descriptor table which contains the physical addresses. In standard mode there can be only 4096 global handles in the entire Windows system, and in protected mode there can be 8192 global handles. Also, the pointer returned from GlobalLock() can refer to a block of any size, but the intrinsic type for a PTR, an LPSTR, limits you from accessing more than 64K bytes. This allows memory pointers from GlobalLock() to be used by Windows API calls. To allow a PTR to access data of more than 64K bytes, we must provide support functions to facilitate indexing into large data blocks. This can be done by providing cross-platform API functions, or it can be done as needed within the scope of the functions used by your application. To properly use an LPSTR-type memory pointer in Windows 3.1 to access more than 64K bytes, you should cast the pointer returned by GlobalLock() to a "char huge *" and assign it to an equivalently declared variable. You are now free to access any byte in the memory block directly or to increment the pointer beyond 64K as needed.

This 64K limit does not exist in Windows NT. All pointers are 32 bits. A handle is a 32-bit pointer into a table of pointers that is maintained by the process.

```
// we only need to lock if we haven't done so before
if (!pMem->u2Lock){

    if (!(pMem->ptr=(PTR)GlobalLock ((HANDLE)pMem->h))){
        // error: unable to lock down memory handle
        return (NULLPTR);
    }
}
```

Before we exit with the valid pointer to the memory block, we increment the lock count for this memory block.

```
// increment lock count
pMem->u2Lock++;

return (pMem->ptr);
}
```

Unlocking a Block of Memory

When you are finished with a block of memory, you unlock it to minimize memory fragmentation and to maximize available memory. Our unlock function, MUnlock(), requires a pointer to a MEM structure and returns this pointer if the unlock was successful or a null pointer if it was not successful. The first step is to check if the memory is already completely unlocked and if it is not, we decrement the lock count.

```
//----------------------------------------------------
PMEM MUnlock (PMEM pMem)
//----------------------------------------------------
// pMem     - pointer to a MEM structure referencing
//              allocated and locked memory
// RETURNS - pMem if successful, NULLPTR otherwise
//----------------------------------------------------
{
    // check if the memory is completely unlocked?
    if (!pMem->u2Lock) return (pMem);

    // decrement the lock count
    pMem->u2Lock--;
```

In the Macintosh we need to unlock the handle if the lock count is zero.

```
    if (!pMem->u2Lock){

        SINT2 s2Result;
        Handle hMem=(Handle)pMem->h;

        asm{
            MOVE.L hMem,A0;
            HUnlock;
            MOVE.W D0, s2Result;
        }

        if (s2Result!=noErr){
            // error: can't unlock memory handle
            return (NULL);

        }else pMem->ptr=NULLPTR;
```

Similarly in Windows 3.1 and Win32 we unlock the handle if the lock count is zero.

```
    if (!pMem->u2Lock){
        GlobalUnlock ((HANDLE)pMem->h);
        pMem->ptr=NULLPTR;
    }
```

Then we exit with the pointer to the MEM structure; a null pointer indicates the block could not be unlocked.

```
    return (pMem);
}
```

Freeing a Block of Memory

Because the MEM structure contains all of the information that is needed to represent a dynamically allocated memory block, we only need to provide the free memory function MFree() with a valid pointer to a memory structure. The function must check to see if the memory block is currently in use (the lock count is nonzero). If the memory block is in use, it is not freed and the function returns successfully.

We begin the free memory function MFree() by declaring the function and passing it a pointer to a valid memory structure.

```
//----------------------------------------------------
ERR MFree (PMEM pMem)
//----------------------------------------------------
// pMem    - pointer to a MEM structure referencing
//           allocated and unlocked memory
// RETURNS - ERR_No if successful
//----------------------------------------------------
{
```

On the Macintosh we check the lock count of the block and free the memory block associated with the handle by disposing the handle. If we are unable to dispose the handle, the function returns an error.

```
    // dispose handle if completely unlocked
    if (!pMem->u2Lock){

        SINT2 s2Result;
        Handle hMem=(Handle)pMem->h;

        asm{
            MOVE.L hMem,A0
            DisposHandle;
            MOVE.W D0, s2Result
        }
        if (s2Result!=noErr){
            // error: can't dispose handle, already freed?
            return (ERR_Yes);
        }
    }
```

In Windows 3.1 and Win32 we also check the lock count and free the memory block associated with the memory handle.

```
//free memory if completely unlocked
if (!pMem->u2Lock){

    if (GlobalFree ((HANDLE)pMem->h)){
        // error: can't free memory, already freed?
        return (ERR_Yes);
    }
}
```

On exiting, we indicate to the caller that the memory was freed successfully.

```
return (ERR_No);
}
```

Retrieving the Size of a Block of Memory

We begin by defining the memory block size function MSize(). It requires a pointer to a valid memory structure, and it returns the size of the memory block in bytes.

```
//------------------------------------------------------
UINT4  MSize (PMEM pMem)
//------------------------------------------------------
// pMem     - pointer to a MEM structure referencing
//            valid memory
// RETURNS - size of the memory block if successful and
//            zero otherwise
//------------------------------------------------------
{
```

In the Macintosh we get the size of a memory handle using the GetHandleSize() function.

```
return ((UINT4)GetHandleSize ((Handle)pMem->h));
```

In Windows 3.1 and Win32 the process of retrieving the size of a memory block is similar, but the returned size of the memory handle might be larger than the size that was originally specified to GlobalAlloc(). This is because Windows might allocate a block larger than necessary to allow for possible growth, because a block might already exist with the approximate size as that requested, or as a side effect of the memory allocation process.

```
return ((UINT4)GlobalSize ((HANDLE)pMem->h));
```

Finally we terminate the function definition and return the size of the memory block in bytes.

```
}
```

Compacting the Heap

Usually you compact the heap because you have either been unable to allocate a memory block of a certain size or because you want to ensure that there is enough memory available to flawlessly allocate a block of memory at a later time. To compact the heap, we define MCompact() which requires the number of bytes that you want to ensure are available. The return value is the number of bytes that have been freed as a result of compaction.

```
//-------------------------------------------------------
UINT4 MCompact (UINT4 u4Bytes)
//-------------------------------------------------------
// u4Bytes - number of bytes that we want available
// RETURNS - number of bytes actually compacted
//-------------------------------------------------------
{
```

In the Macintosh memory is compacted in the following way:

```
return ((UINT4)CompactMem ((Size)u4Bytes));
```

In Windows we compact memory this way:

```
return ((UINT4)GlobalCompact ((DWORD)u4Bytes));
```

Then we end the function definition. The value returned is the number of bytes actually compacted in the heap.

```
}
```

ADVANCED MEMORY MANAGEMENT CONSIDERATIONS

Some other basic memory management functions that are not illustrated in the examples in this chapter but are included in the XPLib software are:

- memory reallocation—to increase or decrease the size of a previously allocated block of memory
- memory copying—to copy the contents of one block of memory to another location
- memory filling—to fill the contents of a memory block with a single value
- memory comparison—to compare the contents of one memory block with the contents of another, byte for byte

To implement the most efficient memory manager for multiple platforms it may be necessary to create an abstracted memory management engine or suballocator. This means that when the application starts up, the memory manager allocates one or more large blocks of memory from the operating system. When the application requests memory from the memory manager, the memory manager will allocate it from the large blocks that have already been reserved. This allows you to minimize platform overhead by minimizing the execution times of memory management functions and minimizing the space associated with each memory block.

Creating an abstracted memory management engine also lets you more accurately control the behavior of memory functions and provides you the broadest range of functionality across all platforms. Unfortunately this suballocator technique comes at a cost—it takes time to design, implement, and debug. On some platforms, such as the Win32 subsystem on Windows NT, it is probably not necessary or efficient to employ a memory suballocator because the memory management facilities of the operating system already provide you with the necessary functionality and flexibility.

For most applications this memory suballocator will probably not be necessary. It really is important if you need to allocate a lot of small memory blocks. In Windows 3.1 the overhead associated with small blocks can be unnecessarily high, at least 32 bytes per block in enhanced mode. Also, you are limited to 4096 memory handles (in standard mode; 8192 memory handles in enhanced mode) for the entire Windows 3.1 operating environment. But unless you will be allocating a lot of memory blocks (2K or more) that are persistent and plan on allowing a lot of other applications to run concurrently, you will probably not have a problem with the limit on the number of memory handles.

Another solution to the cross-platform memory manager problem is to purchase a third-party solution. Micro Quill provides an efficient and well tested memory manager, SmartHeap, that is available for the Macintosh, Windows 3.1, Windows NT, OS/2, and other platforms.

6

File Management

Unless you plan to generate all of your data at run-time for exclusive run-time use, you must provide a way to read and write your data to a file. To do this, you will need to design a set of cross-platform file functions that can provide you with a simple, practical, or advanced solution to the file management problem.

A simple (and quick) file solution involves using the ANSI C Library functions but costs you some flexibility. An advanced file solution is data-smart: the file manager knows how to save data by type, and it might even know the organization of the file to facilitate reading and writing operations. It must also be able to read and write transparently to various platform-specific data organizations, big-endian (byte 0 is the most significant byte) and little-endian (byte 0 is the least significant byte), for example. A practical solution falls somewhere in the middle and requires an understanding of the platform-specific file management functionality but doesn't take a lot of time to implement. It illustrates the nature of the file problem and a way to solve it, and provides a solid base for future enhancements.

A SIMPLE FILE SOLUTION

As with memory management, the simplest solution to the cross-platform file management problem is to use the ANSI C library routines; for example, fopen(), fclose(), fread(), and fwrite(). They provide equivalent functionality in all development environments that support a proper ANSI C implementation, allowing you to implement file management functionality across platforms quickly.

There are some limitations imposed by the ANSI C file functions if you use them with platforms based on graphical user interfaces. GUI-based platforms generally do not support or recommend using a command line to provide input to a program, and there is generally no concept of standard input, output, or error files. Normally the process of selecting a file to read or write is accomplished using dialogs—features not represented by any functions in the standard library.

Another problem with using the ANSI file management functions is that they do not allow you to access all of a platform's necessary file functionality. For example, if you are using THINK C on the Macintosh, you cannot specify the file type or file creator with the ANSI library functions. This may or may not be a problem for your application, but if you need to work with files of various types, it will be a problem.

The ANSI file functions do not allow you to read or write a cross-platform file format directly. You must build a functional layer above the ANSI functions to provide a way to transparently read and write files generated on multiple platforms. (Note that the ANSI functions are already built up from the lower operating system file functions.) This might not be a problem if the files are small and their contents are not too complex, but it could add unnecessary inefficiency to the file access process if your files are large and complex.

Decide if the ANSI C functions are appropriate for your application. If you are producing an application that will not be distributed widely or does not read or write files often, then the simple standard C library solution may be appropriate. Otherwise I recommend that you try a more robust solution.

IMPLEMENTING A PRACTICAL FILE MANAGEMENT SOLUTION

A cross-platform file manager:

- needs to be fast
- should work with the largest possible file sizes
- should read or write arbitrarily large blocks
- needs to allow cross-platform file formats to be read and written
- must represent the highest subset of available functionality
- must allow you to access platform-specific file features

In this section we will discuss a general cross-platform file management solution that should satisfy all of the above criteria except two: largest possible file sizes and cross-platform file access. To keep the following examples simple, I have not included cross-platform file access. This is something that we can add later.

The largest file size on the Macintosh and Windows 3.1 is 4 gigabytes (GB). The largest file size on Windows NT using FAT disk format is 4 GB, but is 2^{64} bytes (16 giga gigabytes, or GGB) using the NTFS disk format. In the file management solution presented in this book and in the XPLib software, we specify the maximum cross-platform file size to be 4 GB, which is the greatest-common denominator.

The examples in this chapter illustrate how to:

- create a file
- open a file
- close a file
- read from a file
- write to a file
- seek into a file or set the file pointer
- get file position or the file pointer
- display an open file dialog to select a file to work with
- display a save file dialog to select a file to save to

On the Macintosh data is assumed to be read to and written from the data fork of the file. The resource fork is not included in the file management functionality presented in this chapter or in the XPLib software. This is a feature of the Macintosh that is not available in Windows.

Also, we won't discuss or implement file sharing. This means that an application has exclusive write access to a file.

Comparing API Functionality

To create a cross-platform file manager, you must first list the functionality that you want to provide and then find the function or functions that provide the functionality on all of your target platforms. The resulting functional map, shown in Table 6.1, provides the backbone for your implementation.

Notice that on the Macintosh sometimes there are two ways to perform the same file functions. The first function listed is the better choice either because it is simpler or because it provides all of the functionality necessary to implement properly the cross-platform solution.

On Windows 3.1 some of the file functionality can only be performed using a software interrupt function call, int 21. The format specified in Table 6.1 for deleting a file, int 21: 0x41, is a shorthand notation that means that the AH register must contain the value 0x41 when the int 21 instruction is executed. Additional register setup may be necessary to perform properly these types of file operations. Consult the *MS-DOS Programmer's Reference* for detailed information about assembly language access to DOS functions.

Disk Formats

Each of our three target platforms supports various disk formats. Usually, a particular disk format is specific to a disk partition. A single hard disk can have many disk partitions, each formatted differently. Table 6.2 shows some of the disk formats available on our platforms.

All of the above disk format types use a 32-bit file pointer, except the NTFS disk format in Windows NT, which uses a 64-bit file pointer. Because 64-bit file pointers are only allowed on the NTFS format in Windows NT, this format is not a common denominator in our target platforms and is not included in this cross-platform solution.

Table 6.1 File manager functions.

Function	*Macintosh*	*Windows 3.1*	*Win32*
create	PBCreate or Create	_lcreat	CreateFile or _lcreat*
delete	FSDelete	int 21: 0x41	DeleteFile
rename	Rename	int 21: 0x56	MoveFile
file size	GetEOF	_llseek	GetFileSize
get attributes	GetFInfo or PBGetFInfo	int 21: 0x43	GetFileAttributes
set attributes	SetFInfo or PBGetFInfo	int 21: 0x43	SetFileAttributes
open	PBOpen or FSOpen	_lopen or _lcreat	CreateFile, OpenFile, or _lopen*
close	PBClose or FSClose	_lclose	CloseHandle or _close*
read	FSRead	_lread or _hread	ReadFile, _lread,* or _hread*
write	FSWrite	_lwrite or _hwrite	WriteFile, lwrite,* or _hwrite*
open-file dialog	SFGetFile	GetOpenFileName	GetOpenFileName
save-file dialog	SFPutFile	GetSaveFileName	GetSaveFileName

* Provided for compatibility.

Actually none of the 64-bit features of Windows NT or the underlying RISC processors are supported in our sample code or the XPLIb software. Even though Windows NT runs on 64-bit processors and has certain 64-bit features, it is only a 32-bit operating system.

Here are a few points about disk formats:

- It is possible to copy files to and from FAT formatted floppy disks on the Macintosh if you use Apple File Exchange, PC Exchange, or a similar product.

- Windows NT supports HPFS so that it can provide the widest file solution to users and because Windows NT supports a text-only OS/2 subsystem that allows OS/2 applications to run under Windows NT.

Table 6.2 Comparison of available hard disk formats.

Macintosh	*Windows 3.1*	*Windows NT*
Macintosh: 4GB file size FAT: 4GB file size	FAT: 4GB file size	FAT: 4GB file size HPFS: (OS/2) 4GB NTFS: 16GGB file size

Table 6.3 File feature specifications.

File Feature	Macintosh	Windows (FAT)	Windows NT: NTFS
name	31 characters	8 characters plus dot plus 3 character extension	255 Unicode characters
directory	31 characters	8 characters plus dot plus 3 character extension	255 Unicode characters
volume	27 characters	1 character (A-Z)	1 character (A-Z)
path	arbitrary (usually < 255)	64 characters	arbitrary
type	4 bytes	not directly specified but generally 3 characters	not directly specified
creator	4 bytes	NA	NA

- The CD-ROM formats are not included in our list. This is because all platforms are able to support them either directly or by using installable device drivers.

It really isn't important which disk format is being used by the operating system. What is important is that we provide a standard way of specifying files and accessing the information in those files.

File Features

In this discussion file features are the features of files on our platforms that are apparent to the user. File features can represent the maximum sizes for the certain aspects of files (see Table 6.3) or can represent the valid or invalid characters that can comprise them (see Table 6.4).

Data Types for File Management

Next we will describe some fundamental simple data types and data structures that are necessary to define and implement a cross-platform file manager.

Table 6.4 Reserved characters for file names

File Feature	Macintosh	Windows (FAT)	Windows NT: NTFS
case sensitivity	case is maintained but ignored	all characters converted to upper case	case is maintained but ignored
valid separators	: ...	: for volume \ for path	: for volume \ for path
disk volume identifiers	any	A through Z	A through Z
invalid name characters	:	* ? / \ + . , SPACE " ; < > = [ ] |	: / \ * ? < > | "

File Management Support Data Types

When a file is created or opened, we receive a handle to the file. The handle is a number (the nature of which is dependent on the platform) that indentifies the application's file to the operating system. It is defined to be:

Data Type	Macintosh	Windows 3.1	Win32
HFYLE	short integer 2 bytes	short integer 2 bytes	HANDLE 4 bytes

When you create a file, you may want to specify its type. Unfortunately this information does not exist in the same form nor is it used in the same way across platforms. In the Macintosh a file type is an intrinsic part of a file's specification that is independent of its name. It is specified as a series of 4 characters, usually enclosed in single quotation marks; for example, 'TEXT' refers to a text-only file.

In Windows 3.1 or Win32 using FAT-type files, the file type is implied by a 3-character extension to a file's name. However, the file's name and extension do not need to map to any specific type of file. For example, MYLETTER.DOC usually refers to a Microsoft Word document, but a user could give that name to a WordPerfect document by mistake.

For our cross-platform file management solution, we will assume Windows 3.1 and Win32 file names to be FAT-type file names (3 characters plus a null-terminator). This does not preclude using the NTFS-type (or HPFS-type) files but limits our choice of names. Thus we define our cross-platform data type for file types to be:

Data Type	Macintosh	Windows 3.1	Win32
FTYPE	OSType 4 bytes	char[4] 4 bytes	char[4] 4 bytes

The Cross-Platform File Structure

Whenever a file is created, opened, or used, we need to maintain some information that gives us an easy and consistent way to reference the file and to allow us to abstract some platform-specific features. We define a data structure, FYLE, that facilitates this. See Table 6.5. The unusual spelling of this data type is not a typographical error. I've spelled it so to avoid confusion with the ANSI C data type, FILE.

Predefined File Values

Table 6.6 lists some commonly used values for file information. FNULL indicates a null or invalid file handle. The default file type, FTYPEDEFAULT, is used whenever the programmer

Table 6.5 Contents of the cross-platform file structure

Component	Field Name	Description
HFYLE	h	handle to the file
MEM	mName	memory block containing the file name and path
FTYPE	ftype	the file type (polymorphic)
ERR	err	the most recent error condition
UINT4	u4NumRW	the number of bytes actually read or written, only valid immediately after a read or write operation
UINT2	u2Attrib	attributes assigned to this file, for example, read-only or hidden; initialized to read-write and not used in the sample code of this book
UINT2	u2Mode	the mode in which the file will be opened, for example, read-only, which means the file can be opened only using a read-only mode
UINT2	u2Options	file access options, for example, truncate/append or text/binary; the only option currently supported is truncate/append
Macintosh		
SINT2	s2VolRefNum	the Macintosh volume reference number
OSType	fcreator	the Macintosh file creator

wants a file with a default file type—this value can be application-specific. For our purposes we define our default file to be text-only.

We also need to specify relative file positions using the FPOS_xxx values, valid file options using the FOPT_xxx values, and file open modes using the FMODE_xxx values.

Table 6.6 Predefined file values.

Value	Macintosh	Windows 3.1	Win32
FNULL	0	−1	INVALID_HANDLE_VALUE
FTYPEDEFAULT	'TEXT'	"TXT"	"TXT"
FPOS_Start	fsFromStart	0	FILE_BEGIN
FPOS_Current	fsFromMark	1	FILE_CURRENT
FPOS_End	fsFromLEOF	2	FILE_END
FOPT_Truncate	0	0	0
FOPT_Append	1	1	1
FMODE_Read	fsRdPerm	OF_READ	0
FMODE_Write	fsWrPerm	OF_WRITE	1
FMODE_ReadWrite	fsRdWrPerm	OF_READWRITE	2

Implementing File Functionality

For clarity the only error codes that the file functions return are ERR_No, no error has occurred, and ERR_Yes, an error has occurred. Though the file management functions of the XPLib software support more detailed error codes, I have not included them in this discussion for clarity's sake.

Creating a File

First let's look at how files are created on our target platforms by defining the FCreate() function. All of the information required by this function is contained in the FYLE structure pointed to by pFile. The FYLE structure can be initialized manually or by using the save file dialog procedure, which is described later in this chapter. If the creation process is successful, an ERR_No value is returned.

The creation process creates a file based on the information provided. The file is not opened after it is created. A file must be opened explicitly. For the purposes of this discussion we will only create files with read/write access. Creating read-only files can be added later.

```
//-------------------------------------------------------
ERR FCreate (PFYLE pFile)
//-------------------------------------------------------
// pFile   - pointer to a valid file structure
// RETURNS - ERR_No if successful
//-------------------------------------------------------
{
```

In the Macintosh we create the file and then set the file type and creator. This necessary second step allows the file to be properly handled by Finder. Notice that creating a file on the Macintosh is a laborious process. This is because we are using the low-level PBCreate() function rather than the Create() function. PBCreate() gives us more flexibility in the way the file is created. Also, the functions StrCtoP() and StrPtoC() perform inline translations of strings from C to Pascal and from Pascal to C.

```
{
    ParamBlockRec pb;

    // the cross-platform file name is null-terminated,
    // convert file name to Pascal format
    StrCtoP (pFile->mName.ptr);

    // set up io parameter block
    pb.ioParam.ioVRefNum=pFile->s2VolRefNum;
    pb.ioParam.ioVersNum=0;
    // create all files as read-write
    pb.ioParam.ioPermssn=fsRdWrPerm;
    pb.ioParam.ioMisc=0;
    pb.ioParam.ioNamePtr=(StringPtr)pFile->mName.ptr;
```

```
PBCreate (&pb, FALSE);

// convert the Pascal file name back to C in case
// we have to exit unexpectedly
StrPtoC((PTRP)pFile->mName.ptr);

if (pb.ioParam.ioResult!=noErr){
    return (pFile->err=ERR_Yes);
}

StrCtoP (pFile->mName.ptr);

// set up file parameter block and read
// current settings so that we can set the file
// type and creator attributes later

pb.fileParam.ioVRefNum = pFile->s2VolRefNum;
pb.fileParam.ioFlVersNum = 0;
// don't give name if open
pb.fileParam.ioNamePtr= (StringPtr)0;
// indicate that we want to get information on
// the file (0 means file, >0 means directory)
pb.fileParam.ioFDirIndex=0;
pb.ioParam.ioNamePtr=(StringPtr)pFile->mName.ptr;
PBGetFInfo (&pb, FALSE);

StrPtoC ((PTRP)pFile->mName.ptr);

// if there was an error, return
if (pb.fileParam.ioResult!=noErr){
    return (pFile->err=ERR_Yes);
}

// modify only the type and creator fields
pb.fileParam.ioFlFndrInfo.fdType=pFile->ftype;
pb.fileParam.ioFlFndrInfo.fdCreator=
    pFile->fcreator;
PBSetFInfo (&pb, FALSE);

// if there was an error, return
if (pb.fileParam.ioResult!=noErr){
    return (pFile->err=ERR_Yes);
}
}
```

In Windows 3.1 we check that the file does not exist, create it with the default attributes (read/write and not hidden), and then close the file.

```
// does the file already exist?
if (FExists (pFile)){
   // error: can't create file, it already exists
   return (pFile->err=ERR_Yes);
}
// create the file and check if the returned file
// handle is valid
if ((pFile->h=
      _lcreat ((LPSTR)pFile->mName.ptr,
         0/*read-write*/)
   )<0
){
   // error: unable to create file
   return (pFile->err=ERR_Yes);
}


// close the file
_lclose (pFile->h);
pFile->h=FNULL;
```

The process of creating a file in Win32 is similar to that in Windows 3.1, except that we use the CreateFile() function instead of _lcreat(). Like Windows 3.1, Win32 creates a file and returns a handle to the open file. So we close the file before we exit.

```
if (FExists (pFile)){
   // error: can't create file, it already exists
   return (pFile->err=ERR_Yes);
}
// create the file and check if the returned file
// handle is valid
if ((pFile->h=CreateFile(
      (LPSTR)pFile->mName.ptr,
      GENERIC_READ|GENERIC_WRITE,
      0          /*no share*/,
      NULL       /*no security info*/,
      CREATE_NEW,   /*create if it doesn't exist*/
      FILE_ATTRIBUTE_NORMAL,/*read-write access*/
      NULL       /*no file template handle*/
   ))
   ==INVALID_HANDLE_VALUE
){
   // error: unable to create the file
   return (pFile->err=ERR_Yes);
```

```
    }
    // close the file
    CloseHandle ((HANDLE)pFile->h);
    pFile->h=FNULL;
```

If we get this far, all has gone well, and we return indicating that the file was created successfully.

```
    return (pFile->err=ERR_No);
}
```

Opening a File

After we have created a file, we need to open it so that we can write data to it. Here we specify our file open function, FOpen(), to use the same FYLE structure that was specified to FCreate() or returned to us from the file open dialog (which will be described later). The file handle is returned in the h field of the FYLE structure.

```
//------------------------------------------------------
ERR FOpen (PFYLE pFile)
//------------------------------------------------------
// pFile   - pointer to a valid FYLE structure that
//           references an unopened file
// RETURNS - ERR_No if successful
//------------------------------------------------------
{
```

In the Macintosh we first open the file with the read/write mode, specified by the u2Mode field of the FYLE structure. Then we seek to the end of the file if the file options indicated that we are opening the file for appending, or we set the end of file to the start if the file options indicated that the file is to be truncated.

```
    {
        ParamBlockRec pb;

        // read the file type
        FTypeRead (pFile);

        // convert file name to Pascal format
        StrCtoP (pFile->mName.ptr);

        // set up io parameter block
        pb.ioParam.ioVRefNum = pFile->s2VolRefNum;
        pb.ioParam.ioVersNum = 0;
        pb.ioParam.ioPermssn = pFile->u2Mode;
        pb.ioParam.ioMisc = 0;
        pb.ioParam.ioNamePtr=(StringPtr)pFile->mName.ptr;
```

```
    PBOpen (&pb, FALSE);

    // convert the Pascal file name back to C
    StrPtoC ((PTRP)pFile->mName.ptr);

    if (pb.ioParam.ioResult!=noErr){
        return (pFile->err=ERR_Yes);
    }
    pFile->h=pb.ioParam.ioRefNum;

    if (pFile->u2Options&FOPT_Append){
        // open for appending
        if (FSeek (pFile, FPOS_End, 0L)!=ERR_No){
            return (pFile->err);
        }

    }else{
        // truncate the file
        if (SetEOF (pFile->h, 0L)!=noErr){
            return (pFile->err=ERR_Yes);
        }
    }
}
```

In Windows 3.1 we open the file with the read/write mode specified by u2Mode and seek to the end of the file if the options tell us to open the file for appending. If the options tell us to truncate the file, we recreate the file so that its contents are truncated.

```
    // are we appending to the file or truncating it?
    if (pFile->u2Options&FOPT_Append){

        //open for appending
        if ((pFile->h=_lopen ((LPSTR)pFile->mName.ptr,
            (WORD)pFile->u2Mode))<0
        ){
            // error: unable to open file
            return (pFile->err=ERR_Yes);
        }
        if (FSeek (pFile, FPOS_End, 0L)!=ERR_No){
            return (pFile->err);
        }

    }else{
        //truncate the file
        if ((pFile->h=_lcreat ((LPSTR)pFile->mName.ptr, 0))
            <0
```

```
    ){
        pFile->err=ERR_Yes;
    }
}
```

In Win32 we open the file by using the CreateFile() function. This allows us to open the file for appending by using the OPEN_EXISTING attribute and then seek to the end of the file or to open the file for truncating by using the TRUNCATE_EXISTING attribute.

```
if ((pFile->h=CreateFile (
        (LPSTR)pFile->mName.ptr,
        GENERIC_READ | (pFile->u2Mode?GENERIC_WRITE:0),
        0    /*no share*/,
        NULL /*no security info*/,
        //decide if we will append or truncate
        pFile->u2Options & FOPT_Append
            ? OPEN_EXISTING : TRUNCATE_EXISTING,
        FILE_ATTRIBUTE_NORMAL,/*read-write access*/
        NULL /*no file template handle*/
    ))==INVALID_HANDLE_VALUE
){
    // error: unable to open file
    return (pFile->err=ERR_Yes);
}
// if we are opening for appending, then seek to the
// end of file
if (pFile->u2Options&FOPT_Append){
    if (FSeek (pFile, FPOS_End, 0L)!=ERR_No){
        return (pFile->err);
    }
}
```

If we get this far, all has gone well and we return indicating that the file was opened successfully. The function would have returned earlier if there was an error.

```
    return (pFile->err=ERR_No);
}
```

Closing a File

When we are done with a file, we need to close it. Our FClose() function assumes that the FYLE structure is valid and the file is open. If the file is not open, then an error value is returned.

```
//-----------------------------------------------------
ERR FClose (PFYLE pFile)
//-----------------------------------------------------
// pFile   - pointer to a valid FYLE structure that
//           references an open file
```

```
// RETURNS - ERR_No if successful
//----------------------------------------------------
{
    //is the file open?
    if (pFile->h==FNULL) return (pFile->err=ERR_Yes);
```

In the Macintosh we close the file by using PBClose() and then flush the disk volume to ensure that all changes are written to disk.

```
    {
        ParamBlockRec pb;

        StrCtoP (pFile->mName.ptr);

        //  set up io parameter block
        pb.ioParam.ioVRefNum = pFile->s2VolRefNum;
        pb.ioParam.ioVersNum = 0;
        pb.ioParam.ioPermssn = pFile->u2Mode;
        pb.ioParam.ioMisc = 0;
        pb.ioParam.ioNamePtr = (StringPtr)pFile->mName.ptr;
        pb.ioParam.ioRefNum=pFile->h;

        // close the file
        PBClose (&pb.ioParam, FALSE);

        StrPtoC((PTRP)pFile->mName.ptr);

        if(pb.ioParam.ioResult==noErr){
            pb.volumeParam.ioVRefNum=pFile->s2VolRefNum;
            pb.volumeParam.ioNamePtr=(StringPtr)0;

            // make sure all changes are recorded
            PBFlushVol (&pb,FALSE);

            pFile->err=ERR_No;

        }else pFile->err=ERR_Yes;
    }
```

In Windows 3.1 we use the _lclose() function to close the file.

```
    // Close the file
    if ((pFile->h=_lclose (pFile->h))<0){
        // error: file not open
        return (pFile->err=ERR_Yes);
    }
```

Similarly, in Win32 we use the CloseHandle() function to close the file.

```
// Close the file
if (!CloseHandle ((HANDLE)pFile->h)){
    // error: file not open
    return (pFile->err=ERR_Yes);
}
```

If all has gone well, we set the file handle to FNULL to indicate that the file is no longer open and then return indicating that the file was sucessfully closed.

```
pFile->h=FNULL;
return (pFile->err=ERR_No);
}
```

Reading from a File

We define our read file function, FRead(), to allow us to read an arbitrary number of bytes from a file to a buffer that we have provided. The FYLE structure also provides a field, u4NumRW, which lets us save the actual number of bytes read from the file so that we can compare it with what we requested. If the number of bytes read does not equal the number of bytes that we requested, our read file function returns an error. This type of error might not actually be an error but allows us to check the condition of the read without actually comparing the numbers.

```
//-------------------------------------------------------
ERR FRead (PFYLE pFile, PTR ptr, UINT4 u4Bytes)
//-------------------------------------------------------
// pFile   - pointer to a valid FYLE structure that
//           references an open file
// ptr     - pointer to a buffer to receive the data
// u4Bytes - number of bytes to read
// RETURNS - ERR_No if successful
//-------------------------------------------------------
{
    //check if we have a valid open file handle
    if (pFile->h==FNULL) return (pFile->err=ERR_Yes);
pFile->err=ERR_No;
```

In the Macintosh reading data from a file is a simple process using the FSRead() function.

```
{
    OSErr oserror;

    pFile->u4NumRW=u4Bytes;
    oserror=FSRead (pFile->h, &pFile->u4NumRW, ptr);
    if (oserror!=noErr) pFile->err=ERR_Yes;
}
```

Reading data from file (and writing to file) in Windows 3.1 is more difficult. Because the API specifies the receive buffer parameter of the _lread() function to be of type LPSTR, we are limited to a buffer of 64K bytes. If we need to read more than that, we need a globally allocated memory block that we must index into 64K blocks at a time using a huge pointer. In our example, we read blocks 32K bytes at a time.

> *We could actually save ourselves a lot of work by using the _hread() function that is provided by the Windows 3.1 API. I have opted to use the _lread() function in this example so that this function will also work in Windows 3.0.*

```c
{
    UINT4 u4NumRead=0L;

    // if we are reading less than 64K bytes we don't
    // need to use a huge pointer
    if (u4Bytes<=0x0000ffff){
        u4NumRead=
            (UINT4)_lread (pFile->h, ptr, (SINT2)u4Bytes);

    // more than 64K bytes to read
    }else{
        SINT2 i;
        SINT2 s2NumIterations;
        SINT2 s2Remainder;
        SINT2 s2Temp;
        char huge * hptr=(char huge *)ptr;

        // calculate the number of whole 32K blocks
        s2NumIterations=(SINT2)(u4Bytes/0x00007fff);
        // calculate the remaining bytes
        s2Remainder=(SINT2)(u4Bytes%0x00007fff);

        // for each 32K block, read it into the buffer
        // relative to the proper index into the larger
        // memory block
        for (i=0,u4NumRead=0L; i<s2NumIterations; i++){
            if ((s2Temp=_lread (pFile->h,
                &hptr[u4NumRead], (SINT2)0x7fff))<0x7fff
            ){
                // error: read error
                pFile->err=ERR_Yes;
                if (s2Temp>0) u4NumRead+=(UINT4)s2Temp;
```

```
            goto DONE;
        }
        u4NumRead+=(UINT4)s2Temp;
    }

    // read in the last block (<32K bytes)
    if (s2Remainder){
        s2Temp=_lread (pFile->h, &hptr[u4NumRead],
            s2Remainder);
        if (s2Temp<s2Remainder) pFile->err=ERR_Yes;
        if (s2Temp>0) u4NumRead+=(UINT4)s2Temp;
    }
}

DONE:
    if (u4NumRead!=u4Bytes){
        // error: read error
        pFile->err=ERR_Yes;

    }
    pFile->u4NumRW=u4NumRead;
}
```

The process in Win32 is straightforward and uses the ReadFile() function.

```
pFile->u4NumRW=0L;

if (!ReadFile (pFile->h, ptr, u4Bytes, &pFile->u4NumRW,
        NULL)
    || pFile->u4NumRW!=u4Bytes
){
    pFile->err=ERR_Yes;
}
```

When we're all done, return the error code that was generated during the write process.

```
    return (pFile->err);
}
```

Writing to a File

We define our write to file function, FWrite(), to allow us to write an arbitrary number of bytes to the file from the buffer that we have provided. The FYLE structure also provides a field, u4NumRW, which lets us save the actual number of bytes written to the file so that we can compare it with what we requested. If the number of bytes written does not equal the number of bytes that we requested, our write file function returns an error.

```
//---------------------------------------------------
ERR FWrite (PFYLE pFile, PTR ptr, UINT4 u4Bytes)
//---------------------------------------------------
// pFile   - pointer to a valid FYLE structure that
//           references an open file
// ptr     - pointer to a buffer holding the data to write
// u4Bytes - number of bytes to write
// RETURNS - ERR_No if successful
//---------------------------------------------------
{
    //check if we have a valid open file handle
    if (pFile->h==FNULL) return (pFile->err=ERR_Yes);

    //initialize the error state (assume OK)
    pFile->err=ERR_No;
```

In the Macintosh writing to a file is a simple process that uses the FSWrite() function.

```
    {
        OSErr oserror;
        pFile->u4NumRW=u4Bytes;

        if ((oserror=FSWrite (pFile->h, &pFile->u4NumRW,
            ptr))!=noErr
        ){
            pFile->err=ERR_Yes;
        }
    }
```

Writing data to file in Windows 3.1 is more difficult. Because the API for _lwrite() specifies the pointer to the buffer to be of type LPSTR, we are limited to writing 64K bytes of data. If we need to write more than that, we need a globally allocated memory block that we must index into 64K blocks at a time using a huge pointer. In our example we write blocks 32K bytes at a time.

We could use the _hwrite() function provided by the Windows 3.1 API to write huge blocks of data. But I am using _lwrite() so that this function will also work in Windows 3.0.

```
    {
        UINT4 u4NumWritten=0L;

        // if we are writing less than 64K bytes we don't
        // need to use a huge pointer
        if (u4Bytes<=0x0000ffff){
            u4NumWritten=(UINT4)_lwrite (pFile->h, ptr,
                (SINT2)u4Bytes);

        // more than 64K bytes to write
```

```
    }else{
        SINT2 i;
        SINT2 s2NumIterations;
        SINT2 s2Remainder;
        SINT2 s2Temp;
        char huge * hptr=(char huge *)ptr;

        // calculate the number of whole 32K blocks
        s2NumIterations=(SINT2)(u4Bytes/0x00007fff);
        // calculate the remaining bytes
        s2Remainder=(SINT2)(u4Bytes%0x00007fff);

        // for each 32K block, write it relative to the
        // proper index into the larger memory block
        for (i=0, u4NumWritten=0L;
            i<s2NumIterations;
            i++
        ){
            if ((s2Temp=_lwrite (pFile->h,
                &hptr[u4NumWritten], (SINT2)0x7fff))<0x7fff
            ){
                pFile->err=ERR_Yes;
                if(s2Temp>0) u4NumWritten+=(UINT4)s2Temp;
                goto DONE;
            }
            u4NumWritten+=(UINT4)s2Temp;
        }

        // write out the last block (<32K bytes)
        if (s2Remainder){
            s2Temp=_lwrite (pFile->h,
                &hptr[u4NumWritten], s2Remainder);

            if (s2Temp<s2Remainder) pFile->err=ERR_Yes;
            if (s2Temp>0) u4NumWritten+=(UINT4)s2Temp;
        }
    }

DONE:
    if (u4NumWritten!=u4Bytes){
        // error: write error
        pFile->err=FERR_Write;
    }
    pFile->u4NumRW=u4NumWritten;
}
```

The process of writing data to file in Win32 is straightforward and uses the WriteFile() function.

```
pFile->u4NumRW=0L;

if (!WriteFile (pFile->h, ptr, u4Bytes,
        &pFile->u4NumRW, NULL)
    || pFile->u4NumRW!=u4Bytes
){
    pFile->err=ERR_Yes;
}
```

When we're all done, return the error code that was generated during the write process.

```
return (pFile->err);
}
```

Seeking into a File

Seeking into a file or setting the file pointer or position is another fundamental file management function, which we name FSeek(). Here we need to specify a file using a pointer to a FYLE structure, indicate the relative starting point of the seek (from the start of the file, from the current position, or from the end of the file), and then the offset (plus or minus) relative to that starting point.

```
//------------------------------------------------------
ERR FSeek (PFYLE pFile, UINT2 u2From, SINT4 s4To)
//------------------------------------------------------
// pFile   - pointer to a valid FYLE structure that
//           references an open file
// u2From  - seek from: start, current, or end
// s4To    - seek to this position relative to u2From
// RETURNS - ERR_No if successful
//------------------------------------------------------
{
```

In the Macintosh we seek from relative position u2From to offset s4To using SetFPos().

```
pFile->err=
    (SetFPos (pFile->h, u2From, s4To)==noErr
      ? ERR_No : ERR_Yes);
```

In Windows 3.1 we seek to offset s4To from relative position u2From using _llseek().

```
if (_llseek (pFile->h, s4To, u2From)==HFILE_ERROR){
    pFile->err=ERR_Yes;
}
```

In Win32 file pointers can be 64 bits long. This allows a file to be 16 GGB in size. Because file pointers are only 32 bits long on the Macintosh and Windows 3.1, we limit the file pointers in our Win32 implementation to 32 bits long by setting the third argument to SetFilePointer() to zero.

```
if (SetFilePointer (pFile, s4To, 0L/*32bit*/,
    (UINT4)u2From)==0xffffffff
){
    pFile->err=ERR_Yes;
}
```

When we're all done, return the error code that was generated during the seek process.

```
    return (pFile->err);
}
```

Getting the Current File Position

The companion function to setting the file position is getting the current file position. Our function, FPos(), requires a pointer to a FYLE structure and returns the current file position or a zero if the file position could not be retrieved.

```
//-------------------------------------------------------
UINT4 FPos (PFYLE pFile)
//-------------------------------------------------------
// pFile   - pointer to a valid FYLE structure that
//             references an open file
// RETURNS - 32-byte file position relative to start
//-------------------------------------------------------
{
UINT4 u4FilePos;
```

To get the current file position in the Macintosh, use the GetFPos() function.

```
    pFile->err=(GetFPos (pFile->h, &u4FilePos)==noErr
        ? ERR_No : ERR_Yes);
    if (pFile->err==ERR_Yes) u4FilePos=(UINT4)0;
```

In Windows 3.1 there isn't a specific function for retrieving the file pointer. Instead, you must use the _llseek() function and specify that you want to seek zero bytes from the current position. The function returns the current file position.

```
    if ((SINT4)(u4FilePos=_llseek (pFile->h, 0L,
        FPOS_Current))==HFILE_ERROR
    ){
        // error: seek error
        u4FilePos=(UINT4)0;
        pFile->err=ERR_Yes;
    }
```

In Win32, as in Windows 3.1, there is no direct way to get the current file position. Instead, you must use the SetFilePointer() function and specify that you want to seek zero bytes from the current position. The function returns the current file position.

```
if ((u4FilePos=SetFilePointer (pFile, 0L, 0L/*32bit*/,
    FILE_CURRENT))==0xffffffff
){
    u4FilePos=(UINT4)0;
    pFile->err=ERR_Yes;
}
```

When we're all done, return the current (absolute) file position. If there was an error, this value will be zero.

```
    return (u4FilePos);
}
```

Putting Up the Open File Dialog Box

In a GUI-based environment the proper way to select a file that you want to open is by using an open file dialog box. Our cross-platform solution, as in XPLib, provides this functionality by defining the FDialogOpen() function. We specify a FYLE structure that will receive the file information returned by the dialog box and indicate if we want to display all file types or just the type specified in the FYLE structure. The hwndParent parameter specifies the handle to the window that will own the dialog box. It is provided for Windows compatibility and is ignored for the Macintosh implementation.

Letting the user select a file to open requires that the user choose a file from a list of existing files. You want to ensure that the user will select a file that exists and is of the proper type. The platform-specific open file dialog boxes provide these features.

```
//-----------------------------------------------------
ERR FDialogOpen (HWND hwndParent, PFYLE pFile,
    BOOL2 b2AllFiles)
//-----------------------------------------------------
// hwndParent - handle to the window that owns the dialog
// pFile      - pointer to a valid FYLE structure that
//              will receive the file information
// b2AllFiles - include all files or just the default
//              type
// RETURNS    - ERR_No if successful
//-----------------------------------------------------
{
```

The Macintosh provides a standard open file dialog box by its SFGetFile() function (Standard File package Get File function). This dialog box is shown in Figure 6.1. In the Macintosh you can specify a list of up to four file types, or all types, that will be included in the dialog's list box. For our implementation, we limit the choices of file types to one or all.

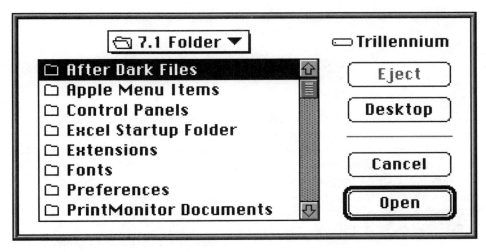

Figure 6.1 Macintosh open file dialog box.

Before we are finished, we need to save the user's file name selection in the FYLE structure by calling FNameSet(). This function simply allocates a memory block large enough to hold the file name that was selected or entered by the user and then copies the string into it. Next we need to check the file's type and save it in the FYLE structure's ftype field. This is done by using FTypeRead().

```
// upper-left corner of the dialog box
Point dlgPt={100,100};

SFReply sfReply;
SINT2 s2NumTypes=1;

if (b2AllFiles) s2NumTypes=-1;

// the supplied type list (arg 5) is ignored if arg 4
// s2NumTypes is -1
SFGetFile (dlgPt, "\p", (ProcPtr)NULL, s2NumTypes,
    &pFile->ftype, (ProcPtr)NULL, &sfReply);


if (!sfReply.good) return (pFile->err=ERR_Yes);

pFile->s2VolRefNum=sfReply.vRefNum;

// set the file name in the FYLE structure to that
// specified by the user's selection
StrPtoC (sfReply.fName);
```

```
FNameSet (pFile,(PTR)sfReply.fName);
StrCtoP ((PTR)sfReply.fName);

//try to read the file's type (if the file exists),
//else use defaults
FTypeRead (pFile);
```

Windows 3.1 and Win32 use a common set of functions that provide dialog boxes for opening and saving a file, selecting a color, selecting a font, and controlling the printing process (the common dialog functions). Here we use the GetOpenFileName() function to get the name of a file to open. This dialog box is shown in Figure 6.2. In Windows we can provide the dialog function with an arbitrary number of file extensions (types) and descriptions of the types. For our implementation of this function we will limit this to either one type, provided in the FYLE structure, or all types. To show all types, we need to construct a custom filter that we will provide to the GetOpenFileName() function.

As in the Macintosh, we need to save the file name that was selected or entered by the user in the FYLE structure by using the FNameSet() function. Then we need to read the file's type by extracting the file extension from the file that the user selected by using the FTypeRead() function.

```
OPENFILENAME ofn;
SINT1 zFilter[32]="All Files (*.*)|*.*|";
SINT1 zFile[128];
SINT1 zFileTitle[128];
SINT1 zDir[128];
UINT1 u1Len=(UINT1)StrLen((PTR)zFilter);
UINT1 u1Wild=zFilter[u1Len-1];
UINT1 i;

if (!b2AllFiles){
    // make a custom filter based on the file type
    // of the file specified by pFile
    //      "XXX Files (*.XXX)|*.XXX|"
    StrCopy (zFilter, pFile->ftype);
    StrCat (zFilter, " Files (*.");
    StrCat (zFilter, pFile->ftype);
    StrCat (zFilter, ")|*.");
    StrCat (zFilter, pFile->ftype);
    StrCat (zFilter, "|");
}
//replace all '|' with '\0'
for (i=0; zFilter[i]!='\0'; i++){
    if ((UINT1)zFilter[i]==u1Wild) zFilter[i]='\0';
}

MemFill ((PTR)&ofn, 0, sizeof (OPENFILENAME));
```

```
    if (pFile->mName.ptr){
        StrCopy ((PTR)zFile, pFile->mName.ptr);
    }else zFile[0]='\0';

    // use the current directory
    StrCopy (zDir, ".");

    // set up the open file name structure
    ofn.lStructSize=sizeof (OPENFILENAME);
    ofn.hwndOwner=hwndParent;
    ofn.hInstance=_ghWinInstance;
    ofn.lpstrFilter=zFilter;
    ofn.nFilterIndex=1;
    ofn.lpstrFile=zFile;
    ofn.nMaxFile=sizeof (zFile);
    ofn.lpstrFileTitle=zFileTitle;
    ofn.nMaxFileTitle=sizeof (zFileTitle);
    ofn.lpstrInitialDir=zDir;
    ofn.Flags=OFN_PATHMUSTEXIST|OFN_FILEMUSTEXIST
        |OFN_HIDEREADONLY;

    if (!GetOpenFileName (&ofn)){
        return (pFile->err=ERR_Yes);
    }
    //get the returned file name from the dialog
    FNameSet (pFile, zFileTitle);

    //then extract the extension from the name
    FTypeRead (pFile);
```

When we're finished, we return the error code that was accumulated during the file selection process.

```
    return (pFile->err);
}
```

Putting Up the Save File Dialog Box

Letting the user select or enter the name of a file to save to is slightly different from letting the user select or enter the name of a file to open. We need to allow the user to see what files are available, and then let him or her type in the name of the file in an edit box. Usually the edit box is initialized with a file name that is either based on the file that the user was working on in his or her application or some default file name or file name series, like "Untitled," or "NONAME1," "NONAME2," etc.

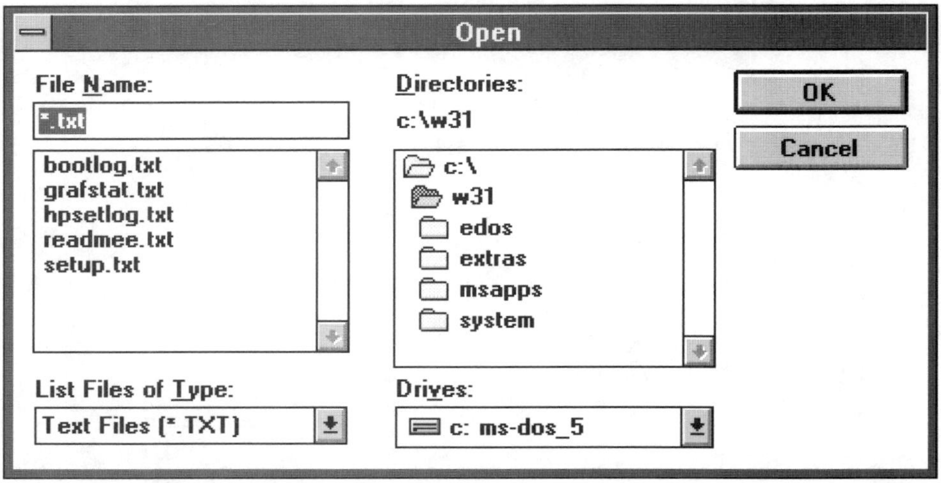

Figure 6-2. Windows open file dialog box.

As with FDialogOpen(), FDialogSave() needs the handle of the parent window that will own the dialog box and the FYLE structure that will receive the information. We also need to specify the default file name that will appear in the edit box.

We don't bother to check if the file already exists when the user clicks OK in the dialog box because the platform-specific Save Dialog functions prompt the user automatically.

```
//-------------------------------------------------------
ERR FDialogSave (HWND hwndParent, PFYLE pFile,
    PTR zDefaultFile)
//-------------------------------------------------------
// hwndParent    - handle to the window that owns the
//                 dialog
// pFile         - pointer to a valid FYLE structure that
//                 will receive the file information
// zDefaultFile  - name of the default file that will be
//                 in the dialog's edit box
// RETURNS       - ERR_No if successful
//-------------------------------------------------------
{
```

The Macintosh provides a standard save file dialog box by its SFPutFile() function (Standard File package Put File function). This dialog box is shown in Figure 6.3. In the Macintosh, you specify a prompt string and a default file name that will be entered into the dialog's edit box. If the user doesn't click Cancel or type COMMAND-'.', SFPutFile() returns success, sfReply.good=TRUE.

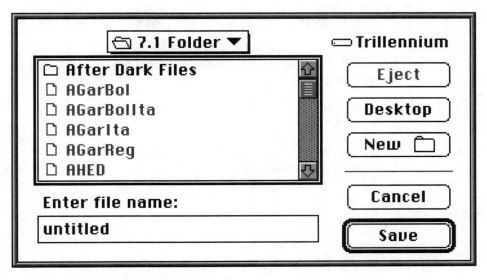

Figure 6.3 Macintosh save file dialog box.

Just as in FDialogOpen(), we need to save the user's file name selection in the FYLE structure by calling FNameSet() and to check the file's type and save it in the FYLE structure's ftype field by calling FTypeRead().

```
// upper-left corner of the dialog box
Point dlgPt={100,100};

SFReply sfReply;
Str255 zPStr;

sfReply.vRefNum=pFile->s2VolRefNum;
if (pFile->mName.ptr){
    StrCopyCtoP (zPStr,pFile->mName.ptr);

}else StrCopyCtoP (zPStr,zDefaultFile);

SFPutFile (dlgPt, "\pEnter file name:", zPStr,
    (ProcPtr)NULL, &sfReply);
if (!sfReply.good) return (pFile->err=ERR_Yes);

pFile->s2VolRefNum=sfReply.vRefNum;

StrPtoC (sfReply.fName);
// allocate space for the file name and copy it over
FNameSet (pFile, (PTR)sfReply.fName);
```

```
StrCtoP ((PTR)sfReply.fName);

//if the file exists, use the type info from the file
//if not, then use the type information provided
//if the caller has not assigned anything
if (FExists (pFile)){
   FTypeRead (pFile);
{
```

As with opening a file in Windows 3.1 and Win32, we use a common dialog box function to retrieve the name of the file to save to, GetSaveFileName(). The save file dialog is shown in Figure 6.4. As in GetOpenFileName(), we can provide the dialog function with an arbitrary number of file extensions (types) and descriptions of the types. Because the Macintosh does not offer this feature (the default behavior is to show all files in its Save Dialog list box), we duplicate this by telling GetSaveFileName() that we want to show all files. We then finish up by setting the file name and extracting the file type.

```
OPENFILENAME ofn;
// Use all files as the default to mimic the behavior
// on the Macintosh.
// We could use the "ftype" field in the FYLE structure
SINT1 zFilter[32]="All Files (*.*)\0*.*\0";
SINT1 zFile[128];
SINT1 zFileTitle[128];
SINT1 zDir[128];
UINT1 u1Len=(UINT1)StrLen ((PTR)zFilter);
UINT1 u1Wild=zFilter[u1Len-1];
UINT1 i;

MemFill ((PTR)&ofn, 0, sizeof (OPENFILENAME));
if (pFile->mName.ptr){
   StrCopy ((PTR)zFile, pFile->mName.ptr);

}else StrCopy ((PTR)zFile, zDefaultFile);

//use the current directory
StrCopy (zDir, ".");

// set up the open file name structure (a bad choice
// of names for a structure that also is used to
// get a save file name!)
ofn.lStructSize=sizeof (OPENFILENAME);
ofn.hwndOwner=hwndParent;
ofn.hInstance=_ghWinInstance;
ofn.lpstrFilter=zFilter;
ofn.lpstrFile=zFile;
```

```
ofn.nMaxFile=sizeof (zFile);
ofn.lpstrFileTitle=zFileTitle;
ofn.nMaxFileTitle=sizeof (zFileTitle);
ofn.lpstrInitialDir=zDir;
// tell the procedure that we want to know if the
// file already exists and to ignore files that
// are write protected
ofn.Flags=OFN_OVERWRITEPROMPT|OFN_HIDEREADONLY;

if (!GetSaveFileName (&ofn)){
    return (pFile->err=ERR_Yes);
}

//get the returned file name from the dialog box
FNameSet (pFile, zFileTitle);

//then extract the extension from the name
FTypeRead (pFile);
```

When we're finished, we return the error code that was accumulated while getting the save-file name.

```
    return (pFile->err);
}
```

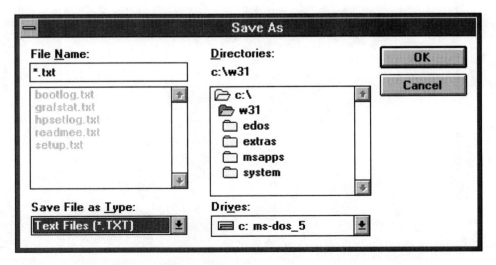

Figure 6.4 Windows save file dialog box.

OTHER FILE MANAGEMENT CONSIDERATIONS

Other basic file management functionality that was not demonstrated in this chapter but is included in the XPLib software includes:

- reading and writing a single byte
- reading and writing a 2-byte integer
- reading and writing a 4-byte integer
- reading and writing a string
- getting the file size
- checking if a file exists
- accessing the file structure fields
- deleting a file
- emptying a file
- renaming a file
- copying a file
- getting and setting the file attributes

There are numerous advanced areas of file management that you will want to consider as you develop your own applications. Among these are reading and writing files created on other platforms as, for example, Microsoft Word on the Macintosh can read and write files in Word for Windows formats and vice versa. You might want to consider allowing file sharing if your application is designed for multiple users and is very data oriented. These topics and others are discussed in more detail in the Advanced File Management section of Chapter 18.

7
Events

From the outside a program is something that accepts input from the user and interacts with the operating system and other programs. You might visualize these relationships as shown in Figure 7.1. But hidden behind this apparent connectivity is an event mechanism that allows a GUI-based platform to process the happenings from the user, from your program, from the operating system, and from other programs that might be running alongside it or interacting with it.

While most platforms maintain the same concept of the event mechanism, they are not usually implemented in the same way. The categorization and parameterization of events are not consistent between platforms (except between sibling platforms like Windows 3.1 and Win32). In this chapter we will discuss the problems of defining a cross-platform event mechanism and present some examples of how you might accomplish it.

DEFINING COMMON EVENT CAPABILITIES

To define properly a common cross-platform event model and implement the required functions, we need to:

- discuss basic event concepts
- describe the Macintosh event model
- describe the Windows 3.1 event model

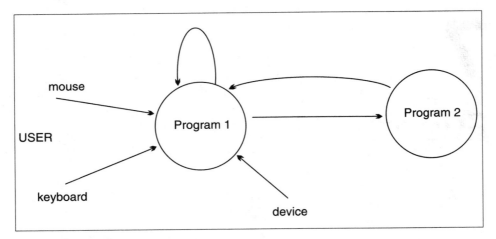

Figure 7.1 Apparent connectivity of a program.

- describe the Win32 event model
- define a cross-platform event model
- define and compare events
- look at some event sequences

Basic Event Concepts

An event or message is a representation of information that a program needs to function. The term *event* is from the Macintosh. In Windows an event is a message. In our cross-platform solution, we refer to the action as the event and the data associated with the event the event record. Within the event record is a message that indicates the specific type of event that has occurred.

Events can come from a variety of sources:

Event Source	Description
user action	from mouse and keyboard activity
I/O devices	drivers associated with low-level activity or hardware
internally generated	events sent from the system
explicitly generated	events sent by an application to itself
other programs	events sent by another application

User action triggers events due to mouse activity or keyboard activity. I/O devices can trigger events when they need to send information to the system. Some events are internally generated; for example, when a window is made active, the system might post an event to an application

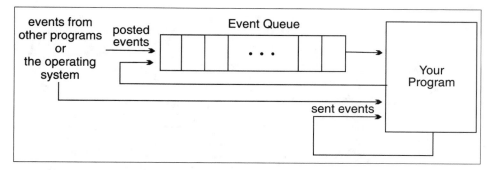

Figure 7.2 Relationship of the event queue and your program.

whose message is to make the window or application active and then to redraw the window contents. A program can explicitly send events to itself or indirectly when it invalidates a region of the window. Sometimes, other programs can send messages to your program or vice versa.

Events can be sent in one of two ways: directly to the function that is processing them or indirectly, or posted, to the system event queue.

The event queue, as shown in Figure 7.2, represents a first-in first-out buffer (FIFO)—the first event that enters the queue is the first event to leave the queue. By definition this is what a FIFO is; however, in event-driven systems the contents of the queue can be selectively emptied either by the priority of the event or by request of the window or application that removes the events from the queue.

Macintosh Event Model

The Macintosh platform System 6 and System 7 operating systems support three distinct but fundamentally similar event architectures. The simplest case, which is shown in Figure 7.3, is System 6 running with Finder. There is a central operating system (OS) event manager that fields

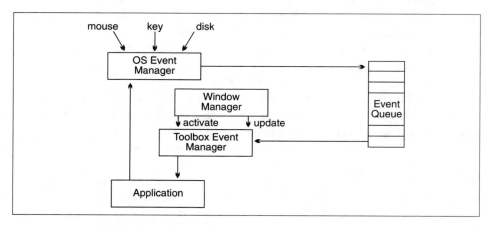

Figure 7.3 System 6 event architecture.

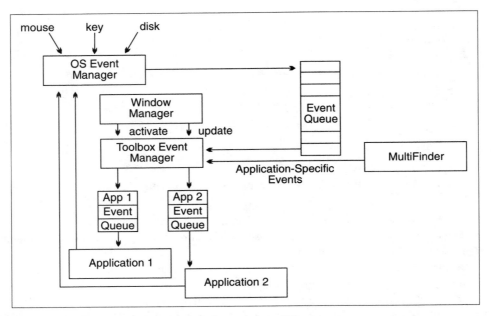

Figure 7.4 System 6 with MultiFinder event architecture.

events from various devices and from the application and puts them in the event queue. The Toolbox Event Manager manages the information in the event queue and fields activate and update events from the Window Manager. These events are read by the application and processed accordingly.

The next architecture, shown in Figure 7.4, is a Macintosh running System 6 with MultiFinder—this model supports multiple applications. Most of the architecture is similar to the previous one, except the Toolbox Event Manager can also get events from MultiFinder to control the activation of different applications. The other difference is that all the events fielded by the Toolbox Event Manager are sent to multiple-event queues, one for each application. Each application reads an event from its corresponding queue and processes it as necessary.

The third Macintosh event architecture is defined in System 7. Although similar in concept to System 6 with MultiFinder, it does have some differences, as shown in Figure 7.5. Instead of MultiFinder feeding messages into the Toolbox Event Manager, the Process Manager does. The Toolbox Event Manager also fields events from the Program-to-Program Communications (PPC) Toolbox, which allows applications to send and receive data with each other. The other difference is that when applications send events to each other (using the Apple Event Manager), the events are sent to the Toolbox Event Manager rather than the OS Event Manager as in System 6 with MultiFinder.

Even though the Macintosh event architectures are different, the underlying model that the application sees is the same. Each application is responsible for reading events from a queue and processing the information. This processing involves determining which of the application's windows the message is for and decoding the contents of the information.

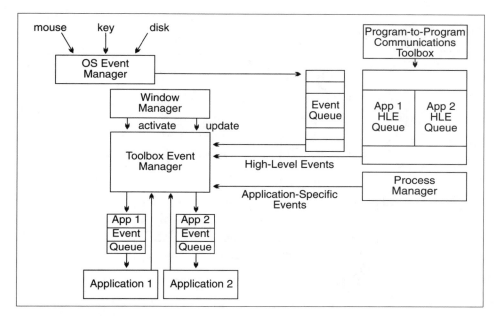

Figure 7.5 System 7 event architecture.

For a thorough discussion of Macintosh events and event processing, see *Inside Macintosh*, Volume VI, Chapter 5.

Windows 3.1 Event Model

The Windows 3.1 operating environment maintains a system queue that receives messages from hardware devices and routes them to one or more application message queues, as shown in Figure 7.6. The messages in an application message queue are removed by the message loop of the corrseponding application. When a message is removed and processed, the corresponding window callback function is called by the system. Only one application can remove messages from its queue at a time.

Architecturally the Windows 3.1 model is very similar to the Macintosh model of System 6 and MultiFinder. The differences lie in the event model that is seen by the application. There are two differences between the Macintosh and Windows models: the higher granularity of events in Windows and the way events are processed. In the Macintosh events are read and processed by the application. In Windows messages are usually read at the application level but the system directs them to the corresponding window handler in the application for processing.

Win32 Event Model

Every environment subsystem in Windows NT maintains its own event model and architecture. The Win32 event model is different from the Windows 3.1 event model and is shown in Figure 7.7. The first difference is that there is no centralized input queue maintained by the operating

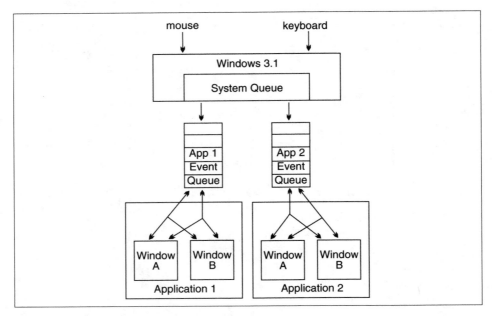

Figure 7.6 Windows 3.1 event architecture.

system. User activity translates into hardware events that are sent directly to an application's message queue. This decentralizes the event-gathering process and prevents one application from misbehaving and stopping the flow of events into the operating system. The other primary difference is that Win32 uses preemptive multitasking. Each application runs as a process that consists of one or more threads. For example, Thread 1 from Process 1 runs for a time, then

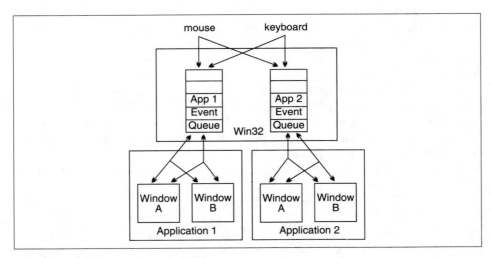

Figure 7.7 Win32 event architecture.

Thread 2 from Process 1, then Thread 1 from Process 2, and back to Thread 1 from Process 1, and so on. (Refer to "Creating, Managing, and Destroying Processes and Threads under Windows NT," *Microsoft Systems Journal*, v. 8, no. 7, July 1993, pp. 55–76.)

Even though there are substantial differences in the architectures, the Win32 event model (as seen by the application) is the same as Windows 3.1. That is, messages are window-centric and dispatched by the operating system during processing and sent to the appropriate window. For this reason, we will consider the Windows 3.1 and Win32 event models the same and refer to them as the Windows event model.

Cross-Platform Event Model

The event model that we have adopted in our discussions in this book and in the XPLib software is based on the Windows model. It was obvious, early on, that it would be much easier to modify the Macintosh event model to be more Windows-like that to make Windows more Macintosh-like. This is because the Macintosh architecture is much simpler in its design. Macintosh applications, typically, have a single event handler that is not window-based but application-based. The application decodes the event entirely. In contrast, the Windows model is window-based—all events are targeted to a window regardless of the type, and event decoding is performed by the operating system. This can sometimes pose a problem in Windows if an application does not have a main window and you want to process events. Normally you would create a window and hide it and let its callback procedure handle the events.

What we do in the Macintosh is to create an application event loop that dispatches events to the appropriate window handler functions, including locally created dialogs. By supplying a pointer to a window handler function (see XPInit() documented in Chapter 3), we were able to define a pseudo window class in the Macintosh à la the Windows class definition. By registering this function with the event system and intercepting events and dispatching them to the appropriate window handler, we are able to make the Macintosh behave like Windows.

If you look closely, you'll notice that the cross-platform events that we have defined are defined in a one-to-one way with those in Windows. If you look in the XPLib documentation, you'll see that the cross-platform events are merely #defined to Windows messages. In the Macintosh, the cross-platform events map to non-Macintosh event codes.

Defining and Comparing Events

The Macintosh maintains a hierarchical event model that is tied to the application's event-dispatching code, shown in Figure 7.8. A small number of events encapsulate the behavior of all of the windows in the application. The standard event set (excluding high-level events) in the Macintosh is small, represented by 16 primary events (of which only 8 are commonly used). Some primary events also have secondary messages and some secondary messages have tertiary messages. The number of secondary event messages depend on the particular primary event; for example, the mouseDown event has 7 secondary events. Some secondary events have other (ternary) events tied to them; for example, a mouseDown inside a window interior produces an inContent message. If the window has controls, the inContent message might also imply one of seven "in control" messages, like inButton, inCheckBox, etc. A more complete diagram of events is shown in Appendix D.

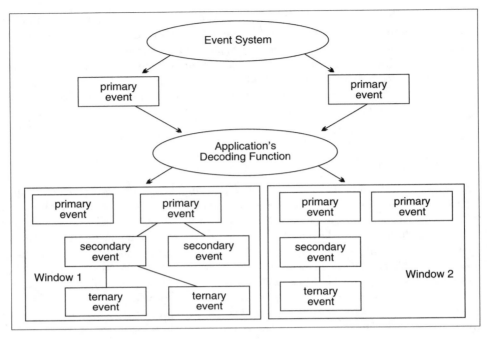

Figure 7.8 Macintosh event-dispatching mechanism.

In Windows the event model for each window is reasonably flat, as shown in Figure 7.9. Each window is an encapsulated entity that can field a broad range of messages. There are a few types of event messages that indicate smaller packets of information. Some events need additional processing to extract secondary messages, such as WM_COMMAND, which contains information about the user's menu or control selection.

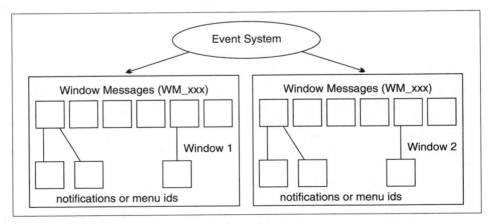

Figure 7.9 Windows event-dispatching mechanism.

The real problem in producing a cross-platform event manager is to select a small group of messages that will give you the functionality that you need without sacrificing flexibility. Many of the specialized messages in Windows, those for specific types of user interface controls, can be hidden by specialized control functions because they are not normally received or processed by the window handler routine (they are sent from a function to a control). Other control messages, called notification codes, are received through the Windows WM_COMMAND message. These are discussed later.

The set of cross-platform events that are listed in Table 7.1 are essential to basic program function. We compare each event to its Macintosh (primary and secondary) message and its Windows message in Table 7.2. Notice that every cross-platform event message maps to a Windows message. We could rename all cross-platform messages to have the Windows naming convention, but we won't because we want to distinguish between events in our discussion (cross-platform events) and those in platform-specific code (platform-specific events). Also, there are some Macintosh events that have no corresponding Windows event; these are listed in Table 7.3.

Table 7.1 Essential events for a cross-platform event manager.

Event	*Meaning*
E_Null	a null event, nothing has happened
EW_Create	a window is being created, but nothing has been displayed yet
EW_Close	a window is closing
EW_Destroy	a window is being destroyed
E_Quit	the application is quitting
EW_M1Down	the 1st mouse button is pressed
EW_M1Up	the 1st mouse button is released
EW_M1Double	the 1st mouse button was double-clicked
EW_M2Down	the 2nd mouse button is pressed
EW_M2Up	the 2nd mouse button is released
EW_M2Double	the 2nd mouse button was double-clicked
EW_M3Down	the 3rd mouse button is pressed
EW_M3Up	the 3rd mouse button is released
EW_M3Double	the 3rd mouse button was double-clicked
EW_MMove	the mouse has moved
EW_Move	the window is being moved
EW_KeyUp	a key has been released
EW_KeyDown	a key has been pressed
EW_Char	a character key has been pressed
EW_Redraw	the contents of the window should be redrawn
EW_ScrollH	the horizontal scroll bar was used (up, down, page up, page down, or thumb)
EW_ScrollV	the vertical scroll bar was used (up, down, page up, page down, or thumb)

(continued)

Table 7.1 (*Continued*)

Event	Meaning
EW_Activate	the window is being made active or inactive
E_ActivateApp	the application is being activated or deactivated
EW_MenuBarInit	the user has clicked in the menu bar (before menu action)
EW_Command	a control was used or a menu item was selected
EW_SysCommand	a system menu item was selected
EW_Show	the window is about to be shown or hidden
EW_Size	the window was sized
EW_TitleGet	a request to retrieve the window's title was made
EW_TitleSet	a request to set the window's title was made
EW_DialogInit	the dialog box is about to be displayed and made active

Table 7.2 **Cross-platform to platform-specific event map.**

	Macintosh		
Event	Primary	Secondary	Windows
E_Null	nullEvent		WM_NULL
EW_Create	NA		WM_CREATE
EW_Close	mouseDown	inGoAway	WM_CLOSE
EW_Destroy	NA		WM_DESTROY
E_Quit	kHighLevelEvent	'quit'	WM_QUIT
EW_M1Down	mouseDown		WM_LBUTTONDOWN
EW_M1Up	mouseUp		WM_LBUTTONUP
EW_M1Double	mouseDown	*plus processing*	WM_LBUTTONDBLCLK
EW_M2Down	NA		WM_RBUTTONDOWN
EW_M2Up	NA		WM_RBUTTONUP
EW_M2Double	NA		WM_RBUTTONDBLCLK
EW_M3Down	NA		WM_MBUTTONDOWN
EW_M3Up	NA		WM_MBUTTONUP
EW_M3Double	NA		WM_MBUTTONDBLCLK
EW_MMove	NA		WM_MOUSEMOVE
EW_Move	mouseDown	inDrag	WM_MOVE
EW_KeyUp	keyUp autoKey		WM_KEYUP
EW_KeyDown	keyDown autoKey		WM_KEYDOWN
EW_Char	keyDown		WM_CHAR

(continued)

Table 7.2 (*Continued*)

Event	Macintosh Primary	Secondary	Windows
	autoKey		
EW_Redraw	updateEvt		WM_PAINT
EW_ScrollH	mouseDown	inContent	WM_HSCROLL
EW_ScrollV	mouseDown	inContent	WM_VSCROLL
EW_Activate	activateEvt		WM_ACTIVATE
E_ActivateApp	kHighLevelEvent	'oapp'	WM_ACTIVATEAPP
	osEvt	suspendResumeMessage	
EW_MenuBarInit	mouseDown	inMenu	WM_INITMENU
	keyDown		
	autoKey		
EW_Command	mouseDown	inContent	WM_COMMAND
	keyDown		
	autoKey		
EW_SysCommand	mouseDown	inMenu	WM_SYSCOMMAND
EW_Show	NA		WM_SHOWWINDOW
EW_Size	mouseDown	inSize	WM_SIZE
	mouseDown	inZoomIn	
	mouseDown	inZoomOut	
EW_TitleGet	NA		WM_GETTEXT
EW_TitleSet	NA		WM_SETTEXT
EW_DialogInit	NA		WM_INITDIALOG

Table 7.3 Macintosh events that don't have Windows equivalents.

Primary	Secondary	Meaning
mouseDown	inDesk	mouse down in desktop or in undefined region of window frame
mouseDown	inSysWindow	mouse pressed in the system window
diskEvt		a floppy was inserted—usually processed if the disk is unformatted
osEvt	mouseMovedMessage	the mouse has moved out of a predefined region (the cursorRgn)
kHighLevelEvent		some of these don't map to Windows events; some are application-specific

Looking at Event Sequences

To provide a cross-platform event system, we need to first understand how events compare in static or feature-only terms. We covered this in the last section; now we need to look at the dynamic aspects of events, or how sequences of events occur. In this section we will look at the sequences of events on the Macintosh and Windows platforms that occur during the following actions:

- creating a window
- switching between applications
- selecting a menu item
- typing a character
- quitting the application

The event sequence tables that we present will show:

- a comparison of the raw (native) event sequences
- roughly how the event sequences are synchronized
- how raw events map to cross-platform events in each platform
- how cross-platform event sequences compare across platforms

The event sequences are not exactly what will happen in every instance of the actions. Some events were removed for clarity, and repetitive events were removed. There might not be complete agreement in the Windows event sequences across the Windows 3.1 and Win32 platforms because event ordering can never be completely guaranteed. Last, in all of the tables of event sequences, events shown in italics indicate events that are synthesized by the cross-platform event system; they either don't exist on the platform or don't correspond in a one-to-one way with a native event.

Creating a Window

One of the first things that happens in a GUI-based application is that a window is created. In Windows the window is associated with the application and makes the application visible to the operating system. It also provides a conduit through which event messages can flow from user actions to the application. Without a window the application cannot receive events. This isn't necessary on the Macintosh. There doesn't need to be a window for the application to gather events.

The process of creating a window generates many events in Windows, which are listed in Table 7.4. We have extracted the corresponding cross-platform events as well. The WM_-CREATE message is special. It is sent to the window callback or handler function to tell it that a new window of its type is being created but hasn't been shown yet. It allows the window handler to initialize and prepare for the new window. The WM_SHOW message is sent to tell the window handler that the window will be shown or hidden depending on the information in the message. The handler can acquiesce or intervene in this process.

Table 7.4 Event sequences during window creation.

| Macintosh | | Windows | |
Raw Event	XP Event	Raw Event	XP Event
		WM_GETMINMAXINFO	
		WM_NCCREATE	
		WM_NCCALCSIZE	
	EW_Create	WM_CREATE	EW_Create
	EW_Show	WM_SHOW	EW_Show
		Undefined Message	
		WM_WINDOWPOSCHANGING	
		WM_NCACTIVATE	
		WM_GETTEXT	EW_TitleGet
activateEvt	EW_Activate	WM_ACTIVATE	EW_Activate
		WM_SETFOCUS	
		WM_NCPAINT	
		WM_GETTEXT	EW_TitleGet
		WM_ERASEBKGND	
		WM_WINDOWPOSCHANGED	
		WM_SIZE	EW_Size
		WM_MOVE	EW_Move
		WM_WINDOWPOSCHANGING	
		WM_NCCALCSIZE	
		WM_NCPAINT	
		WM_GETTEXT	EW_TitleGet
		WM_ERASEBKGND	
		WM_WINDOWPOSCHANGED	
updateEvt	EW_Redraw	WM_PAINT	EW_Redraw

The create and show messages are special in that they occur before the window is actually activated. If we synchronize the Macintosh activate event, activateEvt, with the Windows WM_ACTIVATE event, you'll notice that the create and show process occurs before the Macintosh window is activated. This indicates that not only do we synthesize these events, but they are sent before the activateEvt is processed. This tells us that the function that creates the window must send these messages to the window handler.

The other cross-platform events associated with the window creation process on the Windows side don't need to be synthesized explicitly on the Macintosh. They occur in Windows because they naturally do. But, they are important for the Macintosh implementation and are synthesized by other cross-platform functions; for example:

EW_Show	synthesized when the show window function is called
EW_TitleGet	synthesized when the get window title function is called
EW_Move	synthesized when the move window or change window size function is called
EW_Size	synthesized when the size window function is called

Switching Back and Forth Between Applications

Next let's look at what happens when we click on a window that doesn't belong to our application and then click back to ours (see Table 7.5). There are a few things to note here:

- The Macintosh osEvt event maps to E_ActivateApp (activate or deactivate).
- The Windows nullEvt message maps to EW_MMove (mouse moved).
- The Windows WM_ACTIVATEAPP message maps to E_ActivateApp.

In the Macintosh because there is no activate window message in conjunction with an activate application message, the EW_Active (active and deactivate window) message needs to be synthesized by the Macintosh implementation to emulate what happens in Windows. (The messages that need to be synthesized are italicized on Table 7.5.) It also means that we need to process the nullEvt message and determine if the mouse has moved. If it has, we generate the cross-platform EW_MMove message. The EW_M1Down and EW_M1Up messages aren't generated in the Macintosh because these events are "swallowed" by the Macintosh osEvt message.

Macintosh Note: If you want to receive the mouse events associated with the activation of your application, you need to indicate to the application that you want to receive "front clicks." This will send the mouseDown and mouseUp events to the application (they are simply translated to EW_M1Down and EW_M1Up events).

Table 7.5 Event sequences during application switching.

| Macintosh | | Windows | |
Raw Event	XP Event	Raw Event	XP Event
osEvt		WM_NCACTIVATE	
(suspend)		WM_GETTEXT	EW_TitleGet
	EW_Activate	WM_ACTIVATE	EW_Activate
	E_ActivateApp	WM_ACTIVATEAPP	E_ActivateApp
		WM_KILLFOCUS	
nullEvent		WM_NCHITTEST	
		WM_SETCURSOR	
	EW_MMove	WM_MOUSEMOVE	EW_MMove
		WM_NCHITTEST	

(continued)

Table 7.5 (*Continued*)

Macintosh		Windows	
Raw Event	*XP Event*	*Raw Event*	*XP Event*
		WM_MOUSEACTIVATE	
		WM_WINDOWPOSCHANGING	
osEvt		WM_NCPAINT	
(resume)		WM_GETTEXT	EW_TitleGet
		WM_ERASEBKGND	
		WM_WINDOWPOSCHANGED	
	E_ActivateApp	WM_ACTIVATEAPP	E_ActivateApp
		WM_NCACTIVATE	
	EW_Activate	WM_ACTIVATE	EW_Activate
		WM_SETFOCUS	
		WM_SETCURSOR	
		WM_LBUTTONDOWN	EW_M1Down
nullEvent		WM_NCHITTEST	
		WM_SETCURSOR	
	EW_MMove	WM_MOUSEMOVE	EW_MMove
		WM_NCHITTEST	
		WM_SETCURSOR	
		WM_LBUTTONUP	EW_M1Up
updateEvt	EW_Redraw	WM_PAINT	EW_Redraw
nullEvent		WM_NCHITTEST	
		WM_SETCURSOR	
	EW_MMove	WM_MOUSEMOVE	EW_MMove

Selecting a Menu Item

Another important event sequence to analyze is what happens when the user clicks in the menu bar, drops down a menu list, and selects a menu item (see Table 7.6). Macintosh generates only one event, and again Windows generates many event messages. The important point to note here is the WM_INITMENU message in Windows, which maps to the cross-platform EW_Menu-BarInit message. This event is sent before any menu list is dropped down so that the window handler function can initialize anything in the menu bar before any lists in the menu bar are displayed. The initialize menu bar message must be synthesized in the Macintosh.

The key points of these event sequences are:

- The Windows WM_INITMENU maps to EW_MenuBarInit.
- The Windows WM_COMMAND maps to EW_Command.
- The EW_MenuBarInit event must be synthesized on the Macintosh.

Table 7.6 Event sequences during a menu selection.

| Macintosh | | Windows | |
Raw Event	XP Event	Raw Event	XP Event
mouseDown		WM_NCHITTEST	
(inMenuBar)		WM_SETCURSOR	
		WM_NCLBUTTONDOWN	
		WM_SYSCOMMAND	EW_SysCommand
		Undefined Message	
		WM_SETCURSOR	
	EW_MenuBarInit	WM_INITMENU	EW_MenuBarInit
		WM_MENUSELECT	
		WM_INITMENUPOPUP	
		WM_ENTERIDLE	
		WM_MENUSELECT	
		WM_ENTERIDLE	
		WM_MENUSELECT	
		Undefined Message	
	EW_Command	WM_COMMAND	EW_Command

Typing SHIFT-A

Table 7.7 lists the sequences of events that are related to typing a SHIFT-A on the Macintosh and Windows. The process of typing keys is not usually thought of as a complicated action, and this is true on the Macintosh, where only a single event, keyDown, is usually associated with a key press. It is not true on Windows, which generates a sequence of WM_KEYDOWN messages before the character message (WM_CHAR) associated with the key is sent, and then another sequence of WM_KEYUP messages. The WM_KEYxxx messages refer to virtual key codes. There is no equivalent construct on the Macintosh, so this needs to be created. The subject of virtual keys is discussed in more detail in the Keyboard Events section of this chapter.

The important points to note about this sequence are:

- The Windows WM_KEYDOWN events map to EW_KeyDown events.
- The Windows WM_KEYUP events map to EW_KeyUp events.
- We need to define virtual keys for the Macintosh.
- We need to synthesize EW_KeyDown events for the Macintosh.
- We need to synthesize EW_KeyUp events for the Macintosh.

Also, we ignore the KeyUp events in the Macintosh. This is because they are not consistently generated by all versions of the Macintosh system software.

Table 7.7 Event sequences due to typing SHIFT-A.

| Macintosh | | Windows | |
Raw Event	*XP Event*	*Raw Event*	*XP Event*
keyDown	*EW_KeyDown*	WM_KEYDOWN	EW_KeyDown
	EW_KeyDown	WM_KEYDOWN	EW_KeyDown
	EW_Char	WM_CHAR	EW_Char
	EW_KeyUp	WM_KEYUP	EW_KeyUp
	EW_KeyUp	WM_KEYUP	EW_KeyUp

Quitting the Application

The last sequence of events that an application needs to deal with is what occurs when the user wants to terminate an application. In our example this sequence centers around the user clicking the close box in the Macintosh and selecting the close menu item in the system menu in Windows. This sequence is shown in Table 7.8. There are two things to note in this sequence: A number of messages need to be synthesized by the Macintosh and the "quit" message is never actually processed by the application.

On the Macintosh between the time the user clicks the close box and the time the application quits, there are many events on the Windows side and just one event on the Macintosh side. To provide a window-centric event model, we need to send the window messages that will close, deactivate, and destroy the window and then inactivate and terminate the application. Because the only Macintosh event we receive is mouseDown, we need to synthesize the others.

To perform the actual quitting of the application, we need to do something special. In Windows, the PostQuitMessage() posts the WM_QUIT message. This message is retrieved using GetMessage() and directs the event loop to end and terminate the program; thus the WM_QUIT message is never seen by a window handler function. We need to emulate this on the Macintosh, so we use the application-specific app1Evt message and post ourselves a quit message. We not only synthesize the cross-platform E_Quit message but we also synthesize the Macintosh app1Evt.

IMPLEMENTING CROSS-PLATFORM EVENT MANAGER

The events that we have described and compared in Tables 7.1 and 7.2 are essential to basic event-based program behavior. Outlining the event sequences for particular actions is also important in implementing an event solution. Certain actions will require the synthesis of a number of cross-platform events on the Macintosh. A good example of this is in Table 7.8, which illustrates what happens when an application is terminated.

As with most of the other functional areas, to implement the event functions, we need to define some event-related data types and implement the event functions.

Table 7.8 Event sequences during application termination.

Macintosh Raw Event	XP Event	Windows Raw Event	XP Event
mouseDown		WM_NCHITTEST	
(inGoAway)		WM_SETCURSOR	
		WM_NCLBUTTONDOWN	
		WM_SYSCOMMAND	EW_SysCommand
		Undefined Message	
		WM_SETCURSOR	
		WM_INITMENU	EW_MenuBarInit
		WM_MENUSELECT	
		WM_INITMENUPOPUP	
		WM_MENUSELECT	
		WM_MENUSELECT	
		Undefined Message	
		WM_SYSCOMMAND	EW_SysCommand
	EW_Close	WM_CLOSE	EW_Close
		WM_WINDOWPOSCHANGING	
		WM_WINDOWPOSCHANGED	
		WM_NCACTIVATE	
	EW_Activate	WM_ACTIVATE	EW_Activate
	EW_Destroy		
	E_ActivateApp	WM_ACTIVATEAPP	E_ActivateApp
		WM_KILLFOCUS	
		WM_DESTROY	EW_Destroy
		WM_NCDESTROY	
*app1Evt**	*E_Quit***	WM_QUIT**	E_Quit**

 * This Macintosh event is sent to initiate the termination process.

** This event is never actually processed, but it terminates the program.

Basic Events

We have defined many cross-platform events. Unfortunately there isn't enough room in this book to explain them all. Our discussion in this chapter will consider only the following subset of events:

EW_Activate
EW_Close
EW_Command
EW_Destroy

EW_MMove
EW_MenuBarInit
E_Quit

Describing the various aspects of these events will give you the information you will need to understand the process of implementing a cross-platform event solution.

Event-Related Data Types

There are several basic data types that we need to define for our cross-platform event system. The HWND, MSGDATA, DATA1, and DATA2 types are used to define our cross-platform EVENT structure. On the Macintosh notice that the HWND type (handle to a window) actually refers to a WindowPtr. This is an unfortunate but necessary naming idiosyncrasy. The WindowPtr is the primary reference to a window in the Macintosh environment, so rather than diverge from that, we call a WindowPtr a window handle. This allows us to have a consistent usage with Windows, which employs a window handle, HWND, to identify a window.

Type	*Macintosh*	*Windows 3.1*	*Win32*
HANDLERrtn	SINT4	LRESULT	LRESULT
HWND	WindowPtr (4 bytes)	HWND (2 bytes)	HWND (4 bytes)
MSGDATA	UINT4	UINT (2 bytes)	UINT (4 bytes)
DATA1	UINT4	WPARAM (2 bytes)	WPARAM (4 bytes)
DATA2	UINT4	LPARAM	LPARAM

There is also one data wrapper that masquerades as a data type, HANDLERdecl. It is used to define the window handler function, which is discussed in the next section.

Wrapper	*Macintosh*	*Windows 3.1*	*Win32*
HANDLERdecl	SINT4	LRESULT CALLBACK	LRESULT CALLBACK

Cross-Platform Window Handler Function Declaration

Events are retrieved from the queue and processed by the appropriate window handler function. The declaration of this window handler function is polymorphic, and there are a few peculiarities associated with the its definitions that allow us to define it as such.

The Macintosh defintion of the window handler function is:

```
typedef HANDLERdecl (*HANDLER) (HWND hwnd, MSGDATA msg,
    DATA1 data1, DATA2 data2);
```

The Windows 3.1 definition of the window handler function is:

```
typedef LRESULT (_far _pascal* WNDPROC) (HWND, UINT, WPARAM,
    LPARAM);
#define HANDLER WNDPROC
```

The Win32 definition of the window handler function is:

```
typedef LRESULT (__stdcall* WNDPROC) (HWND, UINT, WPARAM,
    LPARAM);
#define HANDLER WNDPROC
```

Notice that earlier we also defined the HANDLERdecl and HANDLERrtn types. These are used in specific ways to facilitate the declaration of a window handler function, as shown here:

```
// HANDLERdecl is used to declare the function
HANDLERdecl HandlerFunction (HWND hwnd, MSGDATA msg,
    DATA1 data1, DATA2 data2)
{
    // HANDLER rtn is the return value data type
    return ((HANDLERrtn) 0);
}
```

Extra Window Data

It is necessary to provide our cross-platform windows with additional information. To handle events properly, cross-platform windows created on the Macintosh require an additional piece of information: the pointer to the window handler that will process all cross-platform events. No additional information is required by Windows.

The window extra information is packaged in a data structure that we dub WNDX. This structure and its purpose is discussed in more detail in Chapter 14, where we discuss windows. But for the purpose of our discussion of events, we will define the structure as follows:

```
typedef struct _WNDX
{
    HANDLER   fnHandler;
}
WNDX, *PWNDX;
```

Cross-Platform EVENT Data Structure

To define a cross-platform event system, we need to define a cross-platform event data type: the EVENT structure. Because it is cross-platform, some of the fields are independent of the platform and some are not. To maintain compatibility with the native environment, we will also include a copy of the native event that caused the cross-platform event.

Let's begin with the cross-platform fields—the sizes of the fields aren't necessarily the same. The contents of the data1 and data2 fields depend on the particular event that was retrieved.

Type	Field Name	Description
MSGDATA	msg	the message (id) of the event
UINT4	u4Tick	the system time (in ticks) that the event occurred
POINT	ptScreen	the point on the screen where the event occurred
DATA1	data1	the first piece of data needed by the event
DATA2	data2	the second piece of data needed by the event
HWND	hwnd	the handle of the window that received the event

The Macintosh version of the EVENT structure needs these additional fields:

Type	Field Name	Description
EventRecord	_event	native Macintosh event information
_MACSYS7	_sys7	System 7 stuff for processing High Level Events

Notice that the Macintosh requires the _MACSYS7 structure, which maintains the information necessary for the application to process High Level Events. For more information on this topic, consult *Inside Macintosh*, Volume VI, Chapter 5. The _MACSYS7 structure is defined as follows:

Type	Field Name	Description
TargetID	senderID	the id of the sender of the event
UINT4	s4MsgRef	unique number that identifies the received event
UINT4	s4Len	actual length of the message buffer
MEM	mMsgBuf	maintains the buffer to hold the message data
OSErr	err	maintains the Macintosh error code

The Windows version of EVENT structure needs an additional field to save the original Windows message. Notice that the original Macintosh and Windows events that are stored in the EVENT structure are given the same name, _event.

Type	Field Name	Description
MSG	_event	native Windows message information

Event Functions

In our implementation we limit our discussion of event functions to:

- getting an event record from the system queue
- processing an event
- posting an event message to the system queue
- sending an event message to a window handler

Getting an Event

The first step in working with events is being able to get one from the operating system's queue. We define EventGet() to supply a pointer to our cross-platform event record (which will be filled by the function) and a handle to the window whose events we want. This function returns FALSE if the E_Quit message was received and TRUE otherwise. A FALSE value tells the event loop that we want to end the program.

```
//-------------------------------------------------------
BOOL2 EventGet (PEVENT pXPEvent, HWND hwnd)
//-------------------------------------------------------
// pXPEvent  - pointer to a cross-platform EVENT structure
//             that will receive the event information
// hwnd      - handle to a window whose events we are
//             interested in, or NULL if all windows
// RETURNS   - FALSE if the application should quit
//-------------------------------------------------------
{
```

In the Macintosh we need to check if the version of the operating system supports multiple applications (MultiFinder or System 7). If the system is running plain Finder, we call SystemTask() to allow desk accessories to operate, then GetNextEvent() to retrieve the next event from the queue. If the system is running MultiFinder, we use WaitNextEvent(), which lets our application sleep for a while if there are no events, then gets the next event from the queue. This function allows other applications that aren't necessarily in the foreground to receive events.

If the computer is running System 7 we also call WaitNextEvent(), but we call _MacEventHighPrep() first to allow our application to receive High Level Events (HLE). It checks if a HLE is pending, and if so allocates a buffer large enough to receive the information associated with the message. The buffer is later destroyed after the event is processed in the EventProcess() function. The _MacEventHighPrep() function is listed after EventGet().

Once we have an event (an EventRecord) we need to convert it to a cross-platform form (EVENT structure) or sequence of events. The translation from Macintosh and Windows events is based on the information contained in Table 7.2 and is performed by the _MacEventConvertToXP() function. We don't discuss this function in its entirety because it would be very large. But we will discuss some examples of what is involved in the conversion process in the Converting Native Events to Cross-Platform Events section later in this chapter.

```
{
EventRecord _macEvent;
HWND hwndEvent;

// are we running System 6 with MultiFinder or
// System 7?
if (_gb2MacMultiApps){

        if (_gs2MacSysVers>6){
        // running System 7...
        // get any extra data that might be associated
        // with a high-level event...this MUST be done
        // before the WaitNextEvent() call.
        _MacEventHighPrep (pXPEvent);
    }
    WaitNextEvent (everyEvent, &_macEvent, _MACSLEEP,
        NULL);

// System 6 with plain old Finder
}else{
    // for desk accessories
    SystemTask ();

    GetNextEvent (everyEvent, &_macEvent);
}

if (hwnd){
    //if the window is not the active one, make it so
    if(hwnd != FrontWindow ()){
        SelectWindow (hwnd);
    }
}
// this is where the translation from Macintosh events
// to Windows events occurs
return (_MacEventConvertToXP (&_macEvent, pXPEvent));
}
```

In Windows we use GetMessage() to retrieve the next message from the queue. The hwnd parameter can be NULL if we want to retrieve the next message for any window in the application or non-NULL if we want messages for only a specific window. This option is not available in the Macintosh version.

After we've gotten the message, we convert it to a cross-platform form. This is easy in Windows because the event information is the same. We save a copy of the original event and return the value we received from GetMessage(), which is FALSE if the WM_QUIT message was received.

```
    {
MSG _winEvent;
BOOL2 b2Quit;

b2Quit=GetMessage (&_winEvent, hwnd, 0, 0);

// copy over the Windows message information to the
// cross-platform event structure
pXPEvent->msg=_winEvent.message;
pXPEvent->u4Tick=_winEvent.time;
pXPEvent->data1=_winEvent.wParam;
pXPEvent->data2=_winEvent.lParam;
pXPEvent->hwnd=_winEvent.hwnd;

// make a copy of the windows message information
pXPEvent->_event=_winEvent;

return (b2Quit);
    }
```

The event information has been gotten from the queue, and we're finished.

```
}

//---- MAC only! ----------------------------------------
//-------------------------------------------------------
BOOL2 _MacEventHighPrep (PEVENT pxpe)
//-------------------------------------------------------
// pxpe - pointer to a cross-platform EVENT structure
//-------------------------------------------------------
{
    pxpe->_sys7.s4Len=0L;

    // check if any HLEs are pending, if so, call
    // AcceptHLE once to get the length
    pxpe->_sys7.err=
        AcceptHighLevelEvent (&pxpe->_sys7.senderID,
            &pxpe->_sys7.s4MsgRef,
            pxpe->_sys7.mMsgBuf.ptr=NULLPTR,
            &pxpe->_sys7.s4Len);

    // if a HLE is pending, then we need to allocate
    // a buffer to hold the information
    if (pxpe->_sys7.err==bufferIsSmall){

        // allocate the memory for the message...
```

```
        if (!MAlloc (&pxpe->_sys7.mMsgBuf,
            pxpe->_sys7.s4Len)
        ) {
            return (FALSE);
        }
        // ...and lock it down
        MLock (&pxpe->_sys7.mMsgBuf);

        // get the message and put it into our buffer
        pxpe->_sys7.err=
            AcceptHighLevelEvent (&pxpe->_sys7.senderID,
                &pxpe->_sys7.s4MsgRef,
                pxpe->_sys7.mMsgBuf.ptr,
                &pxpe->_sys7.s4Len);

        if (pxpe->_sys7.err!=noErr) {
            return (FALSE);
        }

    }
    return (TRUE);
}
```

Processing an Event

Once an event (an EVENT structure) has been retrieved by the EventGet() function, we need to call EventProcess() so that the appropriate window handler can be called and the event can be processed. This function requires a pointer to a valid EVENT structure and returns the value returned by the window handler function. This function does not send null events to the window; this is normally the case in Windows but not on the Macintosh, where processing nullEvents is used to perform certain background functions.

```
//-------------------------------------------------------
UINT4 EventProcess (PEVENT pXPEvent)
//-------------------------------------------------------
// pXPEvent - pointer to an EVENT structure with
//            information about the event to process
// RETURNS  - unsigned 4-byte integer that depends on
//            the event that was processed
//-------------------------------------------------------
{
    UINT4 u4Return=0;

    // for now, ignore null events
    if (pXPEvent->msg!=E_Null) {
```

Because the concept of a dedicated window handler doesn't naturally exist in the Macintosh architecture, we need to take care of calling the appropriate window handler function ourselves. This means that we need to get the pointer to the WNDX (window extra) data that we attached to the window when it was created (see Chapter 14 for more information) and then call the window handler using the pointer to it that is included in the WNDX structure.

Because this is "the last stop" for an event, we also must check the cross-platform msg field of the EVENT structure to see if this was a High Level Event. If it was, we need to free up any memory associated with its message buffer after the message has been processed. When this is done, we return the return code from the window handler to the caller.

```
// check if we have a valid window
if (pXPEvent->hwnd
    && ((WindowPeek)pXPEvent->hwnd)->windowKind>=0
){
    PWNDX pwndx;

    pwndx=(PWNDX)GetWRefCon (pXPEvent->hwnd);

    // if the window "extra" pointer is valid
    // and the handler too...
    if (pwndx && pwndx->fnHandler){
        // call the window handler procedure
        u4Return=pwndx->fnHandler(
            pXPEvent->hwnd,
            pXPEvent->msg,
            pXPEvent->data1,
            pXPEvent->data2);
    }

    // E_MacHLE can only be sent if we are running
    // System 7, if so...
    if (pXPEvent->msg==E_MacHLE){

        //free up the high level event info
        MUnlock (&pXPEvent->_sys7.mMsgBuf);
        MFree (&pXPEvent->_sys7.mMsgBuf);
    }
}
```

In Windows we use the usual method of processing a message. Don't forget that the _event structure in the Windows version of the cross-platform EVENT structure refers to a MSG structure, which is what we need. This implementation of EventProcess() won't work if you want to process accelerators for the window or keyboard shortcuts for a modeless dialog box; you will need to include calls to TranslateAccelerator() or IsDialogMessage() accordingly.

```
TranslateMessage (&pXPEvent->_event);
u4Return=DispatchMessage (&pXPEvent->_event);
```

We terminate the if statement that excludes null events (at the top of the function definition), and return the result of the window handler function.

```
    }
    return (u4Return);
}
```

Sending an Event

Sending an event to a particular window is really an indirect way of calling the window handler routine. This means that we will wait for the sent event to be processed by the window before we do anything else. Our EventSend() function requires the same arguments that the window handler routine requires: a handle to a window, the message id, and the message-specific data1 and data2 values.

```
//---------------------------------------------------------
UINT4 EventSend (HWND hwnd, MSGDATA msg, DATA1 data1,
    DATA2 data2)
//---------------------------------------------------------
// hwnd    - handle to the window to send the event
//           message to
// msg     - the event message
// data1   - data needed to process the message
// data2   - data needed to process the message
// RETURNS - unsigned 4-byte integer containing the
//           return code from the window handler
//---------------------------------------------------------
{
```

Because the concept of a window handler is not native to the Macintosh, our cross-platform implementation needs to do a little work before we actually call the handler with the event data. First we need to check that the window is the correct kind, then get the extra data that we've tacked on to the window structure. If the pointer to our extra data is valid and the window handler function pointer is OK, we call the handler with the data supplied to EventSend(). If something went wrong, we return a zero; otherwise we return whatever the callback function returns to us—this value is window handler specific.

Basically this is the same as our Macintosh version of the EventProcess() function, except that we don't need to worry about High Level Events.

```
        // check if we have a valid window
        if (hwnd && ((WindowPeek)hwnd)->windowKind>=0){
            PWNDX pwndx=(PWNDX)GetWRefCon (hwnd);
            // if the window "extra" pointer is valid
            // and the handler too...
            if (pwndx && pwndx->fnHandler){

                // call the window handler procedure
                return (pwndx->fnHandler (
```

```
                    hwnd, msg, data1, data2));
        }
    }
    return (0);
```

In Windows the API provides us with a way to send a window a message using the SendMessage() function.

```
    return (SendMessage (hwnd, msg, data1, data2));
```

That's all there is to sending an event message.

```
}
```

> *Note: In Windows, when you specify a window handle with the value 0xffff to the SendMessage() function, the message will be sent to all windows. This capability is not supported by the Macintosh version of our EventSend() function. To do this, you will need to access the WindowList global variable (a pointer to the first window in the application's window list) and send the message to their window handlers (assuming they are windows with window handlers). Otherwise you do nothing.*

Posting an Event

When we post an event message, we want the system to return to us before it actually processes the message, so it just adds the event information in the system queue. We define EventPost() to need all of the parameters that are needed by a handler function because this information will eventually end up in one. This means we supply a window handle (where the message is eventually going), a cross-platform event message, and the corresponding data1 and data2 values. EvenPost() will return TRUE if the event was posted successfully.

We also limit the scope of this function to only windows within our application. We will need to define another function, like EventPostApp(), to handle posting events to other applications. This discussion exceeds the scope of this book.

```
//----------------------------------------------------
BOOL2 EventPost (HWND hwnd, MSGDATA msg, DATA1 data1,
    DATA2 data2)
//----------------------------------------------------
// hwnd    - handle of the window to post the event
//           message to
// msg     - the event message
// data1   - data needed to process the message
// data2   - data needed to process the message
// RETURNS - TRUE means the event message was posted
//----------------------------------------------------
{
```

In the Macintosh we use the PostEvent() function. *Inside Macintosh*, Volume II, Chapter 2, says that we should be careful about the events that we post using this function and that we should only post events for our application. We adhere to this by using the app1Evt event as the guise to post all of our cross-platform messages—the msg parameter indicates the appropriate cross-platform message. When we retrieve the message using GetNextEvent() or WaitNext-Event(), we will have a complete EventRecord set up by the event manager.

The only problem with this technique is that if you are posting an event to a window that is different from the one that is active, this won't work. We don't have any way of letting the event dispatcher know to whom the event was intended. Because the Macintosh msg is 4 bytes, we could use some of the space to indicate the window using the upper 2 bytes (perhaps the window's position in the application's window list). Another possible solution is to create another queue that is parallel to the Macintosh event queue. Whenever an event is removed from the Macintosh queue, the parallel event is removed from our cross-platform event queue. This will let us pass along additional information.

```
// here we post a cross-platform event to ourselves
// with our event id information in the msg parameter
// we wrap all of our posted cross-platform events
// within the Macintosh app1Evt
return (PostEvent (app1Evt, msg) ? FALSE : TRUE);
```

In Windows posting a message is simply a matter of calling PostMessage() with the appropriate data. The callback function defined for the window class during initialization will eventually process the information.

```
return (PostMessage (hwnd, msg, data1, data2));
```

Then we terminate the EventPost() function definition.

```
}
```

Converting Native Events to Cross-Platform Events

Providing a cross-platform application with a cross-platform event system requires that there be a common way to express the information contained in an event. We outlined the comparisons of our cross-platform events with the native Macintosh events and Windows messages earlier in this chapter, now we need to discuss how we will convert a native event to a cross-platform event. This involves more that just mapping from one name to another; it also involves converting the other event information to a common form.

In this section we will discuss:

- converting a Windows message to a cross-platform event
- synthesizing a mouse-moved event (EW_MMove) in the Macintosh
- generating an EW_MenuBarInit and EW_Command sequence from a mouseDown, in-MenuBar event in the Macintosh
- processing a Macintosh mouseDown, inGoAway event to close a window and quit the application

Windows Message to Cross-Platform Event Conversion

Converting a Windows message (MSG structure) to our cross-platform event (EVENT structure) is a simple matter of copying fields. This process is already shown in the discussion of the EventGet() function.

Synthesizing a Mouse-Moved Event

Because we are using the Windows event model, there is a substantial amount of work that needs to be done to convert a Macintosh event into a cross-platform event or sequence of events. We start by looking at a simple example: how do we generate an EW_MMove (mouse-moved) event? Whenever we read a Macintosh event (using our EventGet() function), we need to check the where field of the EventRecord to see if the current location of the mouse has changed from the previous position—saved in a global variable from the last time we received an event.

Let's look at the description of our EW_MMove event shown in Figure 7.10. It indicates when the message is sent and how the data1 and data2 parameters are encoded. The description of the event references some constants that indicate the state of the mouse button (or buttons in Windows) and the SHIFT and CONTROL keys. On the Macintosh, these mouse modifier constants are defined as:

```
#define MOUSE_Button1  1
#define MOUSE_Button2  2   // never used
#define MOUSE_Button3  4   // never used
#define MOUSE_Shift    8
#define MOUSE_Ctl      16
```

The mouse-modifier constants, in Windows, are defined as:

```
#define MOUSE_Button1  MK_RBUTTON
#define MOUSE_Button2  MK_LBUTTON
#define MOUSE_Button3  MK_MBUTTON
#define MOUSE_Shift    MK_SHIFT
#define MOUSE_Ctl      MK_CONTROL
```

Once we have defined the components of the event data, we can specify the means of converting to this form on the Macintosh. We check if the mouse position has changed, and if it has, we copy the Macintosh location to a cross-platform POINT and convert the point that is in Macintosh screen (global) coordinates to coordinates that are relative to the top-left corner of the window pane (the content bounding box). Then we fill in the EVENT structure fields according to the encoding instructions defined in the description of the cross-platform event. Before we leave, we save the current point so we can compare it the next time.

```
//-------------------------------------------------------
// code sample to synthesize an EW_MMove event
//-------------------------------------------------------

// Macintosh format point
static Point _gMacPrevPt={0,0};
```

```
// pMacEvent is a pointer to an EventRecord
// pXPEvent is a pointer to an EVENT structure

if (*((PUINT4)((PTR)&_gMacPrevPt))
    != *((PUINT4)((PTR)&pMacEvent->where))
){
    POINT pt;

    pXPEvent->hwnd=FrontWindow ();

    // convert from global coords to pane coords
    PointSet (&pt, pMacEvent->where.h, pMacEvent ->where.v);
    PointStoP (pXPEvent->hwnd, &pt);

    pXPEvent->msg=EW_MMove;
    // pack the location of the mouse in data2
    pXPEvent->data2=((UINT4)pt.y)<<16; //y in MSW
    pXPEvent->data2+=(UINT4)pt.x;      //x in LSW

    // set up the mouse modifiers in data1
    pXPEvent->data1=0;
    if (pMacEvent->modifiers&controlKey){
        pXPEvent->data1+=MOUSE_Ctl;
    }
    if (pMacEvent->modifiers&shiftKey){
        pXPEvent->data1+=MOUSE_Shift;
    }
    if (!(pMacEvent->modifiers&btnState)){
        pXPEvent->data1+=MOUSE_Button1;
    }
}

// save the current mouse position so that we can check
// for mouse moves the next time through
_gMacPrevPt=pMacEvent->where;
```

There are few other things you might want to do that would make the behavior of the Macintosh mouse-moved event more Windows-like:

- Only send a mouse-moved event if the mouse has moved within the window pane area of the window (analogous to a WM_MOUSEMOVED message, which is only sent when the mouse moves in the client area of the window).

- Only send a mouse-moved event if the window handle of the previous saved point is the same as the current window handle.

EW_MMove

Description

EW_MMove is sent to a window handler when the mouse has moved.

Encoding

Macintosh
```
data1 = (UINT4)  u2Modifiers;
data2 = ((UINT4) s2y)<<16;
data2 += (UINT4) s2x;
```

Windows 3.1
```
data1 = (UINT2)  u2Modifiers;
data2 = ((UINT4) s2y)<<16;
data2 += (UINT4) s2x;
```

Win32
```
data1 = (UINT4)  u2Modifiers;
data2 = ((UINT4) s2y)<<16;
data2 += (UINT4) s2x;
```

Parameters

u2Modifiers is an unsigned 2-byte integer that contains a bit-field collection of mouse modifiers. The valid mouse modifiers are:

MOUSE_Button1	Indicates that the primary mouse button is down.
MOUSE_Button2	Indicates that the secondary mouse button is down.
MOUSE_Button3	Indicates that the tertiary mouse button is down.
MOUSE_Shift	Indicates that the Shift key is down.
MOUSE_Ctl	Indicates that the Control key is down.

s2x is a signed 2-byte integer that is the x value, in window pane coordinates, of the location of the mouse.

s2y is a signed 2-byte integer that is the y value, in window pane coordinates, of the location of the mouse.

Figure 7.10 Description of the cross-platform mouse-moved event.

Processing a Menu Selection

Next let's try something a little more complicated: converting a Macintosh mouseDown, inMenuBar event to the cross-platform EW_MenuBarInit and EW_Command sequence (recall, this emulates the behavior in Windows). We need to look at the description of the events and the encoding of the data1 and data2 parameters; EW_MenuBarInit is shown in Figure 7.11 and EW_Command is shown in Figure 7.12.

EW_MenuBarInit

Description

EW_MenuBarInit is generated when the user has clicked in the menu bar but before the item is highlighted or the menu list is displayed. This gives an application the chance to modify the contents and appearance of the menu before it is accessible to the user.

Encoding

Macintosh
```
data1 = (UINT4) hMenuBar;//4-byte handle
data2 is not used.
```

Windows 3.1
```
data1 = (UINT2) hMenuBar;//2-byte handle
data2 is not used.
```

Win32
```
data1 = (UINT4) hMenuBar;//4-byte handle
data2 is not used.
```

Parameters

hMenuBar is the handle to the menu bar where the item was selected.

Figure 7.11 Description of the cross-platform initialize menu bar event.

When a Macintosh event is retrieved from the queue, we need to call FindWindow() to determine the window in which the event occurred and the location of where the event occurred. If the user mouse downed in the menu bar, the window handle returned from FindWindow() will be NULL, so we need to call FrontWindow() to get the window handle (WindowPtr) of the front-most (top) window.

GetMenuBar() gives us the handle to the menu bar, and we're ready to synthesize our first cross-platform event, EW_MenuBarInit, by setting up the proper arguments to EventSend(). This causes the window handler for the window referenced by pXPEvent->hwnd to be called with the EW_MenuBarInit event message and the appropriate information.

When the EventSend() function returns, the window handler may (or may not) have modified the menu bar, so just to be sure we need to redraw it. Because GetMenuBar() gave us a handle to a copy of the menu bar, we need to get rid of it by calling DisposHandle(). And that ends the first part of the conversion process.

Now, we need to generate the EW_Command message. This process involves calling MenuSelect() to determine which menu list and menu item were selected. If no item was selected, we generate an E_Null message. If an item was selected, we set up the EVENT structure based on the encoding information in Figure 7.12. The last thing we need to do is to call HiliteMenu() to make sure the menu title is unhighlighted.

EW_Command

Description

EW_Command is generated when a menu item has been selected, when a control in a dialog has been used, when a keyboard equivalent to a menu item has been issued, or (for Windows only) when a keyboard equivalent to a dialog control has been issued.

Encoding

Macintosh
```
data1 = ((UINT4) u2NotificationCode)<<16;
data1 += (UINT4) u2id;
data2 = (UINT4) hControl;
```

Windows 3.1
```
data1 = (UINT2) u2id;
data2 = ((UINT4) hControl)<<16;
data2 += (UINT4) u2NotificationCode;
```

Win32
```
data1 = ((UINT4) u2NotificationCode)<16;
data1 += (UINT4) u2id;
data2 = (UINT4) hControl;
```

Parameters

u2id is an unsigned 2-byte identifier of a menu item, a control, or an accelerator (for Windows only).

u2NotificationCode is an unsigned 2-byte integer that is a notification code from a control if hControl is non-zero. u2NotificationCode is zero if the command message is from a menu and is 1 if the command message is from an accelerator (for Windows only).

hControl is a 2-byte handle to a control (in Windows 3.1) and a 4-byte handle to a control (in Win32 and the Macintosh). hControl is NULL if the command is not from a control.

Return Value

An application should return zero if it processes this message.

Figure 7.12 Description of the cross-platform command message.

```
//-------------------------------------------------------
// code sample convert a Macintosh mouseDown/inMenuBar
// to an EW_MenuBarInit and EW_Command sequence
//-------------------------------------------------------

// pMacEvent is a pointer to an EventRecord
// pXPEvent is a pointer to an EVENT structure
```

```
SINT2 s2Where=FindWindow (pMacEvent->where,
    &pXPEvent->hwnd);

switch (s2Where){

    case inMenuBar:
    {
        SINT4 s4MenuSelection;
        SINT2 s2Listid;
        SINT2 s2Itemid;
        Handle hMenuBar=GetMenuBar ();

        // winPtr will be NULL when mouseDown inMenuBar
        // so we assume menu action is for front window
        pXPEvent->hwnd=FrontWindow ();

        // send the EW_MenuBarInit message to the handler
        EventSend (pXPEvent->hwnd, EW_MenuBarInit,
            (UINT4)hMenuBar, 0L);

        // during the EventSend() the window handler
        // might have modified the menu bar, so we redraw it
        SetMenuBar (hMenuBar);
        DrawMenuBar ();
        DisposHandle (hMenuBar);

        // wait until the user has made a selection
        s4MenuSelection=MenuSelect (pMacEvent->where);

        //extract the menu list id
        s2Listid=HiWord (s4MenuSelection);
        //extract the menu item id
        s2Itemid=LoWord (s4MenuSelection);

        // user selected an item
        if (s2Listid && s2Itemid){
            pXPEvent->msg=EW_Command;
            pXPEvent->data1=(UINT2)(s2Listid+s2Itemid);
            pXPEvent->data2=0L;

        // user didn't select anything
        }else{
            pXPEvent->hwnd=0L;
            pXPEvent->msg=E_Null;
            pXPEvent->data1=0L;
```

```
            pXPEvent->data2=0L;
        }
        // make sure the menu is in an unselected state
        HiliteMenu (0);

        // the EW_Command message doesn't need to be sent
        // it will be dispatched by EventProcess()
    }
    break;

}// end of switch
```

Processing a Close Window Event

For our final example we'll try something even more complicated. It illustrates how the process of conversion can be spread out over various function calls, for example, the Macintosh event loop, the window handler function, and the destroy window function (in the cross-platform window manager).

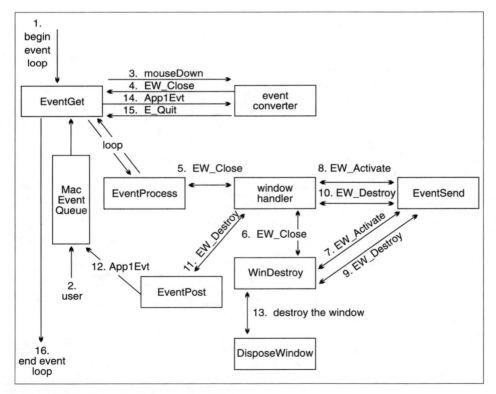

Figure 7.13 Complex event conversion process.

EW_Close

Description

EW_Close is generated in Windows when the user has selected the Close item in the System menu, or double-clicked the System menu icon; an EW_Close is generated in the Macintosh when the user clicks the close box. This event message precedes the actual destruction of the window. The WinDefHandler() function will perform a WinDestroy() in response to this message.

Encoding

Macintosh

There is no encoding for this event message.

Windows 3.1

There is no encoding for this event message.

Win32

There is no encoding for this event message.

Parameters

This event message has no parameters.

Figure 7.14 Description of the cross-platform close window event.

A flow chart illustrating the distributed conversion process, shown in Figure 7.13, shows that the Macintosh event loop can be entered more than once in the cross-platform event converstion process, the cross-platform window handler can be entered more than once, and a non-related function (destroy window) can be involved to send multiple cross-platform events to the handler.

Our example illustrates the processing involved to convert a Macintosh mouseDown, inGoAway event into a cross-platform sequence that will close and destroy the window (generating EW_Close, EW_Activate, and EW_Destroy messages) and terminate the application. Terminating the application isn't necessarily a process that you will associate with the destruction of a window, but we have included this to illustrate how the window handler can be used to link different event sequences together.

The information that we need to properly generate our events are shown in the descriptions of the EW_Close, EW_Activate, and EW_Destroy events in Figures 7.14 through 7.16.

Now, let's describe the conversion process. First we read a Macintosh event from the system queue. If the event indicates that a mouse down occurred, we use FindWindow() to determine where. If it occurred in the "go away" portion of the window, we wait until the mouse button is released. If the mouse is still inside the close box, we know that the user wants to close the window. We set our EVENT structure with the appropriate message (EW_Close) and return— EW_Close doesn't require a data1 or data2 value. The EW_Close message is dispatched by the EventProcess() function, which is called after we have converted the event.

EW_Activate

Description

EW_Activate is generated when a window is activated or deactivated.

Encoding

   Macintosh
```
data1 = (UINT4) s2ActivationCode;
data2 = (UINT4) hwnd;
```

   Windows 3.1
```
data1 = (UINT2) s2ActivationCode;
data2 = (UINT4) hwnd;
```

   Win32
```
data1 = (UINT4) s2ActivationCode;
data2 = (UINT4) hwnd;
```

Parameters

s2ActivationCode is a signed 2-byte integer that is zero if the window is being deactivated and is non-zero if the window is being activated. In Windows, there is some significance to the value of a non-zero activation code. Consult your Windows documentation for more information.

Figure 7.15 Description of the cross-platform activate window event.

EW_Destroy

Description

EW_Destroy is generated when a window is being destroyed, after the window is removed from the screen.

Encoding

   Macintosh

   There is no encoding for this event message.

   Windows 3.1

   There is no encoding for this event message.

   Win32

   There is no encoding for this event message.

Parameters

This event message has no parameters.

Figure 7.16 Description of the cross-platform destroy window event.

```
//--------------------------------------------------------
// code sample convert a Macintosh mouseDown/inGoAway
// to an EW_Close, EW_Activate, and EW_Destroy sequence
//--------------------------------------------------------

// pMacEvent is a pointer to an EventRecord
// pXPEvent is a pointer to an EVENT structure

switch (pMacEvent->what){

    case mouseDown:
    {
        SINT2 s2Where;

        s2Where=FindWindow (pMacEvent->where,
            &pXPEvent->hwnd);

        switch (s2Where){

            // user mouse downed in close box
            case inGoAway:
                // was mouse up still in close box?
                if (TrackGoAway (pXPEvent->hwnd,
                    pMacEvent->where)
                ){
                    pXPEvent->msg=EW_Close;
                }
            break;

        }
    }
    break;

    // process a request made to quit the application
    case app1Evt:
        switch(pMacEvent->message){
            case E_Quit:
                pXPEvent->msg=E_Quit;
                // time to quit the application
                return (FALSE);
            break;
        }
    break;
}

// normal exit (non-quit)
return (TRUE);
```

When the event that we return from EventGet() is processed by EventProcess(), the window handler associated with the indicated window is called. The switch statement in the handler function identifies the EW_Close event and proceeds to destroy the window using the WinDestroy() function.

```
HANDLERdecl MyWindowHandler (HWND hwnd, MSGDATA msg,
    DATA1 data1, DATA2 data2)
{
    switch (msg){

        case EW_Close:
            WinDestroy (hwnd);
            return (0);
        break;

        case EW_Destroy:
            EventPost (hwnd, E_Quit, 0L, 0L);
        break;
    }
}
```

But there are a few things that need to be done before the window is actually destroyed. To emulate the behavior of Windows, we need to generate an EW_Activate message to deactivate the window and an EW_Destroy message to find out if the handler wants us to do anything in response to the destruction of the window. We ignore the EW_Activate message in our example, but we have chosen to have the window handler instruct our application to quit when the window is destroyed by posting an E_Quit message.

This process actually posts an app1Evt to the Macintosh event queue with the E_Quit message attached, but this event isn't actually removed from the queue until some time later. The EventPost() function returns immediately after posting the event, we return from the handler function, and we're back in the WinDestroy() function. We finish up the destruction of the window by calling DisposeWindow().

Now remember WinDestroy() was called in the window handler, so we're back in the handler function in the EW_Close case statement. We exit the window handler again and now we're back in the EventProcess() function. We'll loop around in here until the quit message is removed from the queue. At that time, the Macintosh event, app1Evt, is read, and we check which cross-platform event was posted. If it's the E_Quit message, we exit the EventGet() function with the return value of FALSE. This instructs our cross-platform event loop to terminate, and the application as well.

```
VOID WinDestroy (HWND hwnd)
{
    EventSend (hwnd, EW_Activate, 0L, 0L);
    EventSend (hwnd, EW_Destroy, 0L, 0L);
    HideWindow (hwnd);
```

```
        // you'll want to destroy extra data at this point

        DisposeWindow (hwnd);
}
```

Let's summarize in this simulated function trace what happened when we converted the Macintosh mouseDown, inGoAway event to our EW_Close, EW_Activate, EW_Destroy sequence:

```
XPMain
    XPInit
    EventGet-->mouseDown, inGoAway
        convert to cross-platform -> EW_Close
        return TRUE
    EventProcess
        window handler: EW_Close
            WinDestroy
                window handler: EW_Activate
                window handler: EW_Destroy
                    EventPost: E_Quit
                destroy the window
    EventGet
        no event
        return TRUE
    EventProcess

    EventGet -> app1Evt: E_Quit
        convert to cross-platform -> return FALSE
    XPExit
```

This was a complicated event conversion process. Once you understand how the EventGet(), EventProcess(), window handler, and window management functions interact, the other Macintosh events can be converted into event sequences that emulate Windows without too much trouble.

Decoding Functions

Several event messages include additional information that is encoded in the data1 and data2 parameters received by the window handling procedure. Alas, the three platforms do not necessarily encode this information in the same way. There are some facilities in Windows to hide the Windows 3.1 and Win32 inconsistencies, called "message crackers." We ignore them for our discussion because they only hide the issues that we are trying to describe. Another approach is to write to the Win32s specification, which is common to both Windows 3.1 and Windows NT.

Because we have generated all events in the Macintosh implementation by translating Macintosh events into Windows events, all decoding is dependent on the encoding that we have previously devised. Because there are some similarities in data types between the Macintosh and Windows NT (for example, handles are 32-bit data types, even though they don't represent the same things), we have opted to use the Win32 encoding of information whenever possible.

The Command Message

The EW_Command message can contain various pieces of information, including:

- the identifier of the control or menu item that was selected or used
- the handle of the control
- the notification code (submessage) returned by a control

Unfortunately the three platforms do not encode this information in the same way. (Acually, in this instance the Macintosh and Win32 implementations are the same, but the Windows 3.1 implementation is different.) Figure 7.12 describes the EW_Command in more detail and presents the encoding of information in the data1 and data2 parameters. Our EDecodeCommand() function requires the data1 and data2 values that were passed in to the window handler, a pointer to a 2-byte integer to receive the notification code (if the command is from a control), and a pointer to a handle to receive the control handle that caused the notification. EDecodeCommand() returns the 2-byte identifier of the control or menu item that caused the EW_Command event message to be sent.

```
//------------------------------------------------------
UINT2 EDecodeCommand (DATA1 data1, DATA2 data2,
    PUINT2 pu2Note, HANDLE *phControl)
//------------------------------------------------------
// data1   - data1 parameter from the window handler
// data2   - data2 parameter from the window handler
// pu2Note - pointer to a 2-byte unsigned integer to
//           receive the notification code (if control)
// phControl - pointer to a HANDLE to receive the control
//             handle if the command is from a control
// RETURNS - unsigned 2-byte identifier of the control
//           or menu item that issued the command
//------------------------------------------------------
{
    // this routine assumes that an EW_Command message
    // was received
```

In the Macintosh and Win32, because the data1 and data2 values are set up the same way, we can use the same code to decode the command information. The notification code is in the high word of the data1 parameter, the handle to the control is in the data2 parameter (the Macintosh and Win32 have 4-byte handles), and the control or menu id is in the lower word of the data1 parameter.

```
*pu2Note=(UINT2)HIWORD (data1);
*phControl=(HANDLE)data2;
return ((UINT2)data1);
```

In Windows 3.1 things are bit different. Handles are 2 bytes and the data1 parameter is 2 bytes. The notification code is in the high word of the data2 parameter, the handle to the control is in lower word of the data2 parameter (Windows 3.1 has 2-byte handles), and the control or menu id is in the data1 parameter.

```
*pu2Note=(UINT2)HIWORD (data2);
*phControl=(HANDLE)LOWORD (data2);
return (data1);
```

That's all there is to it.

```
}
```

The Scroll Messages

Some other event messages that encode information are the EW_ScrollH and EW_ScrollV messages. These messages encode:

- the identifier of the scroll bar part that was used
- the handle of the scroll bar
- the position of the scroll bar slider

This information is encoded in the data1 and data2 values provided to the window handler. Our EDecodeScroll() function requires a pointer to a 2-byte signed integer to receive the position of the control, requires a pointer to a handle to receive the handle of the scroll bar, and returns the scroll bar part.

```
//-------------------------------------------------------
UINT2 EDecodeScroll (DATA1 data1, DATA2 data2,
   PUINT2 ps2Pos, HANDLE *phControl)
//-------------------------------------------------------
// data1    - data1 parameter from the window handler
// data2    - data2 parameter from the window handler
// ps2Pos   - pointer to a 2-byte unsigned integer to
//              receive the position of the control
// phControl - pointer to a HANDLE to receive the handle
//                of the control
// RETURNS  - signed 2-byte identifier of the part of
//              scroll bar that the user clicked
//-------------------------------------------------------
{
   // this routine assumes that an EW_ScrollV or an
   // EW_ScrollH message was received
```

In the Macintosh and Win32 the information is encoded in the same way. The handle of the scroll bar is 4 bytes and contained in the data2 parameter, the most-significant word of data1 contains the position of the scroll bar, and the least-significant word of data1 contains the id of the scroll bar part that caused the message.

```
// get the handle of the control
*phControl=(HANDLE)data2;

// get the position of the control
*ps2Pos=HIWORD (data1);

// get the control's id and return it
return ((SINT2)LOWORD (data1));
```

In Windows 3.1 the scroll bar handle is in the most-significant word of data2, the scroll bar position is in the least-significant word of data2, and the id of the scroll bar part that caused the message is in data1.

```
// get the handle of the control
*phControl=(HANDLE)HIWORD (data2);

// get the position of the control
*ps2Pos=LOWORD (data2);

// get the control's id and return it
return ((SINT2)data1);
```

And that's how horizontal or vertical scroll bar messages are decoded.

```
}
```

Keyboard Events

Before we get into virtual keys, let's talk a bit about keyboard encoding in general. Figures 7.17 through 7.19 illustrate the basics of processing keyboard information on the Macintosh, Windows 3.1, and Win32, respectively. Notice that the Macintosh and Windows keyboard processes share two common descriptions of keyboard encoding: key code and character code.

A key code is a number that represents the physical key. In the Macintosh it is called the key code and in Windows it is called a scan code. The meaning of a particular key code value differs with different keyboards.

A character code is a number that represents the character associated with a key or combination of keys (for example, SHIFT-A or ALT-SHIFT-1). There are different character encodings that can be used. The Macintosh supports the standard Roman character set and other double-byte character sets using Scripts. Windows supports the OEM character set (DOS characters) and the ANSI character set. Win32 adds the Unicode character encoding specification.

Windows also adds the virtual key code, which is common numeric representation for certain types of keys across keyboard configurations. It allows you to process key stroke information

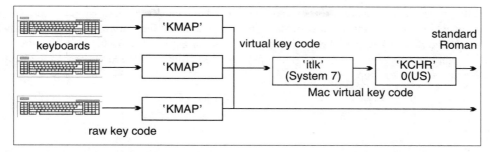

Figure 7.17 Macintosh key process.

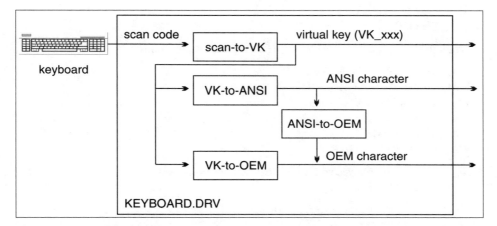

Figure 7.18 Windows 3.1 key process.

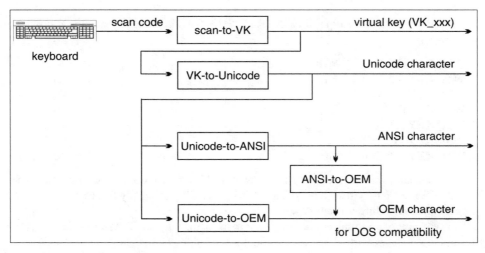

Figure 7.19 Win32 key process.

different from the encoding of key strokes into character sets. Windows uses the VK_xxx nomenclature to reference symbolically certain virtual keys, for example, VK_SHIFT always means the SHIFT key regardless what the scan code might be for a particular keyboard.

Virtual key codes are sent in response to user interaction with the keyboard. In the simplest Windows message loop:

```
while (GetMessage (&msg, NULL, NULL, NULL)){
    DispatchMessage (&msg);
}
```

The following sequence of events are generated and sent to the appropriate window handler routine when the user types the A key:

WM_KEYDOWN: A
WM_KEYUP: A

When the user types a CONTROL-SHIFT-A, the system sends:

WM_KEYDOWN: CONTROL
WM_KEYDOWN: SHIFT
WM_KEYDOWN: A
WM_KEYUP: A
WM_KEYUP: SHIFT
WM_KEYUP: CONTROL

Now in the normal message loop virtual key codes are also translated into character codes. This loop looks like this:

```
while (GetMessage (&msg, NULL, NULL, NULL)){
    TranslateMessage (&msg);
    DispatchMessage (&msg);
}
```

As a result, if the user types a CONTROL-SHIFT-A, the system sends the following to the window handler:

WM_KEYDOWN: CONTROL
WM_KEYDOWN: SHIFT
WM_KEYDOWN: A
WM_CHAR: A
WM_KEYUP: A
WM_KEYUP: SHIFT
WM_KEYUP: CONTROL

The TranslateMessage() function adds a WM_CHAR message to the message stream between a WM_KEYDOWN (virtual key A) and a WM_KEYUP (virtual key A). This message includes the character encoding for the 'A' key.

This concept of a virtual key doesn't exist in the same way on the Macintosh. The cross-platform (à la Windows) virtual key code implies knowledge of which keys correspond to extended keys (numeric keypad). Some virtual keys correspond to their character set encodings too, for

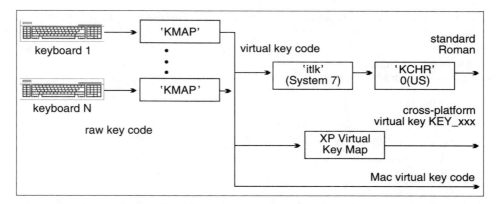

Figure 7.20 Our cross-platform Macintosh key process.

example, VK_A should have the value of 65. The information sent as a Macintosh virtual key code refers to a representation of the raw key information that differentiates between right and left SHIFT, OPTION, and CONTROL keys. This means we need to translate from a Macintosh virtual key code to a cross-platform–type virtual key. Figure 7.20 shows the relationship of this virtual-key conversion with respect to the rest of the Macintosh key process.

Appendix B contains a list of cross-platform virtual key representations and a comparison of virtual keys in Windows.

EVENT SUMMARY

There are many things to consider when you design a cross-platform event system. It is probably the most detail-intensive aspect of a cross-platform solution. You need to ask yourself a few questions before you start:

- What event capability is necessary in your application?
- What event capability is desirable?
- What event solutions are possible relative to the platforms?

I have chosen to model my event solution on Windows. You could choose to model yours after Macintosh or somewhere in between. Porting one platform's event model to another is probably simpler than finding a solution somewhere in the middle. A midway solution involves modifying the event model of two or more platforms. Choosing one platform's model as the cross-platform model allows you to limit the problems of implementation to one less platform. In our case, because Windows 3.1 and Win32 share a common event model (even though the underlying event architectures are different), our three-platform event solution involves only producing code for one platform.

It is probably a good idea to come back to this chapter after you have read the rest of this book. Many of the details of writing a cross-platform event manager will become clearer after you understand more of the issues involved in developing a cross-platform API.

Also, now that you've seen the process of porting the Windows event model to the Macintosh, it isn't outrageous to consider a cross-platform event solution that is identical to Windows. This means that we rename all cross-platform events to the corresponding Windows names and support many of the messages and message sequences that occur in Windows.

In general other areas to consider that would improve the cross-platform solution are:

- supporting a larger subset of events
- providing more thorough support of event sequences
- providing more thorough event decoding
- supporting more notification codes from controls
- supporting interprocess events

These topics are discussed in more detail in Improving Event Support in Chapter 18.

8

Graphics

There are three categories of functions that you must support in your cross-platform API: graphics, text, and bitmaps. In this chapter, we will address graphics, that is, graphical objects such as lines, circles, rectangles, and polygons. We will look at some of the problems of implementing a cross-platform graphics solution by comparing features of graphics objects on all three platforms and then implementing some of the essential graphics functions to illustrate how you might implement your own set of graphics functions.

DEFINING COMMON GRAPHICS CAPABILITIES

The process of defining a cross-platform graphics solution is not as difficult as it is tedious. You need to learn as much as you can about how graphics objects are drawn on the three platforms. This means you need to:

- compare the graphics functionality of each platform
- compare the differences in fill designations
- compare the different rendering models
- consider the differences between the screen and the printer

Once you understand the differences and similarities, implementing the functions to do the work is straightforward.

169

Table 8.1 Graphics terminology.

Term	Macintosh	Windows
draw space	GrafPort	device context (DC)
stroke	pen	pen
fill	pattern	brush
draw space coordinate	local coordinate	logical coordinate
screen coordinate	global coordinate	device coordinate

Comparing Basic Graphics Terminology

Let's begin by defining some cross-platform graphics terminology and compare it to the equivalent terminology on the Macintosh and Windows, as listed in Table 8.1. The most important thing to note here is the term "draw space," which is coined as the cross-platform equivalent to the GrafPort or DC. The draw space is the area where all of the drawing to a window or to a printer occurs. The draw space is an arbitrarily large area that is a superset of the display or printable area.

The stroke is used to draw the border of an object or to connect two points. The fill is applied to the interior of a closed object. A draw space coordinate gives the location of a point in the draw space. A screen coordinate gives the location of a point on the screen.

Comparing Basic Graphics API Functions

Table 8.2 illustrates how some common graphics functions map to the equivalent function or functions on the Macintosh and Windows. Most graphics objects are represented by reasonably equivalent functions on all platforms, but as you move to more complicated types of graphics, the differences become more problematic. Look at the way a rectangle is drawn on all three platforms; then look at how a polygon is drawn.

You will notice that there are no entries in our functional map for arcs, pies, chords, and wedges. These types of graphics objects don't have equivalent representations across platforms (if at all). They are complicated to implement and do little to illustrate the basic issues of cross-platform graphics functionality.

Extracting Common Fill Patterns

Table 8.3 compares some of the standard fill patterns that are available on the Macintosh and Windows. We limit our cross-platform selection of fill patterns to this small subset of possible fills. We ignore the other Windows stock brushes, we do not allow custom fill patterns to be created or used, and we ignore the foreground and background colors (which we assume are black and white). On the Macintosh, we ignore the standard PixPat fills of Color QuickDraw. This simplifies the Macintosh implementation and allows the cross-platform solution to span the largest cross section of Macintosh systems.

Table 8.2 Comparison of graphics functions across platforms.

Function	Macintosh	Windows 3.1	Win32
move to	MoveTo	MoveTo or MoveToEx	MoveToEx
line to	LineTo	LineTo	LineTo
rectangle	FillRect FrameRect	Rectangle	Rectangle
round-corner rectangle	FillRoundRect FrameRoundRect	RoundRect	RoundRect
getting the current point	GetPen	GetCurrentPosition or GetCurrentPositionEx*	GetCurrentPositionEx
ellipse	FillOval FrameOval	Ellipse	Ellipse
polygon	OpenPoly MoveTo LineTo ClosePoly FillPoly FramePoly KillPoly	Polygon	Polygon
polyline	OpenPoly MoveTo LineTo ClosePoly FramePoly KillPoly	Polyline	Polyline
setting the current stroke	PenSize	GetStockObject CreatePen SelectObject	GetStockObject CreatePen SelectObject
getting the current stroke	GetPenState	GetObject	
setting the current fill	NA	GetStockObject SelectObject	GetStockObject SelectObject
getting the current fill	NA	GetObject	GetObject
inverting a rectangle	InvertRect	InvertRect	InvertRect
scrolling the drawing area	ScrollRect	ScrollWindow	ScrollWindow
getting the origin	NA	GetWindowOrg or GetWindowOrgEx	GetWindowOrgEx
setting the origin	SetOrigin	SetWindowOrg or SetWindowOrgEx	SetWindowOrgEx
invalidate rect	InvalRect	InvalidateRect	InvalidateRect
validate rect	ValidRect	ValidateRect	ValidateRect

* This function is not available in Windows 3.0.

Table 8.3 Comparison of standard fill patterns across platforms.

Pattern	Macintosh	Windows
None	NA*	NULL_BRUSH
White	white	WHITE_BRUSH
Black	black	BLACK_BRUSH
Gray	gray	GRAY_BRUSH
Light Gray	ltGray	LTGRAY_BRUSH
Dark Gray	dkGray	DKGRAY_BRUSH

* On the Macintosh there is no explicit null fill pattern. To perform a null fill, on the Macintosh, don't call the QuickDraw function that performs the fill. For example, look at how a rectangle is stroked with the current pen and filled with a gray pattern:

```
// set up the fill pattern and fill the rectangle
PenPat (gray);
PaintRect (&macRect, gray);
// set up the pen pattern and stroke the rectangle
PenPat (black);
FrameRect (&macRect);
```

The filling operation is called first because it fills the entire rectangle without regard to the width of the pen. The stroke will overwrite the filled area based on the pen width, pen pattern, and pen transfer mode (which we assume to be "copy"). Removing the call to PaintRect() prevents the rectangle from being filled.

In general, providing only standard fill patterns limits the functionality provided by the cross-platform solution, but it also greatly simplifies the implementation. If you are going to produce an application that is graphics intensive, you will want to expand on the cross-platform fill model.

> *Note: Gray fill patterns do not always appear the same across platforms, within a platform on different screens, or between screen and printer representations. On some platforms fill patterns can be small (usually 8 pixel by 8 pixel bitmaps), which are used to fill the interior space of closed objects. Consequently, the printed version of these fills can appear denser—this type of fill is always rendered in a pixel-for-pixel way (one screen pixel maps to one printer pixel). This also causes problems if different platforms have displays with different resolutions. Higher resolution displays make gray patterns appear darker than they do on lower resolution displays.*
>
> *Sometimes bitmap versions of gray fills on the screen are rendered as bitmaps but are printed as halftones. Rendering the same gray as a halftone can also produce inconsistent results when printed on different printers. Halftones can be rendered using different algorithms, with different halftone resolutions (screen frequencies), and with different printer resolutions (dots per inch). This can cause some grays on one printer to appear darker or lighter on other printers.*

Let's look at the attributes of a fill:

- pattern
- foreground color
- background color
- transfer operation

In this book and in XPLib we consider only simple patterns with a white background and a black foreground color. We have also assumed that all fills are transferred using a copy-type operation—all pixels behind the fill are obscured. There is a lot of room to improve this type of fill operation. Simple additions include specifying percentages of gray, simple coloration, and support for some basic transfer operations (OR, XOR, for example). If you want to get fancy, you could support custom patterns, custom RGB or other types of colors, and transfer operations that allow you to portray transparent fills and blends.

Comparing the Graphics Rendering Models

The Macintosh uses a stroke that is defined as a rectangular area that hangs down from and to the right of the mathematical point, as illustrated in Figure 8.1. This simple model causes some trouble when you are drawing lines at shallow or steep angles—the end caps of the lines aren't consistently rendered. Another problem, which is especially noticable at 45-degree increments from the x and y axes, is that the width of the line grows by the square root of 2, or 1.414. This produces a line that gets progressively thicker as you move toward the 45- degree point. For our purposes we ignore this annoying feature. If you want to correct it, you will have to modify the dimensions of the pen, based on the angle of the line you are drawing. Finally, when a

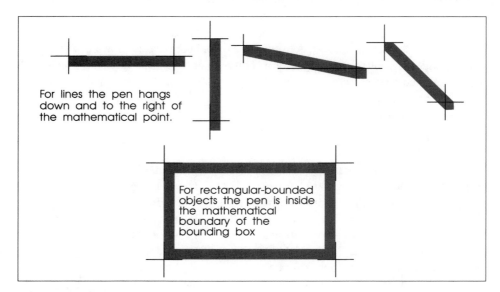

Figure 8.1 Macintosh rendering model.

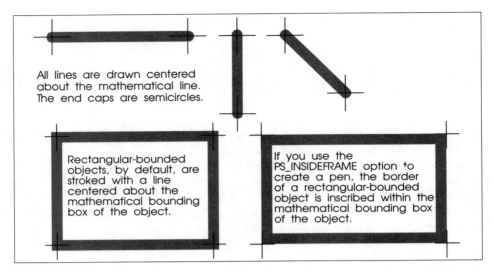

Figure 8.2 Windows rendering model.

rectangular-bounded object is drawn on the Macintosh, the stroke is applied toward the inside of the bounding box (also shown in Figure 8.1).

Windows uses a rendering technique that assumes that the stroke (pen) is round and that the line is drawn centered about the mathematical line that defines it, as illustrated in Figure 8.2. In Windows this technique is also used to draw compound line objects such as polygons or polylines. When Windows renders a rectangular-based object, there are two different ways the stroke can be applied: centered or inside the bounding box. Also, there are no round end caps applied when the border of a rectangular object is drawn.

In addition Windows allows various mapping modes (scalings) to provide a scale to the logical coordinates of the device context. A list of these mapping modes is shown in Table 8.4.

To provide a reasonable cross-platform solution, you will need to decide which model you want to use and have the cross-platform implementation for the other platform map from the

Table 8.4 Windows scaling factors.

Mapping Mode	*Logical Unit*	*Coordinate System*
MM_TEXT	1 unit = 1 pixel	4th quadrant
MM_LOENGLISH	1 unit = .01 inch	1st quadrant
MM_HIENGLISH	1 unit = .001 inch	1st quadrant
MM_LOMETRIC	1 unit = .1 mm	1st quadrant
MM_HIMETRIC	1 unit = .01 mm	1st quadrant
MM_TWIPS	1 unit = 1/1440 inch	1st quadrant
MM_ISOTROPIC	1 unit x = 1 unit y	any quadrant
MM_ANISOTROPIC	1 unit = anything	any quadrant

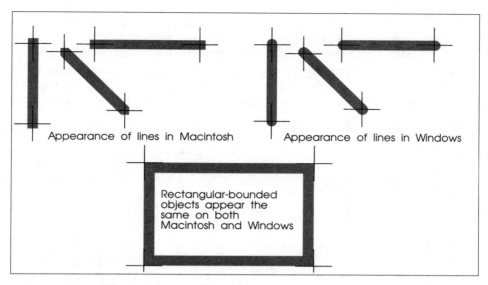

Figure 8.3 Cross-platform rendering model.

chosen rendering model to its rendering model. In this book and the XPLib software, I have chosen the Windows rendering model as the basis for the cross-platform model and the Macintosh local coordinate system. This means that we need to do three things:

- We must shift a Macintosh point by half of the pen width to the left and by half of the pen height upward, as illustrated in Figure 8.3.

- In Windows we must use the MM_TEXT (the default) mapping mode. This provides a coordinate system that is equivalent to the Macintosh local coordinate system, which is a 4th quadrant coordinate system where the logical unit of measure is a pixel. This means x increases to the right and y increases downward.

- Use the PS_INSIDEFRAME option when we create a pen in Windows. This ensures us that any closed, rectangular-based shapes (rectangles and ellipses, for example) are rendered equivalently on the Macintosh and Windows. For simplicity we will ignore any inconsistencies when rendering odd- and even-width lines and any inconsistencies with the placement of lines on even- and odd-pixel boundaries. Examples using the cross-platform rendering model are shown in Figure 8.3.

Don't Forget Printing

What happens when you print your elaborate graphics? That depends on the rendering model that your program uses. You must consider three types of screen-to-printer rendering models:

- pixel-for-pixel
- screen-based
- printer-based

Pixel-for-pixel rendering is the simplest to implement. The resolutions of the screen and the printer are ignored. If the resolution of the printer is two times that of the screen, the printed version will be one half the size of the screen version.

The screen-based rendering model is more difficult to implement than the pixel-for-pixel solution, but it gives you a printed version that is the same size as the screen version. During printing the coordinate values are scaled by the ratio between the printer to screen resolutions:

printer coordinate value = screen coordinate value * (printer res / screen res)

A printer-based model is computationally as complicated as a screen-based solution. The difference is that during the screen drawing process using the printer-based rendering model, the program must know the printer resolution so that it can scale the screen coordinates accordingly.

screen coordinate value = printer coordinate value * (screen res / printer res)

Another difference between the screen-based model and the printer-based model is that with the printer-based model, you need to query the printer for its resolution when your program starts up and you need to modify the printer resolution if the user changes the printer during the course of his or her work so the screen version can be redrawn. In a screen-based solution you don't have to worry about the user changing screens during the course of using your program. (However, on the Macintosh there are some special considerations that need to be taken if you want to support multiple screens.)

In the following examples we will use the pixel-for-pixel rendering model. This keeps the examples simple. The XPLib software uses the screen-based model, which allows the items on a printed page to be the same size as the items on the screen, without requiring all of the work to implement a printer-based rendering solution.

IMPLEMENTING A GRAPHICS SOLUTION

Once we know what the rules for rendering the graphics are and the features that we are going to support, we can concentrate on implementing the graphics functions. The process of implementing a cross-platform graphics API involves:

- defining data structures
- defining global variables and constants
- defining function definitions

Data Structures for Graphics

The cross-platform POINT and RECT data structures were defined in Chapter 4 in the Basic Cross-Platform Data Types section. In addition, we define the draw space (DSP) structure to represent a two-dimensional drawing space in which all drawing occurs. It maps to a GrafPort in the Macintosh (see Table 8.5) and to a device context (DC) in Windows (see Table 8.6). It

Table 8.5 The Macintosh draw space (DSP) structure.

Type	Field Name	Description
SINT2	s2Fill	index of the current cross-platform fill for this DSP
BOOL2	b2Print	TRUE if this is a printer port; FALSE otherwise
HWND	hwnd	handle to the window that owns the DSP (actually maps to a WindowPtr); NULL if the DSP refers to a printer
GrafPtr	pport	pointer to the GrafPort or pointer to a printer port if b2Print is TRUE
GrafPtr	pPrevPort	pointer to previous GrafPort or printer port

maintains the information necessary to render the output to the screen or the printer. A DSP structure is required by all cross-platform graphics and text functions.

When a window receives a redraw message, it is instructed to redraw its contents. This is done by accessing the draw space that is tied to the window and then calling an application-specific function that performs the drawing. When the user wants to print the contents of a window, a suitable printer draw space is created and the same drawing function is called. This redirects all drawing operations to the printer.

The DSP structure is a convenient way to hide platform differences and to add some extra information that makes it easier to provide equivalent graphics capabilities on all platforms.

Necessary Graphics Global Variables and Constants

Because we have limited the scope of the graphics solution to include only the most basic fill patterns, we can provide a simple indexed method of referencing fill patterns on both platforms. On the Macintosh we declare a global variable to contain the list of standard fill patterns:

```
Pattern _gpatMacFillList[6];
```

In Windows we define a variable that contains a list of the standard Windows brush identifiers:

```
SINT _gsWinFillList[6];
```

Both of the fill lists must be initialized with fill patterns in the same order, so we can reference a platform-specific fill using a cross-platform index. We define these indices as:

Table 8.6 The Windows draw space (DSP) structure.

Type	Field Name	Description
SINT2	s2Fill	index of the current cross-platform fill for this DSP
BOOL2	b2Print	TRUE if this is a printer DC; FALSE otherwise
HWND	hwnd	the handle to the window that owns the DSP
HDC	hdc	handle to the device context where the rendering will be directed

```
enum {
   GFILL_None,
   GFILL_Black, GFILL_White,
   GFILL_DarkGray, GFILL_Gray, GFILL_LightGray
};
```

Graphics Functionality

Our implementation of cross-platform graphics functions include:

- setting (moving to) the current point
- getting the current point
- drawing a line from the current point using the current stroke
- drawing a rectangle using the current stroke and fill
- getting and setting the stroke
- getting and setting the fill
- invalidating a rectangular area of a draw space

Setting the Current Point

When you are drawing a line, you need to specify two end points, which are usually specified in two steps: a "move to" the first point and a "line to" the second point. The "move to" sets the current point, which is maintained by the draw space (the GrafPort or the DC). A "line to" draws a line from the current point to the point specified by the "line to."

The first graphics function, GMoveTo(), sets the current point. It requires a pointer to a draw space and the x and y values of the coordinate that will become the current point.

```
//----------------------------------------------------
ERR GMoveTo (PDSP pdsp, SINT sx, SINT sy)
//----------------------------------------------------
// pdsp    - pointer to a draw space
// sx      - x value of the coordinate to move to
// sy      - y value of the coordinate to move to
// RETURNS - currently always returns ERR_No (success)
//----------------------------------------------------
{
```

In the Macintosh the simplest way to set the current point is by using the QuickDraw MoveTo() function. However, we can't just pass the cross-platform coordinate values and maintain a consistent drawing behavior across platforms. Because the Macintosh pen hangs down and to the right of the mathematical point, you have to compensate by moving the point up and to the left by half the pen dimension. So, before we actually call the MoveTo() function, we need to get the pen dimension by calling GetPenState(). The pnSize.h and pnSize.v fields contain the width and height of the pen.

Notice that we do not save the current port and call SetPort() before doing our work. That is because we assume that redraws use the WinPaneDraw() function (described in Chapter 14) or that dynamic drawing is bracketed inside of WinPaneOpen() and WinPaneClose() functions (XPLib functions), which ensure that the proper port is set before drawing operations are performed.

```
PenState _macPenState;
// Get the current pen state so that we can get
// the dimensions of the pen
GetPenState (&_macPenState);
// Modify the point to compensate for the Macintosh
// pen hang
MoveTo (sx-_macPenState.pnSize.h/2,
    sy-_macPenState.pnSize.v/2);
```

In Windows 3.1 we simply call MoveTo() with the HDC from our draw space and the x and y values supplied to GMoveTo(). Actually there is a newer API call in Windows 3.1, MoveToEx(), which is also available in the Win32 API, illustrated in the Win32 code sample. Unless you need to provide Windows 3.0 compatibility, you can use the new function instead of MoveTo().

```
MoveTo (pdsp->hdc, sx, sy);
```

In Win32 we use the new GDI call, MoveToEx(). The first three parameters are the same as in the MoveTo() function for Windows 3.1. The last parameter can be a pointer to a POINT if we want to retrieve the current point or NULL if we don't.

```
MoveToEx (pdsp->hdc, sx, sy, NULL);
```

Currently this function is always successful.

```
return (ERR_No);
}
```

Drawing a Line from the Current Point

After you specify the current point with a call to GMoveTo(), you can draw a line using the current stroke setting with a call to GLineTo(). This function requires a pointer to a draw space and the x and y values of the coordinate that the line will be drawn to. This point becomes the current point after the drawing operations is complete.

```
//----------------------------------------------------
ERR GLineTo (PDSP pdsp, SINT sx, SINT sy)
//----------------------------------------------------
// pdsp    - pointer to a draw space
// sx      - x value of the coordinate to draw a line to
// sy      - y value of the coordinate to draw a line to
// RETURNS - currently always returns ERR_No (success)
//----------------------------------------------------
{
```

In the Macintosh we need to adjust the position of the end point of the line in the same way we modified the start point: using GetPenState() to get the stroke dimensions and then modifying the point by one half the width and height of the pen dimensions before calling LineTo() to draw the line.

```
PenState _macPenState;
// Get the current pen state so that we can get
// the dimensions of the pen
GetPenState (&_macPenState);
// Modify the point to compensate for the Macintosh
// pen hang
LineTo (sx-(_macPenState.pnSize.h/2),
    sy-(_macPenState.pnSize.v/2));
```

In Windows 3.1 and Win32 under Windows NT, the process of drawing a line is the same: a line is drawn from the current point to the point specified by sx and sy.

```
LineTo (pdsp->hdc, sx, sy);
```

This function always returns indicating the line was drawn successfully.

```
    return (ERR_No);
}
```

Getting the Current Point

The current point is maintained by the draw space (either the GrafPort or the DC). GCurrentPt() retrieves the current point and returns it to us in the POINT structure that is referenced by ppt. If the current point was retrieved and the pointer we supplied is valid, this function returns the pointer that we supplied. If there was an error, this function returns a NULL.

```
//----------------------------------------------------
PPOINT GCurrentPt (PDSP pdsp, PPOINT ppt)
//----------------------------------------------------
// pdsp -    pointer to a draw space
// ppt  -    pointer to a POINT structure that will
//           receive the current point
// RETURNS - the value of ppt or NULL if unsuccessful
//----------------------------------------------------
{
    // do some simple error checking
    if (!ppt) return (NULL);
```

In the Macintosh the current point is maintained in the GrafPort in the pnLoc field. We retrieve this location with the GetPen() function, and we then copy the Macintosh point information into our cross-platform POINT form.

```
    {
    Point _macPt;
```

```
GetPen (&_macPt);
PointSet (ppt, _macPt.h, _macPt.v);
}
```

In Windows 3.1 the current point is maintained by the DC and we retrieve the point with the GetCurrentPosition() function. This function returns the coordinates of the current point packed in a 4-byte return value, which we need to copy to the provided POINT structure. Windows 3.1 provides another function—GetCurrentPositionEx()—which allows us to supply a pointer to a POINT. You can use GetCurrentPointEx() if you don't need to be compatible with Windows 3.0.

Note that the copy of the packed point information returned by GetCurrentPosition() assumes that a cross-platform point is a Windows 3.1 POINT and contains 2-byte coordinate values. If you want to extend the cross-platform point values to 4 bytes across all platforms, you must explicitly copy the x and y values of the current point values.

```
{
SINT4 s4Pt=GetCurrentPosition (pdsp->hdc);
// Copy over the current point from 4-byte form to
// point form.
*ppt=*((PPOINT)&s4Pt);
}
```

In Win32 we use the GetCurrentPositionEx() function, which allows us to supply a pointer to a Windows POINT structure that is to receive the current position. Because our cross-platform point and the Windows POINT structure are the same, we just pass on the pointer that is provided to us.

```
if (!GetCurrentPositionEx (pdsp->hdc, ppt)){
    return (NULL);
}
```

When we're done, we return the pointer to the POINT that was supplied to us.

```
    return (ppt);
}
```

Drawing a Rectangle

The next type of graphics object we need to abstract for cross-platform use is a rectangle. Actually, all objects specified by a rectangular bounding box—round-corner rectangles, ellipses, and inverted rectangles—are implemented in a very similar way. Our function for drawing a rectangle, GRect(), needs a pointer to a draw space in which the rectangle will be rendered and two points that indicate the top-left and bottom-right corners of the rectangle. The resulting rectangle is drawn with the current stroke and fill pattern.

We specify the bounds of the rectangle a bit differently than what you are probably familiar with in QuickDraw or GDI. We allow the caller to provide GRect() with the rectangle information in two forms: as two distinct points or as a rectangle. If ppt2 is NULL, the function assumes that the first pointer points to a rectangle instead of a point.

```
//-------------------------------------------------------
ERR GRect (PDSP pdsp, PPOINT ppt1, PPOINT ppt2)
//-------------------------------------------------------
// pdsp      - pointer to a draw space
// ppt1      - pointer to a POINT structure that contains
//              the top-left corner or a pointer to a RECT
//              structure if ppt2 is NULL
// ppt2      - pointer to a POINT structure that contains
//              the bottom-right corner
// RETURNS - the value of ppt or NULL if unsuccessful
//-------------------------------------------------------
{
```

In the Macintosh you specify a rectangular object with a pointer to a Rect structure. In addition you perform the stroke and fill of the rectangle in two steps. In our implementation we fill the rectangle before we frame it. This allows us to draw the frame of the rectangle using the same bounding box that we used to fill it—the stroke is applied over the top of the fill. You can also fill the rectangle in two ways: using PaintRect(), which uses the current fill pattern and mode of the current GrafPort, or using FillRect(), which always fills using the copy (overwrite) mode with the pattern that we specify. We opted to use FillRect() in our implementation.

```
Rect _macRect;
PRECT prect;
if (ppt2){
    SetRect (&_macRect, ppt1->x, ppt1->y, ppt2->x,
        ppt2->y);
}else{
    prect=(PRECT)ppt1;
    SetRect (&_macRect, prect->left, prect->top,
        prect->right, prect->bottom);
}
if (pdsp->s2Fill!=GFILL_None){
    FillRect (&_macRect,
        _gpatMacFillList[pdsp->s2Fill]);
}
FrameRect (&_macRect);
```

In Windows 3.1 and Win32 you create rectangular objects by specifying the left, top, right, and bottom coordinate values as parameters to the function. The translation from cross-platform parameters to Windows requires accessing the fields of the POINT structures or the RECT structure. The current stroke and fill pattern (the currently selected pen and brush objects) are applied when the rectangle is rendered.

```
PRECT prect;

if (ppt2){
    Rectangle (pdsp->hdc, ppt1->x, ppt1->y,
```

```
        ppt2->x, ppt2->y);
   }else{
      prect=(PRECT)ppt1;
      Rectangle (pdsp->hdc, prect->left, prect->top,
         prect->right, prect->bottom);
   }
```

This function always returns indicating the rectangle was drawn successfully.

```
   return (ERR_No);
}
```

Setting the Stroke

The stroke, or pen, determines how a line, a polyline, or the border to an enclosed graphic object is rendered. Some of the common attributes of a stroke are listed in Table 8.7.

We will consider monochrome strokes with variable widths (but with the same x and y dimensions) that are rendered using a copy transfer operation. The default end cap on the Macintosh is defined by the way a line is rendered from point A to point B, as illustrated earlier in Figure 8.3. The default end cap in Windows is a semicircle with its center at the end point and is also illustrated in Figure 8.3. Win32 allows more flexibility in the type of end cap, line join, and miter limit. However, because these capabilities are not available in the Macintosh or Windows 3.1, we will ignore them. Our Win32 implementation will use only the Windows 3.1 subset.

Our function for setting the stroke, GStrokeSet(), requires a draw space that will maintain the stroke information and the dimension of the stroke (the width and height of the stroke). The value supplied to the sDim parameter has the following meanings:

sDim > 0	stroke is as specified by sDim
sDim = 0	null stroke (lines aren't rendered and boxes aren't framed)
sDim = -1	stroke is always 1 pixel

The last option is irrelevent to the examples in this book because screen and printer rendering occur pixel-for-pixel. However, in the XPLib software the screen is the basis for printing. So

Table 8.7 Common stroke attributes.

Stroke Attribute	*Meaning*
dimension	the *x* and *y* dimensions of the stroke
color	simple color or RGB specified
pattern	bitmap pattern appied to the stroke
transfer operation	pnXXX modes in QuickDraw and R2_XXX ops in Windows
end cap	detail of the line at an end point (usually butt, square, or round)
line join	detail of two lines that have a common vertex
miter limit	limit of the length of a line join

sDim=1 on a 75dpi display would map to sDim=4 on a 300 dpi printer, but sDim=-1 would always be a single pixel. Use single pixel width lines carefully because a one-pixel-wide line on a 1200 dpi or 2400 dpi device may be barely visible.

```
//--------------------------------------------------------
ERR GStrokeSet (PDSP pdsp, SINT sDim)
//--------------------------------------------------------
// pdsp   - pointer to a draw space
// sDim   - a signed integer that represents the
//          dimension of the pen stroke (x and y)
// RETURNS- returns ERR_No if successful
//--------------------------------------------------------
{
```

Notice that we reserve a stroke dimension of -1 to indicate a width of 1 pixel. A single pixel stroke is not necessarily useful here, but it demonstrates some additional functionality that you might want to consider in the future. Later, if you decide to provide strokes that depend on a scale—for example, if the scale is inches—a stroke of 1 would mean 1 inch. Setting the stroke to -1, always provides you with a one-pixel–wide line, which is useful if you are drawing a grid or rules. You wouldn't have to know or care what the scale is when you use a -1 stroke.

In the Macintosh we can specify the width and height of a pen. Because we cannot easily do this in Windows, we always set the pen width and height to the same value. Also, setting a pen's dimensions to zero results in nothing being drawn.

```
// we define a special case of a one pixel stroke
// when sDim is -1.
if (sDim==-1) PenSize (1,1);
else PenSize (sDim, sDim);
```

In Windows the process of creating a pen requires that we specifiy its color—we always use black. You might want to extend this functionality to use pens of different colors, but you will have to use different techniques in the Macintosh if you want to support both classic QuickDraw colors and Color QuickDraw RGB colors. Notice that if the caller specifies a zero-width pen, this is a special case. The Windows screen and printer drivers already provide us with a standard pen for this purpose: NULL_PEN.

```
HPEN hPen;
if (sDim==-1){
    // create a single pixel wide pen
    hPen=CreatePen (PS_INSIDEFRAME, 1, RGB (0, 0, 0));
}else if (sDim){
    hPen=CreatePen (PS_INSIDEFRAME, sDim,
        RGB (0, 0, 0));
}else hPen=GetStockObject (NULL_PEN);
// were we able to create the pen?
if (!hPen) return (ERR_Yes);
//select the pen into the DC
SelectObject (pdsp->hdc, hPen);
```

Then we end the function.

```
   return (ERR_No);
}
```

Actually in Windows you will need to do a bit more housekeeping for this solution to work. Every time you create a pen, you use up space in the GDI heap. If you don't delete a pen before you create a new one or provide a way to cache pens, you may create pen after pen after pen. The solution depends on how intricate you want your graphics solution to be. A simple solution involves defining a static variable in the GStrokeSet function that saves the handle of the previous pen handle. Each time you create a pen, you first delete the previous pen. I've used this simple solution in the XPLib software.

However, this approach won't work if more than one drawing window can be opened. Maintaining a single state won't provide you with enough memory of the situation. Instead you will need to create a higher level construct that maintains the pen handle information in an access-by-access way. Each point of access will then keep track of its most frequently used pen. Or you could save the pen handle in the DSP structure.

Alternatively you could maintain a cache of pens that are categorized by size and color. When you need a pen, you search the cache and select the one you want. If it isn't in the cache, then you create it and add it to the cache.

Getting the Stroke

The companion function to setting the stroke is getting the currently selected stroke. Our function, GStrokeGet(), requires a pointer to a draw space and retrieves a single number that indicates the x and y dimensions of the stroke.

```
//--------------------------------------------------------
ERR GStrokeGet (PDSP pdsp, PSINT psDim)
//--------------------------------------------------------
// pdsp   - pointer to a draw space
// psDim  - pointer to a signed integer that represents
//          the dimension of the pen stroke (x and y)
// RETURNS- currently always returns ERR_No
//--------------------------------------------------------
{
```

In the Macintosh the pen dimensions are maintained in the current GrafPort in the pnSize field. This field (and other pen fields) are retrieved by using the GetPenState() function. We read the h field of the pnSize field (the x dimension of the stroke) and return it through the psDim parameter. Note that we could have directly accessed the pen dimension in the current port and copied it to our parameter by using:

```
*psDim=thePort->pnSize.h;
```

I've done it the long way to show you a functional way to get the information. This allows Apple to change the port structure without us worrying about the format for the information.

```
PenState penState;
GetPenState (&penState);
*psDim=penState.pnSize.h;
```

In Windows, if we let the DC maintain the information about the current pen, we need to get a handle to the pen to get information about its dimension. To do this, we have to select a temporary pen into the DC, which does two things: it gives us the handle to the previous pen and sets up a default. Then we use GetObject() on the returned pen to get the information about it using a LOGPEN (logical pen) structure. We read the *x* dimension and then select the previous pen back into the DC.

```
LOGPEN logPen;
HDC hdc=pdsp->hdc;
HPEN hCurPen;
// select a dummy pen so that we can get the handle
// to the current pen
hCurPen=SelectObject (hdc, GetStockObject (BLACK_PEN));
// fill the logical pen structure with the information
// about the current pen
if (GetObject (hCurPen, sizeof(LOGPEN), &logPen)){
    // read the x dimension of the pen
    *psDim=logPen.lopnWidth.x;
}
//set the pen back to what it was
SelectObject (hdc, hCurPen);
```

If we save the pen information or the handle to the pen in the draw space structure, then the process is much simpler. For example, if we have previously saved the pen handle in the draw space, we can do the following:

```
// fill the logical pen structure with the information
// about the current pen
if (GetObject (pdsp->hPen, sizeof(LOGPEN), &logPen)){
    // read the x dimension of the pen
    *psDim=logPen.lopnWidth.x;
}
```

Or if you save the pen dimension in the draw space:

```
*psDim=pdsp->sPenDim;
```

Your choice is whether it's better for GDI or your program to keep track of the information. We opted to let GDI do it for us.

Whichever way you decide to do it, when the stroke dimension has been retrieved successfully, we return.

```
    return (ERR_No);
}
```

Setting the Fill

Any closed rectangular-based object (rectangles, round rectangles, and ellipses) or polygon can be filled. We limit the fill options to none, black, white, and three shades of gray because this level of capability is easily abstracted. We need only to provide our fill setting function, GFillSet(), with a draw space and a cross-platform index into one of two tables of platform-specific fill descriptors.

```
//-------------------------------------------------------
ERR GFillSet (PDSP pdsp, SINT2 s2Fill)
//-------------------------------------------------------
// pdsp   - pointer to a draw space
// s2Fill - cross-platform index of the fill to set
// RETURNS- currently always returns success
//-------------------------------------------------------
{
    // save the cross-platform fill index
    pdsp->s2Fill=s2Fill;
```

In the Macintosh we don't need to set the fill pattern in the GrafPort because, as we saw in the GRect() function, we always explicitly tell the Macintosh fill function which fill pattern we want to use.

In Windows we need to do a couple more things besides saving the information in the draw space structure. We need to get the handle to the fill pattern that has been selected and then select the brush object into the DC referenced by our draw space. We don't need to be careful about accumulating too many brush handles in our implementation here because all of our fill patterns are based on default Windows brushes, which are predefined by the underlying screen or printer driver.

```
SelectObject (pdsp->hdc,
    GetStockObject(_gsWinFillList[s2Fill]));
```

When we're done, we return, indicating that the fill was successfully set.

```
    return (ERR_No);
}
```

Getting the Fill

Because we have provided a common place to store current fill information in the DSP structure on all platforms, we don't need to do a lot of work to retrieve the current fill state. GFillGet() is implemented the same way on all three platforms. It requires a pointer to a draw space structure and returns the cross-platform index of the current fill in the 2-byte integer pointed to by ps2Fill.

```
//-------------------------------------------------------
ERR GFillGet (PDSP pdsp, PSINT2 ps2Fill)
//-------------------------------------------------------
// pdsp    - pointer to a draw space
// ps2Fill - pointer to a signed integer that will
```

```
//              receive the cross-platform fill index
// RETURNS - currently always returns success
//----------------------------------------------------
{
    *ps2Fill=pdsp->s2Fill;
    return (ERR_No);
}
```

Invalidating the Draw Space

When a user interacts with an application, usually two types of drawing operations can take place: redrawing everything or redrawing portions that have changed.

In GUI-based systems a request for redrawing is maintained in the event queue. This allows the inefficient redraws to occur when the system is less active (when user activity slows) or when a number of things need to be redrawn. Internally, the programmer invalidates portions of the draw space. These areas can be grouped together by the system so that a redraw operation will take care of all areas at the same time.

In our implementation of the invalidation process, we define a function, GRectInval(), which invalidates all of the draw space or any rectangular portion of it and, optionally, erases the area that was invalidated.

Erasing the invalidated area is useful for cleaning up an area that might have gotten mottled by a lot of modifications. It is also useful when you want to redraw the entire window because you don't want to redraw over the top of something that might have changed.

GRectInval() requires a pointer to a draw space, a pointer to a rectangle (a null pointer indicates the entire draw space), and a boolean to indicate if the invalidated area is to be erased.

```
//----------------------------------------------------
ERR GRectInval (PDSP pdsp, PRECT pRect, BOOL2 b2Erase)
//----------------------------------------------------
// pdsp    - pointer to a draw space
// pRect   - pointer to a RECT structure that indicates
//           the area to invalidate, or NULL if the
//           entire draw space should be invalidated
// b2Erase - TRUE means erase the invalidated area
// RETURNS - currently always returns ERR_No
//----------------------------------------------------
{
```

In the Macintosh we need to convert a cross-platform rectangle to a Macintosh Rect structure and optionally to use EraseRect() to erase the specified rectangular area of the GrafPort. Then we invalidate the rectangle. EraseRect() erases the rectangle by filling the area with the default erase fill pattern (white)—the bkPat field of the GrafPort.

```
    GrafPtr oldPort;

    // save the pointer to the current GrafPort
    // just to make sure we invalidate the right rect
```

```
GetPort (&oldPort);
SetPort (pdsp->pport);
if(pRect){
    Rect rect;
    // copy the cross-platform rectangle to a Mac rect
    SetRect (&rect, pRect->left, pRect->top,
        pRect->right, pRect->bottom);
    // erase the rectangle if we're supposed to
    if (b2Erase) EraseRect (&rect);
    InvalRect (&rect);
// invalidate the entire port rectangle
}else{
    if (b2Erase) EraseRect (&pdsp->pport->portRect);
    InvalRect (&pdsp->pport->portRect);
}
// restore the previous GrafPort
SetPort (oldPort);
```

In Windows the process is a little more complicated. Invalidation is a term applied to the client area of the window (in cross-platform terms, the window pane). Because we specify the invalidation rectangle in draw space coordinates (logical coordinates in GDI), we need to convert them to pane coordinates (device coordinates in GDI). Once we have the bounds of the rectangle that we want to invalidate in device coordinates, we invalidate the area. The Windows InvalidateRect() function provides a boolean parameter for erasing, so we don't have to bother checking and possibly erasing the area ourselves.

```
if (pRect){
    POINT pts[2];
    RECT r;
    // convert the rectangle in draw space (logical)
    // coordinates to client rect (device) coordinates
    PointSet (&pts[0], pRect->left, pRect->top);
    PointSet (&pts[1], pRect->right, pRect->bottom);
    LPtoDP(pdsp->hdc,pts,2);
    // make a rectangle out of the two points
    SetRect (&r, pts[0].x, pts[0].y, pts[1].x,
        pts[1].y);
    // invalidate away!
    InvalidateRect (pdsp->hwnd, &r, b2Erase);
// a NULL RECT pointer indicates the entire client
// area of the Window is to be invalidated
}else InvalidateRect (pdsp->hwnd, pRect, b2Erase);
```

For now we always return indicating that the invalidation was successful.

```
    return (ERR_No);
}
```

OTHER GRAPHICS CONSIDERATIONS

The samples in this chapter do not describe a complete graphics solution. However, they do illustrate some of the things that you need to consider when you implement your own solution. Some additional functions that are included in XPLib are:

- implementing the other rectangular-based objects: round-cornered rectangles and ellipses
- implementing polygons and polylines
- implementing functions to scroll the draw space and its contents
- getting and setting the drawing origin
- saving and restoring the graphics state

Other important features to consider are:

- implementing color
- providing transfer operations
- supporting regions

These and other advanced graphics topics are discussed in Extending Graphics Capabilities in Chapter 18.

9

Text and Fonts

A cross-platform API must provide a way to work with text and fonts and allow the user to select fonts. The ability to work draw text in a variety of fonts is an important part of many GUI-based applications. In this chapter, we will discuss some of the issues and problems in specifying a cross-platform text solution and then implement some of the necessary functions.

DEFINING COMMON TEXT CAPABILITIES

To define a set of cross-platform font and text functions, we need to look at:

- the types of font technologies that are available
- the text capabilities of the various platforms
- the definitions of text metrics used by each platform
- the different font styles that are available

Think about a font. What is essential to its description? Its name, its style, its size, and its color. How is a font used? To display text along a line or inside a box. The text can be aligned along the left side or along the right side, can be centered, or can be justified. Sometimes you want to rotate the text or wrap it along a curve.

Now what do we absolutely need to describe and use a font? We need to select a font by its name and its size. We need to be able to draw text from a starting point along a line—other ways of drawing text can be implemented later. We need to left-align the text. Other alignments aren't really necessary. Let's throw in specifying the font style and retrieving the size of the individual characters in a font. That's it!

Font Technologies

Table 9.1 describes the five types of font representation: bitmap, vector, outline, multiple outline, and parametric. Bitmap fonts are copied directly to the screen and printer. They occupy a lot of disk space if you want to have a large selection of fonts, sizes, and styles. Vector and outline fonts are scalable. This means that one description can be used to generate fonts of a variety of sizes. Some scalable font descriptions allow some of the font styles to be used as modifiers to produce bold, italic, or underlined versions of the characters.

Multiple outline and parametric font descriptions are used to generate many different fonts. The difference between multiple outline and parametric fonts is that multiple outline fonts are defined using from 1 through 16 special outline fonts that provide the bounds for all generated fonts. Parametric font descriptions require a series of numbers (parameters) that are used to synthesize outline fonts; there are no internal outlines that are used as the basis for the generated fonts.

Table 9.1 Descriptions of font representations.

Font Representation	*Description*
bitmap	A pixel-for-pixel bitmap is required for every character in a font in every size and style of the font for every device on which the font will be used.
vector	The characters in a font are defined as a series of polygons. Defining a character using line segments allows a certain amount of scaling, but small or overly large font sizes will not be rendered accurately. Vector fonts are normally used by plotters.
bezier or outline	The characters in a font are defined using bezier curves or outlines. This type of font description can be scaled to produce very small to very large fonts. Examples of this type of scalable font are PostScript Type 1 and TrueType 1.0 fonts. A rasterizer is used to convert an outline font into a bitmap representation.
multiple outlines	A number of master outlines describe a mathematical collection of fonts. This representation uses interpolation to create multiple font descriptions based on from 1 through 16 outlines that bound the characteristics of all generated fonts. A rasterizer is sometimes used to generate a bitmap for screen use. Adobe Systems Inc. has a technology called Multiple Master font technology that uses this technique.
parametric	A method of describing a font using parameters that instruct a font synthesizer to generate bezier (outline) fonts. A rasterizer can also be used to convert the outline font into a bitmap. This technogy is available from ElseWare Corporation and Ares Software Corporation.

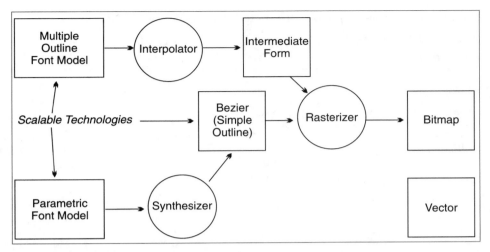

Figure 9.1 Relationships between font technologies.

Figure 9.1 illustrates the relationships between the font technologies. The boxes represent a font (or font technology) and the circles represent a process that is needed to convert one font representation into another. Notice that a bitmap is the final form of outline, multiple outline, and parametric fonts. Vector fonts are in a league of their own; they are neither produced by another font technology, nor are they used to produce fonts in other forms.

Table 9.2 compares how the font technologies are supported on the Macintosh and Windows.

For our purposes it is sufficient to ignore the underlying font technology and base our description of a font on its name, style, and size. Using only the font name to specify a particular font allows you to work with fonts on different platforms but doesn't work across platforms unless the same font name is available on all platforms.

Comparing API Functionality

Here we will outline the necessary cross-platform font and text functions and compare them to equivalent functions on all platforms, as shown in Table 9.3. Notice that there is general support for most of the functions across the three platforms. We won't know what is actually involved in implementing our font and text functions until later.

Comparing Font Metrics

Font metrics are numbers used to describe various aspects of a font. Font metrics provide a way to relate the details of one font to those of another. There are numerous pieces of information that comprise font metrics. Some of these pieces of information are defined the same across platforms, some are different, and some don't exist in all platforms. Table 9.4 compares various font metrics and terminology across platforms.

Table 9.2 Comparison of available font technologies across platforms.

Font Representation	Macintosh Screen	Macintosh Printer	Windows Screen	Windows Printer
bitmap	yes	yes	yes	yes
vector	NA	NA	yes	yes
TrueType 1.0 (outline)	System 7.x	System 7.x converts to bitmap or PostScript Type 1.	Windows 3.1 or NT	Windows 3.1 or NT converts it to a bitmap, maps it to an existing PostScript Type 1, or converts to a PostScript Type 1.
PostScript Type 1 (outline)	ATM, SuperATM, or System 7.1	ATM, SuperATM, System 7.1, or a PostScript printer	ATM	ATM or requires a PostScript printer
TrueType GX (multiple outline)	System 7.1	System 7.1	NA	NA
Multiple Master (multiple outline)	ATM, SuperATM, or System 7.1	ATM, SuperATM, or System 7.1	NA	NA
parametric	System 7.x	System 7.x converts to bitmap or PostScript Type 1.	Windows 3.1 or NT	Windows 3.1 or NT converts it to bitmap, maps it to an existing PostScript Type 1, or converts to a PostScript Type 1.

Figure 9.2 illustrates the basic Macintosh font metrics. The origin is located at the base line to make it easy to output text. The ascent and descent are built into the font description, while the leading is added by the application to provide interline spacing.

The Windows font model includes more font metrics, as illustrated in Figure 9.3. There are several things that distinguish the Windows font model from the Macintosh:

- The origin is at the top-left corner of the cell rather than at the intersection of the baseline and left edge of the cell.

- The ascent includes the internal leading.

- The height of the font may or may not include the internal leading.

Table 9.3 Comparison of font and text functionality across platforms.

Function	Macintosh	Windows 3.1	Win32
text in a box	TextBox	FillRect DrawText or ExtTextOut	FillRect DrawText or ExtTextOut
text on a line	DrawText or DrawString	TextOut or ExtTextOut	TextOut or ExtTextOut
size of text	GetFontWidth TextWidth	GetTextExtent or GetTextExtentPoint	GetTextExtentPoint
get character widths	CharWidth	GetCharWidth	GetCharWidth
get font name	GetFontName	GetTextFace	GetTextFace
set font name (by name not ID)	GetFNum TextFont	CreateFont or CreateFontIndirect	CreateFont or CreateFontIndirect
get font style	NA	GetTextMetrics	GetTextMetrics
set font style	TextFace	CreateFont or CreateFontIndirect	CreateFont or CreateFontIndirect
get font size	NA	GetTextMetrics	GetTextMetrics
set font size	TextSize	CreateFont or CreateFontIndirect	CreateFont or CreateFontIndirect
font dialog	NA	ChooseFont	ChooseFont
font metrics	GetFontInfo	GetTextMetrics	GetTextMetrics

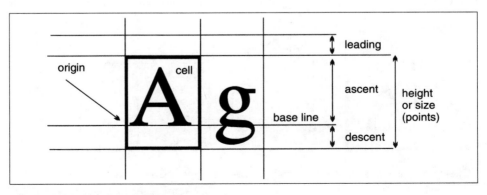

Figure 9.2 Basic Macintosh font metrics.

Table 9.4 Comparison of font terminology and metrics across platforms.

Term	Macintosh Meaning	Windows Meaning
cell	bounding box of the character	bounding box of the character
size	point size of the font	point size of the font
width	horizontal dimension of the cell	horizontal dimension of the cell
baseline	drawing line of the text	drawing line of the text
height	NA	size + internal leading or size
origin	intersection of base line and left cell edge	intersection of top cell edge and left cell edge
ascent	height-descent	height-descent-internal leading
descent	height-ascent	height-ascent-internal leading
leading	added by application	a combination of internal and external leading
internal leading	NA	internal leading included in height
external leading	NA	external leading added by application

Having looked at the differences and similarities of the Macintosh and Windows font models, we can extract a minimal cross-platform font metric set that we can use to specify fonts. These metrics are illustrated in Figure 9.4. We use the size so that we can create an appropriately sized font. We use the origin and base line to place a line of text. We use the descent so that we know how much space we need to provide between lines, and we need the dimensions of the cell so that we can accurately place characters along a line and calculate the length of a line of text. Unless you are working on a text-intensive application, you probably won't need to worry about ascent and leading. Most applications need to know only where a character will start being drawn, its descent, and it's dimensions.

Comparing Font Styles

We also need to compare the font styles that are available on the Macintosh and Windows. This information is listed in Table 9.5. Using this information, we can extract the following greatest-

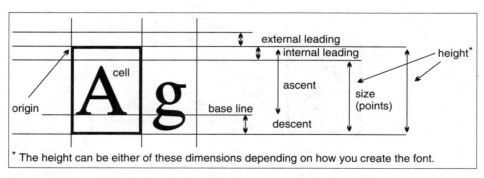

Figure 9.3 Basic Windows font metrics.

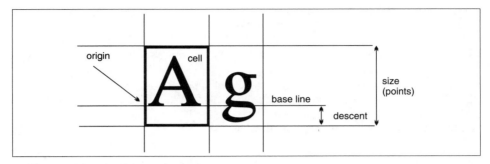

Figure 9.4 Basic cross-platform font metrics.

common denominators for font styles: normal, bold, italic, and underline. If you want to provide the other font styles, you will need to figure out some way to synthesize it. We will limit our discussion to these basic styles.

IMPLEMENTING A TEXT SOLUTION

To properly implement a cross-platform text and font solution, we need to define a cross-platform font state structure and implement the cross-platform functions that will do the work.

The FONTSTATE Data Structure

The only data type that we need for cross-platform font and text support is the FONTSTATE structure. This structure contains the essential information required to define and use a font on multiple platforms. This structure doesn't allow font information to be shared across platforms unless the fonts happen to have the same names. Some methods for using fonts across platforms are discussed in Chapter 18.

Table 9.5 Comparison of supported font styles across platforms.

Style	*Macintosh Designation*	*Windows Designation*
normal	normal	FW_NORMAL
bold	bold	FW_BOLD
italic	italic	TRUE/FALSE
underline	underline	TRUE/FALSE
strikeout	NA	TRUE/FALSE
outline	outline	NA
shadow	shadow	NA
condense	condense	NA
expand	extend	NA

Type	Field Name	Description
UINT1[256]	zName	null-terminated name of the font
UINT2	u2Style	font style bits
UINT2	u2Size	size of the font in points

The cross-platform font styles are defined as:

```
enum{
    FONT_Normal, FONT_Bold, FONT_Italic=2, FONT_Underline=4
};
```

All of the styles are integer powers of two, so they can be applied singularly or in combination with the other font styles, except FONT_Normal, which must be used exclusive of the others.

The default values for the FONTSTATE structure describe a default font that is interpreted in a platform-specific way. The defaults allow you to specify a single, valid font in a cross-platform way:

Field Name	Default Value	Meaning
zName	" "	use the cross-platform system font
		Macintosh: applFont (geneva)
		Windows: System
u2Style	FONT_Normal	plain font (no bold, italic, or underlining
u2Size	12	points

Text Functionality

In this chapter we discuss and illustrate only a subset of text and font functionality. Space prevents us from covering all aspects of this issue. We will implement the following functions, which we think will illustrate the basic concepts of cross-platform font and text functionality:

- drawing text along a line
- getting the dimensions of some text
- displaying a font selection dialog
- getting and setting the font name
- getting and setting the font size
- getting and setting the font style

Drawing Text on a Line

The ability to output text along a horizontal line is fundamental. To accomplish this we define TStrLine(), which requires a pointer to a draw space to draw the text into, the text, and the point at which to start drawing the text. We also want the current point to be unaffected by our text output operation.

```
//-------------------------------------------------------
ERR TStrLine (PDSP pdsp, PTR zText, SINT sLen, SINT sx,
    SINT sy)
//-------------------------------------------------------
// pdsp     - pointer to a draw space
// zText    - null-terminated text to output
// sLen     - number of characters to output, or -1 if
//              we output the entire string
// sx       - x coordinate to start the line of text
// sy       - y coordinate to start the line of text
// RETURNS  - ERR_No if successful, ERR_Yes otherwise
//-------------------------------------------------------
{
```

In the Macintosh we use the DrawText() function to output the text. We could use the DrawString() function, but that would limit us to only 255 characters. DrawText() modifies the current point, so we need to save the current point before we start and then restore it after we are done.

```
    POINT ptCur;

    if (!pdsp || !zText) return (ERR_Yes);

    // save the current point
    GCurrentPt (pdsp, &ptCur);

    MoveTo (sx, sy);
    DrawText (zText, 0, sLen==-1 ? StrLen (zText) : sLen);

    // we don't modify the current point, so go back to
    // where we started
    MoveTo (ptCur.x, ptCur.y);
```

In Windows we use the TextOut() function. This function does not alter the current point. But because Windows specifies the origin of text by the top-left corner of the bounding box, we need to offset the start point that we specify to Windows by subtracting the font's ascent. This allows our cross-platform starting point to represent a point that is the intersection of the baseline and the left edge of the text.

```
    TEXTMETRIC tm;
    if (!pdsp || !zText) return (ERR_Yes);

    GetTextMetrics (pdsp->hdc, &tm);
    TextOut (pdsp->hdc, sx, sy-tm.tmAscent, zText,
        sLen==-1 ? StrLen (zText) : sLen);
```

Then we return indicating that the text was drawn successfully.

```
    return (ERR_No);
}
```

Getting the Dimensions of Text

Knowing the length and height of a string of text allows you to know exactly where the text will be drawn. Our function, TStrSize(), requires a draw space, a pointer to some text, and the number of characters in the string to use. It returns the height and width of the text. This function, when used in conjunction with TStrLine(), will allow you break up a long piece of text and output it in multiple lines.

```
//--------------------------------------------------------
ERR TStrSize (PDSP pdsp, PTR zText, SINT sLen, PSINT psdx,
PSINT psdy)
//--------------------------------------------------------
// pdsp    - pointer to a draw space
// zText   - null-terminated text to output
// sLen    - number of characters to output, or -1 if
//           we output the entire string
// psdx    - pointer to a signed integer to receive the
//           width of the string
// psdy    - pointer to a signed integer to receive the
//           height of the string
// RETURNS - ERR_No if successful, ERR_Yes otherwise
//--------------------------------------------------------
{
    // return the height and width, in pixels, of the
    // text specified
```

In the Macintosh getting the dimensions of text is a two-step operation. First, we need to get the height of the font by calling GetFontInfo(). This gives us some of the metrics of the font and lets us calculate the height by adding the ascent, descent, and leading together. Second, we get the width of the text by calling TextWidth(). We don't use StringWidth() because it works only with strings of up to 255 characters.

```
    FontInfo fontinfo;
    if (!pdsp || !zText || !psdx || !psdy){
        return (ERR_Yes);
    }

    GetFontInfo (&fontinfo);
    *psdy=fontinfo.ascent+fontinfo.descent
        +fontinfo.leading;
    *psdx=TextWidth (zText, 0 /* start offset*/,
        sLen==-1 ? StrLen (zText) : sLen);
```

In Windows 3.1 we use the GetTextExtent() function to retrieve the height and width of the string packed into a 4-byte integer. Then we unpack the text dimensions from the 4-byte number and put the information in our return parameters. Actually, in Windows 3.1 (and Win32) we can use the GetTextExtentPoint () function to retrieve a SIZE structure. We use the GetTextExtent() function to illustrate the differences in functionality and to provide backward compatibility with Windows 3.0.

```
UINT4 u4Temp;

if (!pdsp || !zText || !psdx || !psdy){
    return (ERR_Yes);
}
u4Temp=GetTextExtent (pdsp->hdc, zText,
    sLen==-1 ? StrLen (zText) : sLen);

*psdy=HIWORD (u4Temp);
*psdx=LOWORD (u4Temp);
```

In Win32 we use GetTextExtentPoint() and retrieve a SIZE structure that contains the height and width information for the specified text. Then we transfer the SIZE information to our return parameters.

```
SIZE size;

if (!pdsp || !zText || !psdx || !psdy){
    return (ERR_Yes);
}
GetTextExtentPoint (pdsp->hdc, zText,
    sLen==-1 ? StrLen(zText) : sLen, &size);

*psdx=size.cx;
*psdy=size.cy;
```

We return, indicating that there were no errors and that the dimensions of the text were retrieved successfully.

```
    return (ERR_No);
}
```

Font Selection Dialog Box

To select a font or to change the properties of a font, the user must use a font selection dialog box. In our cross-platform solution we provide this font selection dialog box by defining our TFontDialog() function. The function requires a parent window (which the Macintosh implementation ignores), a draw space, and a font state structure. The initial settings that the dialog will display should be based on the contents of the font state structure. The font state structure returns information about the font that the user selected. If our function returns successfully, the font state information can be used to select or create the font.

```
//----------------------------------------------------
ERR TFontDialog (HWND hwndParent, PDSP pdsp,
    PFONTSTATE pfs)
//----------------------------------------------------
// hwndParent - handle to the window that owns the dialog
// pdsp       - pointer to a draw space
// pfs        - pointer to a FONTSTATE structure that
//              will receive the font selection info
// RETURNS    - ERR_No if successful, ERR_No otherwise
//----------------------------------------------------
{
```

The Macintosh does not have a standard font selection dialog box. Therefore we have to define one. For the sake of our discussion we will keep the font dialog simple, as illustrated in Figure 9.5. When reading the source code for this function, keep in mind:

- OK and Cancel buttons are always items 1 and 2 (for which we define IDOK and IDCANCEL, which is also the same in Windows).

- The font name radio buttons are numbered sequentially, and only one font can be selected.

- The font style check boxes are numbered sequentially, and multiple styles can be selected.

- The number representing the font size is assumed to be in points, and we don't do error checking on the edit box value.

You wouldn't want to include a simple font selection dialog like the one we are describing in this chapter in a product. At the very least you would want to let users select a font from a list of available fonts on their systems and to ensure that the font size specified represents a valid font size. You would also want the dialog box to come up with its contents initialized to the font

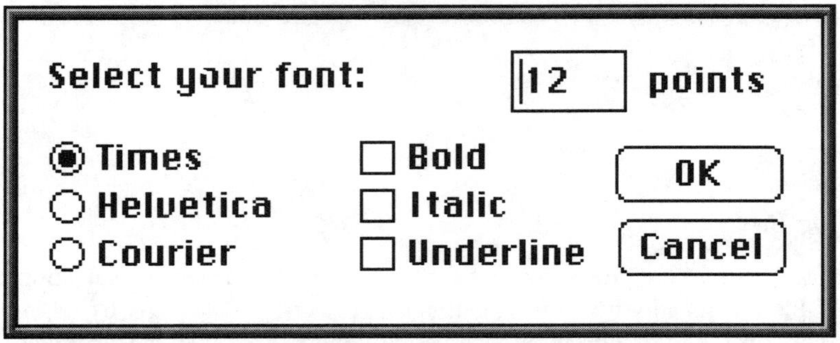

Figure 9.5 Simple Macintosh font selection dialog box.

state setting that you provide to the TFontDialog() function. (This functionality is available in the font selection dialog box that is included with the XPLib software.)

```
ERR err=ERR_Yes;
DialogPtr dlgPtr;
INT iItem;
INT iType;
INT i;
ControlHandle hCtl;
Rect rect;
enum {ID_Times=3, ID_Helv, ID_Courier,
    ID_Bold, ID_Italic, ID_Under,
    ID_Size/*edit box*/};

// read the dialog box from resources
dlgPtr=GetNewDialog (128, NULL, (WindowPtr)-1);

// loop until the user clicks OK or Cancel
do{
    // get a user response
    ModalDialog (NULL, &iItem);

    // determine what it is and what to do with it
    switch (iItem){
        // font name selection
        case ID_Times: case ID_Helv: case ID_Courier:
            // shut them all off...
            for (i=ID_Times; i<=ID_Courier; i++){
                GetDItem (dlgPtr, i, &iType, &hCtl, &rect);
                SetCtlValue (hCtl, 0);
            }
            // then, turn only the desired one on
            GetDItem (dlgPtr, iItem, &iType, &hCtl,
                &rect);
            SetCtlValue (hCtl, 1);
        break;
        // font style checkboxes
        case ID_Bold: case ID_Italic: case ID_Under:
            GetDItem (dlgPtr, iItem, &iType, &hCtl,
                &rect);
            // check/uncheck the right box
            SetCtlValue (hCtl, GetCtlValue (hCtl)
                ? 0 : 1);
        break;
    }
}while (iItem>IDCANCEL);
```

```
    if (iItem==IDOK){ // user clicked OK
        Str255 str;

        // initialize
        pfs->u2Style=0;
        pfs->u2Size=0;
        err=ERR_No;

        // search each font radio button to find out
        // which one was selected
        for (i=ID_Times; i<=ID_Courier; i++){
            GetDItem (dlgPtr, i, &iType, &hCtl, &rect);
            if (GetCtlValue (hCtl)){
                // find out the font name associated with
                // the font number
                GetFontName (i+times-ID_Times, str);
                StrCopyPtoC (pfs->zName, str);
                break;
            }
        }

        // for each style check box, run up a tally
        // of which styles were checked
        for (i=ID_Bold; i<=ID_Under; i++){
            GetDItem (dlgPtr, i, &iType, &hCtl, &rect);
            if (GetCtlValue (hCtl)){
                // convert item number to a style
                pfs->u2Style+=(1<<(i-ID_Bold));
            }
        }
        // read the contents of the edit box...
        GetDItem (dlgPtr, ID_Size, &iType, &hCtl, &rect);
        GetIText (hCtl, str);
        // ...and convert it to a number
        for (i=1; i<=str[0]; i++){
            pfs->u2Size=pfs->u2Size*10+str[i]-'0';
        }
        // if the number is out of range, default to 12 pts
        if (pfs->u2Size<=0 || pfs->u2Size>255){
            pfs->u2Size=12;
        }
    }
    // get rid of the dialog box and return
    DisposDialog (dlgPtr);
    return (err);
}
```

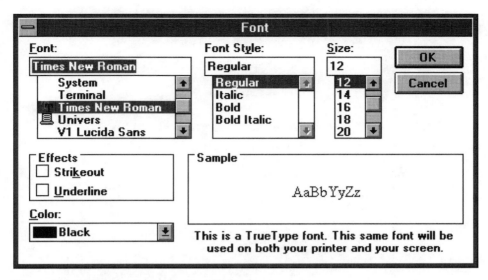

Figure 9.6 Windows font selection dialog box.

In Windows a font selection dialog box is included with the common dialog DLL (COMMDLG.DLL), as illustrated in Figure 9.6. Most of the work you must do involves setting up the CHOOSEFONT data structure that the ChooseFont() function requires. In our code sample we ask ChooseFont() to return us a logical font (LOGFONT) structure, which we use to set up our FONTSTATE structure. The code sample also does not properly handle symbol character sets.

```
ERR err;
LOGFONT lf;
CHOOSEFONT cf;

if (!pdsp || !pfs) return (ERR_Yes);

// initialize the CHOOSEFONT and LOGFONT structures
// to all zeros
MemFill ((PTR)&cf, 0, sizeof (CHOOSEFONT));
MemFill ((PTR)&lf, 0, sizeof (LOGFONT));

// Tell the common dialog function to enumerate the
// font based on the information specified in the
// FONTSTATE structure which we convert to LOGFONT
lf.lfHeight=-(SINT2)(((SINT4)pfs->u2Size
    * (SINT4)GetDeviceCaps (pdsp->hdc, LOGPIXELSY)
    + 36L)/72L);
```

```
lf.lfWidth=0;
lf.lfEscapement=0;
lf.lfOrientation=0;
lf.lfWeight=((pfs->u2Style&FONT_Bold)
   ? FW_BOLD : FW_NORMAL);
lf.lfItalic=((pfs->u2Style&FONT_Italic)
   ? TRUE : FALSE);
lf.lfUnderline=((pfs->u2Style&FONT_Underline)
   ? TRUE : FALSE);
lf.lfStrikeOut=FALSE;
// ignore symbol character sets for now
lf.lfCharSet=ANSI_CHARSET;
lf.lfOutPrecision=OUT_DEFAULT_PRECIS;
lf.lfClipPrecision=CLIP_DEFAULT_PRECIS;
lf.lfQuality=PROOF_QUALITY;
lf.lfPitchAndFamily=FF_DONTCARE|VARIABLE_PITCH;

if (pfs->zName[0]){
   StrCopy (lf.lfFaceName, (PTR)pfs->zName);

// if no font name was specified, use the system font
}else StrCopy (lf.lfFaceName, "System");

cf.lStructSize=sizeof (CHOOSEFONT);
cf.hwndOwner=hwndParent;
cf.lpLogFont=&lf;
cf.Flags=CF_BOTH|CF_EFFECTS|CF_INITTOLOGFONTSTRUCT;
//color defaults to black
cf.nFontType=PRINTER_FONTTYPE|SCREEN_FONTTYPE;

cf.hDC=_WinPrinterIC();
if (!cf.hDC) return (ERR_Yes);

// put up the dialog box and see what happens
err=(ChooseFont (&cf) ? ERR_No : ERR_Yes);

DeleteDC (cf.hDC);

// if all went well...
if (err==ERR_No){
   // save the font name
   StrCopy ((PTR)pfs->zName, lf.lfFaceName);

   // calculate the cross-platform style information
   pfs->u2Style=0;
```

```
        if (lf.lfWeight==FW_BOLD) pfs->u2Style|=FONT_Bold;
        if (lf.lfItalic) pfs->u2Style|=FONT_Italic;
        if (lf.lfUnderline) pfs->u2Style|=FONT_Underline;

        // calculate the font size in points
        {
            SINT4 idpi=
                (SINT4)GetDeviceCaps (pdsp->hdc, LOGPIXELSY);

            pfs->u2Size=(SINT2)(((SINT4)ABS (lf.lfHeight)
                *72L)/idpi);
        }
    }
    return (err);
}


//---- Windows ONLY! ---------------------------------
//----------------------------------------------------
HDC _WinPrinterIC (VOID)
//----------------------------------------------------
// no parameters
// RETURNS - handle to a printer device context or NULL
//           if there was an error
//----------------------------------------------------
{
    PTR zDriver, zDevice, zOutput;
    UINT1 zProfile[64];

    // read some information from WIN.INI
    //      [windows]
    //      device=<printer name>,<file>,<port>
    // in Win32 this information is read from the Registry
    //
    GetProfileString ("windows","device","",zProfile,64);

    zDevice=zProfile;
    zDriver=StrChar (zProfile, ',') +1;
    zOutput=StrChar (zDriver, ',') +1;
    if (!zProfile && !zDriver && !zOutput) return (0);

    // null-terminate the substrings within the
    // original profile string
    zDriver[-1]='\0';
    zOutput[-1]='\0';
```

```
        // create an information context and return
        return (CreateIC (zDriver, zDevice, zOutput, NULL));
    }
```

Getting the Current Font Name

One of the first things we might want to know about the current font is its name. In our cross-platform font solution, the font name is the primary identifier for a font. We don't maintain information about the font attributes (such as serif or sans serif or other specifics about the font's appearance). Our intention is to keep things simple. Later, if necessary, you can add functionality to let you intelligently map a desired font to one that is available.

```
    //------------------------------------------------------
    ERR TFontNameGet (PDSP pdsp, PTR zFont)
    //------------------------------------------------------
    // pdsp    - pointer to a draw space
    // zFont   - buffer to receive the font name string
    // RETURNS - ERR_No if successful, ERR_Yes otherwise
    //------------------------------------------------------
    {
        // Assume that zFont is large enough to hold
        // the largest font name of 255 characters
```

The Macintosh GrafPort maintains information about the currently selected font in the field txFont, which is a font number. GetFontName() takes a font number and returns a Pascal string that contains the font name.

```
        Str255 zpFont;

        if (!pdsp) return (ERR_Yes);

        GetFontName (pdsp->pport->txFont, zpFont);
        // Mac font name is a Pascal string, convert to C
        StrCopyPtoC (zFont, zpFont);
```

In Windows we use GetTextFace() to retrieve the name of the current font in the specified DC. We need to pass it a pointer to a buffer to receive the font name and the size of the largest name that the buffer will hold.

```
        if (!pdsp) return (ERR_Yes);

        if (!GetTextFace (pdsp->hdc, 255, zFont)){
            return (ERR_Yes);
        }
```

If we get here, everything went OK.

```
        return (ERR_No);
    }
```

Setting the Name of the Current Font

The companion function to getting the current font name is setting the name of the current font. This involves more that just copying over a new font name. A font name is not a modifier to a general font description (at least not in our context[1]). Changing the name of the current font requires loading a new font definition. Our syntax hides this on purpose. We don't want to or should not have to care about the specifics of fonts. We only want to be able to specify settings and modifiers and then expect things to work.

Our function, for setting the font name, TFontNameSet(), requires that we provide a pointer to a draw space and a pointer to a null-terminated font name. Remember that we have reserved the null string " " to indicate a cross-platform default font.

```
//---------------------------------------------------
ERR TFontNameSet (PDSP pdsp, PTR zFont)
//---------------------------------------------------
// pdsp     - pointer to a draw space
// zFont    - buffer containing the font name
// RETURNS - ERR_No if successful, ERR_Yes otherwise
//---------------------------------------------------
{
```

In the Macintosh we first check to see if the font name is a null-string. If so, we install the applFont, which is the default application font (usually geneva). If the font name is non-null, then we ask the system to give us the corresponding font number and then install that font into our GrafPort.

```
Str255 zpFont;
SINT2 s2Font;
ERR err=ERR_No;

if (!pdsp) return (ERR_Yes);

// if the supplied font is a null-string
// set up our default
if (!zFont[0]) TextFont (applFont);

// the caller provided us with a non-null font name
else{
    StrCopyCtoP (zpFont, zFont);
    // ask the system what the font number is
    GetFNum (zpFont, &s2Font);
```

---

[1]   A morphable font description, like Adobe's Multiple Master font technology, allows a master font description to generate many font descriptions. It is possible to design an interface to this technology that uses a font name as a modifier to the master font description that, in turn, generates a new font definition.

```
        if (!s2Font) err=ERR_Yes;
        else TextFont (s2Font);
    }


    return (err);
```

In Windows we have to go through some DC gymnastics of selecting a dummy font to get the current font and then asking the system for information about the font by using GetObject(). The LOGFONT structure that we receive represents a valid specifier for the current font. We change the font name to that provided by the zFont parameter, create a new font, and install it. If the font name is a null string, we use the System font as the default—not a particularly attractive font, but it is always available.

```
    HANDLE hNewFont, hCurFont;
    LOGFONT lf;

    if (!pdsp) return (ERR_Yes);

    // get the handle to the current font by
    // selecting another
    hCurFont=SelectObject (pdsp->hdc,
        GetStockObject (SYSTEM_FONT));

    GetObject (hCurFont, sizeof (LOGFONT), &lf);

    if (!zFont[0]) StrCopy (lf.lfFaceName, "System");
    else StrCopy (lf.lfFaceName, zFont);

        hNewFont=CreateFontIndirect (&lf);

    //select the new font if it's valid
    if (hNewFont){
        SelectObject (pdsp->hdc, hNewFont);
        DeleteObject (hCurFont);

    // otherwise select the current font
    }else{
        SelectObject (pdsp->hdc, hCurFont);
        return (ERR_Yes);
    }
    return (ERR_No);
```

That's all there is to do.

```
    }
```

Getting the Font Size

One of the modifiers of a font is its size. A font size is properly specified in points (1/72 of an inch). We ask the system for the font size by using the function TFontSizeGet(), which requires a pointer to a draw space. Our function returns a number that indicates the font size in points.

```
//-----------------------------------------------------
UINT2 TFontSizeGet (PDSP pdsp)
//-----------------------------------------------------
// pdsp     - pointer to a draw space
// RETURNS - the font size in points or 0xffff if an
//               error occurred
//-----------------------------------------------------
{
    UINT2 u2Size;
```

In the Macintosh, the font size is maintained in the txSize field of the GrafPort.

```
    if (!pdsp) return (0xffff);

    u2Size=pdsp->pport->txSize;
```

In Windows 3.1 we need to do a few things to calculate the font size. First we get the resolution of the device referenced by the DC in the draw space, and then we get the text metrics for the current font. The Windows height of a font includes the internal leading which must be subtracted to get the true height of the font. The height of the font is in pixels which we then convert to points:

cross-platform size = ((height-internal leading) * 72 pts/inch) / resolution

```
    TEXTMETRIC tm;
    SINT4 idpi;

    if (!pdsp) return (0xffff);

    // get the resolution of the device
    idpi=(SINT4)GetDeviceCaps (pdsp->hdc, LOGPIXELSY);

    GetTextMetrics (pdsp->hdc, &tm);
    u2Size=(SINT2)(((SINT4)(tm.tmHeight
        -tm.tmInternalLeading)*72L)/idpi);
```

In Win32 the process should be the same as in Windows 3.1, but the Win32 font height seems to include both the internal and external leadings. So we need to subtract both of them from the height to get the font size in points:

leading = internal leading + external leading
cross-platform size = ((height-leading) * 72 pts/inch) / resolution

```
      TEXTMETRIC tm;
      SINT4 idpi;

      if (!pdsp) return (0xffff);

      // get the resolution of the device
      idpi=(SINT4)GetDeviceCaps (pdsp->hdc, LOGPIXELSY);

      GetTextMetrics (pdsp->hdc, &tm);
      // There seems to be a difference between the metrics
      // info in Win32 and 3.1...we need to subtract BOTH
      // leadings from the height
      u2Size=(SINT2)(((SINT4)(tm.tmHeight
          -tm.tmInternalLeading-tm.tmExternalLeading)
      *72L)/idpi);
```

When we're done, we return the point size of the font in u2Size.

```
      return (u2Size);
  }
```

Setting the Font Size

Next we need to set the size of the font that we want to use. Sometimes, just as in setting the font name, this can require creating a new font and deleting the old at the API level. At a lower level, setting or changing the font size just means applying a modifier to a font description or loading the information from a different font file.

Our function, TFontSizeSet(), requires a pointer to a draw space and the point size that we want to set. Be careful if you plan on specifying fonts larger than 127 points because not all font technologies or coordinate systems can handle them.

```
  //-----------------------------------------------------
  ERR TFontSizeSet (PDSP pdsp, UINT2 u2Size)
  //-----------------------------------------------------
  // pdsp    - pointer to a draw space
  // u2Size  - font size in points (72 points/inch)
  // RETURNS - ERR_No if successful, ERR_Yes otherwise
  //-----------------------------------------------------
  {
```

You can set the size of a font on the Macintosh by using TextSize().

```
      if (!pdsp) return (ERR_Yes);

        TextSize (u2Size);
```

In Windows the process is more complicated. Unless you maintain a handle to the current font in the DSP structure (we don't), you need to get the current font from the DC by selecting another font. Next you use the font handle and get the logical font information using GetObject(). Then you use the LOGFONT structure, load in the desired font height, and create a new font. Finally you make the new font the current font.

```
HANDLE hNewFont,hCurFont;
LOGFONT lf;

if (!pdsp) return (ERR_Yes);

// get the handle to the current font by
// selecting another
hCurFont=SelectObject (pdsp->hdc,
    GetStockObject (SYSTEM_FONT));

// get the information on the current font
GetObject (hCurFont, sizeof (LOGFONT), &lf);

// calculate the size of the new font in pixels
// based on the current device
lf.lfHeight=-(SINT2)(((SINT4)u2Size
    *(SINT4)GetDeviceCaps (pdsp->hdc, LOGPIXELSY)+36L)
    /72L);
lf.lfWidth=0;

hNewFont=CreateFontIndirect (&lf);

//select the new font if it's valid
if (hNewFont){
    SelectObject (pdsp->hdc, hNewFont);
    DeleteObject (hCurFont);

// otherwise, select the current font
}else{
    SelectObject (pdsp->hdc, hCurFont);
    return (ERR_Yes);
}
```

If we get here, the font size was successfully set.

```
    return (ERR_No);
}
```

Getting the Font Style

Our, function, TFontStyleGet(), requires a pointer to a draw space and returns the current font style. The available cross-platform font styles are:

FONT_Normal
FONT_Bold
FONT_Italic
FONT_Underline

Some platforms and some font technologies allow other font styles, but we limit ourselves to these because they are represented by all three platforms and font technologies.

```
//--------------------------------------------------------
UINT2 TFontStyleGet (PDSP pdsp)
//--------------------------------------------------------
// pdsp    - pointer to a draw space
// RETURNS - unsigned 2-byte integer representing the
//           style of the current font or 0xffff if an
//           error occurred
//--------------------------------------------------------
{
    UINT2 u2Style=0;
```

In the Macintosh the font style information is readily available in the GrafPort structure's txFace field. We just read the settings in the Macintosh format and convert them to our cross-platform format.

```
    if (!pdsp) return (0xffff);

    if (pdsp->pport->txFace&bold) u2Style|=FONT_Bold;
    if (pdsp->pport->txFace&italic) u2Style|=FONT_Italic;
    if (pdsp->pport->txFace&underline){
        u2Style|=FONT_Underline;
    }
```

In Windows the DC maintains the information about the current font. There is no direct way to access this information, so we use the GetTextMetrics() function. This function returns us a **TEXTMETRIC** data structure that is filled with the information about the current font. We merely read the information about the font style and convert it into our cross-platform form.

```
    TEXTMETRIC tm;

    if (!pdsp) return (0xffff);

    GetTextMetrics (pdsp->hdc, &tm);

    if (tm.tmWeight==FW_BOLD) u2Style|=FONT_Bold;
    if (tm.tmItalic) u2Style|=FONT_Italic;
    if (tm.tmUnderlined) u2Style|=FONT_Underline;
```

When we're done, we return the style information to the caller.

```
    return (u2Style);
}
```

Setting the Font Style

The font style is another modifier to the font description. Our function, TFontStyleSet(), requires a pointer to a draw space and the cross-platform font style.

```
//------------------------------------------------------
ERR TFontStyleSet (PDSP pdsp, UINT2 u2Style)
//------------------------------------------------------
// pdsp    - pointer to a draw space
// u2Style - unsigned 2-byte integer representing the
//           desired style of the current font
// RETURNS - ERR_No if successful or ERR_Yes otherwise
//------------------------------------------------------
{
```

In the Macintosh we can directly set the style of the currently selected font. First we set the font style to normal (clear the style), and then we check our cross-platform style information, one style at a time, and modify the Macintosh font style information accordingly.

```
if (!pdsp) return (ERR_Yes);

TextFace (normal);
if (u2Style&FONT_Bold) pdsp->pport->txFace|=bold;
if (u2Style&FONT_Italic) pdsp->pport-txFace|=italic;
if (u2Style&FONT_Underline){
    pdsp-pport-txFace|=underline;
}
```

In Windows the process is almost the same as setting a new font size. You get the current font from the DC by selecting another font and then use that font handle to get the logical font information (in a LOGFONT structure) with GetObject(). Then you use the LOGFONT structure and load in the desired font styles and create a new font. Finally you make the new font the current font.

```
HDC hdc;
HANDLE hCurFont, hNewFont;
LOGFONT lf;

if (!pdsp) return (ERR_Yes);

// get the handle to the current font by
// selecting another
hCurFont=SelectObject (pdsp-hdc,
    GetStockObject (SYSTEM_FONT));

// get the information about the current font
GetObject (hCurFont, sizeof (LOGFONT), &lf);
```

```
lf.lfWeight=((u2Style&FONT_Bold) ? FW_BOLD: FW_NORMAL);
lf.lfItalic=((u2Style&FONT_Italic) ? TRUE : FALSE);
lf.lfUnderline=((u2Style&FONT_Underline)
    ? TRUE : FALSE);

hNewFont=CreateFontIndirect (&lf);

//select the new font if it's valid
if (hNewFont){
    SelectObject (pdsp-hdc, hNewFont);
    DeleteObject (hCurFont);

// otherwise select the current font
}else{
    SelectObject (pdsp->hdc, hCurFont);
    return (ERR_Yes);
}
```

We exit the function indicating that the font style was successfully set.

```
return (ERR_No);
}
```

OTHER TEXT CONSIDERATIONS

Now that we've covered the basic cross-platform font and text functions, let's list some additional functions that you should also consider implementing (these are provided by the XPLib software):

- drawing text in a box
- getting and setting the complete font state (name, style, and size)
- getting the widths of some or all characters in a font

In addition we might want to think about some other features, such as:

- providing text alignment (left, right, centered, and justified)
- supporting font color (foreground and background)
- providing transfer operations in addition to just copying
- maintaining some font attribute information (for example, monospaced fonts vs. proportional fonts and character fonts vs. symbol fonts)
- providing a mechanism for font substitution
- supporting multi-byte character sets

These topics are discussed in more detail in Extending Text Capabilities in Chapter 18.

10

Bitmaps

Ultimately every graphic object, text string, window frame, or menu bar is rendered as a collection of pixels. Groups of pixels, called bitmaps, are the lowest form of visual information that a GUI-based platform can process. Consequently a cross-platform solution must provide support for them. In this chapter we will look at how our target platforms deal with bitmaps and present solutions to some of the problems.

DEFINING COMMON BITMAP CAPABILITIES

There are two types of bitmaps:

- device-dependent bitmaps—a bitmap in a format specific to one type of device (a screen or a printer)
- device-independent bitmaps—a bitmap in a format (such as Windows DIB, TIFF, and PCX) that can be used by many devices

Table 10.1 lists several forms that either type of bitmap can take. Figure 10.1 illustrates how the bitmap types and forms can be used. Maintaining a device-independent bitmap form lets you read and write the bitmap to file and display or print the bitmap without worrying about the format. Device-dependent bitmaps saved to file are only accurately used on the device that created them. To provide a proper cross-platform bitmap solution, you will need to provide most of the pieces in the figure.

Table 10.1 Descriptions of the various bitmap forms.

Bitmap Form	Description
file	A bitmap that has been saved in a disk file. Usually a bitmap is maintained in a device-independent format when it is saved to file, but files can also be used to hold device-dependent bitmaps when the data represents a device "image" that will be transferred without modification to the target device.
memory	When a bitmap is in memory, it can represent the contents of a bitmap file, a device-independent bitmap, a device-dependent screen image, or a device-dependent printer image. Memory bitmaps are useful when you want to prepare an image that later will be transfered to the screen or printer. Imaging a bitmap in memory is more efficient that imaging a bitmap to a device.
screen	This is a device-dependent bitmap that is imaged into a GrafPort (Macintosh) or DC (Windows) that is tied to a display device.
printer	This is a device-dependent bitmap that is imaged into a TPrPort (Macintosh) or a DC (Windows) that is tied to a printing device.

For our purposes we will limit the scope of the problem to that illustrated in Figure 10.2. Basically we can create, use, and save screen bitmaps without problems. But the bitmaps won't be transportable to other platforms. We can print a screen bitmap to the printer if the bitmap is monochrome or has the same pixel organization as the screen, but we'll end up with either a shrunken or a full-size but distorted (chunky) version of the original.

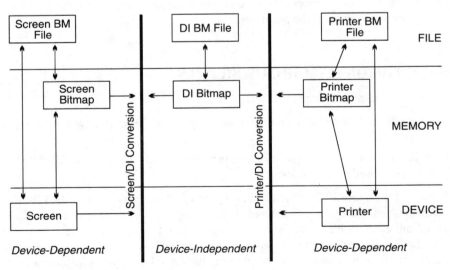

Figure 10.1 Total bitmap solution.

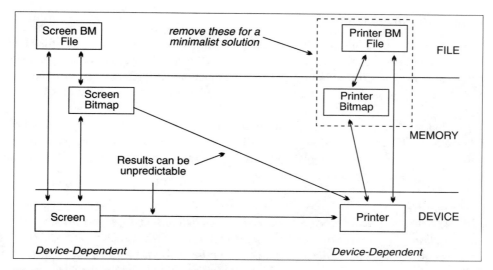

Figure 10.2 Limited bitmap solution.

The area in Figure 10.2 that is enclosed in the dashed rectangle represents the functionality needed to support bitmap operations on the printer. When you transfer a bitmap to a draw space that is tied to a printer, you need to be careful what you do. The printer is a draw-once kind of device. If you do a lot of unnecessary dragging of images, your printed page will look very messy.

The subset in Figure 10.2 allows a user to cut, copy, paste, and drag bitmaps during an application session. This is what most non–bitmap-intensive programs need to do with bitmaps (see Figure 10.3). For example, the user selects an area of the screen and wants to move it somewhere else. Copying the area (or drawing it) into a bitmap and dragging it around is much more efficient than actually redrawing the area over and over.

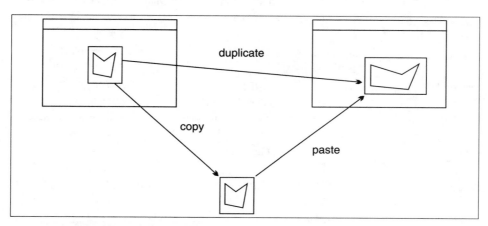

Figure 10.3 Basic bitmap functionality.

Comparing API Functionality

Now let's take a look at Table 10.2 to see how some of the common bitmap functions are performed on each of our three platforms. On the Macintosh there are two ways to perform most bitmap and pixel operations. In the table the first function listed indicates the method used for classic QuickDraw and the second function listed indicates the method used for Color Quick-Draw.

In Windows there are multiple options for performing the bitmap transfer operation. The first two methods are used for device-dependent bitmaps and the second two methods are used to transfer device-independent bitmaps. We need only consider the device-dependent functions, BitBlt() and StretchBlt(), for our purposes.

> *In Windows 3.1, when you work with device-dependent bitmaps and use the CreateCompatibleBitmap() with BitBlt() or StretchBlt(), you are limited to bitmaps of 64K bytes because that is the largest piece of data that can be addressed by a LPSTR pointer type. This can be a problem if you have a 24-bit color display and want to copy a large area of the screen from one place to another. We will ignore this limitation in our example.*

Table 10.2 Comparing bitmap functions across platforms.

Function	Macintosh	Windows 3.1	Win32
allocate bitmap container	NewHandle or NewPixMap	CreateCompatibleDC	CreateCompatibleDC
free bitmap container	DisposHandle or DisposPixMap	DeleteDC	DeleteDC
allocate bitmap	NewHandle or NewPtr	GlobalAlloc CreateCompatibleBitmap or CreateDIBitmap SelectObject	GlobalAlloc CreateCompatibleBitmap or CreateDIBitmap SelectObject
free bitmap	DisposHandle or DisposPtr	DeleteObject	DeleteObject
transfer bitmap	CopyBits	BitBlt or StretchBlt or SetDIBitsToDevice or StretchDIBits	BitBlt or StretchBlt or SetDIBitsToDevice or StretchDIBits
get pixel	GetPixel or GetCPixel	GetPixel	GetPixel
set pixel	SetCPixel (Color QuickDraw only)	SetPixel	SetPixel or SetPixelV

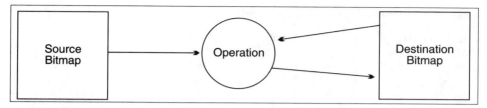

Figure 10.4 Binary transfer operation.

Abstracting Bit Transfer Operations

A source bitmap can be transferred to a destination bitmap in a variety of ways. The manner of bit transfer is called a transfer operation. There are two general types of transfer operations: binary and ternary. Binary transfer operations take a source and destination and combine them to produce the new destination (see Figure 10.4). Ternary transfer operations take a source, a pattern, and a destination and combine them to produce the new destination (see Figure 10.5). Classic QuickDraw has eight binary transfer operations for bitmaps: srcCopy, notSrcCopy, srcOr, notSrcOr, srcXor, notSrcXor, srcBic, and notSrcBic. Windows, which uses ternary operations, has 256 operations. The Macintosh is the limiting case, so our cross-platform subset of bit transfer operations is based on it and is shown in Table 10.3. We have not included the "make white" and "make black" operations because these can be accomplished by drawing a rectangle with a null stroke and a white or black fill.

When transferring bitmaps to a printing device, you will need to be careful with the transfer operations that you use. Most of the time a printer will only recognize a copy type of operation or map other operations to a copy operation. This means that some operations that transfer bits

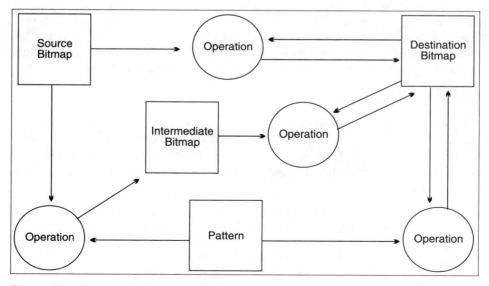

Figure 10.5 Ternary transfer operation.

Table 10.3 Common bit transfer operations.

Transfer Operation	Macintosh	Windows*
copy source to dest	srcCopy	SRCCOPY
OR source to dest	srcOr	0x008800c6
XOR source to dest	srcXor	0x00990066
copy inverted source to dest	notSrcCopy	NOTSRCCOPY
OR inverted source to dest	notSrcOr	0x00220326
XOR inverted source to dest	notSrcXor	SRCINVERT

* The process of determining which Windows ternary raster operation to use is sometimes confusing. You should consult Volume 2, Chapter 11 of the Windows SDK documentation for a thorough discussion of this topic. In our case we can limit the scope of the ternary operation possibilities by ignoring the pattern operand.

won't necessarily be able to clean up a mess that another produced. For example, you can't XOR a bitmap around on a printer device; the bitmap will just get smeared around on the page. The XOR will usually act like a copy, so if a pixel is black, XORing black will leave the pixel black instead of changing it to white.

Macintosh Color QuickDraw offers arithmetic transfer modes in addition to the logical transfer operations we present here. These are designed to allow colors to be blended and to specify transparency. We do not consider these in our discussion.

IMPLEMENTING A MINIMAL BITMAP SOLUTION

We will discuss two classes of functions: bitmap functions and pixel functions. Pixel functions allow you to get and set the value of an individual pixel in a draw space. Bitmap functions let you work on rectangular areas that are filled with pixels. As with the other groups of functionality, we will define the cross-platform data types and then define the cross-platform functions. We loosely group bitmap and pixel functions together as bitmap functions.

Bitmap Data Types

The first data type that we will abstract is a handle to a bitmap. Although the underlying data type on all platforms is a memory handle, we will define a new handle type to identify a bitmap handle, HBMAP. The BLTMODE data type is necessary to abstract the bit transfer operation code that is used to control the action of the bitmap functions. Here is how our bitmap data types compare across platforms:

Type	Macintosh	Windows 3.1	Win32
HBMAP	Handle (4 bytes)	HANDLE (2 bytes)	HANDLE (4 bytes)
BLTMODE	SINT2	UINT4	UINT4

Bitmap Global Data

Our cross-platform bitmap functions require only one global variable, _gb2MacColorQD, which is defined as:

```
BOOL2 _gb2MacColorQD;
```

This is a Macintosh-specific boolean variable that indicates if the system is running Color QuickDraw. Our _gb2MacColorQD variable is TRUE if Color QuickDraw is running or if System 7 QuickDraw is running, and FALSE otherwise.

> *In System 6 there are three flavors of QuickDraw: classic, Color, and 32-bit. Classic QuickDraw came into being in 1984 when the Macintosh was first introduced, Color QuickDraw emerged when the Macintosh II family was introduced in 1987, and 32-bit QuickDraw came out in 1989. In System 7 all of the three versions of QuickDraw were merged into one, called System 7 QuickDraw.*

Bitmap Data Structures

We must define two data structures to implement bitmaps:

- the bitmap container
- a representation for color

The Bitmap Container

The bitmap container type includes everything that is needed by a particular platform to create and manipulate a bitmap. We call this type BMAP. It represents vastly different information between the Macintosh and Windows versions. You will probably never need to directly access the information in this structure (unless you are doing something platform-specific), so most functions that deal with bitmap images will supply you with a handle to the BMAP structure, or HBMAP.

The data type for color, RGBCOLOR, is a cross-platform way to represent color. In our implementation the need for color is insignificant compared to what you ultimately might require.

Here is how our bitmap data structures compare with native structures across platforms:

Type	Macintosh	Windows 3.1	Win32
BMAP	BitMap or Pixmap	NA	NA
RGBCOLOR	RBGColor	COLORREF	COLORREF

The cross-platform bitmap container data type, BMAP, can actually refer to two different data types in the Macintosh. If the Macintosh system supports Color Quickdraw, the PixMap data type is used; otherwise, the BitMap data type is used.

In Windows you will notice that we do not indicate a particular native Windows data type that is equivalent to our cross-platform bitmap container. The process of defining and using a bitmap in Windows is more complicated than it is on the Macintosh. There are actually several bitmap data structures that deal with bitmaps, but none are singularly applicable to our solution.

Normally the Windows bitmap structures are used to access bitmaps from files or to act as receptacles for information returned from Windows. For example, GetObject() is used to retrieve information about the logical bitmap that is associated with a bitmap handle. This logical bitmap information is returned in a BITMAP structure.

For Windows we define BMAP to be a structure that contains the following components:

Type	Field Name	Description
HDC	hdcMem	handle to the memory DC that owns the bitmap
HBITMAP	hbm	handle to the bitmap data (image)
SINT	sdx	the x dimension of the bitmap
SINT	sdy	the y dimension of the bitmap

We need the hdcMem parameter to save the memory DC handle with the cross-platform bitmap. This memory DC is equivalent to the device upon which it was based, a real DC based on the screen or a printer. The hbm field contains a handle to a Windows bitmap object that is created by the CreateCompatibleBitmap() function. This ensures that we have a valid bitmap for the device that we are are working with; sdx and sdy indicate the dimensions of the bitmap.

Cross-Platform Color Structure

The Macintosh RGB color data structure, RGBColor, is defined as follows:

Type	Field Name	Description
unsigned short	red	red color value
unsigned short	green	green color value
unsigned short	blue	blue color value

The Windows 3.1 and Win32 RGB color data type, COLORREF, is defined as a DWORD or unsigned long. Each of the color components in the Macintosh structure are 2 bytes, but the color components in Windows are only 1 byte (the RGB values are packed into the lower 3 bytes of the 4-byte integer). The most-significant byte of the COLORREF data type is used to indicate a palette color (an index). In this discussion we ignore color palettes.

For upward compatibility we choose the largest representation for color and define the cross-platform RGB color data structure to have 2-byte components. We also rename the structure to make it consistent with our cross-platform data naming convention and abbreviate the color value components in the structure to single letters. The cross-platform structure is called RGBCOLOR and is defined as follows:

Type	Field Name	Description
UINT2	r	red color value
UINT2	g	green color value
UINT2	b	blue color value

Image Functionality

In this section we will implement four bitmap image functions and two pixel functions for:

- allocating a cross-platform container to hold a bitmap
- freeing a bitmap container
- copying a bitmap into a bitmap container
- duplicating a bitmap from one location to another
- getting the value of a pixel
- setting the value of a pixel

Allocating a Bitmap Container

The first thing we need to do is to allocate a structure that will hold the information that we need to perform cross-platform bitmap operations. Our function, BltInit(), uses a draw space that references the device that is the target of our bitmap operations and the *x* and *y* dimensions of the bitmap container. The bitmap container represents a bitmap that resides in memory.

```
//-----------------------------------------------------
HBMAP BltInit (PDSP pdsp, SINT sdx, SINT sdy)
//-----------------------------------------------------
// pdsp    - pointer to a draw space
// sdx     - x dimension of the bitmap container
// sdy     - y dimension of the bitmap container
// RETURNS - handle to a bitmap container
//-----------------------------------------------------
{
```

On the Macintosh we need to do one of two things, depending on whether the system is running classic QuickDraw or Color QuickDraw. Classic QuickDraw needs to allocate a BitMap and Color QuickDraw needs to allocate a PixMap. In both cases we want to allocate a cross-platform bitmap that has the dimensions specified by sdx and sdy. In Color QuickDraw we also need to make sure our bitmap is deep enough to handle the color information of the device. In this regard we also copy over the current GDevice's color table to ensure that colors are properly represented in our memory bitmap.

```
UINT4 u4Size;

// is this system running Color QuickDraw
if (_gb2MacColorQD){
   PixMapHandle hpm=NewPixMap ();
   PixMapPtr ppm;
   GDHandle hgd=GetGDevice ();
   // get a reference to the graphic device's
   // color table handle
   CTabHandle hct=((**(**hgd).gdPMap)).pmTable;

   // make a copy of the gDevice color table
   // and return it in our handle
   HandToHand (&hct);
   // lock down the new color table
   HLock ((Handle)hct);
   // set it to indicate a PixMap and not a gDevice
   (**hct).ctFlags=0x0000;

   // lock down our PixMap and dereference it
   HLock ((Handle)hpm);
   ppm=*hpm;

   //replace the empty color table with a good one
   DisposHandle (ppm->pmTable);

   // initialize the PixMap fields for a memory bitmap
   ppm->pmTable=hct;
   ppm->pixelType=16;//direct pixel values
   ppm->rowBytes=(ppm->pixelSize*((sdx+15)/16))*2;
   u4Size=(UINT4)ppm->rowBytes*(UINT4)sdy;
   ppm->baseAddr=NewPtrClear (u4Size);
   ppm->rowBytes|=0x8000;//to indicate a pixmap
   SetRect (&ppm->bounds, 0, 0, sdx, sdy);

   return ((HBMAP)hpm);

// classic QuickDraw
}else{
   BitMap bm;
   BitMap **hbm=(BitMap**)NewHandle (sizeof (BitMap));
```

```
BitMap *pbm=*hbm;

// initialize the BitMap fields
bm.rowBytes=((sdx+15)/16)*2;
u4Size=(UINT4)bm.rowBytes*(UINT4)sdy;
bm.baseAddr=NewPtrClear (u4Size);
SetRect (&bm.bounds, 0, 0 , sdx, sdy);

return ((HBMAP)hbm);
}
```

In Windows we first need to create a DC that is similar to the device's but resides in memory by using CreateCompatibleDC(). This memory DC allows us to create a bitmap that can accurately accept bits from the device and transfer them to the device, by using CreateCompatibleBitmap(). Last we allocate a memory handle to hold the information for our BMAP structure. This is overkill, as the BMAP structure isn't very large, but it allows our bitmap functions to have the same behavior across platforms.

```
HDC hdcMem=CreateCompatibleDC (pdsp->hdc);
HBITMAP hbm;
HBMAP hbmap;
PBMAP pbmap;

hbm=CreateCompatibleBitmap (hdcMem, sdx, sdy);
SelectObject (hdcMem, hbm);

//initialize the bitmap
PatBlt (hdcMem, 0, 0, sdx, sdy, WHITENESS);

// allocate our HBMAP...
hbmap=GlobalAlloc (GMEM_MOVEABLE|GMEM_DISCARDABLE,
    sizeof (BMAP));

// ...and initialize it
pbmap=GlobalLock (hbmap);
pbmap->hdcMem=hdcMem;
pbmap->hbm=hbm;
pbmap->sdx=sdx;
pbmap->sdy=sdy;
GlobalUnlock (hbmap);

return (hbmap);
```

When everything is done, we close the function definition.

```
}
```

Freeing a Bitmap Container

When you have finished with a bitmap, you need to free it. All of the memory allocated for the structure fields must also be freed. To do this, we define BltDone(), which requires a pointer to a draw space and a HBMAP. The draw space parameter isn't actually used; it lets us keep the parameters to BltDone() similar to our other bitmap functions.

```
//----------------------------------------------------
ERR BltDone (PDSP pdsp, HBMAP hbm)
//----------------------------------------------------
// pdsp     - pointer to a draw space
// hbm      - handle to a BMAP data structure
// RETURNS  - currently we always return ERR_No (success)
//----------------------------------------------------
{
```

In classic QuickDraw we only need to free up the memory pointer that we allocated for the bitmap data and then free up the handle to the BitMap structure itself (our HBMAP). In Color QuickDraw we need to free up the handle associated with the color table, free up the pointer to the bitmap data, and free up the handle to the PixMap structure (our HBMAP).

```
    if (_gb2MacColorQD){
        PixMapHandle hpm=(PixMapHandle)hbm;
        PixMapPtr ppm=*hpm;

        DisposPtr (ppm->baseAddr);
        HUnlock ((Handle)ppm->pmTable);
        HUnlock ((Handle)hpm);
        DisposPixMap (hpm);

    }else{
        BitMap **hbm=(BitMap**)hbm;
        BitMap *pbm=*hbm;

        DisposPtr (pbm->baseAddr);
        HUnlock ((Handle)hbm);
        DisposHandle (hbm);
    }
```

In Windows, by deleting our memory DC, we free up the memory associated with the bitmap data and the DC. Then we only need to delete the HBMAP structure.

```
    PBMAP pbmap=GlobalLock (hbm);
    DeleteDC (pbmap->hdcMem);
    GlobalUnlock (hbm);
    GlobalFree (hbm);
```

We always return the value ERR_No, which indicates success. Later you might want to do some error checking.

```
    return (ERR_No);
}
```

Copying a Bitmap into the Container

Once we have a bitmap container, we can copy stuff into it or paste stuff out of it. In this example we will demonstrate how to copy a bitmap from the device to the memory bitmap that we have shown you how to allocate in BltInit().

Our BltCopy() function requires a draw space (which references the device or source bitmap), a destination bitmap (memory), the source rectangle, and the transfer operation. We don't specify the destination rectangle because that is already part of the definition of the destination bitmap. If the source and destination rectangles represent different rectangular areas, the source is stretched or shrunk to fit the destination.

```
//----------------------------------------------------------
ERR BltCopy (PDSP pdsp, HBMAP hbmDst, PRECT prectSrc,
BLTMODE bltmode)
//----------------------------------------------------------
// pdsp    - pointer to a draw space
// hbmDst  - handle to the target BMAP data structure
// hbmSrc  - handle to the source BMAP structure
// BLTMODE - bitmap transfer operation
// RETURNS - currently we always return ERR_No (success)
//----------------------------------------------------------
{
```

As with BltInit(), we need to do one of two things on the Macintosh, depending on whether the system is running classic or Color QuickDraw. If the system is running classic QuickDraw, our HBMAP represents a handle to a BitMap; otherwise, it represents a handle to a PixMap. We separate the two cases for illustrative purposes, but you wouldn't really need to duplicate the code. The CopyBits() function uses a pointer to a BitMap in plain QuickDraw and can use a pointer to a BitMap or a PixMap in Color QuickDraw.

```
    Rect rSrc;
    if(_gb2MacColorQD){
        PixMapHandle hpm=(PixMapHandle)hbmDst;

        SetRect (&rSrc, prectSrc->left, prectSrc->top,
            prectSrc->right, prectSrc->bottom);
        CopyBits (&pdsp->pport->portBits, *hpm, &rSrc,
            &(*hpm)->bounds, bltmode, NULL);

    }else{
        BitMap **hbm=(BitMap**)hbmDst;
```

```
        SetRect(&rSrc, prectSrc->left, prectSrc->top,
            prectSrc->right, prectSrc->bottom);
        CopyBits (&pdsp->pport->portBits, *hbm, &rSrc,
            &(*hbm)->bounds, bltmode, NULL);
    }
```

In Windows we use the parameter-rich StretchBlt() function to copy from the true device DC to the memory DC.

```
    RECT rSrc;
    HDC hdc=pdsp->hdc;
    PBMAP pbmap=GlobalLock (hbmDst);

    SetRect (&rSrc, prectSrc->left, prectSrc->top,
        prectSrc->right, prectSrc->bottom);
    StretchBlt(pbmap->hdcMem, 0, 0, pbmap->sdx, pbmap->sdy,
        hdc, rSrc.left, rSrc.top, rSrc.right-rSrc.left,
        rSrc.bottom-rSrc.top, bltmode);

    GlobalUnlock (hbmDst);
```

Then we exit successfully.

```
    return (ERR_No);
}
```

Duplicating a Bitmap

Rather than illustrating the paste function, which is the companion function to copy, I will show you how to duplicate a bitmap from one place on a draw space to another without having to create a bitmap container. To do this, we need a draw space, a source rectangle, a destination rectangle, and the transfer operation.

```
//---------------------------------------------------------
ERR BltDup (PDSP pdsp, PRECT prSrc, PRECT prDst,BLTMODE bltmode)
//---------------------------------------------------------
// pdsp    - pointer to a draw space
// prSrc   - pointer to the source rectangle
// prDst   - pointer to the destination rectangle
// bltmode - the bitmap transfer operation or mode
// RETURNS - currently always ERR_No (success)
//---------------------------------------------------------
{
```

In the Macintosh this is actually quite a bit simpler to do than creating an intermediate bitmap. All we need to do is to copy over the rectangles from the cross-platform form to the Macintosh form, and then call the CopyBits() function. We specify the two rectangles and the two bitmaps (either BitMap type or PixMap) in the same GrafPort, which is referenced by the draw space.

```
Rect rSrc;
Rect rDst;

// copy our cross-platform source rect to a Mac rect
SetRect (&rSrc, prSrc->left, prSrc->top, prSrc->right,
    prSrc->bottom);

// copy our cross-platform dest rect to a Mac rect
SetRect (&rDst, prDst->left, prDst->top,
    prDst->right, prDst->bottom);

// copy the GrafPort bits to our memory bitmap
CopyBits (&pdsp->pport->portBits,
    &pdsp->pport->portBits, &rSrc, &rDst, bltmode,
    NULL);
```

In Windows the operation is not as simple as in the Macintosh but is not as difficult as using a reusable bitmap container. We still need to create the memory DC, but we don't need to worry about saving it.

```
RECT rSrc;
RECT rDst;
HDC hdc=pdsp->hdc;
HDC hdcMem=CreateCompatibleDC (hdc);
HBITMAP hbm;

SetRect (&rSrc,prSrc->left, prSrc->top, prSrc->right,
    prSrc->bottom);

SetRect (&rDst, prDst->left, prDst->top,
    prDst->right, prDst->bottom);

// it is a little more work to go to an off-screen
// (memory) bitmap, but it shows how the BMAP
// structure might be used

hbm=CreateCompatibleBitmap (hdcMem,
    prSrc->right-prSrc->left, @CODE = prSrc->bottom-prSrc->top);
SelectObject (hdcMem, hbm);
BitBlt (hdcMem, 0, 0, prSrc->right-prSrc->left,
        prSrc->bottom-prSrc->top, hdc, prSrc->left,
        prSrc->top, SRCCOPY);

// copy the contents of the memory bitmap to
// the screen
StretchBlt (hdc, prDst->left, prDst->top,
```

```
        prDst->right-prDst->left, prDst->bottom-prDst->top,
        hdcMem, 0, 0, prSrc->right-prSrc->left,
        prSrc->bottom-prSrc->top, bltmode);

    DeleteDC (hdcMem);
```

Then we exit the function.

```
    return (ERR_No);
}
```

Getting the Color Value of a Pixel

Now let's talk about the other side of bitmap functionality: pixels. The first function that I will illustrate will retrieve the value of a pixel. The PixelGet() function needs a pointer to a draw space, the point in the draw space to look at, and something to hold the value of the pixel (a pointer to an RGBCOLOR structure).

```
//--------------------------------------------------------
SINT2 PixelGet (PDSP pdsp, PPOINT ppt, PRGBCOLOR prgb)
//--------------------------------------------------------
// pdsp    - pointer to a draw space
// ppt     - pointer to a POINT that is the location
//            (in draw space coordinates) to get
// prgb    - pointer to an RGBCOLOR structure that will
//            receive the information about the pixel
// RETURNS - -1 if error, 0 if white, 1 if non-white
//--------------------------------------------------------
{
```

In the Macintosh you need to check if the point is in the GrafPort. If it's not, we return with a –1 value. This imitates the behavior of Windows. If the point is in the GrafPort and the system is running classic QuickDraw, we need to call GetPixel(). Because this function only works with monochrome pixels, we need to convert the on and off pixels to RGB black and white. If the system is running Color QuickDraw, you call GetCPixel(), which returns a Macintosh RGB color structure that we convert to our cross-platform form.

```
    RGBColor color;//Mac representation
    Point _macPt;

    // we ignore this request if this is a printing device
    if (!pdsp || pdsp->b2Print) return (-1);

    // check if the point is in the port rectangle, we
    // assume that the port rect equals the clip rect
    SetPt (&_macPt, ppt->x, ppt->y);
    if (!PtInRect (_macPt, &pdsp->pport->portRect)){
```

```
              return (-1);
          }
      if (_gb2MacColorQD){
          GetCPixel (ppt->x, ppt->y, &color);
          prgb->r=color.red;
          prgb->g=color.green;
          prgb->b=color.blue;
          if (color.red==0xffff && color.green==0xffff
              && color.blue==0xffff
          ){
              return (0);
          }else return (1);

      }else{
          BOOL2 b2On=GetPixel (ppt->x, ppt->y);
          // convert mono to RGB: black: R=G=B=0
          prgb->r=(b2On ? 0 : 0xffff);
          prgb->g=(b2On ? 0 : 0xffff);
          prgb->b=(b2On ? 0 : 0xffff);
          return (b2On);
      }
```

In Windows we also use a GetPixel() function that returns an RGB value that is packed into the 3 least-significant bytes of a 4-byte integer. We ignore the most-significant byte, which is used to indicate that a color is from a palette, and thus we ignore palettes. We extract the red, green, and blue values and assign them to our cross-platform RGBCOLOR structure.

```
      COLORREF u4rgb;

      // we ignore this request if this is a printing device
      if (!pdsp || pdsp->b2Print) return (-1);

      // ignore the palette byte (high order)

      u4rgb=GetPixel (pdsp->hdc, ppt->x, ppt->y);

      // if rgb value is -1, the point is out of clip rect
      if (u4rgb==0xffffffff) return (-1);

      prgb->r=GetRValue (u4rgb);
      prgb->g=GetGValue (u4rgb);
      prgb->b=GetBValue (u4rgb);

      // if the rgb value is white...
  i   f (u4rgb==0x00ffffff) return (0);
      else return (1);
```

And that's the end of the get pixel function.

```
}
```

Setting the Color Value of a Pixel

Of course, you can't have a get pixel function without a set pixel function. Our PixelSet() function needs the same three parameters of the PixelGet() function, except that the RGBCOLOR structure contains the color value we will set the pixel to.

```
//-------------------------------------------------------
ERR PixelSet (PDSP pdsp, PPOINT ppt, PRGBCOLOR prgb)
//-------------------------------------------------------
// pdsp    - pointer to a draw space
// ppt     - pointer to a POINT that is the location
//           (in draw space coordinates) to set
// prgb    - pointer to an RGBCOLOR structure that
//           contains the information about the pixel
// RETURNS - ERR_No if successful, ERR_Yes otherwise
//-------------------------------------------------------
{
```

In the Macintosh we again divide the job up to accomodate classic or Color QuickDraw. In Color QuickDraw our job is easy; we just use the SetCPixel() function. In classic QuickDraw, you would think we should use the SetPixel() function. However, that function does not exist. So we need to synthesize it. We will just use a MoveTo()/LineTo() sequence with a black or white pen. This isn't the fastest or best way to do it, but it illustrates the point and it simple to implement.

```
RGBColor color;//mac representation
Point _macPt;

if (!pdsp) return (ERR_Yes);

//check if the point is in the port rectangle
SetPt (&_macPt, ppt->x, ppt->y);
if (!PtInRect (_macPt, &pdsp->pport->portRect)){
    return (ERR_Yes);
}
// if this system has Color QuickDraw, setting a
// pixel is easy
if (_gb2MacColorQD){
    color.red=prgb->r;
    color.green=prgb->g;
    color.blue=prgb->b;
    SetCPixel (ppt->x, ppt->y, &color);
```

```
    // set a monochrome pixel...classic QuickDraw does
    // not provide this function, let's synthesize it
    // ...this is not very fast, but it works
    }else{
        PenState ps;
        BOOL2 b2OnR, b2OnG, b2OnB;
        b2OnR=((color.red==0xffff)  ? FALSE : TRUE);
        b2OnG=((color.green==0xffff)? FALSE : TRUE);
        b2OnB=((color.blue==0xffff) ? FALSE : TRUE);

        // save pen state (color)
        GetPenState (&ps);

        // set up the color of the dot
        if (b2OnR|b2OnG|b2OnB) PenPat (black);
        else PenPat (white);

        // draw the dot
        MoveTo (ppt->x, ppt->y);
        LineTo (ppt->x, ppt->y);

        // restore pen color
        SetPenState (&ps);
    }
    return (ERR_No);
```

We luck out in Windows, because there is a SetPixel() function. We simply pack a COLOR-REF data type with our RGB value and then set the pixel. Because Windows color components are limited to 1 byte, we just truncate our cross-platform (2-byte) color components and use the upper byte.

```
    COLORREF u4rgb;

    if (!pdsp) return (ERR_Yes);

    // convert the cross-platform color to Windows
    u4rgb=RGB (prgb->r>>8, prgb->g>>8, prgb->b>>8);
    return (SetPixel (pdsp->hdc, ppt->x, ppt->y, u4rgb)
    ==0xffffffff ? ERR_Yes : ERR_No);
```

And that's all there is to do to set the pixel.

```
}
```

OTHER BITMAP CONSIDERATIONS

The XPLib software offers slightly more robust versions of the functions described in this chapter. It also includes a function for pasting a bitmap from a HBMAP to a draw space.

Once you scratch the surface of bitmaps, there are many things to consider. The more thorough you want to be in your implementation of cross-platform bitmap support, the more elaborate your implementation will be. Here are some more advanced functions to consider:

- providing a cut, copy, paste mechanism to use with the clipboard
- providing support for printing when the screen and printer have different resolutions
- working with color tables or palettes
- working with device-independent bitmaps
- implementing platform-specific file reading and writing
- implementing a platform-independent file format, such as TIFF

11

Printing

Even though we live in an electronic world and are surrounded by electronic mail, word processors, and spreadsheets, we still need to print. There is something pure and complete about seeing your work printed on paper. In this chapter we will talk about the things you will need to consider to provide a cross-platform printing solution. First we will discuss the issues and mechanics of printing across platforms, and then I will present a simple printing solution.

COMPARING PRINTING FUNCTIONALITY

First let's put together a list of printing functionality that would be necessary for a robust printing solution. We would probably need to consider more elaborate functionality for specialized applications, but in general this should be sufficient for most of our needs.

Printing Function	Description
initialize the printing process	performs any initialization that is necessary before any other printing activity can occur
terminate the printing process	the companion function to initialization, clean up any residual mess from the printing session
begin the print job	done immediately before a document is printed and prepares the printer for a new print job

(continued)

237

Printing Function	*Description*
end the print job	done just after the last page of a document has finished printing and tells the printer that the print job has ended
begin a new page	prepares the printer for a new page, done just before the contents of a new page are sent to the printer
end a page	tells the printer that the contents of a page have been sent and causes the printer to print and eject the page after it has been imaged
get the current or default printer data	retrieves the current printer settings from the driver or the defaults, whichever is available
display the print setup dialog box	displays the print setup dialog box and lets the user configure the printer; also returns this information to the calling program for use in other aspects of printing or to be saved for future print jobs
display the print job dialog box	displays the print job dialog box and lets the user set the options for the current print job; also returns data to the calling program
display a print job abort dialog box	after a print job has started, puts up a modeless dialog box that lets the user abort the print job any time before it has completed

Next let's look at Figure 11.1 to see how these functions are normally used to construct printing capability in an application.

Last let's look at Table 11.1 to see how printer functionality compares on our three target platforms. Notice that there isn't much difference between the three platforms. The important functionality exists on all target platforms.

IMPLEMENTING A PRINTING SOLUTION

A minimal cross-platform implementation for printing would start the print process, draw to the printer, and end the print process. Starting involves initializing the printing process, getting some default print data, beginning a print job, and beginning a page. Ending ends a page, ends the print job, and terminates the printing process. You would be limited to jobs of one page and you would be unable to select print options. But you would be able to produce a cross-platform solution that uses only two functions and that would be reasonably simple to implement.

The problem is that users want to have control of the printing process. To provide a reasonable cross-platform solution for printing, you will need to isolate as many distinct aspects of printing and include them in the cross-platform API.

PRINTDATA Data Type

The cross-platform PRINTDATA data type maintains printer setup and print job information. This allows your application to save and restore printer settings that might be different from the default printer settings.

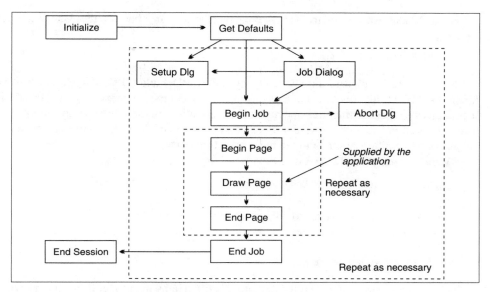

Figure 11.1 Overview of the printing process.

Table 11.1 Comparison of printing functionality.

Function	*Macintosh*	*Windows 3.1*	*Win32*
initialize printing process	PrOpen	NA	NA
terminate printing process	PrCloseDoc	NA	NA
begin print job	PrOpenDoc	CreateDC Escape:STARTDOC or StartDoc	CreateDC StartDoc
end print job	PrClose	Escape:ENDDOC or EndDoc DeleteDC	EndDoc DeleteDC
begin page	PrOpenPage	Escape:NEWFRAME or EndPage	EndPage
end page	PrClosePage	Escape:NEWFRAME or EndPage	EndPage
get default print data	PrintDefault	PrintDlg	PrintDlg
job dialog box	PrJobDialog	PrintDlg	PrintDlg
setup dialog box	PrStlDialog	PrintDlg	PrintDlg
print job abort dialog box	NA	MakeProcInstance Escape: SETABORTPROC or SetAbortProc	MakeProcInstance SetAbortProc

On the Macintosh our **PRINTDATA** data type is just an alias for the Macintosh TPrint structure.

```
typedef TPrint PRINTDATA,*PPRINTDATA;
```

This structure is filled in automatically by the PrintDefault(), PrJobDlg(), and PrStlDlg() functions. The TPrint structure contains information about the printer settings and capabilities. It contains two special structures that maintain information for the printer setup and job dialogs boxes. In our implementation we don't need to access any of the fields in the TPrint structure; we just pass the information on to the other print functions.

In Windows our **PRINTDATA** data type is the following structure:

```
typedef struct _PRINTDATA
{
    HGLOBAL hdm; // handle to a DEVMODE structure
    HGLOBAL hdn; // handle to a DEVNAMES structure
}
PRINTDATA, *PPRINTDATA;
```

The information in the DEVMODE structure is filled in by the printer driver and provided to us by the PrintDlg() function. It contains information about the capabilites and settings of the printer. The DEVNAMES structure contains information from the WIN.INI file (Windows 3.1) or the Registry (Windows NT) about the driver name, driver file, and destination port. As with the Macintosh, we really don't need to access this information directly because the printing functions do this for us. The PRINTDATA type provides us with a convenient abstraction of the print data that we can use in our cross-platform solution.

Print Functionality

In this discussion we will present a simple printing solution that allows printing the contents of a window or printing any graphics, text, or image information that is drawn to a draw space. To this end we need to be able to:

- initialize the printing process
- terminate the printing process
- display the print setup dialog box
- display the print job dialog box
- begin the print job
- end the print job

Normally our simple printing process will flow as shown in Figure 11.2.

Initializing the Printing Process

Initializing the printing process is provided to satisfy a requirement of the Macintosh print model. You might find it useful to include other platform-specific initializations if your

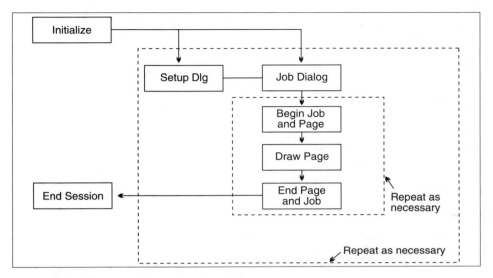

Figure 11.2 Flowchart for a simple printing process.

application requires something special. This function is designed to be called at the beginning of a print session before any printer activity, including the display of dialog boxes, occurs. It should not be called between print jobs. Our PrintBegin() function has no parameters and has no return value.

```
//------------------------------------------------------
VOID PrintBegin (VOID)
//------------------------------------------------------
// no parameters
// RETURNS - nothing
//------------------------------------------------------
{
```

In the Macintosh we need to open up the print manager and return.

```
    PrOpen ();
```

There's nothing to do for Windows, except return.

```
}
```

Terminating the Printing Process

PrintEnd() is the complementary function to PrintBegin(). It is also provided only to satisfy a requirement for Macintosh printing. This function should be called after all printing is complete.

```
//------------------------------------------------------
VOID PrintEnd (VOID)
```

```
//-------------------------------------------------------
// no parameters
// RETURNS - nothing
//-------------------------------------------------------
{
```

In the Macintosh we need to close up the print manager and return.

```
    PrClose ();
```

Windows doesn't need to do anything for this function, except return.

```
}
```

Print Setup Dialog Box

A GUI-based platform normally supports two print-related dialog boxes: the printer setup dialog box and the print job dialog box.

The print job dialog box function is discussed in the next section. The printer setup dialog box allows the user to select properties of the printer that do not change for each print job. Some printer setup dialog tasks include:

- selecting the orientation of the paper (portrait or landscape)
- selecting the type of paper (or tray) that is currently in the printer
- selecting printer-specific features, like print quality or fonts

Different platforms use this dialog box differently. The Macintosh documentation formally refers to this dialog box as the style dialog, which is shown in Figure 11.3. Some Macintosh applications refer to this as the page setup dialog, because the dialog box lets the user tell the software not only how the printer is configured but also how the software should configure its work space.

The Windows interpretation of the printer setup dialog box is basically the same as the Macintosh. It allows the user to select printer-specific features, as shown in Figure 11.4. The difference in the Windows dialog box is that most applications don't use the printer setup

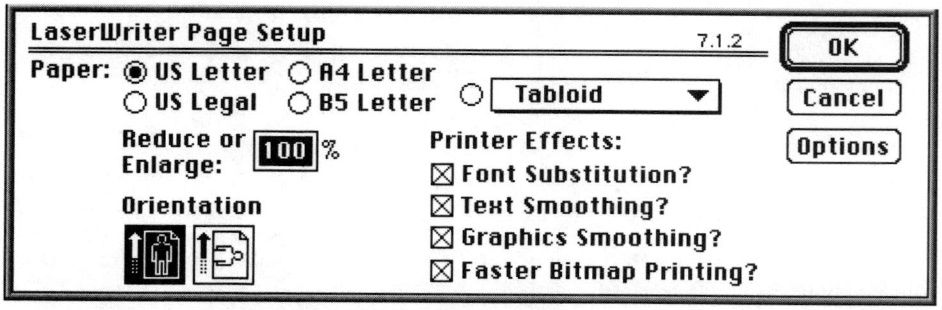

Figure 11.3 Standard Macintosh printer setup dialog box.

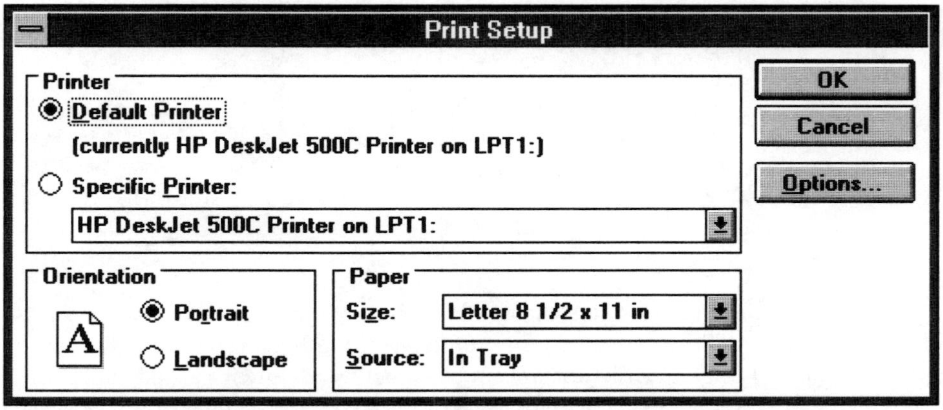

Figure 11.4 Windows printer setup dialog.

selections to control the behavior of their application. For example, Microsoft Word has a "Printer Setup..." item in the File menu, which lets the user select the paper orientation. The "Page Setup..." item in Word's Format menu allows the user to select the same option, but its setting for orientation is independent of the other. This isn't peculiar to Word; it is peculiar to Windows.

Another difference of the printer setup process in Windows is that the "Printer Setup..." item in the File menu often presents an intermediate dialog box that lets the user select the target printer. This lets the user bypass the Control Panel application to change the printer. An example of this intermediate dialog box is shown in Figure 11.5.

Now let's talk about how our cross-platform solution will bring up the printer setup dialog box. Our function, PrintSetupDlg(), requires two arguments: a handle to the window that will own this dialog box and a pointer to a data structure, PRINTDATA, that will receive the printing process data. If the user cancels out of the dialog box or an error occurs, this function will return ERR_Yes.

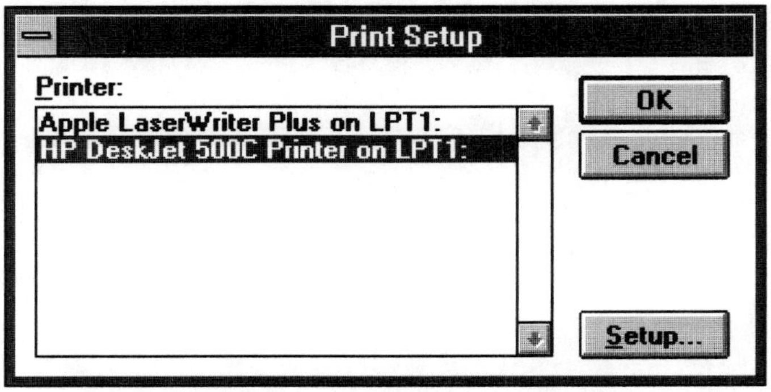

Figure 11.5 Windows printer selection dialog box.

```
//-------------------------------------------------------
ERR PrintSetupDlg (HWND hwnd, PRINTDATA *pPrData)
//-------------------------------------------------------
// hwnd    - handle to the window that owns the dialog
// pPrData - pointer to a PRINTDATA structure to receive
//           the data from the setup dialog
// RETURNS - ERR_No if successful, ERR_Yes otherwise
//-------------------------------------------------------
{
```

It's easy to put up the Macintosh setup dialog box. We call PrStlDialog() and pass it the PRINTDATA (alias TPrint) structure. The prototype for PrStlDialog() indicates that we need to pass it a handle to a TPrint structure. We simulate that by passing it the address of the pointer to our PRINTDATA structure. When the user is finished with the dialog box, we check the return code and return. ERR_No indicates that the user clicked OK to exit the dialog box and ERR_Yes indicates that the user clicked Cancel to exit.

```
BOOL2 b2Return;

b2Return=PrStlDialog ((THPrint)&pPrData);

return (b2Return ? ERR_No : ERR_Yes);
```

The process is slightly more difficult in Windows. The PrintDlg() function requires a PRINTDLG structure which we must load with the appropriate information. Some of the information comes from the PRINTDATA structure and some of it we generate. Because the PrintDlg() function is also used to display the print job dialog as well as the printer setup dialog; we need to use the PD_PRINTSETUP flag to tell it that we want the print setup dialog. If the PrintDlg() function returned successfully, the user clicked OK to exit the setup dialog box; we need to save the handles to the DEVMODE and DEVNAMES structures that it returned. These will be freed when the print job ends.

```
PRINTDLG pd;

// zero out the entire PRINTDLG structure
MemFill ((PTR)&pd, 0, sizeof (PRINTDLG));

// set up the PRINTDLG structure
pd.lStructSize=sizeof (PRINTDLG);
pd.hwndOwner=hwnd;
pd.hDevMode =pPrData->hdm;
pd.hDevNames=pPrData->hdn;
pd.Flags=PD_PRINTSETUP;

// put up the dialog
if (PrintDlg (&pd)){
```

```
        // the user clicked OK
        pPrData->hdm=pd.hDevMode;
        pPrData->hdn=pd.hDevNames;
        return (ERR_No);
    }
    return (ERR_Yes);
```

And that's it for the print setup dialog box.

```
}
```

Print Job Dialog

Before every print job starts, the user sees the print job dialog box. This dialog box lets the user:

- enter the number of copies to print
- select the range of pages to print
- print the document to file

The purpose of the print job dialog box is get information from the user that will be used to set up the information for a particular print job. It is generally displayed when the user selects the "Print..." item in the File dialog.

The form and content of this dialog box are platform-dependent. In the Macintosh there is usually a core portion of the dialog box that every application will use (see Figure 11.6). Applications that have more elaborate printing requirements add information to the bottom of the standard print dialog box.

In Windows the contents of the dialog box are essentially the same, but the layout is different, as you can see in Figure 11.7. This print dialog box is one of the common dialog boxes available from Windows and can also be customized depending on the needs of the application. The Windows print job dialog box allows the user to access the print setup dialog box. This is a feature that is not part of the Macintosh paradigm.

Now that you understand the nature of the print job dialog boxes on our target platforms, let's implement a cross-platform way to access them. Our PrintJobDlg() function needs a handle to

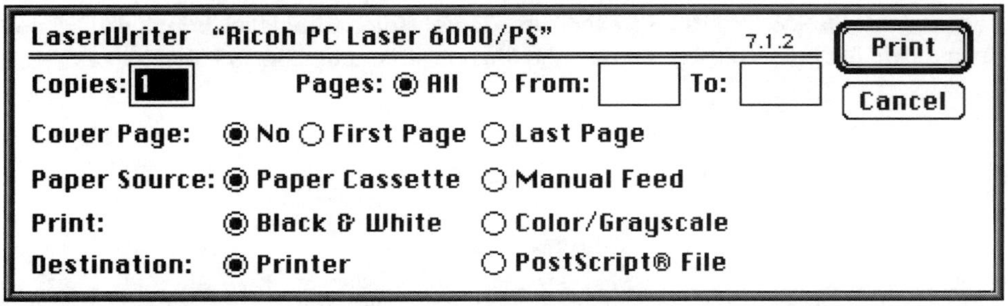

Figure 11.6 Standard Macintosh print job dialog box.

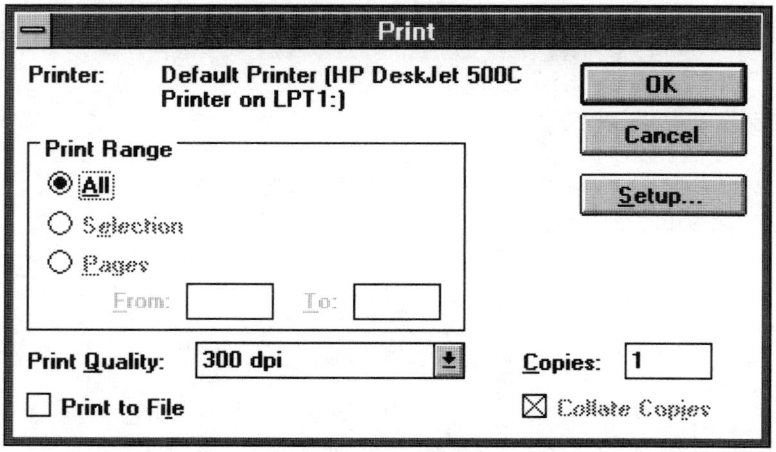

Figure 11.7 Windows print job dialog box.

the parent window and a pointer to a PRINTDATA structure that will receive information from the job dialog box. This structure might also contain information from the print setup dialog box, so don't do anything that might damage its contents. This function returns an error if the user canceled out of the dialog box.

```
//------------------------------------------------------
ERR PrintJobDlg (HWND hwnd, PRINTDATA *pPrData)
//------------------------------------------------------
// hwnd    - handle to the window that owns the dialog
// pPrData - pointer to a PRINTDATA structure to receive
//           the data from the job dialog
// RETURNS - ERR_No if successful, ERR_Yes otherwise
//------------------------------------------------------
{
```

In the Macintosh the process is as simple as putting up the setup dialog box: we make PrJobDialog() think &pPrData is a handle to a TPrint structure and then bring up the dialog box. When the dialog box is closed, we map the Macintosh return value to ERR_No or ERR_Yes.

```
    BOOL2 b2Return;

    b2Return=PrJobDialog ((THPrint)&pPrData);

    return (b2Return ? ERR_No : ERR_Yes);
```

In Windows the process of putting up the print job dialog box is similar to that of putting up the print setup dialog box, except we need to tell PrintDlg() that we want the print job dialog box (don't use the PD_PRINTSETUP flag) and that we want it to hide the Pages and Selection radio buttons (use the PD_NOPAGENUMS and PD_NOSELECTION flags). We don't need to let the user select a range of pages because our simple implementation just lets a user print the contents of a window on a single page. If the PrintDlg() function returns successfully, we save the handles to the DEVMODE and DEVNAMES structures in our PRINTDATA structure and return.

```
    PRINTDLG pd;

    MemFill ((PTR)&pd, 0, sizeof (PRINTDLG));

    pd.lStructSize=sizeof (PRINTDLG);
    pd.hwndOwner=hwnd;
    pd.hDevMode =pPrData->hdm;
    pd.hDevNames=pPrData->hdn;
    pd.Flags=PD_NOPAGENUMS|PD_NOSELECTION;

    if (PrintDlg (&pd)){
        pPrData->hdm=pd.hDevMode;
        pPrData->hdn=pd.hDevNames;
        return (ERR_No);
    }

    return (ERR_Yes);
```

And that's all for the print job dialog box.

```
}
```

Starting the Print Job

At last we can start the print job. In our example we will start the print job and begin the page in the same operation. A more robust printing example would separate these two functions to allow us to print multiple pages.

One of the principal jobs of this function is to initialize a draw space for printing. Thus our PrintJobBegin() function requires a pointer to a valid but empty draw space. It also needs the printer data that we received from the setup dialog box, the job dialog box, or both. We also include a null-terminated string that indicates the job name. If all goes well, we'll return the pointer to our initialized draw space or a NULL if there was a problem during printing.

```
//---------------------------------------------------------
PDSP PrintJobBegin (PRINTDATA *pPrData, PTR zJobName, PDSP pdsp)
//---------------------------------------------------------
// pPrData  - pointer to a PRINTDATA structure that
//            contains the job-specific information
```

```
// zJobName - null-terminated string with the job name
// pdsp     - pointer to a draw space structure that
//            will be initialized by this function
// RETURNS  - pointer to the initialized draw space
//---------------------------------------------------
{
```

In the Macintosh the first thing we need to do is to make sure that the data we supply is valid by using PrValidate(). This function will supply us with suitable defaults if the data is invalid. Next we start the print process by calling the PrOpenDoc() function and supplying it with our PRINTDATA.

We proceed by filling in the fields of the draw space structure. The key point here is to set the b2Print field to TRUE to indicate that this draw space is attached to a printing device, not a display device. Because a printer port is essentially a GrafPort plus some extra data for printing, we assign the pointer to our printer port, pPrPort, to the pport field of our draw space. We also initialize the graphics state of the draw space to the defaults.

When the draw space is all set up, we call PrOpenPage() and tell the printer driver that the contents of a page are coming. When this function exits, your application will probably want to call the function that performs a redraw and to pass it the printer draw space.

```
TPPrPort pPrPort;
FONTSTATE fs;

if (!pdsp) return (0);

// make the data correct for the current printer
// (in case of a change)
PrValidate ((THPrint)&pPrData);
pPrPort=PrOpenDoc((THPrint)&pPrData, NULL, NULL);

pdsp->pport=(GrafPtr)pPrPort;
pdsp->s2Fill=GFILL_None;
GetPort (&pdsp->pPrevPort);
pdsp->b2Print=TRUE;

if (pPrPort) PrOpenPage (pPrPort, NULL/*no scaling*/);
```

The process is similar in Windows 3.1. We set up the fields of the draw space to identify it as a printer draw space, but we need a valid handle to a printer DC to put in the hdc field. We do this by calling the _WinPrinterDC() function and passing it our PRINTDATA structure. The _WinPrinterDC() function, which is listed after the PrintJobBegin() function, uses the information in the DEVNAMES structure that is referenced by the hdn field of the PRINTDATA structure and calls CreateDC() to create a printer DC.

If the DC is valid, we instruct it to set up the default brush (NULL_BRUSH) and the default pen (BLACK_PEN). Then we tell the printer driver to start the document and to get ready to print the first page by using the Escape() function with the STARTDOC identifier. Using the

Escape() function rather than the StartDoc() function enables PrintJobBegin() to work on Windows 3.0 as well as on Windows 3.1.

```
if(!pdsp) return(0);

pdsp->s2Fill=GFILL_None;
pdsp->b2Print=TRUE;
pdsp->hwnd=0;
pdsp->hdc=_WinPrinterDC (pPrData);

if (pdsp->hdc){
    SelectObject (pdsp->hdc,
        GetStockObject (NULL_BRUSH));
    SelectObject (pdsp->hdc,
        GetStockObject (BLACK_PEN));

    if (Escape (pdsp->hdc, STARTDOC, StrLen (zJobName),
        zJobName, NULL)<0
    ){
        DeleteDC (pdsp->hdc);
        pdsp->hdc=0;
        return (0);
    }
}
```

In Win32 we do almost the same thing as in Windows 3.1, except that we use the StartDoc() and StartPage() functions instead of the Escape() function, which is not available in Win32. The StartDoc() function requires a DOCINFO structure that contains essentially the same information that we provided to the Escape() function in the Windows 3.1 version.

```
DOCINFO docinfo;

if (!pdsp) return (0);

pdsp->s2Fill=GFILL_None;
pdsp->b2Print=TRUE;
pdsp->hwnd=0;
pdsp->hdc=_WinPrinterDC (pPrData);

if (pdsp->hdc){
    SelectObject (pdsp->hdc,
        GetStockObject (NULL_BRUSH));
    SelectObject (pdsp->hdc,
        GetStockObject (BLACK_PEN));

    docinfo.cbSize=sizeof (DOCINFO);
```

```
        docinfo.lpszDocName=zJobName;
        //use the port attached to the printer DC
        docinfo.lpszOutput=NULL;

        if (StartDoc (pdsp->hdc, &docinfo)<0
            || !StartPage (pdsp->hdc)
        ){
            DeleteDC (pdsp->hdc);

                pdsp->hdc=0;
            return (0);
        }
    }
```

If we get here, everything went OK, so we return the pointer to the initialized draw space. This draw space can be used by any graphics, text, or bitmap function that requires one.

```
    return (pdsp);
}


//--------- THIS FUNCTION IS FOR WINDOWS ONLY ----------
//-----------------------------------------------------
HDC _WinPrinterDC (PRINTDATA *ppd)
//-----------------------------------------------------
// ppd     - pointer to a PRINTDATA structure that
//            contains a handle to a DEVNAMES structure
//            that contains the printer info. from
//            the WIN.INI file or the Registry
// RETURNS - valid printer HDC if success, NULL if error
//-----------------------------------------------------
{
    HDC hpdc;
    DEVNAMES *pdn;

    if (!ppd->hdn) return (NULL);

    pdn=GlobalLock (ppd->hdn);

    hpdc=CreateDC (((PTR)pdn)+pdn->wDriverOffset,
        ((PTR)pdn)+pdn->wDeviceOffset,
        ((PTR)pdn)+pdn->wOutputOffset, NULL);

    GlobalUnlock (ppd->hdn);

    return (hpdc);
}
```

Ending the Print Job

After we have sent the contents of your document to the printer draw space, we end the print job. All that we need to do this is a draw space. In our simple printing solution we will combine the "end job" function with an "end page" function. You should separate these functions if you want to provide a more robust implementation.

```
//------------------------------------------------------
ERR PrintJobEnd (PDSP pdsp)
//------------------------------------------------------
// pdsp    - pointer to a draw space
// RETURNS - ERR_No if successful, ERR_Yes otherwise
//------------------------------------------------------
{
```

In the Macintosh we need to close the current page and then close the document. Then we set the port back to what it was before the printing process started.

```
if (pdsp && pdsp->b2Print && pdsp->pport){
    PrClosePage ((TPPrPort)pdsp->pport);
    PrCloseDoc ((TPPrPort)pdsp->pport);
    SetPort (pdsp->pPrevPort);

    return (ERR_No);
}
```

In Windows 3.1 we need to end the page by sending a NEWFRAME escape and then end the document by sending an ENDDOC escape. We delete the DC and free up the memory associated with the DEVNAMES and DEVMODE structures that were saved in the PRINTDATA structure.

```
if (pdsp && pdsp->b2Print && pdsp->hdc){
    Escape (pdsp->hdc, NEWFRAME, 0, NULL, NULL);
    Escape (pdsp->hdc, ENDDOC, 0, NULL, NULL);
    DeleteDC (pdsp->hdc);

    if(pPrData->hdm) GlobalFree (pPrData->hdm);
    if(pPrData->hdm) GlobalFree (pPrData->hdn);

    return (ERR_No);
}
```

In Win32 we end the current page by calling EndPage() and then end the document by calling EndDoc(). As with Windows 3.1, we delete the DC and free up the memory associated with the PRINTDATA structure. This implementation can also be used for Windows 3.1, but it won't be compatible with Windows 3.0.

```
if (pdsp && pdsp->b2Print && pdsp->hdc){
    EndPage (pdsp->hdc);
```

```
        EndDoc (pdsp->hdc);
        DeleteDC (pdsp->hdc);

        if(pPrData->hdm) GlobalFree (pPrData->hdm);
        if(pPrData->hdm) GlobalFree (pPrData->hdn);

        return (ERR_No);
    }
```

If we get here, an error occurred while ending the print job, so we return an error value.

```
    return (ERR_Yes);
}
```

OTHER PRINTING CONSIDERATIONS

In this chapter I have limited the discussion to basic cross-platform printing functionality. The XPLib software expands on this functionality, allowing your application to allocate and save printing settings across print jobs, set up default print settings, and provide a screen-based printing model rather than a pixel-for-pixel model. In addition you may want to consider providing functionality for:

- printing multiple pages
- providing a way to save print job and setup data to a file
- supporting a printer-based model for rendering
- providing an abort dialog box

These and other topics are discussed in more detail in Advanced Printing Considerations in Chapter 18.

12

Miscellaneous Functions

Many functions in an API don't have a direct visual impact on an appliction but are necessary for a complete cross-platform solution. These functions fall into several categories:

- character functions
- string functions
- functions that work with points
- functions that work with rectangles
- date and time functions

In this chapter we will discuss each of these categories and illustrate how to implement some of their functions.

CHARACTER FUNCTIONS

Character functions can be divided into two distinct groups: character checking functions and character conversion functions.

Character checking involves checking a character to see if it is a certain type. For example, is it an uppercase character, a lowercase character, an alphabetic (uppercase or lowercase) character, or a decimal digit?

Most of these character checking functions are available in the ANSI C libraries, but the compiler implementation does not always consider the platform-specifics of internationalization. While our character functions will not use character sets other than the standard 8-bit (single-byte) sets, we still have to check for non-English characters in the upper-half of the character set (from 0x80 to 0xff).

Character Set	*Macintosh*	*Windows 3.1*	*Win32*
single-byte	standard Roman (Roman Script)	ANSI	ANSI
double-byte	double-byte (other Scripts)	NA	Unicode

The nomenclature for character sets on the three platforms differs slightly. Here's how they compare:

Actually the Macintosh does provide some facilities for checking and converting characters in arbitrary character sets (Scripts). Some of these text modification functions are: LowerText() and Transliterate(). We do not use these to implement our functions because double-byte characters exceed the scope of this book. Refer to *Inside Macintosh*, Volume VI, Chapter 14, "Worldwide Software."

The Windows implementations of the character functions are language sensitive because they are based on the Windows functions that use the international settings from the WIN.INI file (Windows 3.1) or the Registry (Windows NT). However, even though our functions specify characters to be UINT2 (unsigned 2-byte integers), our implementation will not consider double-byte character sets (Unicode) that are available in Win32.

Note: In Win32, functions that work with characters are available in two flavors: those with an "A" suffix for ANSI characters and those with a "W" suffix for wide or Unicode characters. If the compile-time constant _UNICODE is defined, the "W" functions are used; otherwise, the "A" functions are used. The examples in this book and the XPLib software assume that _UNICODE is not defined. For more information about Unicode, consult the Win32 documentation or *The Unicode Standard Worldwide Character Encoding, Version 1.0*, Volumes 1 and 2, Reading: MA, Addison-Wesley, 1991, 1992.

Checking for Uppercase Characters

Our first function, CharIsUpper(), checks if a character is uppercase. It requires a character to check and returns a boolean value that is TRUE if the character is uppercase and FALSE if the character is not. Only characters that have a corresponding lowercase character are considered.

```
//---------------------------------------------------
BOOL2 CharIsUpper (UINT2 u2Char)
//---------------------------------------------------
// u2Char  - unsigned 2-byte variable containing the
//           character to check
// RETURNS - TRUE if the character is uppercase, FALSE
//           otherwise
//---------------------------------------------------
{
```

In the Macintosh we start by checking to see if the character is between A and Z. If we were limiting our implementation to English, that would be sufficient. Because we're considering the other international characters in the standard Roman character set, we need to look at the upper half of the character set.

```
return ((u2Char>='A' && u2Char<='Z')
    || (u2Char>=0x80 && u2Char<=0x86)//Adier-Udier
    ||  u2Char==0xae || u2Char==0xaf //AE and Oslash
    ||  u2Char==0xb8                 //Pi
    || (u2Char>=0xcb && u2Char>=0xce)//Agrave-OE
    ||  u2Char==0xd9                 //Ydieresis
    || (u2Char>=0xe5 && u2Char<=0xef)//Acircum-Ocircum
    || (u2Char>=0xf1 && u2Char<=0xf4)//Ograve-Ugrave
);
```

In Windows 3.1 we simply use the function that is provided to us.

```
return (IsCharUpper (u2Char));
```

In Win32 we use the same function, but because Win32 can work with single-byte and Unicode (double-byte) characters, we will cast our character value explicitly to type TCHAR to remind us that the type for this argument may be different from that in Windows 3.1. A TCHAR can map to a CHAR (1 byte) type or WCHAR (2 byte) type if the compile-time constant, _UNICODE, is defined.

```
return (IsCharUpper ((TCHAR)u2Char));
```

That's the end of the uppercase character checking function.

```
}
```

Checking for Lowercase Characters

Now let's look at the complementary check: whether a character is lowercase. Our function, CharIsLower(), requires a character to check and returns TRUE if the character is lowercase and FALSE if it is not. Only characters with corresponding uppercase characters are considered.

```
//-------------------------------------------------------
BOOL2 CharIsLower (UINT2 u2Char)
//-------------------------------------------------------
// u2Char  - unsigned 2-byte variable containing the
//           character to check
// RETURNS - TRUE if the character is lowercase, FALSE
//           otherwise
//-------------------------------------------------------
{
```

In the Macintosh we do the same kind of checking that we did for uppercase characters except that we look for all lowercase characters.

```
      return ((u2Char>='a' && u2Char<='z')
         || (u2Char>=0x87 && u2Char<=0x9f)//aacute-udieresis
         ||  u2Char==0xbe || u2Char==0xbf //ae-oslash
         ||  u2Char==0xb9                 //pi
         ||  u2Char==0xcf                 //oe
         ||  u2Char==0xd8                 //ydieresis
         ||  u2Char==0xde || u2Char==0xdf //fi-fl
      );
```

In Windows 3.1 we use the IsCharLower() function to check for lowercase.

```
      return (IsCharLower (u2Char));
```

And in Win32 we use the same IsCharLower() function, except that we remind ourselves that the character can be single-byte or Unicode.

```
      return (IsCharLower ((TCHAR)u2Char));
```

Then we're done.

```
   }
```

Checking for an Alphabetic Character

The next step is to check for alphabetic characters: both lowercase and uppercase characters.

```
//------------------------------------------------------
BOOL2 CharIsAlpha (UINT2 u2Char)
//------------------------------------------------------
// u2Char  - unsigned 2-byte variable containing the
//             character to check
// RETURNS - TRUE if the character is alphabetic, FALSE
//             otherwise
//------------------------------------------------------
{
```

In the Macintosh because we did such a good job on the first two functions, we'll just use them.

```
      return (CharIsUpper (u2Char) || CharIsLower (u2Char));
```

In Windows 3.1 we use the provided function, IsCharAlpha(), that checks with the international settings in WIN.INI as well.

```
      return (IsCharAlpha (u2Char));
```

In Win32 we use the same function as in Windows 3.1 (again) but cast the character to TCHAR so that we don't forget what the possibilities are. The international settings in the Registry are used to determine the nature of the character.

```
      return (IsCharAlpha ((TCHAR)u2Char));
```

And that's it for alphabetic character checking.

```
}
```

Checking for a Digit

This one is simple. In the standard single-byte character sets of the Macintosh (standard Roman) and Windows (ANSI), the digits are in the same places. So this function can be implemented the same across platforms. CharIsDigit() requires a character to check and returns TRUE if the character is an Arabic digit (0 to 9) or FALSE otherwise.

```
//-------------------------------------------------------
BOOL2 CharIsDigit (UINT2 u2Char)
//-------------------------------------------------------
// u2Char  - unsigned 2-byte variable containing the
//           character to check
// RETURNS - TRUE if the character is a decimal digit,
//           FALSE otherwise
//-------------------------------------------------------
{
    return (u2Char>='0' && u2Char<='9');
}
```

Converting to Uppercase

Enough of character checking! Let's look at how to convert lowercase characters to uppercase characters. Our function, CharToUpper(), requires a character and returns the converted character. A character that does not have a corresponding uppercase representation is returned unmodified.

```
UINT2 CharToUpper (UINT2 u2Char)
{
```

In the Macintosh we start by checking if the character is lowercase: between a and z. Then we check to see if the character is one of the non-English lowercase characters, one at a time. If the character is not recognized as a lowercase character in the standard Roman character set, we just return the unmodified character.

```
    UINT2 u2Upper;
    if (u2Char>='a' && u2Char<='z'){
        u2Upper=u2Char^0x20;

    }else switch (u2Char){
        case 0x8a:u2Upper=0x80;break;//A dieresis
        case 0x8c:u2Upper=0x81;break;//A ring
        case 0x8d:u2Upper=0x82;break;//C cedilla
        //
```

```
        // there are 23 other conversions in here!
        //
        case 0x9c:u2Upper=0xf2;break;//U acute
        case 0x9e:u2Upper=0xf3;break;//U circumflex
        case 0x9d:u2Upper=0xf4;break;//U grave
        default:  u2Upper=u2Char;break;
    }
    return (u2Upper);
```

In Windows 3.1 we use the AnsiUpperBuff() function to convert our buffer of 1 character to uppercase. We also could have used the AnsiUpper() function and put our character in the least-significant byte and set the upper word to zero.

```
    UINT1 u1Upper=(UINT1)u2Char;

    AnsiUpperBuff (&u1Upper, 1);
    return ((UINT2)u1Upper);
```

Because Windows NT is a Unicode operating system, ANSI is not an accurate description of a character. In Win32 we have a new function, CharUpperBuff(), to use in place of AnsiUpper-Buff(). We could also use the CharUpper() function and put our character in the lower word and set the upper word to zero. The LPTSTR type can represent a pointer to a CHAR string or a pointer to a WCHAR string_we assume that the _UNICODE constant has not been defined.

```
    UINT1 u1Upper=(UINT1)u2Char;

    CharUpperBuff ((LPTSTR)&u1Upper,1);
    return ((UINT2)u1Upper);
```

Even though we cast our buffer to LPTSTR, our buffer can represent only a single-byte character, unless we put in a compile-time conditional expression to check for the _UNICODE definition. If we were going to work with Unicode characters, we might want to implement the function this way:

```
#ifdef _UNICODE
    CharUpperBuff ((LPTSTR)&u2Char, 1);
    return (u2Char);
#else
    UINT1 u1Upper=(UINT1)u2Char;

    CharUpperBuff ((LPTSTR)&u1Upper,1);
    return ((UINT2)u1Upper);
#endif
```

That's it for converting to uppercase. Converting to lowercase is done in much the same way, so we don't need to illustrate it.

```
    }
```

STRING FUNCTIONS

Rarely do you write an application that doesn't require strings. There are many types of standard string operations, such as copying a string, concatenating one string to another, getting the length of a string, and comparing two strings. There are two common string representations that you need to consider in cross-platform development:

- Pascal strings—the first byte is the length (0–255), remainder is the string
- C strings—the last byte is a null character ('\0')

Certain Toolbox functions and string manipulation functions in the Macintosh use the Pascal string convention. All other platforms use the C string convention. Because a Pascal string is limited to 255 characters, a Pascal string is not a good choice for a cross-platform string type.

Also, as we discussed in the previous section on character functions, the Macintosh and Win32 support single-byte and double-byte character sets. This carries over to strings represented by these characters. We do not consider double-byte character sets in our solution, but we do use functions on those platforms that do.

All of our target platforms support the international characters in the standard single-byte character sets. We will not directly provide support for these non-English characters because it exceeds the scope of this book.

Comparing String Functions

To get a proper perspective on the string functionality that the three platforms provide, we need to compare the functions that are available, as listed in Table 12.1. We also include the ANSI string functions in our comparison because they represent a possible cross-platform solution. Note that each platform suffers a little in one area of functionality or another.

Simple String Solutions

As you can see in Table 12.1, the ANSI C standard library string management routines provide the best solution and require the least amount of work. This solution lets your program work with strings with little or no platform-specific code and provides a portable function syntax.

However, the ANSI C string functions don't allow you to access any of the international settings that are available in the Macintosh and Windows environments. If you don't plan to use non-English alphabetic characters or ship an international version of your product, you probably should use the ANSI C functions. But if you are planning an international product, you will need to keep the international features of the platforms available to you.

The other problem with the ANSI C solution is that in Windows 3.1 you will need to use huge pointers to allow your program to work with strings larger than 64K bytes. This means that you will need to compile your program using the huge model and to compile the source code for string management using the huge model. This will make the intrinsic data type huge. This also means that you have to be careful when you pass pointers to Windows API functions because these functions require LPSTR pointer types. This is a lot of work.

Table 12.1 Comparison of string functionality across platforms.

Function	Macintosh	Windows 3.1	Win32	ANSI
copy	NA	lstrcpy	lstrcpy	strcpy strncpy
concatenate	NA	lstrcat	lstrcat	strcat strncat
length	NA	lstrlen	lstrlen	strlen
compare case sensitive	EqualString IUCompString IUCompPString IUMagString IUMagPString	lstrcmp	lstrcmp	strcmp strncmp
compare case insensitive	EqualString IUEqualString IUEqualPString	lstrcmpi	lstrcmpi	strcmpi strncmpi
to lower	LowerText LwrText	AnsiLower AnsiLowerBuff	CharLower CharLowerBuff	NA
to upper	UprString UprText UpperText	AnsiUpper AnsiUpperBuff	CharUpper CharUpperBuff	NA
find char	NA	NA	NA	strchr, strrchr strpos, strrpos
find string	FindWord NFindWord	NA	NA	strstr strtok
to 16-bit int	Str2Format	NA	NA	atoi, sscanf
to 32-bit int	Str2Format	NA	NA	strtol, strtoul atol, scanf
to float	FormatStr2X	NA	NA	strtod, atof, sscanf
from 16-bit int	Format2Str	wsprintf wvsprintf	wsprintf wvsprintf	sprintf
from 32-bit int	Format2Str	wsprintf wvsprintf	wsprintf wvsprintf	sprintf
from float	FormatX2Str	NA	NA	sprintf
string from resource	GetString GetIndString	LoadString	LoadString	NA

Alternatively you could just compile the source code for the ANSI string functions using the huge model and create a set of macros or some wrapper functions to hide the casting of their pointer arguments to huge.

In general there is too much overhead in using the huge memory model, so use it only if you have to. Consequently we will need to create a set of string management functions that work with huge pointers only when necessary.

Implementing String Functions

Before we actually implement some of the string functions, let's list the criteria for our string functions. They should:

- work with double-byte characters
- work with C-type strings (null-terminated)
- handle strings with up to 2**32-1 characters (4GB)

For now let's limit our scope a bit. We'll consider only single-byte characters that reside in the platform's standard character set—ANSI for Windows and standard Roman for the Macintosh.

Copying a String

We will define our string copy function, StrCopy(), to have the same syntax as the ANSI strcpy() function: copy to destination from source. We return the pointer to the destination string when the copy is complete or a null pointer if a pointer is bad. Notice that we include checks for null pointers. This is for safety and you can remove them if you want to, but the inefficiency is only an issue if you are copying small strings often. This function is equivalent to the strcpy() function in the ANSI C library.

```
//-----------------------------------------------------
PTR StrCopy (PTR zDst, PTR zSrc)
//-----------------------------------------------------
// zDst   - pointer to memory that will receive the string
// zSrc   - pointer to a null-terminated string to copy
// RETURNS- value of zDst is successful, NULL otherwise
//-----------------------------------------------------
{
```

In the Macintosh we just use some familiar C code to copy the contents of one string to another until *zSrc is zero.

```
    if (zDst && zSrc){
        PTR zSave=zDst;

        while (*zDst++ = *zSrc++);
        return (zSave);

    }else return (NULLPTR);
```

In Windows 3.1 we could use the lstrcpy() function, but that only works with strings with a maximum of 64K bytes. So to illustrate how to copy strings up to 4 GB long, we need to cast our PTR pointers, which are LPSTRs, to huge pointers. Copying a string this way is going to be a bit slower than using lstrcpy(), but you don't have to worry about boundaries in case you are using very long strings.

```
char huge *hzSrc=(char huge *)zSrc;
char huge *hzDst=(char huge *)zDst;

if (hzDst && hzSrc){
        PTR zSave=zDst;

        while ((*hzDst++ = *hzSrc++)!=0);
        return (zSave);

}else return (NULLPTR);
```

In Win32 we don't have the 64K limit on LPSTRs (the L is to maintain compatibility with Windows 3.1). But there is something that we need to consider: Namely, lstrcpy() can refer to the lstrcpyA() or the lstrcpyW() function, depending on if the _UNICODE constant is defined. The lstrcpyA() function works with ANSI (1 byte) characters and the lstrcpyW() function works with wide (Unicode) characters. Because our implementation of strings assumes only single-byte character strings, we explicitly use the lstrcpyA() function to remind us and to ensure that in case the _UNICODE constant is defined, we won't have any problems.

```
if (zDst && zSrc){
    return (lstrcpyA (zDst, zSrc));

}else return (NULLPTR);
```

That's it for a cross-platform string copy function.

```
}
```

Getting the Length of a String

To get the length of a string, we define StrLen(), which requires a pointer to a string and returns the string's length. The length of a string does not include the null-terminator. This function is equivalent to the ANSI C, strlen(), function.

```
//-------------------------------------------------------
UINT4 StrLen (PTR z)
//-------------------------------------------------------
// z       - pointer to a null-terminated string
// RETURNS - number of characters (single byte) in the
//           string
//-------------------------------------------------------
{
```

In the Macintosh there isn't a provided function for getting the length of a string. Many of the functions use Pascal strings and getting the length requires looking at the first position of the string: Pascal string length = string [0]. So, we'll just use a simple while loop to count the number of characters in the string.

```
        if (z){
            UINT4 i=0;

            while (*z++) i++;
            return (i);

        }else return ((UINT4)0);
```

In Windows 3.1 we could use the lstrlen() function to get the length of a string. But because this only works with strings with a maximum of 64K characters, we'll write a function that will work with arbitrarily large strings. We do this by casting the pointer to the string (which is by default a LPSTR) to a huge pointer. This allows incrementing safely across any 64K boundary.

```
        char huge * hz=(char huge *)z;
        if (hz){
            UINT4 i=0;

            while (*hz++) i++;
            return (i);

        }else return ((UINT4)0);
```

In Win32 we use the lstrlenA() function to calculate the length of a string. We could have used the lstrlen() function, but this function is a macro that is compile-time defined to either lstrlenA() or lstrlenW(), if the _UNICODE constant is defined. Because we only want to work with single-byte characters, we will explicitly use the ANSI version of the function.

```
        if (z){
            return ((UINT4)lstrlenA (z));

        }else return ((UINT4)0);
```

Then we terminate the function and we're done.

```
        }
```

Comparing Two Strings

The last of the basic string operations that we will illustrate is comparison. In our example we will show how to compare two strings in a case-sensitive manner. Our StrComp() function requires two strings and will return zero if the strings are the same, less than zero if string 1 is less than string 2, and greater than zero if string 1 is greater than string 2. This is equivalent to the ANSI C function, strcmp().

```
    //---------------------------------------------------- -
    SINT2 StrComp (PTR z1, PTR z2)
    //----------------------------------------------------
    // z1      - pointer to the first string
```

```
// z2        - pointer to the second string
// RETURNS -   zero if the strings are the same,
//              < zero if string 1 is less than string 2
//              > zero if string 2 is less than string 1
//-------------------------------------------------------
{
```

In the Macintosh we don't use the International Utilities (IU) string functions in our example because we aren't in a position to deal completely with Scripts and how they interact with all of the other functions in our cross-platform solution. So we will concentrate on a single-byte, standard Roman character set solution to string comparison. This implementation ignores language-specific sorting orders.

```
if (z1 && z2){
    for (;*z1 == *z2; z1++, z2++){
        // if string 1 ends before string 2...
        if (*z1 == '\0') return (0);
    }
    return (*z1 - *z2);

}
```

In Windows 3.1 we will use the lstrcmp() function to perform the string comparison. Even though it is only useful for 64K byte strings, we will not implement a custom solution because lstrcmp() takes into account the international settings in WIN.INI and only works with single-byte characters. This is a reasonable compromise between time and functionality. You probably won't need to compare strings larger than 64K bytes very often.

```
if (z1 && z2){
    // only good for 64K long strings
    return (lstrcmp (z1, z2));
}
```

In Win32 we will use the lstrcmpA() function, which compares two ANSI (single-byte) characters. As with StrLen(), we don't use the lstrcmp() function because its meaning is dependent on the _UNICODE constant. Also, the basis of comparison comes from the international settings in the Registry.

```
if (z1 && z2){
    return (lstrcmpA (z1, z2));
}
```

If either of the pointers is null, this function returns zero.

```
return (0);
}
```

Reading Strings from Resources

Another important thing you need to do with strings is read them from the resource area of your application's file. If you want to provide a version of your program for specific localities (a localization), you will need to put all of your application's strings in resources. At first this can be a bit of a nuisance if you aren't accustomed it, but after a while it will become a natural consideration and it will make your life a lot easier in the long run.

Unfortunately the functions you are given in the various platform APIs aren't always easy to work with. Because of this, we need to design a "get string from resource" function that is easier to use and more useful.

Our load string function, StrLoadAny(), requires the string id, a pointer to a buffer to receive the string (which must be large enough to hold the largest string resource, usually 255 characters), and the base id of the string. The function will return the pointer that we provided.

Let's explain what we mean by a base and string id. Some strings are best grouped together and referred to in a group, thus the base id. But there are differences in the way string resources are managed on the Macintosh and Windows (Windows 3.1 and Win32 are the same) that affect the interpretation of the base and string ids.

In the Macintosh all resource strings are Pascal strings and can only be 255 characters. There are two ways to specify a string resource in the Macintosh:

- *as individual strings, 'STR ' resources*
- *as a group of indexed strings, 'STR#' resources*

In Windows a string resource can also be only 255 characters long, but all string resources are stored by arbitrary resource ids. In the Macintosh we can use individual strings exclusively, except they are a bit more wasteful of disk space. Because resources increase the size of your application, it's always a good idea to minimize their size; thus use indexed resources whenever possible.

In our cross-platform solution we specify the following mapping between Macintosh and Windows individual and grouped string resources:

String Resource Type	Macintosh	Windows
individual	'STR '	STRINGTABLE entry
grouped	'STR#'	STRINGTABLE entry

Each 'STR ' resource on the Macintosh has a unique resource id (starting from 1). Each 'STR#' collection of strings has a unique resource id (starting from 1). Every STRING-TABLE entry in Windows has a unique ID (starting from 1).

Specifying a base id of zero indicates a 'STR ' resource with the id of the string id, and specifying a non-zero base id indicates a particular 'STR#' resource with that id and the particular string being the difference. In Windows the base id is ignored. For example:

Base id	String id	Macintosh	Windows
0	1	'STR ' with id=1	STRINGTABLE id=1
0	23	'STR ' with id=23	STRINGTABLE id=23
1000	1000	'STR#' with id=1000 index=1000-1000+1=1	STRINGTABLE id=1000
1000	1001	'STR#' with id=1000 index=1001-1000+1=2	STRINGTABLE id=1001

```
//-------------------------------------------------------
PTR StrLoadAny (UINT2 u2id, PTR zStr, UINT2 u2Base)
//-------------------------------------------------------
// u2id    - resource id that is used with the base id to
//           identify a string resource
// zStr    - pointer to buffer to receive the string
// u2Base  - base id of the string resources
//-------------------------------------------------------
{
```

So in the Macintosh we first check if the base id is null; if it is, we assume a 'STR ' resource and use GetString() to access it. If the base id is non-null, we know it's a 'STR#' resource and use GetIndString() to read the string.

```
// STR# resources have a base id and strings
// with relative ids starting at 1
// (as the user sees it in ResEdit)

if (u2id<u2Base) return (NULL);
if (!u2Base){
   StringHandle hStr=GetString (u2id);
   SINT2 i;
   if (!hStr) return (NULL);
   //make a local copy
   for (i=0; i<=(*hStr)[0]; i++) zStr[i]=(*hStr)[i];

}else GetIndString ((PTRP)zStr, u2Base, u2id-u2Base+1);

if (!zStr[0]) return (NULL);
StrPtoC ((PTRP)zStr);
```

In Windows we ignore the base id parameter, u2Base and just use the string id. The contents of the _ghWinInstance variable was given to our application through the XPMain() entry point when the program started up; it is used to locate the resources for our application.

```
SINT2 s2Len=LoadString (_ghWinInstance, u2id, zStr, 255);
if (!s2Len) return (NULL);
```

If we get here, we found the resource and we return the pointer to the string.

```
    return (zStr);
}
```

Additional String Functionality

In addition to the functionality that we listed in Table 12.1, there are some other functions that you might find useful:

- providing a cyclic resource-string buffer so that you don't need to provide a buffer to load a string from resources
- providing support for double-byte characters
- supporting international number conversions

FUNCTIONS THAT WORK WITH POINTS

A point is a common entity in a GUI-based platform. It is represented by a data structure that provides a field for the x and y components of the point. In this section we will discuss some of the different defintions of points and the functionality that is provided to support them. We also give some examples of some cross-platform point functions.

Comparing Available Functionality

We'll start by looking at Table 12.2 for a comparison of some of the functionality that is available on our target platforms.

Comparing Point Data Structures

Next we'll look at the definitions of the point data type on our three platforms.

Table 12.2 Comparing point functionality across platforms.

Function	*Macintosh*	*Windows*	*Description*
initialize point	SetPt	NA	Set the x and y coordinate values of the point.
add 2 points	AddPt	NA	Add the x's and y's of the two points. subtract 2 points
are points the same?	EqualPt	NA	Check if two points are equal.
point in rectangle?	PtInRect	PtInRect	Check if the point is inside the rectangle.

Macintosh		*Windows 3.1*		*Win32*	
Point	(4 bytes)	POINT	(4 bytes)	POINT	(8 bytes)
Type	*Field*	*Type*	*Field*	*Type*	*Field*
int	v	int	x	LONG	x
int	h	int	y	LONG	y

Let's look at the differences:

- The Macintosh defintion puts the y component of the point first.
- Both forms of Windows use the designation POINT; the Macintosh uses Point.
- Macintosh and Windows 3.1 use signed 2-byte x and y components.
- Win32 uses signed 4-byte x and y components.

Common Point Structure

There aren't any similarities common to all three platform defintions except that they all have an x and y component. We use the name POINT to define our cross-platform point structure. This name is already used in Windows 3.1 and Win32, so we will extend this polymorphism to the Macintosh by defining a POINT structure as:

Type	*Field*
SINT	x
SINT	y

With the designation of POINT, we can access points on all three platforms even though the underlying defintion of the POINT varies from platform to platform. As long as you don't need to have the size of the structure equivalent on all three platforms, this is a reasonable solution.

Also, you can use the SINT data type to define individual coordinate values because it is polymorphic across our three platforms. On the Macintosh and Windows 3.1 SINT is a signed 2-byte integer, and on Win32 it is a signed 4-byte integer.

Functions That Work with POINT Structures

Many of the functions that manipulate points are straightforward to implement. We will illustrate only a couple of them to show you what we mean.

Initializing a POINT Structure

Initializing, or setting, a point's values is the most basic of the point functions. It is missing in Windows and needs to be redefined for the Macintosh. So our defintion of this function,

PointSet(), contains no platform-dependent sections. It requires a pointer to the POINT structure that will be initialized and the *x* and *y* values to be assigned to the point.

```
//------------------------------------------------------
PPOINT PointSet (PPOINT ppt, SINT sx, SINT sy)
//------------------------------------------------------
// ppt     - pointer to a POINT structure to be initialized
// sx      - signed x value to assign to the point
// sy      - signed y value to assign to the point
// RETURNS- the value of ppt
//------------------------------------------------------
{
    if (ppt){
        ppt->x=sx;
        ppt->y=sy;
    }
    return (ppt);
}
```

Are the Two Points Equal?

Another common function with points is to check if two points are equal. As with PointSet(), it is simplest to define this function in a cross-platform manner. PointEqual() requires pointers to two points that will be checked for equality and returns TRUE if the points are the same or FALSE if they are different.

```
BOOL2 PointEqual (PPOINT ppt1, PPOINT ppt2)
{
    if (!ppt1 || !ppt2) return (FALSE);
    return (ppt1->x==ppt2->x && ppt1->y==ppt2->y);
}
```

Additional POINT Structure Functionality

Most of the other point functionality that we described earlier in this chapter can be implemented in a cross-platform manner. There are a few other functions that you might want to consider:

- checking if a point is on the border of a rectangle
- checking if a point is on a line
- checking if two points are almost the same

FUNCTIONS THAT WORK WITH RECTANGLES

Another commonly used structure in GUI-based platforms is the rectangle. It is used in graphical drawing functions and to describe the bounds of a window and the bounds of a control.

Table 12.3 Comparing rectangle functionality across platforms.

Function	Macintosh	Windows	Description
initialize rectangle	SetRect	SetRect	Set the top-left and bottom-right coordinates of the rectangle.
are rectangles same?	EqualRect	EqualRect	Are the two rectangles the same?
is rectangle empty?	EmptyRect	IsRectEmpty	Check if the rectangle is empty: Is the bottom<=top or right<=left?
inset rectangle	InsetRect	InflateRect	Inset (shrink) or outset (expand) the rectangle by the x and y amounts specified.
move rectangle	OffsetRect	OffsetRect	Move the rectangle by the x and y amounts specified.
union rectangles	UnionRect	UnionRect	Calculate the union of two rectangle (smallest rectangle that encloses both rectangles).
intersect rectangles	SectRect	IntersectRect	Calculate the intersection of two rectangles (largest rectangular area common to both rectangles).
subtract rectangles	NA	SubtractRect	Calculate the area not in common between two rectangles.
empty rectangle	NA	SetRectEmpty	Initialize a rectangle to (0,0) (0,0).

Comparing Available Functionality

Let's look at Table 12.3 and see how Macintosh and Windows differ in their support of rectangles. Notice that there is general agreement in functionality and representation between the Macintosh and Windows. The only real problem here is in the representation of the rectangle itself.

Comparing Rectangle Data Structures

Now we'll look at how the rectangle structure is defined on our three target platforms:

Macintosh		Windows 3.1		Win32	
Rect	(8 bytes)	RECT	(8 bytes)	RECT	(16 bytes)
Type	Field	Type	Field	Type	Field
int	top	int	left	LONG	left
int	left	int	top	LONG	top
int	bottom	int	right	LONG	right
int	right	int	bottom	LONG	bottom

Let's examine the differences:

- The Macintosh defintion puts the *y* components of the rectangle before the *x*.
- Both forms of Windows use the designation RECT; the Macintosh uses Rect.
- Macintosh and Windows 3.1 use signed 2-byte *x* and *y* components.
- Win32 uses signed 4-byte *x* and *y* components.

Common Rectangle Structure

The only similarity across all three platforms is that the names for the fields are the same, even though the order isn't the same. We use the name RECT to define our cross-platform rectangle structure. This name is already used in Windows 3.1 and Win32, so we will extend this polymorphism to the Macintosh by defining the RECT structure as:

Type	*Field*
SINT	left
SINT	top
SINT	right
SINT	bottom

With the designation of RECT, we have an equivalent way to work with rectangles on all three platforms even though the underlying defintion of the RECT varies from platform to platform (actually, the Macintosh and Windows 3.1 definitions are the same). As long as you don't need to have the size of the rectangle structure equivalent on all three platforms, this is a reasonable solution.

Functions That Work with RECT Structures

Most of the functions that are used with rectangles can be written without a lot of trouble. Many will not require any platform-specific code. In this section we will show you some examples of a cross-section of the functions that work with rectangles.

Initializing a RECT Structure

The most important thing that we need to do is to initialize the fields of the rectangle structure. Our function, RectSet(), requires a pointer to a RECT structure and a left, top, right, and bottom value to assign to the rectangle. We return the pointer to the rectangle that we are initializing.

In Windows we could use the SetRect() function and pass it all of the parameters to RectSet(), except the extra function call probably isn't any faster than what we have already done.

```
//-----------------------------------------------------
PRECT RectSet (PRECT pRect, SINT sLeft, SINT sTop,
    SINT sRight, SINT sBottom)
```

```
//---------------------------------------------------------
// pRect    - pointer to a RECT structure to be  initialized
// sLeft    - x value to assign to the left edge
// sTop     - y value to assign to the top edge
// sRight   - x value to assign to the right edge
// sBottom  - y value to assign to the bottom edge
// RETURNS  - the value of pRect
//---------------------------------------------------------
{
    if (pRect){
        pRect->left=sLeft;
        pRect->top=sTop;
        pRect->right=sRight;
        pRect->bottom=sBottom;
    }
    return (pRect);
}
```

Shrinking or Growing a Rectangle

Another common rectangle function is shrinking or growing a rectangle by a specified *x* and *y* amount. This inset amount is applied uniformly to opposite edges. RectInset() requires a pointer to the RECT to inset, an x amount to move the left and right edges, and a y amount to move the top and bottom edges. The function returns the pointer to the RECT. We could have implemented this function with the Macintosh InsetRect() and the Windows InflateRect() functions, but it would hardly be worth the effort.

```
//---------------------------------------------------------
PRECT RectInset (PRECT prect, SINT sx, SINT sy)
//---------------------------------------------------------
// pRect    - pointer to a RECT structure to be inset
// sx       - x amount to grow or shrink the rectangle
// sy       - y amount to grow or shrink the rectangle
// RETURNS  - the value of pRect
//---------------------------------------------------------
{
    if (prect){
        prect->left+=sx;
        prect->right-=sx;
        prect->top+=sy;
        prect->bottom-=sy;
    }
    return (prect);
}
```

Determining the Intersection of Two Rectangles

Now let's show a function that uses some platform-specific code. We'll show you how to implement a cross-platform rectangle intersection function. RectIntersect() requires three rectangles: a pointer to the destination rectangle (receives the intersection rectangle) and pointers to the two rectangles that we are checking. Incidently, the destination rectangle can be one of the sources. If the rectangles don't intersect, our function will return FALSE and also set the destination rectangle to all zeros.

```
//----------------------------------------------------
BOOL2 RectIntersect (PRECT prect, PRECT prect1,
   PRECT prect2)
//----------------------------------------------------
// pRect   - pointer to the destination RECT structure
// pRect1  - pointer to the 1st rectangle
// pRect2  - pointer to the 2nd rectangle
// RETURNS - TRUE if the rectangles intersected
//----------------------------------------------------
{
    if (!prect || !prect1 || !prect2) return (FALSE);
```

In the Macintosh we first need to copy over our cross-platform rectangles to Macintosh Rect structures. Then we use the SectRect() function to do the work and copy over the resulting Macintosh Rect to our cross-platform destination RECT. The SectRect() function returns a null rectangle if the two source rectangles do not intersect.

```
    {
    Rect rect,rect1,rect2;
    BOOL2 b2;

    SetRect (&rect1, prect1->left, prect1->top,
       prect1->right, prect1->bottom);
    SetRect (&rect2, prect2->left, prect2->top,
       prect2->right, prect2->bottom);

    // perform the intersection
    b2=SectRect (&rect1, &rect2, &rect);

    // copy over the intersection rectangle
    RectSet (prect, rect.left, rect.top, rect.right,
       rect.bottom);

    return (b2);
    }
```

In Windows we don't need to reassign the contents of the rectangles because the cross-platform RECT structure is the structure provided by the Windows API. We call the IntersectRect()

function and have it return the intersection rectangle in an intermediate rectangle. This is because the Windows API does not specify the behavior of its function if one of the source rectangles is also the destination. We save the boolean result code from the Windows function, copy over the intersection rectangle to the rectangle specified by the first parameter, and then return the boolean.

```
// Windows SDK does not specify behavior if dest is
// one of the sources, so we ensure that this instance
// is handled correctly
{
BOOL2 b2;
RECT rect;

b2=IntersectRect (&rect, prect1, prect2);
*prect=rect;

return (b2);
}
```

And that ends the RectIntersect() function.

```
}
```

Is the Point in the Rectangle?

In XPLib this function is actually listed in the point function category, but we include it here to show you an example of using cross-platform POINT and cross-platform RECT structures. PointInRect() checks if the specified point is inside a rectangle (the rectangle is considered without regard for the thickness of its border). PointInRect() requires a pointer to a POINT and a pointer to a RECT and returns TRUE if the point is inside the rectangle and FALSE otherwise.

```
//-------------------------------------------------------
BOOL2 PointInRect (PPOINT ppt, PRECT prect)
//-------------------------------------------------------
// ppt     - pointer to a POINT to check
// prect   - pointer to a RECT
// RETURNS - TRUE if point is inside the rectangle and
//           FALSE otherwise
//-------------------------------------------------------
{
    if (!ppt || !prect) return (FALSE);

    // thickness of the rectangle skin is ignored
    // (no border assumed)
    return (ppt->x>=prect->left &&ppt->x<=prect->right
        && ppt->y>=prect->top && ppt->y<=prect->bottom);
}
```

Additional RECT Structure Functionality

There are a few other rectangle functions that you might want to implement:

- initializing a rectangle with two points rather than two x and two y values
- fixing a rectangle so that left<right and top<bottom
- shrinking or growing a rectangle holding one of the corners fixed

DATE AND TIME FUNCTIONS

Another popular area of functionality is time. Providing cross-platform functions that provide a solution to the date and time problem can be important if your application needs to keep track of time. In this section we will look at how our platforms get this information, how they represent it, and how we can provide a reasonable cross-platform solution.

Comparing Functionality

Let's start by comparing how our three target platforms and the ANSI functions work with time, as shown in Table 12.4. We include the ANSI functions because they represent a possible solution. It is evident from the table that all of the desired date and time functions are reasonably represented across all platforms and in the ANSI standard library.

Comparing Time Representations

We know the functions are available on our target platforms; let's look at the following representations of date and time structures:

Table 12.4 Comparing date and time functions across platforms.

Function	*Macintosh*	*Windows 3.1*	*Win32*	*ANSI*
setting the time	SetDateTime SetTime	int 21h:AH=0x2D	SetSystemTime	NA
getting the time	GetDateTime GetTime	int 21h:AH=0x2C	GetSystemTime	time + gmtime, mktime, or localtime
setting the date	SetDateTime SetTime	int 21h:AH=0x2B	SetSystemTime	NA
getting the date	GetDateTime GetTime	int 21h:AH=0x2A	GetSystem Time	(same as getting time)
wait	Delay	NA	NA	NA
get tick count	TickCount	GetTickCount	GetTickCount	clock

- the ANSI tm structure
- the Macintosh DateTimeRec structure
- the Win32 SYSTEMTIME structure

There is no date and time structure defined for Windows 3.1 because the date and time values are retrieved using calls to the int 21h function.

ANSI tm structure

Type	Field	Description
int	tm_year	number of years since 1900*
int	tm_mon	month of the year (from 0 to 11)
int	tm_mday	day of the month (from 1 through 31)
int	tm_hour	hour of the day (from 0 through 23)
int	tm_min	minute of the hour (from 0 through 59)
int	tm_sec	seconds (from 0 through 61**)
int	tm_wday	day of the week from Sunday (from 0 through 6)
int	tm_yday	day of the year from Jan 1 (from 0 through 365)
int	tm_isdst	daylight savings time flag (<0 don't know, 0 not DST, >0 if DST)

*   In THINK C this number is relative to 1904.

**   Seconds 60 and 61 are used to keep track of leap seconds.

Macintosh DateTimeRec structure

Type	Field	Description
int	year	number of years since 1904 (maximum of 2040)
int	month	month of the year (from 1 through 12)
int	day	day of the month (from 1 through 31)
int	hour	hour of the day (from 0 through 23)
int	minute	minute of the hour (from 0 through 59)
int	second	seconds (from 0 through 59)
int	dayOfWeek	day of the week from Sunday (from 1 through 7)

Win32 SYSTEMTIME Structure

Type	Field	Description
WORD	wYear	current year (absolute)
WORD	wMonth	month of the year (from 1 through 12)

(continued)

Type	Field	Description
WORD	wDay	day of the month (from 1 through 31)
WORD	wHour	hour of the day (from 0 through 23)
WORD	wMinute	minute of the hour (from 0 through 59)
WORD	wSecond	seconds (from 0 through 59)
WORD	wDayOfWeek	day of the week from Sunday (from 0 through 6)
WORD	wMilliseconds	number of milliseconds (from 0 through 999)

Cross-Platform DATETIME Structure

We need to define a cross-platform time representation for a couple of reasons: None of the representations are totally equivalent (even the ANSI representation can differ in measurement), and none of the representations are the same size.

It isn't essential for the representation of the date and time to be the same size, but it is a helpful thing to have if you are saving this information to disk. Also, we could wrap the ANSI routines in a cross-platform API that fixes up any platform-specificity. We opt to implement our own solution to illustrate the differences in the ways the platforms access the date and time and the way they represent it. We define our cross-platform DATETIME structure as:

Type	Field	Description
SINT2	s2Year	current year (absolute)
UINT1	u1Month	month of the year (from 1 to 12)
UINT1	u1Day	day of the month (from 1 through 31)
UINT1	u1Hour	hour of the day (from 0 through 23)
UINT1	u1Minute	minute of the hour (from 0 through 59)
UINT1	u1Second	seconds (from 0 through 59)

Examples of Some Time Functions

Now that we have defined a cross-platform represenatation of a date and time structure, let's use it. Not all functions that work with time need to use the DATETIME structure. We will illustrate one of these functions in this section.

Getting the Current Date and Time

Let's illustrate how we use the information about the platform-specific date and time formats, the available platform-specific functionality, and our cross-platform date and time format to get the current date and time. In our example our TimeGet() function requires a pointer to a DATETIME structure that will receive the date and time information from the system and returns nothing.

```
//-------------------------------------------------------
VOID TimeGet (PDATETIME pdt)
//-------------------------------------------------------
// pdt      - pointer to a DATETIME structure to receive
//             the date and time information
// RETURNS - nothing
//-------------------------------------------------------
{
    DATETIME dt;
```

In the Macintosh call the GetDateTime() function and convert the Macintosh DateTimeRec structure to our cross-platform DATETIME format.

DateTimeRec dateTimeRec;

```
    // get the Macintosh version date and time
    GetTime (&dateTimeRec);

    // convert to our cross-platform form
    pdt->s2Year=dateTimeRec.year;
    pdt->u1Month=dateTimeRec.month;
    pdt->u1Day=dateTimeRec.day;
    pdt->u1Hour=dateTimeRec.hour;
    pdt->u1Minute=dateTimeRec.minute;
    pdt->u1Second=dateTimeRec.second;
```

In Windows 3.1 there isn't a function in the API to get the date and time, so we use the DOS interrupt 21h method. Using function AH=0x2A, we can get the date; save the year, month, and day; and then use function AH=0x2C to get the hour, minute and second.

```
    SINT2 s2Year;
    UINT1 u1Month;
    UINT1 u1Day;
    UINT1 u1Hour;
    UINT1 u1Minute;
    UINT1 u1Second;

    _asm{
        mov    ah,2ah ;//get system date
        int 21h
        // save the date information
        mov    s2Year,cx
        mov    u1Month,dh
        mov    u1Day,dl

        mov    ah,2ch ;//get system time
        int 21h
        // save the time information
```

```
        mov     u1Hour,ch
        mov     u1Minute,cl
        mov     u1Second,dh
    }

    // convert to our cross-platform form
    pdt->s2Year=s2Year;
    pdt->u1Month=u1Month;
    pdt->u1Day=u1Day;
    pdt->u1Hour=u1Hour;
    pdt->u1Minute=u1Minute;
    pdt->u1Second=u1Second;
```

In Win32 we just call the GetSystemTime() function and then convert the SYSTEMTIME format of the date and time to our cross-platform DATETIME format.

```
    SYSTEMTIME sysTime;

    // get the Win32 version of date and time
    GetSystemTime (&sysTime);

    // convert to our cross-platform form
    pdt->s2Year=sysTime.wYear;
    pdt->u1Month=(UINT1)sysTime.wMonth;
    pdt->u1Day=(UINT1)sysTime.wDay;
    pdt->u1Hour=(UINT1)sysTime.wHour;
    pdt->u1Minute=(UINT1)sysTime.wMinute;
    pdt->u1Second=(UINT1)sysTime.wSecond;
```

And that ends the get date and time function.

```
}
```

Waiting a Specific Time Interval

The other time function that we will show is TimeWait(), which is a function that will wait a certain number of milliseconds and then return. This probably won't be used very often, except to pause a certain number of milliseconds for some user interface activity. It does illustrate how to manipulate the different time bases of the underlying platforms: The Macintosh has a tick equal to 1/60 of a second, and Windows has a tick equal to 1/1000 of a second.

```
//-----------------------------------------------------
VOID TimeWait (UINT4 u4ms)
//-----------------------------------------------------
// u4ms      - unsigned 4-byte integer containing the
//             number of milliseconds to wait
// RETURNS - nothing
//-----------------------------------------------------
```

```
{
    UINT4 u4TickCur;
```

The Macintosh provides us with a function to wait a specified number of ticks. We need to convert our requested time, in milliseconds, to Macintosh ticks:

$$t_{\text{Mac ticks}} = t_{\text{ms}} * 16.67 = t_{\text{ms}} * 100/6$$

The conversion ratio 100/6 is accurate, but it limits the total delay to about 50 days.

```
    Delay (((u4ms*100L)+3L)/6L, &u4TickCur);
```

In Windows we get the current tick count and then wait until the tick count increases by the delay amount. Notice that we ignore the possibility of the tick count wrapping around from 0xffffffff to zero. This occurs only once every 50 days of uninterrupted system operation.

```
    UINT4 u4TickStop;

    // get the current tick count
    u4TickCur=GetTickCount ();
    // calculate the stop count
    u4TickStop=u4TickCur+u4ms;

    // now wait the specified number of milliseconds
    while (GetTickCount ()<u4TickStop);
```

That's the end of the delay function.

```
}
```

Additional Date/Time Functionality

There are some other things you might want to add to your date and time functionality. These include:

- getting the time and date in seconds
- converting between the structure form and seconds
- being able to add and subtract times
- specifying a base year for our seconds-only representation
- formatting the date and time in a readable text string

Part 3

User Interface
Implementation

13

Menus

In the second part of the book, we discussed some of the basic subsystems of our cross-platform API. Now we need to look at some of the user interface components that are necessary to construct cross-platform GUI-based platforms. In this chapter we will talk about menus and how they are supported across platforms and then present some examples of how you might implement some of the cross-platform menu functions. A more thorough implementation of menu functionality is provided in the XPLib software and is discussed in Part 5 of this book.

DEFINING COMMON MENU CAPABILITIES

Before we can intelligently implement cross-platform menu functions, we need to do a few other things, such as:

- look at some basic menu terminology
- compare the appearances of menus across platforms
- compare the available menu functionality
- define a basic cross-platform menu solution

Menu Terminology

Before we go too far in our discussion on menus, we first need to talk about some of the terminology associated with menus.

Term	Description
menu bar	This is the top area of the screen (on a Macintosh) or top area of a window (in Windows) that contains a horizontal list of menus.
menu list	When the user clicks on a menu title in the menu bar, a list of menu items drops down from which the user can select other items. In Windows, this list is a submenu.
menu item	This is one of the entries in a menu list that represents an option, a selectable feature, or brings up a dialog box with more options.
separator	An entry in a menu list, this is a horizontal line that visually separates one group of menu items from another. Separators are not usually selectable.
check	This mark (usually a check) appears to the left of a menu item and indicates that the feature of that item has been selected. A checked menu item maintains its state until the user selects the item again, which causes the menu item to be unchecked.
submenu	A menu list that is accessed from a menu item, this is also called a hierarchical menu in the Macintosh. In Windows a submenu is also used to describe menu lists that pull down from a menu bar.
icon	An icon is attached to a menu item and pictorially provides information to the user about the contents or state of a menu item. In Windows this feature is installed in a menu item as a bitmap.
state	A menu bar, a menu list, or menu item can be enabled, disabled, or grayed out. In the Macintosh disabling and graying are equivalent; in Windows graying implies disabling, but a disabled item is not necessarily grayed.
popup	This is a menu list that appears beyond the confines of a menu bar or a submenu that is attached to an item in a menu list. It is used in dialog boxes or windows to provide a popup list of selectable options.
key equivalent	This is a single keystroke that activates a particular menu item without pulling down a menu list. It is called an accelerator in Windows and a key command (or menu key) in the Macintosh.
key sequence	This is a Windows-only feature that allows a combination of ALT + other keys to select and pull down a menu list and select a menu item. It is different from a key equivalent because it requires more than one keystroke to initiate. The keys are designated in the menu title or menu item text by an underscore.
system menu	Most platforms maintain a menu list that contains information pertinent to the application in general. In the Macintosh this is called the Apple menu

Comparing Menu Features

We can see some of the differences in menu features in the terminology above, but you'll get a better idea of how the Macintosh and Windows menus differ by looking at the differences between them. The basic Macintosh menu components are shown in Figure 13.1, and the basic Windows menu components are shown in Figure 13.2.

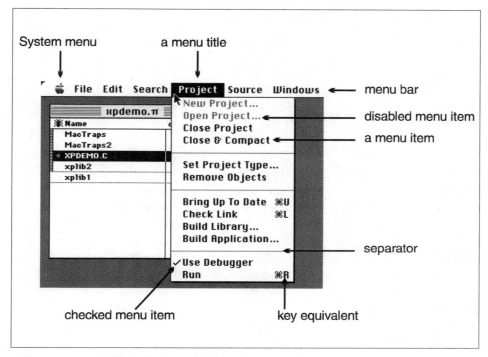

Figure 13.1 Macintosh menu components.

Comparing Menu Functionality

Now that we've talked about the features of menus, let's look at Table 13.1 and see how the Macintosh and Windows APIs let us access and work with menus. As you can see, most of the

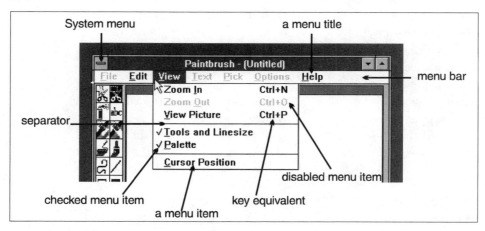

Figure 13.2 Windows menu components.

Table 13.1 Menu functionality across platforms.

Function	Macintosh	Windows
create a menu bar	GetMenuBar	CreateMenu
destroy a menu bar	DisposHandle	DestroyMenu
load a menu bar	GetNewMBar	LoadMenu or LoadMenuIndirect
draw a menu bar	DrawMenuBar	DrawMenuBar
get menu bar of a window	GetMenuBar	GetMenu
set menu bar of a window	SetMenuBar	SetMenu
highlight a menu bar item	HiliteMenu	HiliteMenuBarItem
create a menu list	NewMenu	CreateMenu
destroy a menu list	DisposMenu or ReleaseResource	DestroyMenu
load a menu list	GetMenu	LoadMenu or LoadMenuIndirect
add a menu list	InsertMenu	AppendMenu
insert a menu list	InsertMenu	InsertMenu
delete a menu list	DeleteMenu	RemoveMenu or DeleteMenu
add a menu item	AppendMenu	AppendMenu
add a separator	AppendMenu	AppendMenu
insert a menu item	InsMenuItem	InsertMenu
delete a menu item	DelMenuItem	DeleteMenu
get a menu item's text	GetItem	GetMenuString
set a menu item's text	SetItem	ModifyMenu
check an item using a menu bar	NA	CheckMenuItem or ModifyMenu
check an item using a menu list	CheckItem	CheckMenuItem or ModifyMenu
enable an item using a menu bar	NA	EnableMenuItem or ModifyMenu
enable an item using a menu list	EnableItem or DisableItem	EnableMenuItem or ModifyMenu
item in a menu bar checked?	NA	GetMenuState
item in a menu list checked?	GetItemMark	GetMenuState
item in a menu bar enabled?	NA	GetMenuState
item in a menu list enabled?	NA	GetMenuState
set a menu item's icon	SetItemIcon	SetMenuItemBitmaps
get a menu item's icon	GetItemIcon	NA
does an item have a submenu?	GetItemCmd	GetSubMenu
assign a submenu to an item	InsMenuItem, AppendMenu, or SetItemCmd	InsertMenu, AppendMenu, or ModifyMenu
create a popup menu	NewMenu	CreatePopupMenu
process popup menu	PopUpMenuSelect	TrackPopupMenu

functionality is available on all platforms. Many of the differences are related to the accessing of menu items. Windows allows items to be accessed by position and identifier. Macintosh only let's you access them by position. Also, Windows lets you access an item by identifier from a menu bar handle. You can't do this in the Macintosh using the provided functionality. You will need to search all of the lists for an appropriate match.

Choosing the Basic Feature Set

For our purposes we will limit the menu functionality to:

- menu bar: create, destroy, load from resource, add list
- menu list: create, destroy, load from resource, add item, add separator
- menu item: get and set text, determine if it's checked, check it, determine if it's enabled, and enable it

This means we don't consider icons, submenus, and popup menus. For most applications this is a reasonable subset to work with. Icons are nice, but not really necessary if the item's text is thought out. Submenus allow more options to be available but can appear as groups of items between separators or in dialog boxes. Popup menus are convenient ways to include a list (possibly time varying) in a dialog that doesn't clutter up the dialog design. But again it isn't really necessary.

We also don't include the functions to install a menu bar and retrieve the current menu bar. This is because in the Macintosh the menu bar is something global to an application. In Windows a menu bar is specific to a class of windows. It is better to think of a menu bar as something that is window-specific rather than application-specific. Every window might have some different user interface needs and require a different menu, menu configuration, or initialization. We will consider menu bar installation as part of a window's functionality, which is discussed in Chapter 14.

IMPLEMENTING A PRACTICAL MENU SOLUTION

The process of implementing cross-platform menu functionality involves:

- defining menu-related data types
- implementing menu bar functions
- implementing menu list functions
- implementing menu item functions

Menu-Related Data Types

Before we can show some examples of cross-platform menu functions, we need to define some data types. There are two things to consider:

- Menu bars represent two different types of data on the Macintosh and Windows.
- The menu handle data type names aren't the same.

The second consideration, differences in menu handle data types, is simple to fix; simply rename the Macintosh menu handle name. The first item, different menu bar data types, requires that we limit the scope of a menu handle in Windows. In Windows a menu handle is a menu bar, a menu list, or any submenu. You can install a menu as a menu bar, as a menu list, or as a menu item. In the Macintosh a menu handle refers to a menu list or to a submenu (provided the menu id is a number less than 235). Also, on the Macintosh a menu bar is something that is more of a fixture to an application that you install and modify, but its contents cannot be used as a menu list.

Windows menu functions don't distinguish between menu bars or menu lists, but Macintosh functions do. We can rewrite the Macintosh menu mechanism or in Windows provide a special wrapper for the menu handle that lets the cross-platform functions think there is a difference between menu bar handles and menu handles. To the Windows functions the types are still the same. We choose the latter, and we define our menu data types accordingly:

Data Type	Macintosh	Windows 3.1	Win32
HMBAR menu bar handle	Handle (4 bytes)	HMENU (2 bytes)	HMENU (4 bytes)
HMENU menu list handle	MenuHandle (4 bytes)	HMENU (2 bytes)	HMENU (2 bytes)

Menu Bar Functions

We won't illustrate all of the menu bar functionality here, but we will show you the basics:

- creating a menu bar
- destroying a menu bar
- adding a list of items to a menu bar

Creating a Menu Bar

The first thing you'll need to create is a menu bar that will hold all of the items and lists that your program will need. We define our function, MenuBarCreate(), to do this. It requires no arguments and returns a handle to a new and empty menu bar.

```
//---------------------------------------------------------
HMBAR MenuBarCreate (VOID)
//---------------------------------------------------------
// no parameters
// RETURNS - a handle to a new menu bar
//---------------------------------------------------------
{
    HMBAR hmbar;
```

The process of creating a new menu bar in the Macintosh is a little confusing. The Get-MenuBar() doesn't create an empty, new menu bar; rather it creates a copy of the menu bar that is currently installed. We need a way to create an empty menu bar with the Apple (system) menu in it.

First we save a copy of the existing menu bar using GetMenuBar(). Then we empty out the real menu bar using ClearMenuBar()—we use the application's menu bar as the mechanism for creating a new menu bar. We add the Apple menu that we defined during the initialization of the application in XPInit() and then get a copy of our new menu bar. We copy back the original menu bar that we saved and then dispose the handle to the memory associated with it. Our new menu bar handle can now be used by other menu functions to create a complete menu bar. It represents an empty cross-platform menu bar, which means it only contains an Apple (system) menu list.

```
extern MenuHandle _ghMacAppleMenu;
Handle hCurMBar=GetMenuBar ();

ClearMenuBar();
// insert the Apple menu list (with DA list)
InsertMenu (_ghMacAppleMenu, 0);

hmbar=GetMenuBar ();
// restore the original menu bar
SetMenuBar (hCurMBar);
DisposHandle (hCurMBar);
```

In Windows a menu bar is really just another kind of menu, so we use the CreateMenu() function.

```
hmbar=CreateMenu ();
```

We return the menu bar handle to the caller and we're done.

```
    return (hmbar);
}
```

Adding a Menu List to a Menu Bar

Now that we have a menu bar, we need to add some menu lists to it. Our MenuBarAdd() function requires a pointer to a menu bar handle, the handle to a menu list that we're adding, and the text associated with the menu list, its title (which appears in the menu bar). The menu list is added after all other menu lists in the menu bar.

```
//---------------------------------------------------------
VOID MenuBarAdd (HMBAR *phmbar, HMENU hmenu, PTR zText)
//---------------------------------------------------------
// phmbar  - pointer to a menu bar handle that will
//             receive the additional menu list
// hmenu   - handle to the menu list that will be added
```

```
// zText    - title of the menu list that will appear in
//             the menu bar
// RETURNS - nothing
//-------------------------------------------------------
{
```

In the Macintosh we need go through a few gymnastics to add a menu list. We get a copy of the current menu bar and a handle to it by a call to GetMenuBar(). We set the menu bar to the one that was provided to us. Installing this menu bar allows us to work on it; we'll later remove it. We free up the menu bar that was provided to us because a copy of it was installed in the application's bar.

Then we add the new menu list to our menu bar using InsertMenu(). We get a copy of the new menu bar and a handle to it and replace the menu bar handle that was supplied to us. Finally we replace the application's menu bar with a copy of the original menu bar and free up our copy of the saved original.

Going through all this allows us to add a menu list to a menu bar, but the resulting menu bar handle isn't necessarily the same menu bar handle that we started with. As long as the menu lists in the menu bar don't get destroyed or altered, any copies made from these menu bars will be valid.

Notice that the Macintosh version does not require the zText parameter. This is because this information was provided to the menu list when it was created. The menu list title, zText, provided to this function is used by Windows.

```
// get a copy of the current menu bar
Handle hCurMBar=GetMenuBar ();

// install the menu bar we want to modify
SetMenuBar (*phmbar);
DisposHandle (*phmbar);

// add the new menu list
InsertMenu (hmenu, 0/*append*/);

// get a copy of the new (modified) menu bar handle
*phmbar=GetMenuBar ();

// replace the active menu bar
SetMenuBar (hCurMBar);
DisposHandle (hCurMBar);
```

In Windows the process is simple. We use the AppendMenu() function, tell it we're adding a menu list (by using the MF_POPUP flag), and give it the menu list handle and the text that will appear in the menu bar. The Windows implementation of the MenuBarAdd() function requires the zText parameter because when a menu list is created, using CreateMenu(), we don't need to give it any text information and so we need to do it now. This is a little awkward when you use the MenuListCreate() and MenuBarAdd() functions. You'll need to provide the text information once in each function call to properly set up the menu list and menu bar for the Macintosh and Windows. For example:

```
HMENU hmenu=MenuListCreate (u2MenuID, "New List");
MenuBarAdd (&hmbar, hmenu, "New List");
```

This is unfortunate but necessary. The alternative is to create a new data type that will maintain this information and hide it from you so you don't see that it is required at two separate points of the menu construction process.

```
AppendMenu (*phmbar, MF_POPUP, (UINT)hmenu, zText);
```

And that's the end of MenuBarAdd().

```
}
```

Destroying a Menu Bar

After you're done with a menu bar, you'll need to destroy it. Our MenuBarDestroy() function requires a handle to a menu bar.

```
//-----------------------------------------------------
VOID MenuBarDestroy (HMBAR hmbar)
//-----------------------------------------------------
// hmbar   - handle to the menu bar to destroy
// RETURNS - nothing
//-----------------------------------------------------
{
```

In the Macintosh a menu bar handle is just a memory handle (a Handle), so we get rid of it using DisposHandle().

```
DisposHandle (hmbar);
```

In Windows a menu bar handle is really a menu handle (an HMENU), so we free it up by using DestroyMenu().

```
DestroyMenu (hmbar);
```

The menu bar is destroyed and we end the function.

```
}
```

Menu List Functions

As with the menu bar, we won't illustrate all of the menu list functionality in this chapter, but we will show you the basics. This includes:

- creating a menu list
- destroying a menu list
- loading a list from resources

- adding an item to the list
- adding a separator

Creating a Menu List

To create a menu list, we need to specify the menu id and the text (or title) to be associated with the menu list. The title is what appears in the menu bar. Our function will return a handle to the newly created menu list.

```
//-------------------------------------------------------
HMENU MenuListCreate (UINT2 u2MenuID, PTR zText)
//-------------------------------------------------------
// u2MenuID - unsigned 2-byte integer containing the
//            identifier of the menu list
// zText    - title of the menu list that will appear in
//            the menu bar
// RETURNS  - handle to the new menu list, or NULL if
//            there was an error
//-------------------------------------------------------
{
    HMENU hmenu;
```

In the Macintosh we need to use the NewMenu() function and supply it with the menu identifier and the title of the list (which will appear in the menu bar). Because the menu list title needs to be in Pascal string format, we convert it inline using StrCtoP() in our call to NewMenu() and convert it back when we're done.

```
    hmenu=NewMenu (u2MenuID, StrCtoP (zText));
    StrPtoC ((PTRP)zText);
    if (!hmenu) return (NULL);
```

In Windows we use the CreateMenu() function (which was also used to create a menu bar) to create our menu list handle. We don't need the menu identifier or the name of the list at this point in a menu list's life. These are needed when the list is added to the menu bar. This is different from the Macintosh because the identifier and name are supplied when the list is created; adding the list to the menu bar only requires providing it with the handle.

```
    hmenu=CreateMenu ();
    if (!hmenu) return (NULL);
```

The menu list was created successfully, so we return the handle.

```
    return (hmenu);
}
```

Loading a Menu List

Loading a menu list from resources is often a convenient way to set up the contents of a menu bar quickly. We define our MenuListLoad() function to require one argument that indicates the resource id of the list and to return a handle to the newly loaded menu list.

```
//----------------------------------------------------
HMENU MenuListLoad (UINT2 u2Resid)
//----------------------------------------------------
// u2Resid - unsigned 2-byte integer that is the resource
//           identifier of the menu list to load
// RETURNS - handle to the new menu list, or NULL if error
//----------------------------------------------------
{
    HMENU hmenu;
```

In the Macintosh we use the GetMenu() function to load the resource.

```
    if (!(hmenu=GetMenu (u2Resid))) return (NULL);
```

Similarly in Windows we use the LoadMenu() function, which we provide with the _ghWinInstance variable, supplied to us through XPMain(), and a pointer to the resource name of the menu. Because we specify the menu list by a numeric resource id, we need to convert that id to pointer form (LPSTR) by using MAKINTRESOURCE().

```
    if (!(hmenu=LoadMenu( _ghWinInstance,
       MAKEINTRESOURCE (u2Resid)))
    ){
        return (NULL);
    }
```

If we get here, the menu list was loaded successfully and we return a handle to the list to the caller.

```
    return (hmenu);
}
```

Destroying a Menu List

When we're finished with a menu list, we need to destroy it. Our MenuListDestroy() function requires a handle to a menu list to destroy and returns nothing.

```
//----------------------------------------------------
VOID MenuListDestroy (HMENU hmenu)
//----------------------------------------------------
// hmenu   - handle to the menu list to destroy
// RETURNS - nothing
//----------------------------------------------------
{
```

In the Macintosh it's simple to destroy a menu list by using DisposeMenu().

```
DisposeMenu (hmenu);
```

And it's just as simple to destroy a menu list in Windows, using DestroyMenu().

```
DestroyMenu (hmenu);
```

And that's all there is to it.

```
}
```

Adding a Menu Item

After you've created a menu list, you need to add some items to it. Our function, MenuListAddItem(), requires a handle to a menu list, the text to be associated with the item, and the numeric identifier for the menu item. Adding a menu item means that the item is added at the end of the menu list, after all other items.

```
//-------------------------------------------------------
VOID MenuListAddItem (HMENU hmenu, PTR zText, UINT2 u2id)
//-------------------------------------------------------
// hmenu   - handle to the menu list to add to
// zText   - text to be associated with the new item
// u2id    - unsigned 2-byte integer that will be the
//           identifier for the new item
// RETURNS - nothing
//-------------------------------------------------------
{
```

In the Macintosh we use the AppendMenu() function and supply it with our menu list handle and a Pascal-type string. We don't need the u2id parameter because all menu items are referenced by position in the list, starting at zero. We convert the string back to C format before we leave.

```
AppendMenu (hmenu, StrCtoP (zText));
StrPtoC ((PTRP)zText);
```

In Windows we also use an AppendMenu() function. This one requires that we specify the menu handle, the MF_STRING flag (which tells the function that the last parameter refers to a string), the identifier, and the text to assign to the menu item. In Windows each menu item is assigned a unique identifier, but an item can also be accessed by its position in the menu list, starting at one.

```
AppendMenu (hmenu, MF_STRING, (UINT)u2id, zText);
```

And that's the end of the add item function.

```
}
```

Adding a Separator

Another useful thing to add to a menu list is a separator. This gives you a way to visually group items in a list. We specify our MenuListAddSep() function to require a handle to a menu list. The separator is added at the very end of the list of menu items.

```
//-------------------------------------------------------
VOID MenuListAddSep (HMENU hmenu)
//-------------------------------------------------------
// hmenu   - handle to the menu list to add a separator to
// RETURNS - nothing
//-------------------------------------------------------
{
```

In the Macintosh we use the AppendMenu function, as we did in our MenuListAdd() function. We indicate that we are appending a separator by using a special menu item string that is constructed out of the meta-character '(' to indicate a disabled item and '-' to indicate that the item is a separator. The \p tells the compiler that the string is constructed as a Pascal-type string.

```
AppendMenu (hmenu, "\p(-");
```

In Windows we also use its AppendMenu() function, but we supply the MF_SEPARATOR flag, which tells it that we're adding a separator.

```
AppendMenu (hmenu, MF_SEPARATOR, 0, NULL);
```

Then, we end the function.

```
}
```

Menu Item Functions

Table 13.1 showed a number of functions that work with menu items. We pare that down quit a bit to these essential functions:

- checking or unchecking a menu item
- determining if an item is checked
- enabling or disabling a menu item
- setting the text of a menu item

While the list is not complete, it does show you how the most useful menu item functions are implemented. Also, recall that in Windows menu items can be accessed by positon or identifier from the menu list handle or the menu bar handle. In our examples all of the menu items are accessed by their position in the menu list and not by their identifier. The XPLib software provides a more flexible implementation of these functions.

Checking a Menu Item

Let's start out by showing you how to check a menu item. We require the handle to a menu list, the position (starting from zero), and a boolean that indicates whether we are going to check or uncheck the menu item.

```
//-------------------------------------------------------
VOID MenuCheck (HMENU hmenu, UINT2 u2Pos, BOOL2  b2Checked)
//-------------------------------------------------------
// hmenu     - handle to a menu list
// u2Pos     - position of the item in the list (from 0)
// b2Checked - TRUE = check it, FALSE = uncheck it
// RETURNS   - nothing
//-------------------------------------------------------
{
```

In the Macintosh we use the CheckItem() function and modify the position information to start from one, not zero as our cross-platform function specifies.

```
//Mac position begins at 1 not 0
CheckItem (hmenu, u2Pos+1, b2Checked);
```

In Windows we use the CheckMenuItem() function, telling it that our menu item is specified by position (the MF_BYPOSITION flag) and then indicating whether we want to check or uncheck the item (using the MF_CHECKED or MF_UNCHECKED flags).

```
CheckMenuItem (hmenu, (UINT)u2Pos,
   MF_BYPOSITION
      | (b2Checked ? MF_CHECKED : MF_UNCHECKED));
```

Then we return.

```
}
```

Is a Menu Item Checked?

Sometimes you might want to use the menu item's check state to maintain some state information. You will need to query the menu item to use this information. We define the MenuIsChecked() function to do this. It needs a handle to a menu list and the position of the item (starting from zero) to query. We return a TRUE if the item is checked and a FALSE if it is not checked.

```
//-------------------------------------------------------
BOOL2 MenuIsChecked (HMENU hmenu, UINT2 u2Pos)
//-------------------------------------------------------
// hmenu     - handle to a menu list
// u2Pos     - position of the item in the list (from 0)
// RETURNS   - TRUE if the item is checked, FALSE if not
//-------------------------------------------------------
{
```

In the Macintosh we use the GetItemMark() function and check if the mark character that it returns to us is equal to the noMark constant. If it is equal, the menu item is not checked; if it's not, the item is checked. We map this information to boolean form and return the boolean value to the caller.

```
CHAR cMark;

GetItemMark (hmenu, u2Pos, &cMark);
return (cMark==noMark ? FALSE : TRUE);
```

In Windows we use the GetMenuState() function and tell it that the item we are querying is referenced by position (the MF_BYPOSITION flag) and that the query we are performing is for the check state (by using the MF_CHECKED flag). A return value of MF_CHECKED indicates that the item is checked. Because this is non-zero, we simply check for this and convert to a boolean form.

```
return (GetMenuState (hmenu, (UINT)u2Pos,
    MF_BYPOSITION&MF_CHECKED) ? TRUE : FALSE);
```

And then we end the function definition.

```
}
```

Enabling a Menu Item

Another quality of a menu item is whether it is enabled or disabled. We provide the ability to set the enable state of a menu item using our MenuEnable() function. When a menu item is disabled, a user cannot select the item and no event message, EW_Command, is generated. Our function requires a handle to menu list, the position of the item in the list, and a boolean that indicates if we are enabling or disabling the item.

```
//-------------------------------------------------------
VOID MenuEnable (HMENU hmenu, UINT2 u2Pos,
    BOOL2 b2Enabled)
//-------------------------------------------------------
// hmenu     - handle to a menu list
// u2Pos     - position of the item in the list (from 0)
// b2Enabled - TRUE = enable the item, FALSE = disable it
// RETURNS   - nothing
//-------------------------------------------------------
{
```

In the Macintosh, depending on the value of the b2Enabled parameter, we call EnableItem() or DisableItem(). We supply the function with the position of the menu item in Macintosh form (relative to one) by increasing the position value by one.

```
//the menu item exists...
if (b2Enabled) EnableItem (hmenu, u2Pos+1);
else DisableItem (hmenu, u2Pos+1);
```

In Windows we use the EnableMenuItem() function. We tell it that the menu item is referenced by position (by the MF_BYPOSITION flag) and tell it to enable or disable the item by the MF_ENABLED or MF_GRAYED flags.

```
EnableMenuItem (hmenu, (UINT)u2Pos,
    MF_BYPOSITION|(b2Enabled ? MF_ENABLED : MF_GRAYED));
```

And that's all for enabling or disabling a menu item.

```
}
```

Setting a Menu Item's Text

The last function that we'll show is how to set the text of a menu item. This allows you to change the appearance of a menu. For example, if you have an item whose text is "Show Window" and which can be checked to indicate the option is on or unchecked to indicate the option is off, it might be better to change the text depending on the state you want to indicate. "Show Window" tells us that if you want to show the window, select the item. Once the item is selected, the text is changed to "Hide Window," which tells us the next operation will hide the window.

We specify our function, MenuTextSet(), to require a pointer to a menu list, the position of the item in the list, and a null-terminated string that represents the new text of the menu item.

```
//-----------------------------------------------------
VOID MenuTextSet (HMENU hmenu, UINT2 u2Pos, PTR zText)
//-----------------------------------------------------
// hmenu   - handle to a menu list
// u2Pos   - position of the item in the list (from 0)
// zText   - null-terminated text
// RETURNS - nothing
//-----------------------------------------------------
{
```

In the Macintosh we use SetItem() to change the text of a menu item. We make the position relative to one and provide it with a Pascal string version of the new menu item text.

```
SetItem (hmenu, u2Pos+1, StrCtoP (zText));
StrPtoC ((PTRP)zText);
```

In Windows we use ModifyMenu() and tell it that our menu item is referenced by position (MF_BYPOSITION flag) and that we are modifying the string associated with the menu item by using the MF_STRING flag. We also need to tell it the id of the item and provide it with the new text for the menu item.

```
ModifyMenu (hmenu, (UINT)u2Pos,
    MF_BYPOSITION|MF_STRING,
    GetMenuItemID (hmenu, u2Pos), zText);
```

The menu item's text is changed, and we end the function.

```
}
```

OTHER MENU FEATURES

To provide a represenative subset of menu functionality, you will need to make a few additions to the functionality that we illustrated in this chapter. You will need to work with menu items by id or position and to access menu items from a menu list or a menu bar.

These are essential for providing a solution that works with the event system that we discussed in Chapter 7. When the user clicks in the menu bar, an event should be generated that allows your application to look at and possibly modify the contents of a menu list before it actually dropped down. This event, which we called EW_MenuBarInit, provides us with a menu bar handle (this event is equivalent to the WM_INITMENU in Windows). To initialize the contents of a menu list in a menu bar, you need to be able to access menu items using the menu bar information. And because you can't associate a menu item by position relative to a menu bar (only a menu list), you need to access menu items by id as well as position.

Some advanced areas of menu functionality that should be supported were presented in Table 13.1 but not discussed in this chapter. These include:

- allowing submenus as menu items
- supporting popup menus in windows and dialog boxes
- providing support for keyboard equivalents (accelerators in Windows)
- supporting color in menu items
- allowing icons to appear with a menu item

14

Windows

Most of what the user sees and performs his or her work in is a window. A window represents the portal to the soul of your application, and it is essential that any cross-platform solution provide efficient and robust support for it. In this chapter we will discuss and compare the window features and functions of our three platforms and present some examples of how cross-platform window management functions are implemented.

DEFINING COMMON WINDOW CAPABILITIES

Before we can implement a cross-platform window solution, we need to look at what is available on our three platforms. This means that we need to:

- define some of the terms associated with a window
- look at some of the styles and attributes of windows
- compare window functionality across platforms

Defining Window Terminology

It is important to understand some of the common terms associated with a window before you implement a cross-platform solution.

Term	Description
caption	A thin strip reserved at the top of the window for a string that identifies the window, this is also referred to as the title bar.
zoom	This is a user interface feature that can be added to a window that lets the user choose one of two window size states: full size (zoomed out) or current size (zoomed in).
size	A user interface feature can be added to a window that lets it be incrementally sized by the user. The user usually mouses down in a special area of the window frame and drags the cursor to change the dimensions of a window.
scroll bar	Either a horizontal or vertical scoll bar allows the user to move (scroll) the contents of a window left or right or up and down. A scroll bar consists of a thumb (which the user drags), a line up and down (for moving the contents in small increments), and a page up and down (for moving the contents in large increments).
pane	This is the internal content area of the window where all drawing and user activity is concentrated.
frame	This is the external border of the window that includes the caption, scroll bars, and the window pane. The frame of a window can be drawn in different ways to indicate different types of windows.
close	This user interface feature can be added to a window, allowing it to be closed without using the window's menu bar.
shrink	A user interface feature can be added to a window that allows it to be shrunk to an icon (iconized). This ability is unique to Windows.
handler	Every window has a window handler function that is called by the event manager whenever there are events that the window needs to process.
redraw	A window is redrawn when an area of the screen has been invalidated. Invalidated areas are accumulated into the update region. When no other higher priority events are in the event queue, the redraw event is sent to the window handler, and the update region of the window is redrawn.
activate	This process of making a window the receiver of user input involves a visual change in some of the attributes of a window. A window is usually activated by the user clicking in an inactive window.
inactivate	The process of making another window the receiver of user input, this involves some changes in the appearance of a window. A window is usually inactivated by the user clicking in another inactive window.

Comparing User Interface Features of Windows

Now that we've defined some terms, let's look at how some of these apply to the Macintosh and Windows platforms. In this section we will look at some of the window styles and some of their visual features and compare them across our target platforms.

Styles of Windows

There are numerous styles of windows on a platform. For our purposes we limit the choices of these styles to the following:

Style	Description
normal	window includes a caption or title bar
double	window has a double border and no caption
simple	window has a simple border and no caption

These styles are visually compared in Figure 14.1.

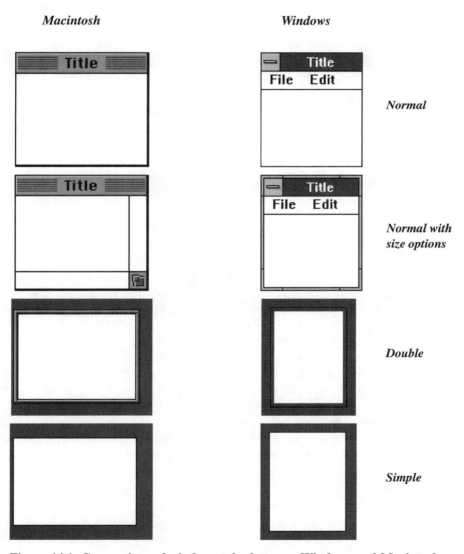

Figure 14.1 Comparison of window styles between Windows and Macintosh.

Visual Features of a Window

Table 14.1 lists the visual features of Macintosh and Windows windows. Figure 14.2 shows some of the Macintosh features and Figure 14.3 shows some of the Windows features.

Comparing API Functionality

Most of the window functions are available and reasonably equivalent on our target platforms, give or take a little, as listed in Table 14.2. Windows 3.1 and Win32 provide an equivalent API to work with windows. So we compare the functions between the Macintosh and Windows.

Table 14.1 Comparison of window visual features.

Visual Feature	*Macintosh*	*Windows*
visible	the window can be made completely visible or invisible	the window can be made completely visible or invisible
size	grow icon in lower-right corner of window plus lines reserving placement for scroll bars	a narrow border around the perimiter of the window that allows stretching of a side or corner to size the window; this requires the WS_THICKFRAME option
close	close box on left end of window caption bar	the Close item in the system menu; requires the WS_SYSMENU option; allows double-clicking the system menu icon to close the window
horizontal scroll	located at the bottom edge of a window, a separate control that needs to be sized and placed at bottom of the window; requires that the window have a grow icon	located at bottom edge of a window, an integral part of the window creation process; this feature requires the WS_VSCROLL option
vertical scroll	located at the right edge of a window, a separate control that needs to be sized and placed at right of the window; requires that the window have a grow icon	located at right edge of a window integral, an integral part of the window creation process; requires the WS_HSCROLL option
zoom	zoom box on the right end of the window caption bar	arrow-up button on the right end of the window caption bar
shrink	NA	arrow-down button on right end of window caption bar
inactive window	close box, zoom box, and grow icon not visible	scroll bar contents not visible, and detail in the window caption bar gone; title still visible but grayed out

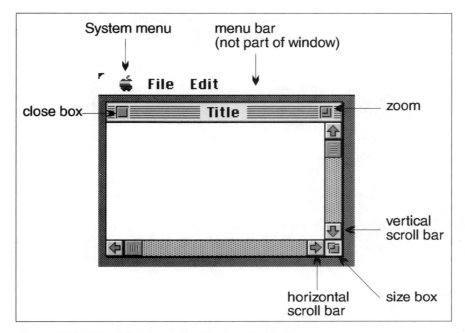

Figure 14.2 Visual features of a Macintosh window.

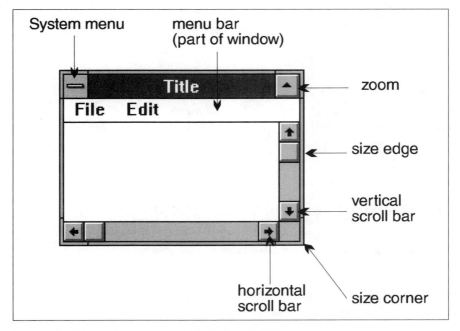

Figure 14.3 Visual features of a Windows window.

Table 14.2 Comparison of window functions across platforms.

Function	Macintosh	Windows
create	NewWindow NewCWindow	CreateWindow
destroy	DisposeWindow	DestroyWindow
show/hide	ShowWindow HideWindow	ShowWindow
set title	SetWTitle	SetWindowText
get title	GetWTitle	GetWindowText
get frame rect	NA	GetWindowRect
set frame dim	SizeWindow	SetWindowPos
set frame pos	MoveWindow	SetWindowPos
get pane rect	NA	GetClientRect
set pane rect	NA	NA
erase pane rect	EraseRect	FillRect
begin redraw	BeginUpdate	BeginPaint
end redraw	EndUpdate	EndPaint
set menu bar	SetMenuBar	SetMenu
get menu bar	NA	GetMenu
draw menu bar	DrawMenuBar	DrawMenuBar
enable scroll bar	HiliteControl	ShowScrollBar
set scroll range	SetCtlMin SetCtlMax	SetScrollRange
get scroll range	GetCtlMin GetCtlMax	GetScrollRange
set scroll position	SetCtlValue	SetScrollPos
get scroll position	GetCtlValue	GetScrollPos
get window extra data	GetWRefCon	GetWindowWord or GetWindowLong
set window extra data	SetWRefCon	SetWindowWord or SetWindowLong

IMPLEMENTING A PRACTICAL WINDOW SOLUTION

After we have organized all of the information about what windows features are necessary and the functionality that is available on our platforms, we can begin to implement a window solution. This process involves:

- determining window-related data types, simple and complex
- defining some necessary data values
- implementing the window management functions

Simple Window Data Types

There are several simple data types that we need to define to provide window functionality across our three platforms:

Type	Macintosh	Windows 3.1	Win32
HWND	WindowPtr (4 bytes)	HWND (2 bytes)	HWND (4 bytes)
HANDLERdecl	SINT4	LRESULT CALLBACK or LONG _far _pascal	LRESULT CALLBACK or LONG __stdcall
HANDLERrtn	SINT4	LRESULT or LONG	LRESULT or LONG
MSGDATA	UINT4	UINT (2 bytes)	UINT (4 bytes)
DATA1	UINT4 (4 bytes)	WPARAM or UINT (2 bytes)	WPARAM or UINT (4 bytes)
DATA2	UINT4	LPARAM or LONG	LPARAM or LONG

Now we need to define the data type for the window handler function. This type of function is the receiving station for all event messages. In the Macintosh we define it as:

```
typedef HANDLERdecl (*HANDLER) (HWND hwnd, MSGDATA msg,
    DATA1 data1, DATA2 data2);
```

In Windows we define it this way:

```
// WNDPROC is defined by Windows
typedef LRESULT (CALLBACK* WNDPROC) (HWND, UINT, WPARAM,
    LPARAM);
#define HANDLER WNDPROC
```

The handler function data types are used in different ways. We define a variable of the HANDLER type:

```
HANDLER fnHandler;
```

We define a function of the HANDLER type:

```
HANDLERdecl MyHandlerFunction (HWND hwnd, MSGDATA msg,
    DATA1 data1, DATA2 data2);
```

We define a variable to contain the return information from a HANDLER type function:

```
HANDLERrtn handlerReturnData=0;
```

We also specify a data type for the function type that is used to redraw the contents of a window.

```
typedef UINT4 (*DRAWPROC) (PDSP pdsp, PTR pData);
```

A pointer to this type of function is included as an argument to the redraw function so that a window can be redrawn using a cross-platform syntax.

Window Extra Data Structure

The window extra data structure, WNDX, contains information that is needed by our cross-platform window defintion. The contents of this structure are platform-specific. The Macintosh version of the WNDX structure is defined as follows:

Type	Field	Description
HANDLER	fnHandler	previously defined in Chapter 7 on events, contains the pointer to the function that will process events for this window
UINT4	u4Attrib	a place to save our cross-platform window attributes
UINT2	u2Magic	identifies this as a cross-platform window

And the Windows version of the WNDX structure is defined as follows:

Type	Field	Description
UINT4	u4Attrib	a place to save our cross-platform window attributes
UINT2	u2Magic	identifies this window as one of ours

The Macintosh extra data is passed on the window data structure, WindowRecord, through the refCon field. This field is accessed using the SetWRefCon() and GetWRefCon() functions.

In Windows the extra window data is stored in a private area of the window definition data. The size of the extra data is allocated when the window is created and is specified by a field in the window class structure, the WNDCLASS type, when the class is registered. All windows created using a class contain the same extra space. To retrieve the information in the window extra area, you use the GetWindowWord() and GetWindowLong() functions. To install information in the extra space, you use the SetWindowWord() and SetWindowLong() functions.

Data Values and Constants

First we need to define some constants that let you indicate the window attributes to include in a window when it is created. (Additional constants are defined for XPLib.)

```
#define WINSTYLEMASK    0x000000ff
#define WINISVISIBLE    0x00000100
#define WINCANSIZE      0x00000200
#define WINCANDESTROY   0x00000400
#define WINCANZOOM      0x00000800
```

Now we need something to identify uniquely a window that has been created by our cross-platform solution. We really don't use it in our discussion, but it's long-term usefulness is essential. It enables a cross-platform window to be distinguished from one that is not.

```
#define WINDOWMAGIC 12345
```

Let's define some constants that let us specify the frame style of the window that we will create.

```
enum {WINSTYLE_Normal, WINSTYLE_Double, WINSTYLE_Simple};
```

And then we define a map that will relate our cross-platform window style to a Macintosh window style.

```
static SINT2 gWinStyleMap[]={
   noGrowDocProc,dBoxProc,plainDBox,
   documentProc//internal use
};
#define _MACGROWWIN 3
```

We define another map to relate our cross-platform window style to Windows.

```
static UINT4 gWinStyleMap[]={
   WS_OVERLAPPED|WS_SYSMENU,
   WS_POPUP|WS_DLGFRAME,
   WS_POPUP|WS_BORDER
};
```

This produces the following relationship between our cross-platform window styles and their Macintosh and Windows equivalents:

Style	Macintosh	Windows
WINSTYLE_Normal	noGrowDocProc	WS_OVERLAPPED|WS_SYSMENU
WINSTYLE_Double	dBoxProc	WS_POPUP|WS_DLGFRAME
WINSTYLE_Simple	plainDBox	WS_POPUP|WS_BORDER
_MACGROWWIN	documentProc	NA

In Windows we need a way to access some of the extra window information, so we define these GWx_xxx constants that map to their offsets into the WNDX data structure.

```
#define GWL_Attrib  0
#define GWW_Magic   4
```

Window Functions

In this section we will show examples of:

- creating a window
- destroying a window
- implementing a window handler function

- redrawing a window
- implementing the redraw function
- retreiving, installing, and redrawing a menu bar

Creating a Window

The first window procedure that we need is the one to create a window. We define our WinCreate() function to require the rectangular bounds of the window in screen coordinates, the attributes to apply to the window, and the window title. If everything goes OK, we'll return a handle to the new window.

There are a few things that we need to do before we move to the platform-specific code. If the window style indicates a double or simple window (no caption), then we turn off the attributes for sizing, destroying, and zooming the window. These attributes aren't really relevant to these types of windows. Next we need to convert the packed attributes into individual variables. This makes it easier to work with them.

Notice that our example does not support scroll bars or the minimize (iconize) capability of Windows. These features add a substantial amount of complexity to the solution.

```
//----------------------------------------------------
HWND WinCreate (PRECT pRect, UINT4 u4Attrib, PTR zTitle)
//----------------------------------------------------
// pRect    -  pointer to a RECT that contains the bounding
//             box of the window in screen coordinates
// u4Attrib -  attributes of the window
// zTitle   -  title (caption) of the window
// RETURNS  -  handle to the new window if successful,
//             NULL otherwise
//----------------------------------------------------
{
   HWND hwnd;
   //attributes: style,visible,grow,zoom,close
   SINT2 s2Style;
   BOOL2 b2Vis;
   BOOL2 b2Size;
   BOOL2 b2Destroy;
   BOOL2 b2Zoom;

   if ((u4Attrib&WINSTYLEMASK)==WINSTYLE_Double
      || (u4Attrib&WINSTYLEMASK)==WINSTYLE_Simple
   ){
      // clear the necessary bits in the attribute
      u4Attrib&=(~WINCANSIZE);
      u4Attrib&=(~WINCANDESTROY);
      u4Attrib&=(~WINCANZOOM);
   }
```

```
// set up some individual attributes variables
s2Style=(SINT2)u4Attrib&WINSTYLEMASK;
b2Vis=((u4Attrib&WINISVISIBLE)!=0);
b2Size=((u4Attrib&WINCANSIZE)!=0);
b2Destroy=((u4Attrib&WINCANDESTROY)!=0);
b2Zoom=((u4Attrib&WINCANZOOM)!=0);
```

In the Macintosh we allocate a new pointer to hold the extra window data and we initialize this window extra structure. We do a little tweaking of the window style and attributes to make sure that they map properly to a Macintosh window. If the window style is WINSTYLE_Normal and we want to size the window, we change the Macintosh style to _MACGROWWIN, which maps to the documentProc type of window.

Then we make a Pascal-string copy of the window title and copy over the bounding box of the rectangle (we check if the coordinates specify a window that is obscured by the menu bar and fix them if necessary). The _gb2MacColorQD and _gb2MacColorGD are Macintosh-specific globals that tell us if this system has Color QuickDraw and if the device we are drawing to supports color. Depending on the configuration of the Macintosh, we create a new window or a new color window and specify the Macintosh window style by mapping the cross-platform window style to a Macintosh style using the gWinStyleMap[ ] array. We install the window extra data into the window record using SetWRefCon() and then send our window handler two messages.

Before the window is shown, we tell our handler that the window is being created. This allows an application to do anything extra that might be necessary before the window is displayed. And then we send another message to the handler that tells it whether the window is to be displayed. These two messages are sent to emulate part of the event sequence in a Windows application. This allows both the Macintosh and Windows versions of an application to provide the same response to the window creation process.

> *Note: Actually, there are quite a few other event messages that are sent to a handler during the creation of a Windows window. We don't include them because the EW_Create and EW_Show are the most important.*

```
{
Rect rect;
Str255 pzTitle;
PWNDX pwndx=(PWNDX)NewPtr(sizeof(WNDX));

pwndx->u4Attrib=u4Attrib;
pwndx->fnHandler=_gfnMacHandler;
pwndx->u2Magic=WINDOWMAGIC;

if (b2Size && s2Style==WINSTYLE_Normal){
    s2Style=_MACGROWWIN;
}
```

```
    // make a copy of the title in Pascal format
    StrCopyCtoP (pzTitle, zTitle);

    // copy the cross-platform RECT to a Mac Rect
    rect.top=(pRect->top<40)?40:pRect->top;
    rect.bottom=pRect->bottom;
    rect.left=pRect->left;
rect.right=pRect->right;

    // create the window, use the appropriate window
    // creation function depending on the system
    hwnd=(_gb2MacColorQD && _gb2MacColorGD)
        ? (WindowPtr)NewCWindow (0L, &rect, pzTitle, FALSE,
            gWinStyleMap[s2Style]+(b2Zoom?8:0),
            (WindowPtr)-1L, b2Destroy, 0)

        : NewWindow (0L, &rect, pzTitle, FALSE,
            gWinStyleMap[s2Style]+(b2Zoom?8:0),
            (WindowPtr)-1L, b2Destroy, 0);

    if (!hwnd) return (NULL);

    // set up the extra window information
    SetWRefCon (hwnd, (UINT4)pwndx);

    // send some events to our window handler to get
    // things started (to emulate Windows)
    EventSend (hwnd, EW_Create, 0L, 0L);
    EventSend (hwnd, EW_Show, b2Vis, 0);
    }
```

In Windows we convert the rectangular bounding box to the top, left, width, and height format that Windows requires. Then we map the cross-platform style to a Windows style using the gWinStyleMap[] array and convert our cross-platform attributes to Windows attributes. We create the window using CreateWindow(), which sends the WM_CREATE and WM_SIZE messages to the handler; these map to our EW_Create and EW_Size messages. Then we fill in the window extra data that is attached to the window.

> *Notice that we can't initialize the window extra data until after the CreateWindow() function returns. This means that we won't have access to the extra data until after the window creation process—after the EW_Create and EW_Size messages. Actually the extra data isn't available until after the first EW_Redraw (WM_PAINT) message is processed. To ensure a consistent source code base, you shouldn't access the extra window data at all. If you need to, you should wait until the first EW_Redraw has been processed.*

```
    {
    UINT4 u4Style;//Windows style not cross-platform
    SINT x, y, dx, dy;

    x=pRect->left;
    y=pRect->top;
    dx=pRect->right-pRect->left;
    dy=pRect->bottom-pRect->top;

    u4Style=gWinStyleMap[s2Style]|(b2Vis?WS_VISIBLE:0)
            |(b2Size?WS_THICKFRAME:0)
            |(b2Zoom?WS_MAXIMIZEBOX:0);

    hwnd=CreateWindow (_gzWinClassName, zTitle, u4Style,
        x, y, dx, dy,
        NULL/*no parent*/,
        NULL,/*no menu*/
        _ghWinInstance,
        NULL/*no extended style information*/);

    // the window could not be created!
    if (!hwnd) return (NULL);

    // identify our window as such (only valid AFTER
    // the first WM_PAINT message)
    SetWindowWord (hwnd, GWW_Magic, WINDOWMAGIC);

    // set up the window extra stuff
    SetWindowLong (hwnd, GWL_Attrib, u4Attrib);
    }
```

We return to the caller with the handle to the new window.

```
    return (hwnd);
    }
```

Destroying a Window

Now let's look at how a window is destroyed. Our function, WinDestroy(), requires a handle to the window that we want destroyed and returns ERR_No if the window was destroyed. We want to check that the window handle is valid before we go too far with this process.

```
//---------------------------------------------------------
ERR WinDestroy (HWND hwnd)
//---------------------------------------------------------
// hwnd    - handle to the window to destroy
```

```
// RETURNS - ERR_No if everything went OK
//---------------------------------------------------
{
    if (hwnd){
```

In the Macintosh the first thing we need to do is to send the window handler a message that the window is going to be destroyed and then hide the window. This is done to emulate the behavior of a Windows application. Then we get the pointer to the extra window data using GetWRefCon() and free up the memory allocated for it. We end the destroy process by calling DisposeWindow(), which frees up the memory that was allocated for the window and removes the window from the application's window list.

```
    {
    PWNDX pwndx;

    // send ourselves a destroy message in advance
    // of the actual destruction, to prepare for it
    EventSend (hwnd, EW_Destroy, 0L, 0L);
    HideWindow (hwnd);

    // free up the extra data that we allocated
    // AFTER sending the destroy
    // message, else the handler would be garbage
    pwndx=(PWNDX)GetWRefCon (hwnd);
    DisposePtr (pwndx);

    DisposeWindow (hwnd);
    }
```

In Windows we first verify that we have a valid window and then call DestroyWindow() to do all of the work.

```
    if (!IsWindow (hwnd)) return (ERR_Yes);
    DestroyWindow (hwnd);
```

If everything went OK, we return ERR_No, which indicates the window was destroyed successfully.

```
    }
    return (ERR_No);
}
```

The Window Handler

The window handler is the function that was designated to handle all event processing during the application initialization process—a parameter to the XPInit() function. All event messages to a window are sent to this function. Our sample window handler function, WinHandler(), receives a handle to a window, the event message, and two data values that are dependent on the event message that was received. The return value is also dependent on the event message.

```
//-----------------------------------------------------
HANDLERdecl WinHandler (HWND hwnd, MSGDATA msg,
    DATA1 data1, DATA2 data2)
//-----------------------------------------------------
// hwnd     - handle to the window
// msg      - the event message that we need to process
// data1    - first data that this message needs
// data2    - second data that this message needs
// RETURNS  - value depends on event, but usually zero if
//              the handler processed the message
//-----------------------------------------------------
{
    switch (msg){
        case EW_Create:
            return (0);

        case EW_Redraw:
            // redraw the window using the DRAWPROC
            // pointed to by WinDrawProc
            WinPaneDraw (hwnd, WinDrawProc, NULLPTR);
            return (0);

        case EW_Command:
            // process all menu action here
            return (0);

        case EW_Destroy:
            return (0);
    }
    // anything that we don't handle, send to the
    // default window handler
    return ((HANDLERrtn)WinDefHandler (hwnd, msg, data1,
        data2));
}
```

A minimal implementation of a window handler function would look like this:

```
HANDLERdecl WinHandlerMinimum (HWND hwnd, MSGDATA msg,
    DATA1 data1, DATA2 data2)
{
    return ((HANDLERrtn)WinDefHandler (hwnd, msg, data1,
        data2));
}
```

The WinDefHandler() is something that defines the standard, default behavior of a window handler function. In Windows this is equivalent to:

```
DefWindowProc (hwnd, msg, data1, data2);
```

You will need to implement a suitable version of this for the Macintosh side. A bare minimum default window handler might look like this:

```
// this is for the Macintosh
HANDLERdecl WinDefHandlerMinimum (HWND hwnd, MSGDATA msg,
    DATA1 data1, DATA2 data2)
{
    switch (msg){
        case EW_Redraw:
            BeginUpdate (hwnd);
            EndUpdate (hwnd);
            return (0);
        break;
        case EW_Show:
            if (data1) ShowWindow (hwnd);
            else HideWindow (hwnd);
            return (0);
        break;
        case EW_Close:
            WinDestroy (hwnd);
            return (0);
    }
    return (1);
}
```

Invalidating a Window

The process of invalidating all or part of a window is handled by the GInvalidateRect() function that we described in Chapter 8. The invalidated area is specified in draw space coordinates and can be larger than the window pane. The invalidiated rectangle is added to the currently accumulated area and will be redrawn during the next EW_Redraw message.

Drawing to a Window

When your window handler receives an EW_Redraw event message, you need to redraw the window contents. To hide the platform-specific baggage of this process, we define WinPane-Draw(). It requires a window handle, a pointer to the function that will perform the actual drawing (of DRAWPROC type), and a pointer to some data that the draw procedure needs.

```
//--------------------------------------------------------
UINT4 WinPaneDraw (HWND hwnd, DRAWPROC fnDraw, PTR pData)
//--------------------------------------------------------
```

```
// hwnd       - handle to the window to draw
// fnDraw     - pointer to the draw procedure
// pData      - pointer to some data needed by draw proc
// RETURNS    - always returns zero
//-------------------------------------------------------
{
```

In the Macintosh the first thing that we need to do is create and initialize a draw space (GrafPort) that can be used by the draw procedure. We set the Macintosh pen to it's normal state (one pixel, black line, in copy mode) and then signal the Macintosh operating system that we are beginning the update process. We erase the GrafPort rectangle and then call the caller-supplied draw procedure. When the contents of the window have been drawn, we end the update and leave. We do not support scroll bars, other controls, or the grow icon in this example, but these features are supported in the XPLib version of this function.

```
      DSP dsp;

      // initialize the draw space
      GetPort (&dsp.pPrevPort);
      SetPort (hwnd);
      dsp.s2Fill=GFILL_None;
      dsp.b2Print=FALSE;
      dsp.pport=hwnd;

      //set up the default drawing state
      PenNormal ();

      BeginUpdate (hwnd);
      //redraw background
      EraseRect (&hwnd->portRect);

      if (fnDraw) fnDraw (&dsp, pData);

      EndUpdate (hwnd);

      //restore to previous window
      SetPort (dsp.pPrevPort);
```

The process of redrawing the window contents is similar in Windows. We need to create and initialize a draw space (a device context) and then initialize the pen and brush of the corresponding device context (DC). Then we call the draw procedure, draw the window contents, and end the paint process (validate the update region and release the DC).

```
      PAINTSTRUCT ps;
      HBRUSH hOldBrush;
      HPEN hOldPen;
      DSP dsp;
```

```
dsp.s2Fill=GFILL_None;
dsp.b2Print=FALSE;
dsp.hwnd=hwnd;
dsp.hdc=BeginPaint(hwnd,&ps);

hOldBrush=SelectObject (dsp.hdc,
    GetStockObject (NULL_BRUSH));
hOldPen=SelectObject (dsp.hdc,
    GetStockObject (BLACK_PEN));
DeleteObject (hOldBrush);
DeleteObject (hOldPen);

if (fnDraw) fnDraw (&dsp, pData);

EndPaint (hwnd, &ps);
```

Then we end the function defintion.

```
    return (0L);
}
```

Defining a Draw Procedure

When we process an EW_Redraw message and use the WinPaneDraw() function, we provide it with a pointer to a draw function. This draw function is a cross-platform function and requires a window handle and a pointer to some data that is needed by it. Here is how the simplest draw function will look.

```
//-----------------------------------------------------
UINT4 fnDraw (HWND hwnd, PTR pData)
//-----------------------------------------------------
// hwnd    - handle to the window
// pData   - pointer to data need by this function
// RETURNS - depends on the draw function
//-----------------------------------------------------
{
    // put in here what you want to draw to the window

    return (0L);
}
```

Installing a Menu Bar

As we alluded to in the previous chapter on menus, installing a menu bar is more appropriately categorized as a window function. Here we define our WinMenuSet() function to require a handle to a window and the handle of a menu bar to install.

```
//----------------------------------------------------------
VOID WinMenuSet (HWND hwnd, HMBAR hmbar)
//----------------------------------------------------------
// hwnd    - handle to the window
// hmbar   - handle to a menu bar to install
// RETURNS - nothing
//----------------------------------------------------------
{
```

In the Macintosh we use the SetMenuBar() function to install the new menu bar. We don't use the window handle because a menu bar is global to all windows in the application.

```
SetMenuBar (hmbar);
```

In Windows we use the SetMenu() function, which requires the window handle and the menu bar handle. A window can use either the menu handle specified during the RegisterClass() function, the menu handle specified during the CreateWindow() process, or the menu handle specified directly using the SetMenu() function.

```
SetMenu (hwnd, hmbar);
```

An then we're done.

```
}
```

Drawing the Menu

If you've modified the menu bar, you will need to redraw it before any of the changes are visible and available to the user. This is done using the WinMenuDraw() function, which requires the handle to a window.

```
//----------------------------------------------------------
VOID WinMenuDraw (HWND hwnd)
//----------------------------------------------------------
// hwnd    - handle to the window whose menu we will draw
// RETURNS - nothing
//----------------------------------------------------------
{
```

In the Macintosh the DrawMenuBar() function has no arguments and redraws the menu bar that is referenced by the MenuList global variable.

```
DrawMenuBar ();
```

In Windows the DrawMenuBar() function requires the handle to the window.

```
DrawMenuBar (hwnd);
```

That ends the draw menu bar function.

```
}
```

Retrieving the Window's Menu Bar

When you want to modify the contents of the menu bar or save a menu bar in total, you need to get a handle to it. The WinMenuGet() function does this for you and requires a handle to a window (the window whose menu bar you want to get).

```
//------------------------------------------------------
HMBAR WinMenuGet (HWND hwnd)
//------------------------------------------------------
// hwnd    - handle of the window with the menu bar to get
// RETURNS - handle to the menu bar
//------------------------------------------------------
{
```

In the Macintosh the global variable MenuList is the handle to the currently active menu bar, so we return it to the caller. Our example assumes that menu bar referred to by MenuList is associated with the window indicated by hwnd and is the active window. This might not always be a valid assumption but can many times be true. Usually you modify the menu of a window that the user is currently working in or has just made active, so there is no problem with the assumption.

A thorough implementation of this function would either make the specified window active, save the menu list (or make a copy of it), and reactivate the previous window; or it would store a copy of a menu bar handle for the window in the window extra data, which it would retrieve. When you set the menu bar, you would copy the new information to the window extra data and then install it in the system, but only if that window is active.

```
        return (MenuList);
```

In Windows we get the menu bar from the window by using GetMenu().

```
        return (GetMenu (hwnd));
```

Then we end the WinMenuGet() function.

```
}
```

Usually when you modify a menu bar, you will do something like this:

```
HMBAR hmbar=WinMenuGet (hwnd);

// modify the menu

WinMenuSet (hwnd, hmbar);
WinMenuDraw (hwnd);
```

OTHER WINDOW FEATURES

Here are some of the additional window-related functionality that you might want to consider for your cross-platform solution (also provided by the XPLib software):

- support for horizontal and vertical scroll bars
- the ability to get and set the window title
- the ability to erase the window pane area
- moving and changing the dimensions of a window
- support for shrinking (iconizing) a window (Windows only)
- the option of redrawing the contents of a window in the background (applicable only in Win32)
- the ability to open the window pane for drawing at times other than during the processing of a EW_Redraw message
- a fully featured default window handler (Macintosh)

You might also want to provide a cross-platform way to access the extra window data. This is probably necessary if you hide a lot of interesting features in there. Or you might just want to provide a cross-platform mechanism to allow the programmer to define and use his or her own extra data (in addition to that needed by the cross-platform functions).

15

Dialogs

Other than the menu bar, a dialog box is the primary method for the user to select options for, enter information into, and to obtain feedback from your application. They are specialized windows that can take on one of three forms:

- the alert or message box
- the modal dialog box
- the modeless dialog box

Each has its own purpose in an application. In this chapter we will discuss the different dialog forms across our three selected platforms and then present some examples of how some cross-platform dialog functionality is implemented.

DEFINING COMMON DIALOG CAPABILITIES

Of the three forms of dialogs, the alert (commonly called a message box in Windows) is the simplest in form and required by most applications. It presents the user with information and allows a limited response. The modal dialog box is variable in form and content and most applications have at least one. It is used to present the user with choices and allow him or her to enter information that is needed by an application. The modeless dialog box is variable in form and function but is usually used to keep the user informed about information that is changing.

In this section we will look at Macintosh and Windows alerts, discuss some forms of dialogs, and compare the dialog functionality across platforms.

Comparing Alert Features

Let's start by looking at some of the attributes of an alert. An alert is made of four basic components:

- the title of the alert
- the message contained in the alert
- an icon indicating the type of alert
- one or more push buttons to field responses from the user

The title indicates the general category for the information contained in the message. The message contains information in one of three forms:

- an informative note—something the user might need to know
- a warning—something the user needs to be aware of
- a notice that something serious has happened

Each of these three types of alerts is represented by a distinctive icon. The icon used for a particular type of alert is platform-specific. These are shown in Figure 15.1.

Now let's look at some of the push button options that you will typically find:

- OK—give the user the choice to acknowlege the alert (usually in notes)
- Cancel—the user clicks to cancel a process, usually found singly in modeless dialogs
- OK and Cancel—the user has a choice between two courses of action
- Yes and No—same as OK with Cancel

For our purposes we limit the choices to OK and OK with Cancel.

Figure 15.1 Comparison of alert icons.

Discussing Dialog Form

Dialogs appear as any other kind of window. They can have a caption, a double border, or a simple single-line border. Dialog boxes cannot usually be sized and do not normally have scroll bars. They maintain a static form that a user can depend on, and the contents of many dialog boxes maintain some informational state that is consistent between invocations.

Most platforms specify a set of user interface guidelines that indicate the proper methods of designing and coding the behavior of dialog boxes. If you are defining a cross-platform look and feel for your product, you may want to define your own common rules for dialog boxes (and other user interface items). For information on the Macintosh GUI for System 6, see *Inside Macintosh*, Volumes I, IV, and V, and *Human Interface Guidelines: The Apple Desktop Interface*. For information on user interface issues related to System 7, see *Inside Macintosh*, Volume VI, Chapter 2. Information on Windows user interface issues can be found in *The Windows Interface: An Application Design Guide*, and in *The GUI Guide: International Terminology for the Windows Interface*, which discusses international issues.

Comparing Dialog Functionality

Table 15.1 lists some of the common dialog functions and maps out how these functions are implemented on the Macintosh and Windows platforms. Most of the needed functionality is

Table 15.1 Comparison of dialog functionality.

Function	*Macintosh*	*Windows*
display an alert	Alert, StopAlert, NoteAlert, or CautionAlert	MessageBox
create a modal dialog	GetNewDialog, NewDialog, or NewCDialog	MakeProcInstance, DialogBox, DialogBoxIndirect, DialogBoxParam, or DialogBoxIndirectParam
destroy a modal dialog	CloseDialog or DisposDialog	EndDialog
create a modeless dialog	GetNewDialog, NewDialog, or NewCDialog	MakeProcInstance, CreateDialog, CreateDialogIndirect, CreateDialogParam, or CreateDialogIndirectParam
destroy a modeless dialog	CloseDialog or DisposDialog	DestroyWindow
process modal dialog events	IsDialogEvent	IsDialogMessage

adequately represented on all platforms. The differences lie beneath the functional interface, in how the systems use dialogs and how they are defined.

IMPLEMENTING A PRACTICAL DIALOG SOLUTION

To implement a cross-platform dialog solution, we need to use some of the information presented above, but more important we need to understand what a dialog really is and how you will use it in your application.

The Macintosh and Windows both expect the visual and component pieces of the dialog to be predefined as a resource template. The Macintosh uses 'DLOG' and 'DITL' (a list of the items in the dialog) resources in the resource fork of a file. Windows uses the DIALOG statement in a resource source (RC) file, which is compiled and included in the executable (EXE) file.

The biggest difference between the Macintosh and Windows is in the way the platforms interact with dialogs. In the Macintosh you construct a loop that waits for user action with any of the controls in a dialog. When this occurs, information about the action is returned that your program needs to handle. This is similar to Windows, except that the interaction of a dialog with the user is controlled not by a loop in the application but at the system level. A dialog is another classification of a window that can receive almost all of the messages that any other window can receive. This makes a Windows dialog a bit more flexible but also more complicated to implement. The Windows dialog window handler is called until it signals to the system that the dialog box should be destroyed.

What we need to do is to make the Macintosh dialog model more like Windows and create a common dialog handler function that can describe the reaction of the dialog to user action in a cross-platform way.

In this section we will look at:

- the data needed for cross-platform dialogs to work
- some data values that need to be defined
- an example of a cross-platform alert function
- an implementation of modal dialog functionality

Dialog-Related Data Types

To implement modal dialogs for the Macintosh in a cross-platform manner (à la Windows), we need to add two more fields to the WNDX structure (defined in the previous chapter) that are used exclusively by dialogs. These fields are:

Type	Field Name	Description
BOOL2	b2DlgRun	TRUE means the dialog is still running
SINT2	s2DlgResult	value returned from the dialog

They are necessary because a modal dialog box is self-destructing. It tells itself when it wants to end and passes a value back to indicate the reason for the destruction.

The process of destroying a modal dialog is very asynchronous. That is, at some point while the dialog is processing events, something happens that signals the dialog handler that the dialog needs to end—the context is defined in the code and usually related to user action. At this point it sets up the return value and resets its run flag to indicate that, at the next chance, we need to end the dialog.

Nothing addional is needed for Windows.

General Dialog-Related Data Values

We need to define some default responses from dialogs that are represented equivalently across platforms. They refer to the ids of the buttons used to field user response and represent the user's choice, usually when a dialog is being closed. We are fortunate that the Macintosh and Windows designate certain numbers for these purposes that just happen to be the same. We simply provide a symbolic designation for them.

Button	Designation	Value
OK	IDOK	1
Cancel	IDCANCEL	2

In the Macintosh this means that a push button designated with OK must be the first item in the dialog item list ('DITL') and the Cancel push button must be the second dialog item. In Windows IDOK and IDCANCEL are predefined in the development header files, so we only need to define them for the Macintosh.

Dialog Data Values for Alerts

Our first group of data values indicate the type of alerts that our cross-platform alert function will support:

```
enum{
    ALERT_Stop, ALERT_Note, ALERT_Warn
};
```

These values map to functions in the Macintosh and to parameter values on Windows. The relationships are shown here:

Type of Alert	Macintosh	Windows MessageBox()
ALERT_Note	NoteAlert	MB_ICONINFORMATION
ALERT_Warn	CautionAlert	MB_ICONEXCLAMATION
ALERT_Stop	StopAlert	MB_ICONHAND

Next we define the values that indicate the types of alerts that we are supporting.

```
enum{
    ALERT_OK,
    ALERT_OKCancel
};
```

These map to resource ids in the Macintosh and parameter values on Windows. These relationships are shown below:

Mode of Alert	Macintosh	Windows MessageBox()
ALERT_OK	'ALRT' id=1	MB_OK
ALERT_OKCancel	'ALRT' id=2	MB_OKCANCEL

Alert Function

In the Macintosh we need to define two alert templates as resources, one for the OK-only alert and the other for the OK/Cancel alert. The general form for these alerts is (in REZ format):

```
resource 'ALRT' (1) {
    {40, 48, 170, 348},
    1,
    {  /* array: 4 elements */
        OK, visible, sound1,/* [1] */
        OK, visible, sound1,/* [2] */
        OK, visible, silent,/* [3] */
        OK, visible, silent /* [4] */
    }
};

resource 'DITL' (1) {
    {  /* array DITLarray: 2 elements */
        {100, 121, 120, 179},/* [1] */
        Button {
            enabled,
            "OK"
        },
        {7, 80, 88, 287},    /* [2] */
        StaticText {
            disabled,
            "^0:\n\n^1^2^3"
        }
    }
};
```

Figure 15.2 Example of a Macintosh alert.

Parameter zero, designated as "^0" defines the caption for the alert. Parameters 1, 2, and 3 are reserved for portions of the alert message.

The first thing we do is to initialize the text substitution parameters—these are four global Pascal strings that are maintained by the Macintosh Dialog Manager. The parameters are applied to the ^0 through ^3 identifiers in any static text string in the dialog item template ('DITL') defined for a dialog.

Depending on the type of alert, we call the corresponding alert function and pass it the proper alert mode (which maps to the appropriate 'DITL' resource in the resource file). The alert functions—for example, StopAlert()—are modal and wait for the user to respond. The response code is the dialog item that was selected, which should be IDOK or IDCANCEL. Figure 15.2 shows an example of a note alert with an OK button.

Next we need to define a function that lets us display an alert and return a response, independent of the platform. Our DlgAlert() function requires the type of alert that we want to display, the mode of the alert (configuration of the buttons in the alert), the caption, and the message. It will return one of our default response identifiers of IDOK or IDCancel.

```
//-------------------------------------------------------
SINT2 DlgAlert (SINT2 s2Type, SINT2 s2Mode, PTR zCaption,
    PTR zMessage)
//-------------------------------------------------------
// s2Type   - type of alert: note, warning, stop
// s2Mode   - OK or OK with Cancel
// zCaption - pointer to the caption string
// zMessage - pointer to the message string
// RETURNS  - IDOK if user clicked OK, IDCANCEL if Cancel
//-------------------------------------------------------
{

    SINT2 s2Result=IDOK;

  // format the text for the alert box fields
  ParamText (StrCtoP(zCaption), StrCtoP(zMessage),
    "\p", "\p");
```

```
ResetAlrtStage ();

// map the cross-platform alert types to Mac types
// the mode allows either resource 1 or 2 for each
// of the types to be accessed (OK or OK/Cancel forms)
switch (s2Type){
    case ALERT_Stop:
        s2Result=StopAlert (s2Mode+1, NULL);
    break;
    case ALERT_Note:
        s2Result=NoteAlert (s2Mode+1,NULL);
    break;
    case ALERT_Warn:
        s2Result=CautionAlert (s2Mode+1,NULL);
    break;
}

// reset everything
ParamText ("\p", "\p", "\p", "\p");
StrPtoC ((PTRP)zCaption);
StrPtoC ((PTRP)zMessage);

return (s2Result);
```

In Windows we first need to define an array to map our cross-platform alert types to Windows message box types. This allows the appropriate icon to be displayed when the message box is displayed.

We map the alert type to the Windows form then add in the alert mode (OK or OK/Cancel). Then we call the MessageBox() function and give it the caption, message, and appropriate message flags. We add in the MB_TASKMODAL option to make the behavior of the Windows message box the same as the Macintosh alerts. Task modal means that the user has to respond to the message box to resume work on the application that owns the alert, but you can switch out of the application into another if you want. The return values from the MessageBox() function are either IDOK or IDCANCEL. Figure 15.3 shows an example of a note alert with an OK button.

Figure 15.3 Example of a Windows alert.

```
// our cross-platform message box types don't map
// directly to Windows, therefore a map is needed
static _gu2WinMBType[]={
    MB_ICONHAND, MB_ICONINFORMATION, MB_ICONEXCLAMATION
};
// take the cross-platform type and map to Windows
UINT2 u2Temp=_gu2WinMBType[(s2TypeALERT_Warn
    || s2Type<ALERT_Stop) ?ALERT_Stop:s2Type];

// take the cross-platform mode and map to Windows
u2Temp+=((s2Mode<ALERT_OK||s2ModeALERT_OKCancel)
    ? ALERT_OK : s2Mode);
// put up the message box
return (MessageBox (NULL, zMessage, zCaption,
    MB_TASKMODAL|u2Temp));
```

And then we end the function.

```
}
```

Implementing Modal Dialogs

Defining an alert was easy. Now let's look at something a little more difficult, a cross-platform way to deal with modal dialog boxes. In this section we'll discuss three functions that let you:

- display a modal dialog
- destroy a modal dialog
- process the event messages for a modal dialog

Displaying a Modal Dialog

The first step in supporting modal dialogs is to display one. This process also involves waiting until the dialog box is destroyed and then retrieving the information returned from it. We define our DlgModal() function to required a handle to its parent window, the pointer to the dialog resource identifier (a number), and the pointer to the function that will be the handler for events generated for the dialog.

This handler function pointer is going to be different from the one that is given to normal window functions. In effect, we create a separate class of window expressly for the purpose of servicing the events for the dialog.

```
//-----------------------------------------------------
SINT2 DlgModal (HWND hwndParent, UINT2 u2Dlgid,
    HANDLER pfnHandler)
//-----------------------------------------------------
// hwndParent - handle to the window that owns the dialog
// u2Dlgid    - unsigned 2-byte resource id of the dialog
```

```
// pfnHandler - pointer to the dialog handler function
// RETURNS    - -1 if invocation error, else value
//               specified in the DlgEnd() parameter
//-------------------------------------------------------
{
```

In the Macintosh the process is similar to that of creating a window. The difference is that we load the dialog and its contents from resources using GetNewDialog() rather than creating it piece by piece. After we have the dialog box pointer, we load up the extra information that it needs and wait until our dialog gets an event. We use our cross-platform EventGet() and EventProcess() functions to get and field dialog events to our dialog's handler. After an event is processed, we go back and get another one. If the dialog was terminated, the b2DlgRun flag will be FALSE, and we exit.

We ignore the hwndParent in our example. For now a Macintosh modal dialog prevents any other window in our application from being switched to—in Windows terms, it is task modal.

```
DialogPtr pdlg;
PWNDX pwndx=(PWNDX)NewPtr (sizeof (WNDX));
SINT2 s2DlgResult;

// read and create the dialog
pdlg=GetNewDialog (u2Dlgid, NULLPTR, (WindowPtr)-1);

// set up the extra data needed for a dialog
pwndx->s2DlgResult=0;
pwndx->b2DlgRun=TRUE;
pwndx->fnHandler=pfnHandler;
SetWRefCon ((WindowPtr)pdlg, (UINT4)pwndx);

// now we need to wait until the dialog ends
// we set up a small event loop and wait until
// the window extra dialog flag, b2DlgRun,
// tells us to stop
{
    EVENT event;

    while (EventGet (&event, (HWND)pdlg)
       && pwndx->b2DlgRun
    ){
        EventProcess (&event);
        pwndx=(PWNDX)GetWRefCon ((WindowPtr)pdlg);
    }
}
// retrieve the result posted by DlgEnd()
s2DlgResult=pwndx->s2DlgResult;

// free up the extra data
```

```
pwndx=(PWNDX)GetWRefCon ((WindowPtr)pdlg);
DisposePtr (pwndx);
// close and free up the dialog
// (deletes the handle to dialog items too)
DisposDialog (pdlg);

return (s2DlgResult);
```

In Windows we need to prepare our dialog handler function to be called by the Windows message system by calling MakeProcInstance(). This gives us a pointer to a proper Windows callback function. If we get a valid address, we can proceed by loading the dialog box from the template defined in the application's resources and displaying the dialog box. In Windows the DialogBox() function waits until the dialog has been terminated and then returns us the result supplied by the DlgEnd() function—which is equivalent to the Windows EndDialog() function.

```
DLGPROC fnCallback;
SINT2 s2Result=-1;

if (pfnHandler){
    // prepare a proper Windows callback function
    fnCallback=(DLGPROC)MakeProcInstance (
        (FARPROC)pfnHandler, _ghWinInstance);

    if (fnCallback){

        // put up the dialog box and wait until it's
        // over, the DlgEnd() or EndDialog() function
        // provides the value for s2Result.
        s2Result=DialogBox (_ghWinInstance,
            MAKEINTRESOURCE (u2Dlgid),
            hwndParent, fnCallback);

        // when we're done, free up the callback
        FreeProcInstance ((FARPROC)fnCallback);
    }
}
return (s2Result);
```

Then we end the create modal dialog box function.

```
}
```

Ending a Modal Dialog

If you create a modal dialog, you need to destroy one. Because an argument is passed back to indicate the context in which the dialog was closed, we can't just use WinDestroy() to get rid of the window. We have to provide a way to destroy the dialog after we have set aside some information for the caller. This mechanism is provided by the DlgEnd() function and requires the handle to the dialog that is about to end and the result code that we want to relay to the caller.

Actually the DlgEnd() function isn't the one that destroys the dialog box. It merely indicates that the dialog box should be destroyed. The dialog box is destroyed at some point after the DlgEnd() procedure returns, probably after the next event message has been processed.

```
//------------------------------------------------------
VOID DlgEnd (HWND hdlg, SINT2 s2DlgResult)
//------------------------------------------------------
// hdlg        - handle to the modal dialog that is ending
// s2DlgResult - modal dialog result code
// RETURNS     - nothing
//------------------------------------------------------
{
```

In the Macintosh we get the extra window information that we included in the dialog when it was created and set its dialog result field to that provided by the s2DlgResult parameter to this function and also set the b2DlgRun flag to FALSE to tell the event loop that we want to end the dialog.

```
PWNDX pwndx=(PWNDX)GetWRefCon ((WindowPtr)hdlg);
pwndx->s2DlgResult=s2DlgResult;
pwndx->b2DlgRun=FALSE;
```

Windows already provides this functionality in its EndDialog() function.

```
EndDialog (hdlg, s2DlgResult);
```

That's all there is to ending a modal dialog.

```
}
```

Modal Dialog Handler

The handler function required for a modal dialog is defined the same as a standard window handler. For the most part it is identical in form to a window handler, except that when you want to end the dialog you call DlgEnd() instead of WinDestroy().

```
//------------------------------------------------------
HANDLERdecl DlgHandler (HWND hwnd, MSGDATA msg,
    DATA1 data1, DATA2 data2)
//------------------------------------------------------
// hwnd    - handle to the dialog
// msg     - the event message that we need to process
// data1   - first data that this message needs
// data2   - second data that this message needs
// RETURNS - value depends on event, but usually zero if
//           the handler processed the message
//------------------------------------------------------
```

```
{
    switch (msg){
        case EW_Command:
            switch ((UINT2)data1){
                case IDOK:
                case IDCANCEL:
                    DlgEnd (hwnd, (UINT2)data1);
                    return (1);
            }
        break;
    }
    return (0);
}
```

OTHER DIALOG CONSIDERATIONS

No doubt you noticed that we did not discuss a solution for modeless dialogs. This was done for two reasons:

- modeless dialogs are not used as often as modal dialogs
- a normal window will probably work instead

These indicate that a modeless dialog isn't as high a priority as alerts and modal dialogs. They have their place, and the ability to define a dialog template in resources that defines the contents of the dialog is much simpler, in the long run, than creating the contents on the fly.

You will probably want to implement some support for modeless dialogs if your application needs this feature or if you want to design a full-featured cross-platform solution. The XPLib software provides functions for modeless dialogs. You might want to look at the functional interface for some ideas on what these dialogs require.

A couple of things that you might want to consider for alerts are to provide a way to produce formatted messages and to support more variations on push buttons. And you might want to think about adding additional functionality for modal dialog boxes. For example:

- support for parent windows rather than task modal dialogs
- provide a default dialog handler to make standard behavior easier to implement (needs to implemented for the Macintosh but can use DeDflgProc() for Windows)
- support a special initialize dialog message, such as the Windows WM_INITDIALOG message, to let you set up the state of a dialog's contents after they have been added but before they have been shown
- provide a way to indicate when controls have the keyboard focus (as in Windows)

16

Controls

A control is the mechanism through which the user enters information or selects the options available in a dialog box or window. There are numerous types of controls, each serving a special purpose. Controls also indicate the level of polish that your application has attained. Many times companies spend a lot of time designing and organizing the controls that comprise their products' dialog boxes. A cross-platform application needs to support controls, but because there are so many types you need to learn as much about them as possible, decide how many and which you need to support, and then implement the functions to do the work. This is what we will do in this chapter.

DEFINING A REASONABLE CONTROL SUBSET

We need to define the set of control functions that we will support in your cross-platform solution. To do this we need to:

- define control terminology
- compare available controls
- compare control visuals
- compare control functionality
- extract a basic control subset

Control Terminology

radio button	Modeled after the buttons on a car radio, this type of control allows you to select one button from a collection of others.
check box	This indicates an option that can be on or off (checked or unchecked).
push button	A momentary button that when pushed causes some other action to occur (like putting up a dialog, or closing a dialog), this is not used to maintain state, although sometimes the text inside the button changes to indicate that the action associated with the button has also changed.
static text	This is informative text that is not selectable and not modifyable by the user.
edit text	Text that is entered and altered by the user, This is usually in a box, can contain multiple lines of text, and can sometimes be scrolled up or down, or left or right.
list box	A list of items contained in a box, this list can be larger than the physical size of the box, in which case there are scoll bars to let the user access all of the items. Usually one item can be selected from the list, although some boxes allow multiple items to be selected.
popup list	This is list of items that pops up when the user clicks in a certain rectangular area (hot spot) of a window or dialog. It lets the user choose from a list without the list being constantly displayed. The selection is usually visible in the hot spot of the control or near it.
button	A radio button, check box, or push button control is of this type.
text control	This is either a static or an edit text control.
list controls	These are list box, popup list, or a combination list box with edit text or popup list with edit text.
graphic	A line, box, or box with text is used to separate visually or to group items in a window or dialog box.
visible	This is an attribute of a control that lets it be visible or invisible to the user.
enable	This is an attribute of a control that lets it be accessed by the user. A disabled control cannot be clicked, checked, edited, or popped up.
state	An attribute of a control that indicates its on, off or enabled state, this usually applies to button controls that toggle from one visual form to another. For example, a radio button has an on and an off state, and a check box can be in its checked or unchecked state.
selection	An attribute of an edit text or list control, this indicates the subset of text entered in an edit text control or the line item or items selected in a list control.
tab stop	This is a control that can be tabbed to. When the user types the TAB key, the next control that is designated a tab stop will be active. In the Macintosh tab stops aren't defined by a dialog; rather they are inherently defined based on the type of control (either edit text or list boxes). In Windows a tab stop can be assigned to any item in a dialog box using the WS_TABSTOP modifier in the resource script.
group	This is a collection of controls in a dialog that accept keyboard input and is available in Windows only. You can move to items in the group using special keys without moving out of the group. It gives you a way to concentrate the user's focus on one portion of a dialog.

Comparing Controls Capabilities

Now let's look at Table 16.1 and see how our platforms stack up in terms of the types of controls they support. Windows supports a larger set of control types. We will no doubt want to concentrate our attention on the set of controls that Macintosh and Windows have in common. Let's also look at how some of the controls appear on the Macintosh and Windows platforms. Figure 16.1 shows a comparison of some of the visuals for the controls.

Comparing Control Functionality

Table 16.2 shows a comparison of various control types and the corresponding Macintosh and Windows functionality. As you can see, there are vast differences in the ways controls are created and accessed and several gaps in available functionality on the Macintosh side.

> *Notice that on Windows there isn't a facility for directly accessing the predefined control types as individual resources—you are limited to including descriptions of icon-type controls in the RC file, using the ICON statement. You can include other types if you use the user-defined resource mechanism or the RCDATA statement. References to controls are limited to control statements within a description of a dialog box, within the confines of the DIALOG statement.*

Choosing the Control Subset

There are several things to consider when we choose our subset of controls and control functionality. Controls are most often found in dialog boxes and sometimes used in normal

Table 16.1 Comparison of available control types across platforms.

Control	*Macintosh*	*Windows*
radio button	x	x
check box	x	x
push button	x	x
static text	x	x
edit text	x	x
list box	x	x
popup list	x	x
popup edit/list		x
icon	x	x
static line		x
static box		x
group box		x
tab stops	limited	x

Figure 16.1 Comparison of control types.

Table 16.2 Comparison of control functionality across platforms.

Function	*Macintosh*	*Windows*
create button	NewControl or GetNewControl	CreateWindow
show/hide button	ShowControl or HideControl	ShowWindow
button visible?	NA	IsWindowVisible
enable/disable button	HiliteControl	EnableWindow or SendMessage*
button enabled?	NA	IsWindowEnabled or SendMessage or IsDlgButtonChecked
turn button on/off	SetCtlValue	EnableWindow or SendMessage or CheckDlgButton
button on/off?	GetCtlValue	IsWindowEnabled or SendMessage or IsDlgButtonChecked
set button text	SetCTitle	SetDlgItemText
get button text	GetCTitle	GetDlgItemText
destroy button	DisposeControl	DestroyWindow
create scroll bar	NewControl or GetNewControl	CreateWindow
show/hide scroll bar	ShowControl or HideControl	ShowScrollBar
scroll bar visible?	NA	IsWindowVisible

(continued)

Table 16.2 (*Continued*)

Function	Macintosh	Windows
enable/disable scroll bar	HiliteControl	EnableWindow
scroll bar enabled?	NA	IsWindowEnabled
set scroll bar position	SetCtlValue	SetScrollPos
get scroll bar position	GetCtlValue	GetScrollPos
set scroll bar range	SetCtlMin and SetCtlMax	SetScrollRange
get scroll bar range	GetCtlMin and GetCtlMax	GetScrollRange
destroy scroll bar	DisposeControl	DestroyWindow
create static text	NA	CreateWindow or CreateWindowEx**
destroy static text	NA	DestroyWindow
create edit text	TENew	CreateWindow or CreateWindowEx
enable/disable edit text	TEActivate or TEDactivate	EnableWindow
edit text enabled?	NA	IsWindowEnabled
set contents	TESetText or SetIText	SendMessage: WM_SETTEXT or SetDlgItemText or SetDlgItemInt
get contents	TEGetText or GetIText	SendMessage: WM_GETTEXT, SendMessage: EM_GETLINE, or GetDlgItemText or GetDlgItemInt
set selection	TESetSelect or SelIText	SendMessage: EM_SETSEL
get selection	NA	SendMessage: EM_GETSEL
scroll contents	TEScroll	SendMessage: EM_LINESCROLL
destroy edit text	TEDispose	DestroyWindow
create icon	NA	CreateIcon
load icon	GetIcon	LoadIcon
display icon	PlotIcon	DrawIcon
destroy icon	NA	DestroyIcon
create list box	LNew	CreateWindow
add item	LAddRow LSetCell	SendMessage: LB_ADDSTRING
delete item	LDelRow	SendMessage: LB_DELETESTRING
find item	LSearch	SendMessage: LB_FINDSTRING
select item	LSetSelect	SendMessage: LB_SETSEL
get selected item	LGetSelect	SendMessage: LB_GETSEL
destroy list box	LDispose	DestroyWindow
create popup list	NewMenu or GetMenu	CreateWindow
insert list	InsertMenu	NA

(continued)

Table 16.2 (*Continued*)

Function	Macintosh	Windows
add item to list	AppendMenu orInsMenuItem	SendMessage: CB_ADDSTRING or SendMessage: CB_INSERTSTRING
delete item from list	DelMenuItem	SendMessage: CB_DELETESTRING
track selection	PopUpMenuSelect	SendMessage: CB_SHOWDROPDOWN
destroy popup list	Delete Menu	DestroyWindow
create popup list with edit text	NA	CreateWindow
other popup list functions (see above)	NA	*similar to popup list* (see above)
destroy popup list with edit text	NA	DestroyWindow
create graphic	NA	CreateWindow
destroy graphic	NA	DestroyWindow

*   In Windows, whenever SendMessage() is used, you can also use SendDlgItemMessage() if the control is a part of a dialog box.

**   Win32 only

windows. For our purposes we will provide a cross-platform solution for controls that limits their use to dialogs. This means that all controls are arranged and specified in a dialog template where the dialog and its contents can be loaded during the dialog creation process.

This limits some aspects of our control functionality because we don't have to support functions that dynamically create controls and place them in a window or dialog box. It also separates the process of creating and maintaining the dialog box and its contents from the process of supporting the behavior of the dialog. This means you can use the platform-specific tools that are best suited for visually contructing a dialog. It even lets you offload the task of creating the dialogs to marketing persons and graphics designers, who probably have a better idea of the user interface design.

Choosing a reasonable subset of controls to support in our cross-platform API is also a difficult task. Which are the controls that are used more often? Which are essential? Which may be easier to support? The answers to these questions depend on your needs. If you are developing a complete cross-platform solution, you'll want to support as many controls as possible. If you only need to provide a cross-platform solution to develop your application, then you can concentrate on only those controls that you'll need. I have outlined these controls:

- radio buttons
- check boxes
- push buttons
- static text
- edit text

I feel that these controls are the most important to support. Almost every application will want or use these controls, so we will concentrate on a solution for them.

IMPLEMENTING BUTTON CONTROL FUNCTIONS

We define the prefix "Ctl" for all functions that work with controls. This allows us room to support other types of controls and not clutter the API with too many function prefixes. We also assume that the controls are in dialog boxes and have numeric identifiers.

In this section we will:

- define some cross-platform button attribute constants
- implement a function to show or hide a button
- implement a function to get and set a button's text
- implement a function to set the state of a button

Button Data Values

Button controls can maintain three visual states: they can be on, off, or disabled. These attributes for buttons are accessed using these cross-platform predefined attribute constants:

```
enum {CTL_Off, CTL_On, CTL_Gray};
```

Showing or Hiding a Button

Let's start with a function that will show or hide a button control. We call it CtlVisSet(), and it requires the handle to the dialog that contains the control, the id of the control, and a boolean that indicates whether the control is to be shown or hidden.

```
//------------------------------------------------------
ERR CtlVisSet (HWND hwnd, UINT2 u2id, BOOL2 b2Vis)
//------------------------------------------------------
// hwnd      - handle to the dialog that owns the control
// u2id      - identifier of the control
// b2Vis     - TRUE = show the control, FALSE = hide it
// RETURNS   - ERR_No if all went well, ERR_Yes otherwise
//------------------------------------------------------
{
```

In the Macintosh we first need to get some information about the control with the u2id identifier in the dialog specified by hwnd by using the GetDItem() function. The hItem parameter indicates whether there is a control with that id and the s2Type parameter tells us what type of control it is. If the control is a button, then depending on the value of b2Vis, we show or hide the control.

```
ControlHandle hItem;
SINT2 s2Type;
```

```
      Rect rectItem;

      // get the dialog item information
      GetDItem (hwnd, u2id, &s2Type, &hItem, &rectItem);

      // if the item is invalid or the type is not a button
      if (!hItem
          || !(s2Type==ctrlItem+btnCtrl
          || s2Type==ctrlItem+chkCtrl
          || s2Type==ctrlItem+radCtrl)
      ){
          return (ERR_Yes);
      }

      // depending on the visibility flag show/hide control
      if (b2Vis) ShowControl (hItem);
      else HideControl (hItem);
```

In Windows we use the ShowWindow() function and give it the window handle of the control itself by using the GetDlgItem() function and map our b2Vis boolean to **SW_SHOW** if it is TRUE and to **SW_HIDE** if it is FALSE.

```
      ShowWindow (GetDlgItem (hwnd, u2id),
          b2Vis ? SW_SHOW : SW_HIDE);
```

If we get here, all has gone well and we exit.

```
      return (ERR_No);
}
```

Getting a Button's Text

Most button controls have some text that indicates the information that they represent. Radio buttons and check boxes usually have the text to one side and push buttons have the text inside the button. Our CtlTextGet() function requires a handle to the dialog, the id of the control, and a pointer to a buffer to receive the text string from the button.

This function also works for text controls. For static and edit text controls the entire static text string is retrieved. Edit text controls also maintain a selected range of text, which this function does not retrieve.

```
//-------------------------------------------------------
VOID CtlTextGet (HWND hwnd, UINT2 u2id, PTR zText)
//-------------------------------------------------------
// hwnd     - handle to the window that owns the control
// u2id     - identifier of the control
// zText    - buffer to receive the control's text
// RETURNS  - nothing
//-------------------------------------------------------
{
```

In the Macintosh we get information about the control using GetDItem(). If the control is a text control (static or edit), we use GetIText() to set its text. If the control is a button control, we use GetCTitle() to retrieve the text of the button. We convert the Pascal string that these strings return to us into a C string and then we're done.

```
ControlHandle hItem;
SINT2 s2Type;
Rect rectItem;

// get information about the control
GetDItem (hwnd, u2id, &s2Type, &hItem, &rectItem);

// if the control is static or edit text
if (s2Type==statText || s2Type==editText){
   GetIText (hItem, (PTRP)zText);

// if the control is a button...
}else GetCTitle (hItem, (PTRP)zText);

StrPtoC ((PTRP)zText);
```

In Windows getting the text of a dialog control is easy. We just call GetDlgItemText() and pass it the handle to the dialog and the id of the control. It returns to us the text associated with the control. This function works with button and text controls.

```
GetDlgItemText (hwnd, u2id, zText, 255);
```

And that's it.

```
}
```

Setting a Button's Text

Now let's do the opposite; let's set a button's text. We define CtlTextSet() to require a handle to the dialog, the resource id of the control, and a pointer to a null-terminated string that will be the new text for the control.

```
//-------------------------------------------------------
VOID CtlTextSet (HWND hwnd, UINT2 u2id, PTR zText)
//-------------------------------------------------------
// hwnd    - handle to the window that owns the control
// u2id    - identifier of the control
// zText   - text to assign to the control
// RETURNS - nothing
//-------------------------------------------------------
{
```

In the Macintosh the process is almost identical to getting the text. We get information about the control and its type and handle; if it's a text control, we use SetIText(), and if its a button control, we use SetCTitle(). Because we did an inline conversion of the text string from C to Pascal, before we leave we need to convert the string back to the C format.

Regardless of the type of control, this function replaces the entire string that makes up the text portion of the control. For edit text controls this is different from setting the selection range of the contents of the control or replacing the selected text.

```
ControlHandle hItem;
SINT2 s2Type;
Rect rectItem;

// get information about the control
GetDItem (hwnd, u2id, &s2Type, &hItem, &rectItem);

// if the control is static text or edit text...
if (s2Type==statText || s2Type==editText){
    SetIText (hItem, StrCtoP (zText));

// if the control is a button
}else SetCTitle (hItem, StrCtoP (zText));

// convert the string back to a C type
StrPtoC ((PTRP)zText);
```

In Windows we use the SetDlgItemText() function.

```
SetDlgItemText (hwnd, u2id, zText);
```

After the control's text has been set the function is done.

```
}
```

Setting the State of a Button

When we set a button's state, we turn it on or off or we disable it. Enabling a button is part of turning it on and off. This is different from the user turning a button on or off. When a button is disabled, the user can't turn it on or off; it maintains its previous on- or off-state. But our function CtlStateSet() can set the button's state. It requires a handle to the dialog, the id of the control, and one of our three constants that represent a button's state.

```
//------------------------------------------------------
ERR CtlStateSet (HWND hwnd, UINT2 u2id, SINT2 s2State)
//------------------------------------------------------
// hwnd      - handle to the window that owns the control
// u2id      - identifier of the control
// s2State   - control state: on, off, or disabled
// RETURNS   - ERR_No if all went well, ERR_Yes otherwise
//------------------------------------------------------
{
```

In the Macintosh we get information about the control using GetDItem(), and if the control type is not a button, we return with an error code. Then we mask off the three least-significant bits to get access to only the bits that should matter (at this time). If the state that we want to set is on or off, we make sure the control is enabled by calling HiliteControl(); then we set the control's state using SetCtlValue(). If the caller wants to disable the control, we use HiliteControl() to disable it, but we don't alter the on- or off-state.

```
ControlHandle hItem;
SINT2 s2Type;
Rect rectItem;

// get information about the control
GetDItem (hwnd, u2id, &s2Type, &hItem, &rectItem);

// if the control isn't a button...
if (!(s2Type==ctrlItem+btnCtrl
    || s2Type==ctrlItem+chkCtrl
    || s2Type==ctrlItem+radCtrl)
){
    return (ERR_Yes);
}

// the control is a button,...
s2State&=0x0003;

// if the state we want is on or off
if (s2State==CTL_Off || s2State==CTL_On){
    HiliteControl (hItem, 0);
    SetCtlValue (hItem, s2State);

// if we are going to disable it
}else if (s2State==CTL_Gray){
    HiliteControl (hItem, 255);
}
// ...an invalid control state
else return (ERR_Yes);
```

The process of setting the state of a button in Windows is a little more complicated. We need to do one thing if the button is a radio button or a check box and another thing if the button is a push button.

We start by getting the class name of the window that defines the control using GetClass-Name(). If the class is not a button, we exit with an error. Next we look at the button class window's style field using GetWindowLong() and see what style of button it is. If the style of button is a push button, we need to use EnableWindow(); but we only enable the push button if the state is CTL_On. Because a push button doesn't maintain state, either it's on (ready to be pushed) or it's disabled (can't be pushed).

If the style of button is a radio button or check box, we use SendDlgItemMessage to turn the button on (check it), turn it off (uncheck it), or disable it (make it gray), depending on the value of the s2State variable. (Our cross-platform button state constants are equivalent to Windows.)

```
UINT1 zClass[16];

// get the class name of the dialog control item
GetClassName (GetDlgItem (hwnd, u2id), zClass, 15);
// if it's a button control, then look at the style
if (!lstrcmpi (zClass, "Button")){
    switch (GetWindowLong (GetDlgItem (hwnd,u2id),
        GWL_STYLE) & 0x0000000f
    ){
        case BS_DEFPUSHBUTTON:
        case BS_PUSHBUTTON:
        case BS_OWNERDRAW:
        case BS_GROUPBOX:
        case BS_USERBUTTON:
            // momentary buttons...
            EnableWindow (GetDlgItem (hwnd, u2id),
                (s2State==CTL_On) ? TRUE : FALSE);
        break;

        case BS_AUTOCHECKBOX:
        case BS_AUTORADIOBUTTON:
        case BS_AUTO3STATE:
        case BS_CHECKBOX:
        case BS_RADIOBUTTON:
        case BS_3STATE:
            // on and off buttons...
            SendDlgItemMessage (hwnd, u2id, BM_SETCHECK,
                (UINT)s2State, 0L);
        break;

    }

// wrong type of control
}else return (ERR_Yes);
```

We could also use SendMessage() instead of SendDlgItemMessage(). The call:

```
SendDlgItemMessage (hwnd, u2id, BM_SETCHECK,
    (UINT)s2State, 0L);
```

is the same as this one:

```
SendMessage (GetDlgItem (hwnd, u2id), BM_SETCHECK,
    (UINT)s2State, 0L);
```

If we get here, all has gone well, and we return success.

```
    return (ERR_No);
}
```

IMPLEMENTING EDIT TEXT CONTROL FUNCTIONS

As with button controls, edit text control functions will also begin with the "Ctl" prefix, and we assume that an edit text control is in a dialog box and has a numeric identifier. In this section we present some examples on implementing edit text controls. This includes:

- defining cross-platform data values for edit text controls
- setting the contents of an edit control
- getting the contents of an edit control
- selecting a portion of the contents
- deleting the selected text in an edit control

Edit Text Data Values

The only cross-platform data value that we need for edit text controls is the designation for the "end of text" in the control.

Value	*Macintosh*	*Windows*
ENDOFTEXT	32767	(–1)

Even though we specify ENDOFTEXT as our designation for the last character in the control, we should mention what the range of the contents of an edit text control is.

Value	*Macintosh*	*Windows 3.1*	*Win32*
minimum	0	0	0
maximum	32767	0xFFFF	not specified but defaults to 32767[*]
end of text	32767	(–1)	(–1)

[*] If you send the control an EM-LIMITTEXT message, you can set an edit text control maximum size to 0x7FFFFFFF for single-line controls and 0xFFFFFFFF for multiline controls.

In the Macintosh an edit text control can only contain 32,767 characters. In Windows 3.1 there is some confusion about the values. The printed SDK documentation indicates that the range is from 0 to 32767, but the online help indicates 0 to 65535. We have found no problem with the information in the online help and use its findings as the basis for our decision. Currently in Win32 it is intrinsically set to 32K but can be made much larger. So be careful when you use edit controls. The only common denominator for the maximum size is 32K; you might want to use that as your rule of thumb when using them in your applications.

> *In Windows 3.1 the storage for any and all edit controls comes from the local heap by default, but you can direct it to come from the application's data segment. The size of the local heap, the stack, static data, and the task header is limited to 64K bytes maximum, so if you want to have access to a 32K byte edit control, you will need to pay attention to the sizes of the other players. If you use the DS_LOCALEDIT flag when you create the control or in the dialog template in the resouce file, you can use your application's data segment. But this can be complicated, too. A data segment can only be 64K bytes. If you compile your program in the small or medium memory model, you will only have one data segment. This data segment is shared by the local heap, task header, the stack, and any static data your program might use—the same restriction when you don't use the DS_LOCALEDIT option. These restrictions do not apply to Win32.*

Setting the Contents of an Edit Control

This functionality has already been implemented in the CtlStateSet() function, which was previously discussed in the Setting a Button's Text section.

Getting the Contents of an Edit Control

This functionality has already been implemented in the CtlStateGet() function, which was previously discussed in the Getting a Button's Text section.

Selecting a Portion of the Contents

Now something we haven't done before is to select a portion of an edit text control's contents. If the selection range encloses at least one character, the selection is depicted as a highlited section of the text in the control; otherwise it is a blinking caret. Our CtlTextSelectSet() function requires a handle to the dialog, the id of the control, and the starting and ending positions of the text to mark as the selection. The start point is relative to zero and the end point can be up to the ENDOFTEXT value. Selecting a range from zero to ENDOFTEXT will select the entire contents of the control.

```
//---------------------------------------------------
ERR CtlTextSelectSet (HWND hwnd, UINT2 u2id,
    UINT2 u2Start, UINT2 u2End)
//---------------------------------------------------
// hwnd    - handle to the window that owns the text box
// u2id    - identifier of the control
// u2Start - start position of the selected text
```

```
// u2End   - end position of the selected text
// RETURNS - ERR_No if everything is OK, else ERR_Yes
//------------------------------------------------------
{
```

In the Macintosh, we get information about the control using GetDItem(). We check the type to make sure that the control is an edit text control. If the control is not an edit text control, we return an error. Then we need to make sure the control is the active one by calling GetIText() and SetIText() and select the range of text using SelIText().

```
ControlHandle hItem;
UINT2 u2Textid;
SINT2 s2Type;
Rect rectItem;
Str255 zpText;

// get information about the control
GetDItem (hwnd, u2id, &s2Type, &hItem, &rectItem);

// if the control isn't an edit box, exit
if (s2Type!=editText) return (ERR_Yes);

// make the requested edit box active
GetIText (hItem, zpText);
SetIText (hItem, zpText);

// select the desired portion of text
SelIText (hwnd, u2id, u2Start, u2End);
```

In Windows 3.1 we just use the SendDlgItemMessage() function and send the control the EM_SETSEL message. Because the selection range needs to be packed into a 4-byte integer, we use MAKELONG() to do this.

```
SendDlgItemMessage (hwnd, u2id, EM_SETSEL, 0,
    MAKELONG (u2Start, u2End));
```

In Win32 we also use the SendDlgItemMessage() function and the EM_SETSEL message, but the start point and end point are separate parameters to the function.

```
// convert to SINT4 to sign-extend position
SendDlgItemMessage (hwnd, u2id, EM_SETSEL,
    (SINT4)u2Start, (SINT4)u2End);
```

The work is done, and all is well.

```
    return (ERR_No);
}
```

Deleting the Selection

Finally we'll show how to delete a the selected contents of an edit control using the CtlTextDelete() function. It requires the handle to the dialog and the id of the edit control.

```
//-------------------------------------------------------
VOID CtlTextDelete (HWND hwnd, UINT2 u2id)
//-------------------------------------------------------
// hwnd    - handle to the window that owns the text box
// u2id    - identifier of the control
// RETURNS - nothing
//-------------------------------------------------------
{
```

In the Macintosh we just use the DlgDelete() function. It will delete the selection range in the currently active edit text control.

```
    DlgDelete (hwnd);
```

As with the other edit text control processes in Windows, we use the SendDlgItemMessage(), this time passing it the WM_CLEAR message, telling the control that we want to clear the selected range of text.

```
    SendDlgItemMessage (hwnd, u2id, WM_CLEAR, 0, 0L);
```

An then we end the function definition.

```
}
```

OTHER CONTROL CONSIDERATIONS

Even though we presented some of the basic control functionality, there are many other things that you could do. The XPLib software provides support for these functions plus the ability to do cut, copy, and paste operations on edit text controls. You might also want to consider:

- supporting cut, copy, and paste to and from the clipboard
- providing functionality to show or hide, enable or disable all types of controls
- supporting other control types: static text, list boxes, popups, scroll bars, and icons
- implementing dynamic (run-time) control creation
- supporting controls in all window types, not just dialogs

Refer to the Broaden User Interface Options section in Chapter 18 for more information about controls and other user interface considerations.

17

Cursors

The ability to manipulate the cursor doesn't exactly represent a group of essential functionalities. But it does add a lot of polish to an application when you change the cursor for different types of tasks. It also gives the user feedback about what is happening in the program—indicating what type of task is being performed or that the user needs to wait for something to happen. For example, when you type text you have one type of cursor and when you draw graphics you have another. In this chapter we look at how cursors differ on our three target platforms and how they are alike. Then we present some functions to provide a cross-platform way to use cursors.

COMPARING PLATFORM CURSORS

We begin our discussion on cursors by comparing how cursors look on our selected platforms and how cursors are functionally supported by the APIs.

Comparing Cursor Appearances

Figure 17.1 shows some of the common cursors on the Macintosh, Windows 3.1, and Win32. You'll notice that they are generally equivalent. The Macintosh also directly supports animated cursors. An animated cursor is represented by a sequence of component cursors that allow the cursor to appear to move. An example of an animated cursor is shown in Figure 17.2. A cross-platform application may need special cursors for its tasks, and you can define them to be

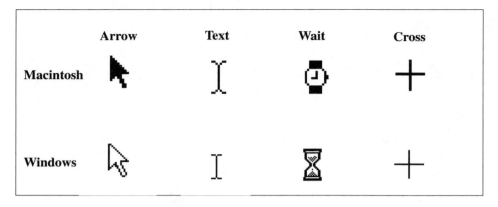

Figure 17.1 Comparison of cursors.

the same across platforms. This allows your application to maintain a certain look and feel independent of the platform it is running on.

Comparing Cursor Functionality

There aren't a lot of cursor functions. Table 17.1 shows how the Macintosh and Windows cursor functions compare. You'll find that for the common cursor functionality our platforms are equally supported.

IMPLEMENTING A CURSOR SOLUTION

To provide cross-platform access to cursors we need to:

- define a cross-platform cursor data type
- provide a way to access some common cursors
- define any necessary global variables
- implement the cursor functions

As a developer, you need to remember that cursors are usually shared resources. A cursor should be set up whenever your application is activated. This ensures that your application will always be working with the proper cursor and not one from another program.

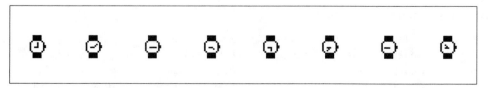

Figure 17.2 An animated cursor.

Table 17.1 Comparison of cursor functions across platforms.

Function	Macintosh	Windows
initialize	InitCursor	NA
get cursor	NA	SetCursor, GetCursor*
set cursor	SetCursor	SetCursor
load cursor from resources	GetCursor	LoadCursor
show cursor	ShowCursor, HideCurosr	ShowCursor
get cursor position	GetMouse	GetCursorPos
set cursor position	NA	SetCursorPos
hide cursor until movement	ObscureCursor	NA
restrict cursor to rectangle	NA	ClipCursor
create a cursor	NA	CreateCursor
destroy a cursor	NA	DestroyCursor

* Win32 only

A Common Cursor Data Type

The only data type that we need to support cursors is a cross-platform definition of a cursor handle, which is defined as:

Type	Macintosh	Windows 3.1	Win32
HCURSOR	Cursor ** (4 bytes)	HCURSOR (2 bytes)	HCURSOR (4 bytes)

Cross-Platform Cursor Identifiers

When you request a particular cursor resource, you usually provide a resource id that refers to a cursor in the resource portion of your program. There are a few standard cursors that you don't really need to define because they are available on the Macintosh and Windows. So we define a set of cross-platform identifiers that refer to these resource ids:

Cursor	Macintosh	Windows
arrow or pointer	0	IDC_ARROW
text insertion	iBeamCursor	IDC_IBEAM
wait	watchCursor	IDC_WAIT
cross	crossCursor	IDC_CROSS

Notice that in the Macintosh we define the arrow cursor with a value of zero. This is not a valid resource id in the Macintosh. We use the zero value as a flag so that our function will be able to identify a request to load this cursor, which is defined in memory and is not a resource.

Global Cursor Variables

In the Macintosh we don't have a handle to the arrow cursor (the default), only the reference to the structure that defines it. So we create a holding variable, with type Cursor*, that is the address of the arrow cursor structure (a pointer to it), and another variable, of type HCURSOR or Cursor**, that contains the address of the pointer to the cursor structure—in effect a handle to the arrow cursor. This allows us to reference all cursors using a handle.

```
Cursor *_gpMacArrowCursor=&arrow;
HCURSOR _ghMacArrowCursor=&_gpMacArrowCursor;
```

Also, in the Macintosh we need to keep track of the current cursor by defining a variable to maintain its handle. This allows us to retrieve the information whenever we need it and give us the same functionality as Windows.

```
//handle to the currently selected cursor
HCURSOR _ghMacCursor;
```

Windows doesn't require any global variables.

Implementing the Cursor Functions

Now that the formalities are out of the way, let's look at how we are going to implement our cross-platform cursor functions. In this section, we will look at examples of the most essential cursor functions, such as:

- loading a cursor from resources
- installing or setting a new cursor
- retrieving the current cursor
- showing or hiding the cursor

Loading a Cursor from Resources

This is the first thing that you need to do. Before you can install a new cursor, you have to have a handle to it. Our CursorLoad() function takes a resource id of a cursor and returns a handle to the cursor. The resource id can represent any valid cursor resource but also refers to the four predefined cross-platform cursor ids (arrow, cross, text insertion, and wait). If you define your own cursors, you should define them to have the same resource id (number) on all platforms; if you don't, you need to provide a constant that maps to the proper id on the corresponding platform.

```
//---------------------------------------------------------
HCURSOR CursorLoad (UINT2 u2id)
//---------------------------------------------------------
// u2id    - resource id of the cursor we want to load
// RETURNS - handle to a cursor
//---------------------------------------------------------
{
```

In the Macintosh we first check if the cursor we want to select is the arrow cursor—this cursor is not identified by a resource constant in the Macintosh development tools, only by a reference to a cursor structure. If the caller wants the arrow cursor, we return our faux handle to the arrow cursor. If any other cursor is desired, we use GetCursor() to load the cursor from resources.

```
if (u2id!=CURS_Arrow) return (GetCursor (u2id));
else return (_ghMacArrowCursor);
```

In Windows all of our cross-platform cursor identifiers represent resource ids to system resources, so we just call LoadCursor() and supply it with the cursor id converted to an LPSTR form by MAKEINTRESOURCE().

```
return (LoadCursor (NULL, MAKEINTRESOURCE (u2id)));
```

Then we end the function.

```
}
```

Setting the Cursor

The process of setting the cursor installs a new cursor and returns the previous one. Our CursorSet() function requires a handle to the cursor that we want to set and returns a handle to the previous cursor.

```
//---------------------------------------------------------
HCURSOR CursorSet (HCURSOR hcursor)
//---------------------------------------------------------
// hcursor - handle to the cursor we want to set
// RETURNS - handle of the previous cursor
//---------------------------------------------------------
{
```

In the Macintosh we use the global _ghMacCursor to save the handle to the current cursor. After we call SetCursor(), _ghMacCursor references the previous cursor. This is copied over to our return variable and we update _ghMacCursor to contain the handle to the current cursor.

```
HCURSOR hcursPrev=_ghMacCursor;

// dereference the cursor to get a ptr to the struct
SetCursor (*hcursor);
_ghMacCursor=hcursor;
return (hcursPrev);
```

In Windows SetCursor() sets the cursor and returns the previous cursor, so we don't have to do anything.

```
return (SetCursor (hcursor));
```

And then we're finished installing a new cursor.

```
}
```

Getting the Cursor

Sometimes we want to get the handle to the current cursor, so we define CursorGet() to do this. It doesn't have any parameters; it just returns a cursor handle.

```
//----------------------------------------------------
HCURSOR CursorGet (VOID)
//----------------------------------------------------
// no parameters
// RETURNS - handle to the current cursor
//----------------------------------------------------
{
```

In the Macintosh there isn't a get cursor function. But when we installed the current cursor, we saved a handle to it in the global variable _ghMacCursor. So all we need to do is return the contents of this variable.

```
return (_ghMacCursor);
```

Windows also doesn't have a function to retrieve the current cursor. What we need to do is call SetCursor() once to get the handle to the cursor and again to reinstall that cursor.

```
HCURSOR hcursCur=SetCursor (NULL);

SetCursor (hcursCur);
return (hcursCur);
```

That's all there is to do.

```
}
```

Showing and Hiding the Cursor

The last thing we need to illustrate, is how to show or hide the cursor. Our CursorShow() function requires a boolean that if true means we want to show the cursor and if false means we want to hide it.

```
//----------------------------------------------------
VOID CursorShow (BOOL2 b2Show)
//----------------------------------------------------
// b2Show  - TRUE means show the cursor, FALSE means
```

```
//              hide it
// RETURNS - nothing
//------------------------------------------------------
{
```

In the Macintosh we use ShowCursor() if b2Show is TRUE and HideCursor() if b2Show is FALSE.

```
if (b2Show) ShowCursor ();
else HideCursor ();
```

In Windows the ShowCursor() function requires the same form of argument that our cross-platform CursorShow() function did, so we just pass on its parameter.

```
ShowCursor (b2Show);
```

That ends the show cursor function.

```
}
```

OTHER CURSOR CONSIDERATIONS

For starters you might want to provide more thorough functional support, such as a function to initialize the cursor and functions to get and set the cursor position.

Some ways to enhance cursor support would involve a bit more coding and perhaps tie in to other functional areas. For example, you might want to provide ways to:

- link a cursor to a window
- provide programmable cursor tracking
- support animated cursors
- provide intelligent cursor mapping to support monochrome and color cursors
- allow for the dynamic creation of cursors (without resources)

Part 4

Advanced Topics

18

The Next Step

You have seen in Parts 2 and 3 of this book that developing a workable cross-platform solution requires a certain amount of critical code-mass to provide even basic cross-platform support. If your product or products have special needs, or you want to provide a more robust cross-platform solution to encompass future projects, you will need to invest considerable time and resources to be successful. This is the point where you will need to evaluate your needs and compare them with what you can reasonably provide, what an existing cross-platform solution provides, and what your long-term needs might be. If your needs are moderate, you might settle for a basic solution. If your needs are broad, you might want to purchase a solution. If your needs are specific, you will need to provide your own solution.

A next step in a cross-platform solution is to enhance the feature set that we have so far outlined in this book. This would provide:

- more complete event support
- broadened user interface options
- more standard dialogs
- extended graphics capabilities
- extended text capabilities
- some advanced printing considerations

You may also need to consider a couple of new functional areas that we have not talked about, for example:

- multiple document control
- advanced file management
- clipboard support
- initialization information
- support for compound documents

IMPROVING EVENT SUPPORT

By increasing the number and improving the quality of events supported by a cross-platform solution, you will extend the usefulness of your cross-platform API. Some particular things that you could do are:

- support a larger subset of events
- increase the granularity of generated events (Macintosh)
- provide better ways to decode event information
- support more notification codes (from controls)
- define a cross-platform interprocess event mechanism

Provide a Larger Subset of Events

The list of cross-platform events that we looked at in Chapter 7 represents a small subset of events that are possible. Because our event model is based on Windows, there are many event messages that we haven't considered. Windows messages fall into several categories:

WM_NCxxx	non-client area (window frame) messages
WM_MDIxxx	multiple document interface messages
WM_COMMAND	command messages that can contain submessages (notification codes)
WM_SYSCOMMAND	system commands
WM_DDE_xxx	dynamic data exchange messages
WM_xxx	other window messages

The number of native Macintosh events is small compared to Windows. To provide a better Windows-like solution, you will need to expand the Macintosh-to-Windows event conversion mechanism.

Provide Finer Event Granularity

To provide support for a Windows-like event model, we need to increase the number of events that we support. But to do this, we also need to look at how these messages are used and the context in which they appear. For various common Windows processes you will need to look at the flow of messages and see how important an event message actually is. If it is important for your project, then you will need to support it.

This also overlaps the support for certain window functionality. Remember how destroying a window involved our Macintosh function to send additional events to emulate more accurately the behavior in Windows. You will need to do this on a larger scale and see how normal Windows functions cause messages to be generated in addition to the events generated by user actions.

Support More Notification Events

Notification events or codes are submessages sent by a control to the window handler. In Windows they are encoded in the WM_COMMAND message. In the implementation of the Macintosh cross-platform solution that we have outlined, they are synthesized. The number of notification codes that you need to support depends on the number of controls that you want to provide and the degree to which you need to support them. As you add user interface improvements and increase the number of available controls, it will be obvious which codes need to be supported and which do not.

More Powerful Event Decoding

As more notification codes are sent, there will need to be a way to decode the information that is encoded in the data1 and data2 parameters of the window handler function. This means you will need to write additional EDecode-type functions that extract the information in a platform-independent way. Another type of event decoding might involve a less linear way to process event messages in a window handler. It might make sense to provide an indexed table method of accessing a function that processes a certain event message. Each type of event message or notification code might comprise a slot in the table. If you choose to support the event, you would supply a pointer to a function; otherwise some default processing would occur.

Support Interprocess Events

Interprocess events allow one application to send events to another and are a way to interchange data. These events are represented and supported for the Macintosh by:

- Apple Events—High Level Events that abide by the Apple Event Interprocess Messaging Protocol (AEIMP)
- the Apple Event Manager
- Program-to-Program Toolbox

For Windows 3.1 or Win32 these events are represented and supported by:

- the PostAppMessage() function
- the Dynamic Data Exchange (DDE) messages (WM_DDE_xxx) and functions DdeXXX()
- the Object Linking and Embedding (OLE) functions, OleXXX()

MULTIPLE DOCUMENT CONTROL

Some applications, such as word processors and spreadsheets, allow you to open up multiple documents. This is convenient when you are working on many different documents and need to have all of them accessible to you or if your task involves maintaining information from many sources. Windows provides the Multiple Document Interface, or MDI, that lets an application maintain a desktop of sorts on which multiple documents (windows) can be conveniently iconized. Although the implementation is really inadequate for many application needs, you might want to provide a similar mechanism on the Macintosh.

A better solution is to construct a multiple document mechanism that is written entirely using cross-platform code. This assumes that a more powerful, general event mechanism is in place. It might take you a bit longer to construct it, but in the long run it will probably be better than reverse-engineering MDI and having to provide workarounds for its idiosyncrasies.

SUPPORTING THE CLIPBOARD

The clipboard is a repository for data that allows an application to perform cut, copy, and paste operations and that allows one application to transfer data to another application. A cross-platform solution should support at least basic clipboard features. Some of the common types of data that are transferred into and out of the clipboard are:

- simple text (a series of characters)
- formatted text
- graphics objects
- bitmap images

More advanced clipboard support will consider:

- custom data types
- embedded objects from other applications
- the ability to convert one type of data to another
- the ability to cut, copy, and paste across platforms

Support Simple Text

The simplest form of clipboard support that your application should provide is simple text—normal, unformatted character strings. Both the Macintosh and Windows (Windows 3.1 and Win32) provide a standard mechanism for doing this. The Macintosh supports the 'TEXT' clipboard data type, and Windows supports the CF_TEXT clipboard format. Windows also supports the CF_OEMTEXT, which allows transfer of text information between a Windows window and a DOS-type window. Win32 also supports the CF_UNICODETEXT format to work with double-byte character strings. On the Macintosh the clipboard format actually represents a resource format. This allows you to use the resource management facilities of the Macintosh to cut and paste to and from disk.

Support Formatted Text

Next you might want to consider using the clipboard to tranfer formatted text. The standard support for this type of data is through the 'PICT' clipboard data type on the Macintosh and the

CF_METAFILEPICT clipboard format on Windows. Win32 also supports the CF_ENHMETAFILE format to support the new features of GDI provided by Win32. This type of formatted text support allows you to include sequences of QuickDraw or GDI function calls that generate formatted text into the clipboard. Any other type of formatted text would need to be provided using a custom clipboard format. The standard support for formatted text does not provide a way to transfer information across platforms.

Support Graphics Objects

The standard method of incorporating graphics objects into the clipboard also uses the 'PICT' clipboard format in Macintosh, the CF_METAFILEPICT clipboard format for Windows, and the CF_ENHMETAFILE for Win32. Because the formats for Macintosh PICTs and Windows Metafiles (WMFs) are not the same, this method cannot be used to transfer information across platforms.

Support Images

Another standard form of information is a bitmap image. Again the Macintosh supports this using the 'PICT' clipboard format; Windows provides the CF_BITMAP format for device-dependent bitmaps, the CF_DIB format for device-independent bitmaps, and the CF_TIFF format to support the TIFF (Tag Image File Format) representation of images. The only format with the potential to transfer information across platforms is TIFF. Because this clipboard format is only supported on Windows, a suitable mechanism needs to be constructed for the Macintosh.

Comparison of Basic Clipboard Functionality

A basic implementation of cross-platform clipboard functionality requires supporting only a few functions. A comparison of clipboard functions is shown in Table 18.1. A breakdown of some of the standard ways to support text, graphics, and image information in the clipboard is listed in Table 18.2.

This type of basic implementation, however, will not provide a means of transferring information across platforms. You will probably need to add another functional layer between the application and these low-level clipboard functions to support a cross-platform clipboard format.

Table 18.1 Comparing clipboard functions across platforms.

Function	*Macintosh*	*Windows*
open clipboard	NA	OpenClipboard
close clipboard	NA	CloseClipboard
empty clipboard	ZeroScrap	EmptyClipboard
writing to clipboard	PutScrap	SetClipboardData
reading from clipboard	GetScrap	GetClipboardData

Table 18.2 Summary of basic clipboard support across platforms.

Format	Macintosh	Windows 3.1	Win32
plain text	'TEXT'	CF_TEXT CF_OEMTEXT	CF_TEXT CF_OEMTEXT CF_UNICODETEXT
formatted text	'PICT'	CF_METAFILEPICT	CF_METAFILEPICT CF_ENHMETAFILE
graphics objects	'PICT'	CF_METAFILEPICT	CF_METAFILEPICT CF_ENHMETAFILE
images	'PICT'	CF_BITMAP CF_DIB CF_TIFF	CF_BITMAP CF_DIB CF_TIFF

BROADEN USER INTERFACE OPTIONS

To improve general user interface features of our cross-platform API that we have discussed, we need to:

- support true window classifications
- support a broader range of menu features
- support more types of controls
- allow controls to be created at run-time

Support Window Classifications

In the presentation of the cross-platform solution in this book and the XPLib software, we have only allowed cross-platform windows to be created within a single window classification. Further, the implementation of the Macintosh window class represents only a superficial type of window class compared to a Windows window class. A proper implementation of window classes (including parent and child window capabilities) would allow more flexibility in the creation and use of windows on the Macintosh.

Advanced Menu Features

As we discussed in Chapter 13, there are numerous menu features that we have not addressed. Supporting submenus is an important way to compact the information in a menu list and can reduce the likelihood of the user having to use a dialog box. This speeds up the process of using your application and eliminates unnecessary visual clutter. Another important timesaver is to allow keyboard shortcuts. They are supported by key commands in the Macintosh (COMMAND-key) and supported in Windows through an accelerator table (resource). Keyboard shortcuts are supported in the XPLib software but are not demonstrated in the sample code in this book.

Another way to improve a user's understanding of the items in a menu list is to use color or icons. Certain types of selection processes are more clearly indicated using visual cues.

You will need to consider additional menu features based on the user interface needs of your product. There is no sense in adding a feature to your cross-platform API unless you need to.

More Control Support

In Chapter 16 of this book and the XPLib software, we have presented a limited solution for using controls. There are three things that can be done to improve the use of controls:

- allow controls in normal windows (non-dialogs)
- increase the functionality of available controls
- increase the set of available controls

To provide control placement in normal windows implies that either the window layout can be done in a resource editor or that controls can be created at run-time. The Macintosh allows window layout in ResEdit, but Windows does not provide a direct way to do this. Run-time creation of controls is discussed in the next section.

Increasing the functionality of the controls we have already defined is probably the easiest way to improve support for controls. This could mean allowing edit text boxes to cut, copy, and paste to the clipboard and providing equal support for modifying the appearance of controls (for example, the programmer doesn't need to know what type of control is involved in hiding or enabling it).

To the user the most obvious improvements will be in the types of controls that are allowed. We have only described support for radio buttons, check boxes, push buttons, static text, and edit text. There are other useful controls to support:

- list boxes—display lists of information and allow selections (very important!)
- icons—perform actions and indicate state
- scroll bars—other than the scroll bars in a document window
- popup lists—remove visual clutter from a dialog

Popup lists are different in Macintosh and Windows. We can define two types of popup lists:

Type	Macintosh	Windows
popup list	popup menu	drop-down list combo box
popup list with edit text	popup menu plus edit text box	drop-down combo box

A popup list always shows the current selection from the list. The difference between the two types is that a popup list with edit text box allows you to type in a selection in the provided edit box to either select that item from the list, add it to the list, or use it as a custom value that's not in the list.

Dynamic Control Creation

Another thing that we left out of our control functions is the ability to create and destroy controls at run-time. Our solution has assumed that the controls are in a dialog that was defined in a resource editor. This dialog plus controls constitutes a dialog template, something that all three of our platforms supported. Unfortunately Windows does not provide an easy way to create a window template.

The process of creating a window with controls is, therefore, a run-time problem. You might also want to create controls at run-time in a dialog if the content of the dialog changes depending on some user action or state, although this can be accomplished using multiple dialog templates as well.

MORE STANDARD DIALOGS

In the design that we have specified in Chapters 6, 9, and 11 of this book, and in the XPLib software, we have provided support for:

- an open file dialog
- a save file dialog
- a printer or page setup dialog
- a print job dialog
- a font selection dialog

These dialogs represent the majority of dialogs that are commonly used in most applications. There are a few other dialogs that could be provided to make a developer's life easier:

- a find text dialog
- a search and replace dialog
- a color selection dialog

Most applications will find that the common dialogs provided for these purposes, either by a platform or by the cross-platform solution, will suffice for most applications. For applications that are very particular about form or function in a specific area or areas, you will need to customize some or all of the common dialogs.

Find and Replace Dialogs

Many applications that work with text require that the user be able to search for specific runs of text. The Windows 3.1 and Win32 API provide a common dialog for this purpose, and if you want to extend this capability across platforms, you will need to provide this functionality on the Macintosh.

Similarly, if you provide a means to search for text, you will probably need to provide the means to replace a run of text with another. Again, this is a common dialog that is part of the Windows API, and you will need to provide this across platforms.

The current form of the Windows find and replace dialogs are very simple and should not require much effort to port. Some issues that you might want to consider, though, are the availability of these dialogs in different languages and a design that will accomodate string growth due to translation.

Also, if you want to provide the means to search and replace attributes and other parameters of text (font type, size, etc.) you will need to write these on all platforms. This capability is used in text-intensive applications such as PageMaker and Microsoft Word, so you will probably not need to provide this capability unless you really have a specific need to.

Color Selection Dialog

A major feature that is missing from many functional areas in our discussion of cross-platform design is color; the graphics and text functions ignore color, for example. If you decide to support color, you will need to provide a means to specify and select colors. To do this, you will need to provide a dialog. Both Macintosh and Windows provide this capability, but you will probably need to ensure that the representation of color that is returned to you is in a common format and based on the same numerical model of color. This will guarantee that the behavior of color in your application, across platforms, and on various screens and printing devices will be as consistent as possible.

EXTENDING GRAPHICS CAPABILITIES

To provide a solution for most graphics needs, you will need to extend the graphics functionality that is specified in Chapter 8 of this book and the XPLib software. This includes:

- supporting all of the common graphics entities
- supporting more image transfer operations
- supporting color
- supporting both a screen- and printer-based representation
- providing 2D graphics transformations

Support Other Graphic Entities

You probably noticed that certain graphic entities were not included in the discussion and the XPLib software. While all of the graphics capabilities are essential, some are less important than others. But if you are developing a program that is graphics-intensive, you will need to support other graphics entities that are not mentioned in this book, as, for example:

- circular subsections, such as arcs, wedges, pies, and chords
- regions
- complex polygons, sometimes called poly-polylines
- path creation
- bezier curves
- marks at points

While there is a certain amount of overlap among these graphics entities across the Macintosh, Windows 3.1, and Win32, certain categories of functionality are missing on some platforms. For example, the Macintosh does not include support for outlined wedges, chords, poly-polylines, paths, bezier curves, or marks. While some of this missing functionality is easy to synthesize, such as outlined wedges, chords, poly-polylines, and marks, paths and beziers are more complicated. In Windows 3.1 there is no support for paths or bezier curves as there is in Win32.

Support More Image Transfer Capabilities

Also missing from the discussion and software in this book is complete support for image transferring. This means the ability to specify how pens, fills, text, and bitmaps are transferred to the screen or printer display surface. This is a little complicated because there are a lot of differences between the Macintosh and Windows, as indicated in Table 18.3.

In addition, in Color QuickDraw on the Macintosh you have the ability to perform arithmetic operations when transferring a source image, whether as a stroke, fill, text, or bitmap. You also can specify if the source image is transparent. Some of this ability to blend images is available in Windows using some of the many ROP3 operations. You will have to determine manually which operations map to the specific operations that you want to provide.

Support Color

In this book we have provided a monochrome solution to graphics and bitmaps—the available colors are either black or white and fills can have shades of gray. If you are developing an application that presents visual information to the user, you will want to include some support for color. In the simplest case this means support for the eight standard colors: black, white, red, green, blue, cyan, magenta, and yellow. You will also want to be able to specify the foreground and background colors of fills and text. See the Extending Text Capabilities section of this chapter for more information about color.

If your application demands more color support, you may want to allow the user to create and specify palettes of color; specify colors in RGB, CMYK, or HSB color models; and provide

Table 18.3 Comparison of transfer operations across platforms.

Type of Transfer	*Macintosh*	*Windows*
stroke	8 pat operations	16 ROP2[*] operations
fill	8 pat operations	256 ROP3[**] operations
text	8 src operations	2 operations[***]
bitmaps	8 src operations	256 ROP3 operations

[*]   ROP2 refers to an operation that involves a source and destination bitmap.

[**]   ROP3 refers to an operation that involves a source, a pattern, and a destination bitmap.

[***]   The valid text operations in Windows are background transparent or opaque.

support for displaying colors independent of the color capabilities of the output device by using dithering if necessary.

Support Screen and Printer Models

A subtle but annoying point of displaying and printing graphics and text is that typically the resolution of the screen and printing device are not the same. Some applications, such as PageMaker, use the printer as the basis for displaying information on the screen or the printer. This ensures that the printed result is always what the user has specified and visualized on the screen. Other applications—paint programs, for example—give you the option of specifying if the drawing is to be based on a screen model or a printer model.

Knowing the target device is important to establishing the consistency the user perceives your application to have. As a developer, it is important to know what the user expects so that you can satisfy the market to which you will be selling your product.

Recall the three types of graphics rendering models from Chapter 8:

- pixel-for-pixel rendering
- screen-based rendering
- printer-based rendering

In this book we have assumed that the resolutions of the screen and printer are the same. The coordinate values always indicated pixels regardess if you are drawing to the screen or to the printer. This simplifies the implementation but also limits the usefulness. If you have a 72 dpi screen and a 300 dpi printer, a 72-dot line (1 inch) on the screen will be printed as 72 dots but will only be about 1/4 inch long. However, this technique does allow all bitmaps to print undestorted.

In the XPLib software the screen-based model is used. A 1-inch line will print as 1-inch, but an image will be stretched to fit to the printer resolution. A proper implementation will allow you to specify the model (either internally in the source code or externally by a dialog check-box for the user) as screen-based or printer-based. If you need to provide a printer-based model, you will need to know the printer's resolution before you start drawing anything. You will also need to scale font information when drawing to the screen, because font metric information will be given to you based on the printer's resolution. If the user changes the target printer, the locations of the screen contents will have to be recalculated and contents of the screen redrawn.

Provide 2D Graphics Transformations

If your application needs to perform arbitrary operations on graphics objects, such as translation, scaling, rotation, and shearing, you might want to consider a more general 2D model for representing graphics objects. Any point in a 2D space can be modified or transformed using a 3×3 transformation matrix. The general form is:

$$point\ A' = \begin{bmatrix} a & b & 0 \\ c & d & 0 \\ t_x & t_y & 1 \end{bmatrix} point\ A'$$

Here point A is the original point and point A′ is the transformed point. The t_x and t_y elements in the 3×3 matrix allow the point to be translated (moved), the a and d parameters control the scaling (size), and rotation is controlled by the *a*, *b*, *c*, and *d* elements.

To provide this capability, all graphical components must be defined using a series of individual points that are interconnected using lines, probably a polygon. When all of the points of a graphic object are transformed, the entire object is also transformed. For more information on this topic you should consult *Fundamentals of Interactive Computer Graphics*, by J. D. Foley and A. van Dam, published by Addison Wesley.

Metafiles

A common way to transfer graphics information between applications on the same platform is to use metafiles. On the Macintosh metafiles represent PICT or PICT2 resources. On Windows they represent the Windows Metafile (WMF) format. Win32 also includes the Enhanced Metafile (EMF) format. Metafiles give you a convenient way to copy and paste graphic information to and from the clipboard. Saving metafiles to disk allows your program a convenient way to export graphics (and some formatted text) information to other applications.

One way to share program data across platforms is to use a metafile format. There are a few options to consider:

- Choose one platform metafile format as the standard. Other platforms need to convert from it to their internal representation. For example, if the WMF format is the standard, the Macintosh needs to convert from WMF to PICT.

- Allow applications to read and write various metafile formats.

- Design a cross-platform metafile format that can be easily and accurately interpreted on various platforms.

EXTENDING TEXT CAPABILITIES

The font and text functionality that we presented in Chapter 9 represents only the tip of the iceberg of the text and font features of our three target platforms and font technology. Other text capabilities to consider are:

- supporting text alignment

- supporting color

- supporting transfer operations

- supporting transformations (e.g., rotation)

- supporting font substitution

- considering international issues

Table 18.4 Comparison of text alignment functions across platforms.

Function	*Macintosh*	*Windows*
setting the alignment	TESetJust	SetTextAlign
setting character extra	NA	SetTextCharacterExtra
setting word extra	SpaceExtra	SetTextJustification

Support Text Alignment

We have not considered text alignment in our discussion of text functionality. International applications will need to consider the writing direction when implementing text alignment. But in general you need to provide the ability to align text in several ways:

- left-aligned text
- right-aligned text
- centered text
- justified text

We have only considered left-alignment (the default) in our discussion. Table 18.4 compares some of the functionality for text alignment on the Macintosh and Windows.

Support Text Color

Our previous discussion of text (in Chapter 9) assumed that the text color (foreground) was black and the background color was white. Many times this is sufficient. But you can easily add the ability to specify the foreground and background color when you render text. Table 18.5 shows a comparison of color functions on the Macintosh and Windows. Changing the foreground and background colors also affects how bitmaps are transferred.

Table 18.5 Comparison of color functions across platforms.

Color Function	*Macintosh*	*Windows***
set foreground	ForeColor RGBForeColor*	SetTextColor
set background	BackColor RGBBackColor*	SetBkColor

*   Available in Color QuickDraw.

**   In Windows the foreground color of pens and brushes is determined when you create the pen or brush.

Table 18.6 Methods for selecting text transfer modes across platforms.

Transfer Mode	Macintosh	Windows
opaque	TextMode(srcCopy)	SetBkMode(OPAQUE)
transparent	TextMode(srcOr)	SetBkMode(TRANSPARENT)
	TextMode(srcCopy+transparent)*	

* With Color QuickDraw

Support Text Transfer Operations

So far we have only considered transferring text using a "copy" operation. Two standard methods of transferring text exist on the Macintosh and Windows: transferring text with an opaque background and transferring text with a transparent background.

The Macintosh and Windows API functions used to perform these basic transfer modes are compared in Table 18.6. There are other ways to transfer text on the Macintosh using the addXXX, subXXX, adXXX, and blend modifiers in combination with the other srcXXX transfer operations; unfortunately these are not directly available in Windows. You will need to render the text to a memory bitmap and transfer the memory bitmap to the screen (or printer) bitmap using the ternary raster operations available for bitmap transfers.

Support Text Transformations

Some graphic arts applications need to have a lot of control over the way text is drawn. This means that you may need to support text rotation, outlining, or wrapping along a path. In Windows you can specify rotation when you create a font, and some of this functionality is provided by the TrueType extensions to the Windows API (available in Windows 3.1), although non-TrueType fonts cannot be rotated or outlined. In the Macintosh generating outlines is provided by additional TrueType functionality provided in System 7. There is no direct way to perform text rotation. There is no direct way in either the Macintosh or Windows to wrap text along a curved line. You will need to implement this feature yourself.

Consider a Font Substitution Strategy

One of the biggest problems with fonts is that you cannot guarantee that all users have the same fonts. This problem is even more prevalent when a document is moved from one platform to another. A text-intensive application will need to provide a solution to this problem. Some common solutions are:

- to know enough about a font so that you can choose a similar one on another machine or platform
- to save information about the end points of either the characters in a string or of the entire string

These will let you choose a similar font and put the characters in approximately the right places. You can do this without relying on external technology, but it doesn't always produce the best results.

Other font products provide better solutions to this problem. For example, with Adobe's Super ATM product your application doesn't need to infer anything about the font. You just make a request to the system about the font you want and if it is there you'll get it. If it's not there, Super ATM will create a substitute font for you.

Products from Ares Software (Font Chameleon) and ElseWare Corporation (Infinifont) allow you to request fonts based on parametric information. A new font can be created to replace one that a document needs but that you don't have on your system. You can also use these products to substitute another font even if you have the font.

ElseWare also markets a font substitution technology that relies on a parametric descriptor of a font (a PANOSE number) that is either embedded in the font definition (TrueType fonts from Microsoft) or provided by a licensed PANOSE data base that contains numbers for over 2600 PostScript and TrueType fonts from Adobe, Bitstream, Microsoft, Corel Systems, and Agfa.

International Issues

If you are writing an application that will be sold internationally, you will need to consider a few things:

- whether the native language requires an 8-bit character set or a 16-bit character set
- if the writing direction is from left to right, right to left
- how the keyboard maps to the character set
- the proper character sorting order for specific languages

The Macintosh provides the International Utilities Package, the Script Manager, and TextEdit to allow you to solve many of these problems. Unfortunately Windows does not yet support all of these capabilities. Windows 3.1 and Win32 both use the language information and keyboard type to control the proper mapping of keys to characters and properly sort and compare character strings. But Windows 3.1 does not support 16-bit characters. Neither Windows 3.1 nor Win32 provides a straightforward way to control arbitrary writing directions and nonstandard text justification schemes. Your application will need to provide this functionality by creating fonts with different escapement and orientation values and modifying the text alignment—refer to the Windows SDK documentation on the LOGFONT structure and the CreateFont() and SetTextAlign() functions for more information.

ADVANCED PRINTING CONSIDERATIONS

Our discussion of printing issues in Chapter 11 dealt with the basic process of starting a print job, printing the job, and ending the print job. We also included a cross-platform way to access the platform-specific print setup and print job dialogs. Most applications require more printing functionality than this. Some advanced printing considerations are:

- providing an "Abort Print Job" dialog
- printing multiple page documents
- using the printer-based document model

Print Job Abort Dialog

When the user decides to print his or her work, it is a good idea to allow them to abort the job before it is "committed" to the printer. If the system supports a print spooler, then the job can always be aborted from the print spooler. If not, or if the job is large and will take a while to be completely spooled out, you will need to provide a print abort dialog so that the user can cancel the job.

Multiple Page Documents

Most of the time, a user's work consists of more than one page worth of information. A proper printing solution needs to address this. You will need to provide at least a couple of extra functions to add this feature:

Function	Purpose
PrintPageBegin()	used to begin a new page
PrintPageEnd()	used to end the current page

Another thing you'll need to think about: what do you do when the contents of a single screen "page" is larger than the physical paper size in the printer? The simplest thing to do is to just let the printer (driver) clip the screen contents to whatever will fit on the paper. Most users won't appreciate this.

The other technique is to "tile" the contents of one screen page so that multiple printed pages are generated—applications such as PageMaker let you do this so that you can get an idea of what a printed page looks like without having the right kind of printer. This sounds great, but it is not an easy job!

A good middle ground solution is to let your application be printer smart. Let the characteristics of the printer and the paper dictate the limitations of what (and where) the user can work. This way every screen page will fit on the printed page.

Screen vs. Printer Resolution

Another printing topic is whether to use the screen-based or printer-based document model. This was discussed in Chapter 8 and in the Extending Graphics Capabilities section earlier in this chapter. Generally users will be happier with a printer-based model if the application is more hard-copy oriented (as are spreadsheets, graphics, word processors, or desktop publishing programs). It eliminates a lot of user confusion because the contents of the screen are based on the target printer. An application that is less hard-copy oriented might not care what the model is (such as a utility or tool that doesn't print, except to generate a report).

You're probably better off using the printer-model if you can afford the time up front to work out the problems. As the user changes printers, the document will need to update itself to reflect the fonts, features, and resolution of the new printer.

Special Features

Some special printing features and capabilities that you might want to consider adding to your cross-platform printing solution are:

- supporting tiling (discussed above)
- supporting titles (headers or footers) for each page
- providing crop marks
- including page numbers

ADVANCED FILE MANAGEMENT

Beyond the facade of simple file creation, deletion, reading, and writing lies a vast region of file management features that we have not discussed. Some of these include:

- supporting more flexible file modes and attributes
- getting directory information
- providing cross-platform file formats
- supporting file sharing
- implementing a record-based file manager

More Flexible File Attributes and Modes

In our discussion of file management issues in Chapter 6, we only considered creating read/write and read/only binary files. There are other types of files that we can consider:

- hidden files
- shared files
- text files
- compressed files
- encrypted files

This information could be specified either during the file creation process or the file open process. Supporting the file capabilities of the native platform API allows a cross-platform application to take advantage of special features and allows it to perform in as familiar manner as possible to native applications. Some features are supported by the Macintosh and Windows (hidden file attribute, text/binary file access, and file sharing). Decompression is available in

Windows using the LZEXPAND.DLL library, but you still have to implement compression. Encryption is not directly available on any of the platforms.

Directory Functionality

From time to time an application will need to get a list of files or to search for specific files or specific contents of files. If your application needs to work with directories and files, you will need to provide some additional file functions, such as:

- getting the current directory
- traversing the directory tree
- getting the list of files in a directory

Cross-Platform File Access

Because a cross-platform application will often have to cope with low-level data representation differences (organization or byte order), you might find it useful to provide a file input/output layer that translates between internal run-time representations of data and disk-based representations and vice versa. This will allow you to write out your program data to file on one platform and read it in on another without needing (or caring) to know about where it came from or where it is going. Adding a cross-platform layer will make it simpler to implement higher-level file management features for your application and probably result in a smaller code size, but it will probably be slower than a dedicated read/write function for each platform.

This brings up the other method of solving cross-platform file access: providing read and write modules for each platform that your program supports. Platform A can read and write Platform A files and Platform B files, Platform B can read and write Platform B files and Platform A files. This will allow you to read and write faster but will take up more space.

File Sharing

File sharing allows all or a portion of a file to be accessed by more than one application or user at the same time. The Macintosh and Windows operating systems support file sharing. We did not consider this in our earlier discussion of files. If your product is going to be used so that one of its files is used by a single user running multiple applications all sharing the same data or used by multiple users on a network all sharing the same data, then you will want to consider supporting file sharing. A work flow or groupware application will require this feature. Most networkable applications or those that support some form of document linking feature may also find file sharing useful. For the Windows version of your products, you might want to also consider the capabilities of Windows for Workgroups or Windows NT Advanced Server.

Record-Based File Manager

The last advanced file management topic deals with a mechanism for reading and writing simple and complex data types to file. This way you don't have to worry about the specific issues of each data structure: how large it is, how it is organized, and how to access it. Every data type you create provides some basic information that allows the file manager to know how to read it and write it and where to find it. Couple this technique with a cross-platform access layer, and you will only need to write your file manager once for each platform and for all of your applications.

MAINTAINING INITIALIZATION INFORMATION

There are two types of initialization that an application needs to consider:

- application initialization information
- document initialization information

Application initialization allows your application to maintain state information that it needs across sessions. Windows has the concept of the profile (INI) file. In addition Win32 has the registration database (the Registry) that provides a centralized way to organize application (and document) information by "keys"—the RegXXX() functions. There is no facility for managing application information on the Macintosh.

Document initialization information is document-specific information that is usually maintained in an application's document file. Some document initialization information will be the same for different applications—for example, print job data and search and replace strings. You might save some time in the long run if you provide a way to read and write a standard form of this information to your document files.

INCLUDING DOCUMENTS FROM OTHER APPLICATIONS

Compound documents allow one document to include one or more documents from other applications within them. Two fundamental ways to include a document or drawing from another application are as a linked object and as an embedded object.

Object Linking

When one document uses a reference to the contents of another document within itself, this is called object linking. This allows you to combine multiple sources of information without adding size to your document. It also allows changes in the original document to be available to the compound document.

There are two strategies to object linking: dynamic linking and session linking. Dynamic linking allows your reference to a document to be updated as soon as changes are made to the original. Session linking limits your updates to whenever you start up your compound document or whenever you consciously request it. Dynamic linking is the more ideal method, but it can cause your application to have unpredictable behavior (waiting) when updates occur at inconvenient times.

Embedding Objects

When one document copies another document, or portion of a document into itself this is called object embedding. This allows you to create a compound document and give it to someone else without the other needing to have access to the originals. It results in larger document sizes than object linking but does make a compound document more portable.

Available Technologies

There are currently four vendors that provide solutions for the document inclusion problem:

- Microsoft's OLE 2.0 for Windows and Macintosh (currently network weak)
- Computer Integration Laboratories' (CIL)[1] OpenDoc for Macintosh, PC, UNIX, and Novell networks and systems
- Lotus' TOOLS (Technology for Object-Oriented Linking and Sharing)
- IBM's Distributed System Object Model for OS/2 and AIX systems

CIL's OpenDoc technology incorporates IBM's Distributed System Object Model, and Apple's Bento object storage format. Lotus' TOOLS is expected to work with Microsoft's OLE. At printing, OLE is currently a single-station solution that is available for Windows and will soon be available for the Macintosh. OpenDoc (which uses networking technology from Novell) offers a cross-platform, network solution and will soon be available for the Macintosh with DOS, Windows, OS/2, and UNIX implementations to follow.

The other alternative to using these available technologies is to use Dynamic Data Exchange (DDE) on Windows and Apple Events on the Macintosh to fashion something of your own design. But if you want your application to work with applications that use OLE or OpenDoc, you'll need to support Microsoft's or Apple's linking strategies as well.

OTHER CONSIDERATIONS

We weren't able to provide information on all topics and aspects of cross-platform development. We hope that we were able to provide you with enough information to determine the direction you want to take and some possible ways to get you there.

Some other advanced topics that we have not discussed that should be mentioned are:

- background processing
- multimedia
- gesture recognition
- embedded email support

---

[1]   CIL is a consortium including IBM, Apple, Novell, WordPerfect, Xerox, Borland, Oracle, and Telligent.

For certain applications your need to provide a cross-platform solution for one or more of these topics could be critical. You might need to do considerable work to solve some of these problems because they deal with rather diverse functional specifications and may imply certain capabilities of a native platform that might not be available on other platforms, for example, background processing, which is only available in Win32.

19

Advanced Resource Considerations

Remember that resources are what the user perceives your application to be. The nature, flavor, and level of completion are all portrayed in your product's user interface. An application's ability to support diverse user interface controls goes a long way in making a customer happy. At the same time the fancier a user interface is, the more trouble it is to design and implement. This is even more true in cross-platform products, where you need to consider the look and feel of a platform as well as the look and feel of your product across platforms. By providing stable and consistent resource functionality, you make it easier to polish your product.

CROSS-PLATFORM RESOURCE SOLUTIONS

When you investigate a cross-platform development solution, for purchase or design, you must consider how you will solve the resource problem. This is not a simple problem. There are three facets of the resource problem to consider:

- using resources at run-time
- creating resources at run-time
- managing resources at development-time

Providing a solution to each of the facets of the resource problem is an increasingly difficult problem as you move down the list.

USING RESOURCES

At run-time a program may change cursors or display a dialog box that contains any number of controls. This is the process of using resources. The program does not involve itself in the creation or specification of the resource or resources. It assumes that the resources already exist and merely loads them and uses them as necessary.

CREATING RESOURCES

Also at run-time a program may decide to alter dynamically the content of a dialog box depending on user input. This process involves creating a resource that depends on information provided by the user and requires that the program understand the format and content of the resource.

MANAGING RESOURCES

A program that deals with creating and using resources to provide a way to maintain resources in file form that will later be used at run-time is a resource manager or editor. This process assumes that the program understands the run-time form of resources and the static, file form of resources. This is the most difficult aspect of the resource problem and requires the most knowledge of resources.

RESOURCE SOLUTIONS

To provide a cross-platform resource solution, you need to know the degree to which your program will use resources. Generally, in order of difficulty, you can:

- provide a common API access to already compiled resources, not provide a common resource creation facility, and use the native resource tools (see Figure 19.1), the technique that XPLib uses

- abstract the resource creation and management processes, use the native resource tools and formats, and provide a common API to access the resources

- provide a new resource format that is common to all platforms and provide an API to access the resource features

Providing a common API that lets you load and use resources does not require that you know or understand the format or the content of the resource. This saves time. Good resource management tools are available on most platforms. Because these resource tools require a significant amount of time to develop and debug, you should not consider writing resource tools unless you need to.

An intermediate solution, shown in Figure 19.2, is to specify a common resource script format in which you can describe resources in a cross-platform syntax. This technique involves writing

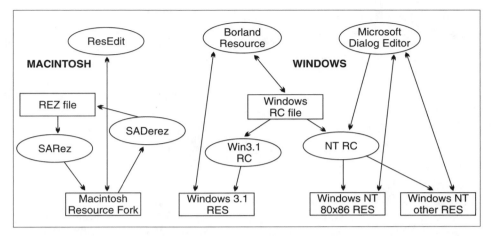

Figure 19.1 Flow chart of the current cross-platform resource process.

a resource preprocessor that converts a cross-platform resource script into a platform-specific format (REZ on the Macintosh and RC on Windows).

A more complicated but generally more useful solution, shown in Figure 19.3, relies on a common resource editor that generates binary resource to any of a number of target platform-specific resource formats—a resource fork in Macintosh and a RES file in Windows.

If you decide that your application has some special resource needs or your development effort is significantly hampered by creating and maintaining resources in a number of formats using a number of tools, you might consider abstracting the resource format and creating your

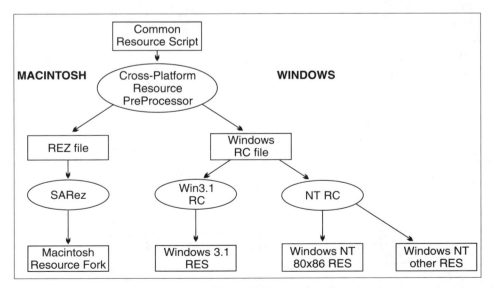

Figure 19.2 Flow chart of the resource solution using a common resource script.

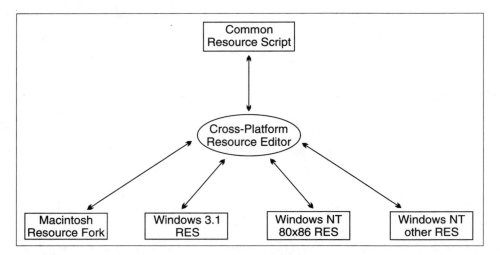

Figure 19.3 Flow chart of the resource solution using a resource cross-compiler.

own solution to the entire resource problem that will be used on all platforms, as illustrated in Figure 19.4. This process involves several engineering tasks:

- designing the file cross-platform resource file format
- specifying the functional interface to the resources
- providing tools to generate cross-platform resources

This means that you will create and maintain your own resource file. The cross-platform API will access this resource file directly. You might also need to provide a way to access certain crucial platform-specific resources, such as icons or cursors, to allow your application to be consistent with other applications on that platform.

Don't underestimate the magnitude of providing a total cross-platform resource solution. It could easily require as much time to develop as the entire cross-platform code solution.

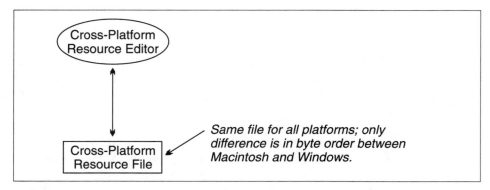

Figure 19.4 Cross-platform resource file solution.

20

Extensions

An extension to your application is something that is added to expand its usefulness. Extensions can be:

- code that adds functionality to your application
- a resource or file that lets your application run in different locations
- code that allows your application to read and write different file formats

Providing a cross-platform way to design and implement extensions to your application will allow you to add functionality or features uniformly to all platform versions of your application simultaneously.

EXTERNAL CODE ACCESS

Providing run-time access to new functions and features is a very efficient way to revise or improve your application without having to release a new version. Your application needs to be designed to take maximum advantange of this capability. It won't do you any good to ship some code extensions if your application doesn't have a way to use any of the features in them.

The common methods of providing run-time code enhancements are different for the Macintosh and Windows. Macintosh applications use code resources, 'CODE', to do this (actually Macintosh programs use code resources for all executable code). Windows programs use Dynamic Link Libraries (DLLs). Windows itself is really just a large collection of DLLs, each performing a specific set of tasks. Your job will be to produce a specification that allows you to develop and use these code extensions in a cross-platform way.

INTERNATIONALIZATION

You have a couple of choices regarding international customization: do it at compile time or do it at run-time. If you choose to internationalize at compile time, then the international extension will be something internal to the product development cycle. If you choose to internationalize at run-time, the international extension will be something that ships with your product.

The first choice is simpler to implement, but many internationalizations can take you a lot of time to put together. This technique is usually employed for simple internationalizations—when you are just changing the text contents of menus and dialogs.

Shipping a run-time international extension with your product will take you longer up front to specify but will make it easier for you to generate many extensions. This technique is better to employ if you are doing more than just simple text replacement—for example, you might want to determine which dialog box designs need to be reorganized for certain locations.

Also, languages that are defined in single-byte character sets have different needs than languages that are defined using double-byte character sets.

Single-Byte Character Set Issues

There are a few basic rules about providing international solutions for languages that can be represented by single-byte character sets, such as putting all strings in resources and allowing room for string growth (2–3X increase in size). You might also want to extend the 255-character limit in resource string size of the Macintosh and Windows resource managers. This will ensure that you can say what you want without worrying about overflowing resource strings and without sounding terse.

Double-Byte Character Set Issues

One problem with double-byte characters is related to string operations. The Macintosh has the Script Manager to help out here, and Windows NT is a Unicode operating system by design. But you are in a bit of trouble if you plan on using Windows 3.1.

Another problem relates to the way text is written. Dialog boxes for right-to-left languages need to be designed differently from dialogs for left-to-right languages. Also, your program will need to be able to work with resource strings that are composed of single- or double-byte characters, which is most easily handled as a compile-time option. You will need to study the particular issues of each location before you decide what you will do—it is probably a good idea to hire someone who is experienced in doing this. Putting these types of troublesome dialog boxes in a run-time linked module will allow you to keep the design of your application clean and easy to maintain.

IMPORT AND EXPORT EXTENSIONS

The ability of an application to read and write (import and export) information in different formats connects it with data from other applications. This makes the application a valuable tool

Table 20.1 Comparison of image file formats.

File Format	Macintosh	Windows	Cross-Platform
Windows bitmaps		x	
CCITT (Group 3 and 4)			x
MacPaint	x		
PICT	x		
Microsoft Paint (MSP)		x	
Tag Image File Format			x
CompuServe (GIF)			x
PaintBrush (PCX)		x	
Encapsulated PostScript			x
Word Perfect (WPG)			x
JPEG			x
FAX			x

that can be used with other applications rather than in isolation. There are three general categories of file types that you should consider:

- formatted text
- bitmap or image
- object graphics

A well-documented formatted-text format is the Rich Text Format, or RTF. If your application can read and write RTF files, you can exchange text information with many word processors. Image data represent bitmaps. A list of common image file formats are compared in Table 20.1. Graphics formats represent pictures composed of collections of graphic objects. Some common graphics file formats are listed and compared in Table 20.2.

Table 20.2 Comparison of graphics file formats.

File Format	Macintosh	Windows	Cross-Platform
MacPaint	x		
PICT	x		
MicroGrafx (DRW)		x	
AutoCAD (DXF)			x
HP Graphics Language			x
Windows Metafile		x	
Lotus 123	x	x	
Encapsulated PostScript			x
Word Perfect (WPG)			x

Index

Product License Agreement
Limited Warranty and Damage Disclaimer

PLEASE READ THIS NOTICE BEFORE OPENING THE PACKAGE CONTAINING THE SOFTWARE PROGRAM AND RELATED DOCUMENTATION (COLLECTIVELY, THE "PRODUCT"). OPENING THE PACKAGE OR USING ITS CONTENTS CONSTITUTES YOUR COMPLETE AND UNCONDITIONAL ACCEPTANCE OF THE TERMS AND CONDITIONS OF THIS PRODUCT LICENSE AGREEMENT ("AGREEMENT"). IF YOU DO NOT AGREE WITH THESE TERMS AND CONDITIONS, PROMPTLY RETURN THE UNOPENED PACKAGE TO THE POINT OF PURCHASE FOR FULL REFUND.

License: Steven J. Petrucci ("Licensor") hereby grants to you, and you accept, a nonexclusive, nontransferable, and nonassignable license, subject to the terms and conditions set forth herein, to use the computer software programs ("Software") and Documentation on a single processing unit for each of the following platforms: Windows 3.1, Windows NT, and the Macintosh. You agree that you will not sublicense, rent, lease, sell, assign, or transfer the Software or share your rights under this license with a third party (whether by network, time-sharing, multiple CPU, or other multiuser arrangement), and any attempt to do so will result in termination of this Product License. You further agree that you will not make changes to, edit, or otherwise modify the Software; nor will you embed, place, or otherwise utilize copies of the Software in subsequent or derivative products, programs, or software without the prior consent of the Licensor. You may make one (1) copy of the Software and Documentation for backup purposes and agree to affix Licensor's copyright and other proprietary rights notices to such copy.

Ownership: You acknowledge and agree that all right, title, and interest in and to the Product are and shall at all times remain with the Licensor. This Agreement conveys to you only a limited right of use revocable in accordance with the terms of this Agreement.

Limited Warranty: Licensor and Random House Electronic Publishing warrant to you that for a period of ninety (90) days from the date you receive this Product the electronic media contains an accurate reproduction of the Software and Documentation. There is no warranty after expiration of the warranty period. This Limited Warranty covers only the original user of the Product, and Licensor's and Random House Electronic Publishing's entire liability and your exclusive remedy shall be, at their option, either (a) return of the price paid for the Product, or (b) repair or replacement of the Product that does not meet the Limited Warranty, provided that the Product is returned with a copy of your receipt. Random House Electronic Publishing and Licensor do not warrant that the Product will be free from error or will meet your specific requirements. Except for the warranties set forth above, the Product is licensed "as is," and RANDOM HOUSE ELECTRONIC PUBLISHING AND LICENSOR DISCLAIM ANY AND ALL OTHER WARRANTIES, WHETHER EXPRESS OR IMPLIED, INCLUDING WITHOUT LIMITATION, ANY IMPLIED WARRANTIES OF MERCHANTABILITY

AND FITNESS FOR A PARTICULAR PURPOSE. SOME STATES DO NOT ALLOW LIMITATION ON HOW LONG IMPLIED WARRANTY LASTS, SO THE ABOVE LIMITATIONS MAY NOT APPLY TO YOU. THIS WARRANTY GIVES YOU SPECIFIC LEGAL RIGHTS, AND YOU MAY ALSO HAVE OTHER RIGHTS THAT MAY VARY FROM STATE TO STATE.

Limitation of Liability: You acknowledge and agree that in no event will Licensor, Random House Electronic Publishing, its affiliates, or any officers, directors, employees, or agents thereof be liable to you or any third party for injury or damages caused directly or indirectly by the Product, including, but not limited to, incidental, special, consequential, indirect, or exemplary damages, damages for loss of business profits, business interruption, loss of business information, and legal expenses or loss of good will, or any other pecuniary loss, whether based on contract, tort, warranty or other legal or equitable grounds, arising out of or resulting from or in connection with the use of or inability to use or performance of the Product, even if Licensor or Random House Electronic Publishing has been advised of the possibility of such damages or costs. Some states do not allow the exclusion or limitation of incidental or consequential damages, so the above limitation or exclusion may not apply to you.

U.S. Government Restricted Rights: This product is provided with RESTRICTED AND LIMITED RIGHTS. Use, duplication, or disclosure by the U.S. Government is subject to limitations contained in this License Agreement and to restrictions as set forth in FAR S52.227-19 (June 1987) Alternate III (8) (3) (June 1987), FAR S52.227-19 (June 1987), or DFARS S52.227-7013 (c) (1) (iii) (June 1987) as applicable.

Term & Termination: The limited license granted to you is effective from the date you open this package and shall continue until terminated. You may terminate it at any time by returning the Product to Random House Electronic Publishing. The license will also terminate automatically if you fail to comply with any term or condition of this Agreement. You agree upon termination for any reason to return the Product together with all copies in whatever form to Random House Electronic Publishing.

Severability: Should any term of this agreement be declared void or unenforceable by any court of competent jurisdiction, such declaration shall have no effect on the remaining terms thereof.

Governing Law: This agreement is governed by and construed in accordance with the laws of the State of New York.

IBM and Macintosh Compatible 3.5" Diskettes

This Random House Software product is also available in IBM and Macintosh compatible 3.5" format. If you'd like to exchange this software for the 3.5" diskettes, please:

- Package your original CD-ROM in a mailer.
- Include a check or money order for US $14.95 ($16.95 Canadian) to cover media and postage and handling. Foreign order: Please send international money order; no foreign checks accepted.
- Include your completed Random House warranty card.

Upon receipt, Random House will immediately send your replacement diskettes via first class mail.

Mail to: Random House Electronic Publishing
          201 E. 50th Street
          New York, NY 10022
          Attn: CPPT/3.5 Diskettes